ICARD DUQUESNE, Bernard Arnaud

The Gospels distributed into Meditations for Every Day in the Year, and arranged according to the Harmony of the four Evangelists, by l'Abbe? Duquesne.

Translated from the French, and adapted to the use of the English Church. Volume

ICARD DUQUESNE, Bernard Arnaud

The Gospels distributed into Meditations for Every Day in the Year, and arranged according to the Harmony of the four Evangelists, by l'Abbe? Duquesne.
Translated from the French, and adapted to the use of the English Church. Volume 1

ISBN/EAN: 9783741183546

Manufactured in Europe, USA, Canada, Australia, Japa

Cover: Foto ©Andreas Hilbeck / pixelio.de

Manufactured and distributed by brebook publishing software (www.brebook.com)

ICARD DUQUESNE, Bernard Arnaud

The Gospels distributed into Meditations for Every Day in the Year, and arranged according to the Harmony of the four Evangelists, by l'Abbe? Duquesne.

THE GOSPELS

DISTRIBUTED INTO MEDITATIONS FOR
EVERY DAY OF THE YEAR

AND ARRANGED

ACCORDING TO THE HARMONY OF
THE FOUR EVANGELISTS

BY

L'ABBÉ DUQUESNE

TRANSLATED FROM THE FRENCH AND ADAPTED
TO THE USE OF THE ENGLISH CHURCH.

VOLUME I.

SOLD BY
JAMES PARKER & CO., OXFORD,
AND 377, STRAND, LONDON;
AND RIVINGTONS,
LONDON, OXFORD, AND CAMBRIDGE.
1881.

TO

Our Mother,

IN WHOM WE WERE NEW-BORN TO GOD,

IN WHOM WE HAVE BEEN FED

ALL OUR LIFE LONG UNTIL THIS DAY,

IN WHOSE BOSOM WE HOPE TO DIE,

The Church of England,

BELOVED AND AFFLICTED,

AND BY AFFLICTION PURIFIED,

ONCE THE PARENT OF SAINTS,

NOW THROUGH OUR SINS FALLEN, YET ARISING,

IN

REVERENT AND GRATEFUL AFFECTION.

THE GOSPELS

DISTRIBUTED INTO MEDITATIONS FOR EVERY DAY IN THE YEAR.

Meditation I.

PREFACE OF S. LUKE.

Of the dispositions of mind with which the study and meditation of the Holy Gospels should be undertaken.—S. Luke i. 1-4.

WE will consider here four of these dispositions, which shall form the four points of this meditation. We must bring with us to our meditation of the Gospels, earnestness, faith, accuracy and confidence.

FIRST POINT.

We must meditate on the Gospel with earnestness.

That which ought to inspire me with this earnestness, is,

1. The example of others. *Forasmuch as many, says S. Luke, have taken in hand to set forth in order a declaration of those things which are most surely believed among us, even as they delivered them unto us, which from the beginning were eyewitnesses, and ministers of the word: it seemed good to me also, having had perfect understanding of all things from the very first, to write unto thee in order, most excellent Theophilus, that thou mightest know the certainty of these things, wherein thou hast been instructed.*

S. Luke was moved to write his Gospel by the example of others: whether by that of the holy Evangelists, S. Matthew and S. Mark, who wrote before him, or by the example of the authors of some writings which the Church had rejected, as not being inspired by the Holy Spirit. In the same way, we ought to stir ourselves up to the study and meditation of the Gospels, by the example both of the saints, and even of worldly people. *Forasmuch as many* read and meditate on the Gospel with such assiduity, and find in it such delight, and draw from it so much benefit, why should I not imitate them? *Forasmuch as many* occupy themselves so earnestly, in such a number of worthless objects, and since I have myself wasted so much time in books, thoughts and reflections, which, if not actually hurtful, were, at least, useless, why should not I do now as much for my salvation, and for eternity, as so many others do and as I have done myself, in the way of sacrifice to the world, and in vain pursuits? My mind is made up. *It seemed good to me,* that is to say, I have at last resolved, and my resolution shall stand firm, to apply myself seriously to the study and meditations of the Holy Gospel.

2. *That which will reanimate unceasingly my zeal in this point, will be the easiness of this exercise:* for it is not a matter here of abstruse or profound speculations. The history of Jesus Christ is within the reach of all the world; and it is this history which I desire to make the subject of my meditations, since it is the foundation of all religion. It is an easy subject; why then should I excuse myself upon my incapacity to meditate? Is there any thing easier than to read a history, to occupy one's thoughts with it, and to reflect on what one reads? It is an agreeable subject; why should I imagine that only weariness and distastefulness are to be met with in meditation? Does not history please every one? And what history can there be more interesting, more ennobling, or more striking than that of Him, Who being God, was made Man, Who lived, worked, and held converse in the midst of us?

3. The importance of this exercise will render me more in earnest to fulfil it. Ah! how I have deceived myself, when I have looked upon the time given to meditation as time wasted, and spent in idleness, when I have said that my occupations would not allow of my meditating! Is it not the most important of our occupations? *The things which are most surely believed among us*, have they not been done for the sake of us all, and for me in particular? Are they not the basis of religion, the object of our faith, the rule of our conduct, the foundation of our hope, and the source of the eternal life which we look for? How otherwise, unless I am filled with these great truths, could I keep myself from the corruptions of the world, and how can I store them up in my mind, save by a diligent, attentive, and careful reading; in a word, by meditation on the Gospels?

SECOND POINT.

We must meditate on the Gospel with faith.

Faith requires of us that we should receive none other Gospel but that which is sanctioned by the authority of the Church, and that we should reject all other Gospels which the Church does not receive, or which she condemns. *Since many*, says S. Luke, *have taken in hand to set forth in order a declaration of these things.* Now, who is it that has given to us as divine and inspired, the four books of the Gospels which we possess? Who has rejected the rest as false and apocryphal? Who has made the choice amongst them? It is the Church, and by this means, she sets forth for our reflections,

1. *An example of her supreme and infallible authority* in all that regards the deposit and the teaching of the faith committed to her keeping, (the pillar and ground of the truth. 1 Tim. iii. 15.). The false Gospels were condemned by the Church, and she cannot have erred in so doing; otherwise the promises of Jesus Christ would be vain, and our faith without foundation. Her authority has never been taken from her, and she will pre-

serve it as long as there are men to be taught, guided, and kept from error.

2. *The tradition of the Gospels goes back to those, who from the beginning were eyewitnesses, and ministers of the word;* that is to say, not only to the apostles, who were instructed by Jesus Christ, and upon whom the Holy Spirit came down in order to give power and virtue to their teaching, but also to those who were irreproachable witnesses of that which took place at the Birth, and during the Infancy of Jesus Christ.

3. *The Church sets before us as an example the submission of the authors of the false gospels.* It is to be presumed that they did not, in any way, rebel against her authority: at least, we find no traces of their having disturbed her with explanations or recriminations, or that they left behind them any defenders of their books, or any who proved, in this point, refractory to her decisions. If the heretics of succeeding centuries have not had the same deference to her authority, let us take care not to participate in their insubordination, by reading their works, and not to withdraw ourselves from the obedience we owe to the Church, and thereby swell the ranks of those who are the partisans of error.

THIRD POINT.

We must meditate on the Gospels with accuracy.

It seemed good to me also, having had perfect understanding of all things from the very first, to write unto thee in order. Every thing that is good comes to us from God, without our deserving it; but we must not abuse this truth, in order thereby to encourage ourselves in idleness. If God has willed that even the inspired authors should bring all their understanding and carefulness to bear, in order to respond faithfully to the inspiration they received, with what far greater reason does He require the same of us, in order that we might profit by this inspiration! A carefulness and accuracy which should extend even to our body, our mind, and our affections.

1. *Accuracy as regards our body*, which consists in forcing ourselves to be punctual and exact in reading and meditating on the Holy Gospels, every day, even at the expense of our rest, our business, our occupations, our pleasures, and our inclinations. If it costs us some trouble, we shall be abundantly rewarded for it.

2. *Accuracy as regards our minds*. The mind, as well as the body, has its indolences which must be overcome by applying ourselves seriously to the subject of our meditation. The mind has an inconceivable levity, which we must bring under control : distractions approach it on all sides; never let us admit willingly any, of which God shall be the witness, by which His Majesty shall be offended, and for which we may be perhaps punished by a dryness and distaste, which may spread itself thence over all our religious exercises, and continue thenceforth through the remainder of our lives. The mind has a secret pride which we must subdue. It sees with grief that it is not always master of itself, that it cannot think as it will, and that a thousand distractions make it think of what it would not. In this case, involuntary distractions, let their number be as great as it may, must never cause us to give up this practice of meditation; let them cause us neither surprise nor disgust; but let them only bring us to humble ourselves before God, to acknowledge our own weakness, and to implore His Help, and offer up to Him our grief. Prayer, which is the oftenest interrupted by involuntary distractions, is only the more meritorious, for the very reason that it costs us a greater effort, and is also more humbling.

3. *Our accuracy in meditation must above all bring our affections into subjection*. The heart combines at the same time the heaviness of the body, and the lightness of the mind. Like the body, it falls by its own weight to the ground: and like the mind, it evaporates into a thousand desires, or chimerical affections. It is

the work of meditation to raise it and to fix it. The accuracy, or attention, which we ought to bring to this work, consists, firstly, in bringing our affections to bear upon the subject of our meditation. The whole work of meditation is directed towards the heart, in order to move it, to elevate it, to soften and purify it. Let us then direct all our thoughts and all our reflections towards this end. If our heart is not moved, the most noble sentiments of our minds would be useless to us. A single word, which penetrates our hearts, is worth more than the most sublime thoughts which do not inspire us with any feeling. This accuracy consists moreover in making, during the course of the meditation, many interior acts of different virtues, according to the subject. These acts are an exercise of our heart, and this exercise puts it into motion, warms it, little by little, and goes sometimes so far as to enkindle it with divine love. It is this affection which we should above all strive to excite in ourselves. The Gospel is the law of love; everything in it tends towards love; miracles, teachings, mysteries, threatenings, promises, everything leads to this. S. Luke, in addressing his Gospel to us, includes all Christians under the name of *Theophilus*, which means, one who loves God. In truth, he who does not love God is not a Christian, or is one only in name. Lastly, this accuracy consists in keeping in mind some point in our meditation which touches us, some living sentiment with which our heart may devoutly occupy itself during the day, and some practical resolution to correct ourselves of some failing, or to promote the exercise of some virtue.

FOURTH POINT.

We must meditate on the Gospel with confidence.

Our confidence and our desire ought to be to draw from the reading and meditation of the Gospel the fruit which God wills that we should gather from it, and this fruit is knowledge of the truth; *that thou mightest know the certainty of those things wherein thou hast been instructed.* We have a general knowledge as to the life, the mysteries, the miracles, and the discourses of our Saviour; but the point in question here is that we should acquire;

1. *A more exact acquaintance with them*, which we shall acquire by reading and meditating connectedly, and by joining together the narratives of the four Evangelists. We shall have before us, the time, the place, the occasion, and the circumstances of each of the events related in the Gospel. This order will make us understand them better, and keep them more easily in mind; we shall understand more thoroughly their relation to one another, and our minds will be more enlightened, our hearts more touched, and our spiritual life strengthened.

2. *A deeper knowledge.* One cannot read the Gospels without admiring them even when one passes rapidly over the facts, and only gives them a slight consideration. But when each day we take some one fact, or a particular discourse, and we arrest our attention to it, and fix it upon it, giving ourselves the time to consider it under all aspects, to meditate on it, to apply ourselves to it, and to extract, so to say, all the substance it contains, we discover wonders in it, and find new lights, and depths, which penetrate and ravish our souls, and for which we should seek in vain elsewhere; and we are forced to acknowledge that all we find there is grand, noble, elevated, touching, inspired, and divine.

3. *A more solid and firmer knowledge.* Faith cannot be wavering in him who meditates in a Christian spirit on the Gospel of Jesus Christ. In truth, in meditating on these sacred works, we are compelled to exclaim, " This is no human invention; this cannot be false; these facts, and this manner of relating them, these discourses and the way in which they have been handed down to us, are beyond the power of man, and can only have God for their Author. Who in truth has ever written with so much grandeur, and such simpli-

city? What other book has ever inculcated a doctrine more elevated, and of which the style and composition bear more fully the characters of truth, strength, simplicity, and nobility? The supernatural character of it is beyond imitation; there is neither art, nor study, nor passion in it, and the events related in it bear the marks of a divine inspiration which proclaim the Grandeur and Majesty of Him, Who is the subject of it, and Who answers to the character therein set forth.

Prayer. I thank Thee, O my God! with all the powers of my heart, that Thou hast made me a partaker of the knowledge of Thy divine Gospel. Shall I be unhappy enough to possess so great a blessing, and yet let it perish in my hands, or shall I possess it only to my shame, and condemnation! No, O Lord! it shall be the joy of my heart, the daily food of my soul, and the support of my life. May I have grace to meditate on it faithfully, to engrave it deeply on my heart, to practise it constantly, that I may have my portion in life everlasting. Amen.

Meditation II.

THE ANGEL APPEARS TO ZACHARIAS.

Appearance of the Angel Gabriel to Zacharias, in order to announce to him the birth of a son, Who was to be forerunner of the Messias,—S. Luke i. 5-25.

The circumstances preceding this appearance, those which accompanied it, and those that followed it.

FIRST POINT.

The circumstances preceding this appearance.

There was in the days of Herod, the king of Judæa, a certain priest named Zacharias, of the course of Abia; and his wife was of the daughters of Aaron, and her name was Elisabeth. And they were both righteous before God, walking in all the commandments and ordinances of the Lord blameless. And they had no child, because that Elisabeth was barren, and they both were now well stricken in years. And it came to pass, that while he executed the priest's office before God in the order of his course, according to the custom of the priest's office, his lot was to burn incense when he went into the temple of the Lord. And the whole multitude of the people were praying without, at the time of incense. Three things here present themselves to our consideration.

1. *The date of this event.* In the reign of Herod, the first foreign king of the ancient part of the kingdom of Judah, there was a priest named Zacharias of the course of Abia; the eighth of the sixteen which had been formed from the sons of Eleazar, the eldest son of Aaron, and his first successor in the pontifical office. What a proof of sincerity and truth! An historian, who gives his dates with such precision, and names the persons, marking their family and origin, cannot intend an imposture, and shews at the same time that he does not fear a charge of falsehood being brought against him. Thus the Jews, who lived in the first centuries after our Saviour's birth, never dared to accuse the Evangelists of inaccuracy, with regard to the dates which they mention, or the illustrious persons whom they are careful to name. If the unbelievers of modern days, who are so zealous in criticising the Gospel, wish to make a successful attack against it, it is in this field that they ought to enter the lists; for to decry unceasingly the miracles of the Gospel, or the incomprehensibility of its mysteries, is only an idle declamation. If the Gospel is false, let them prove it, as in the case of any other book, by applying to it the rules of a just criticism, and pointing out the anachronisms, errors, and contradictions, in it; but that is what neither the ancient nor the modern enemies of Christianity have done, nor will do. This date so simply and so truthfully given by S. Luke, is at the same time, the fulfilment of prophecy. This

Herod was the first foreign king who had ever reigned over the Jews. He was a Philistine by nation, originally from Ascalon, and placed on the throne of Judæa by the authority of the Roman Emperor. The sceptre had departed from Judah, and the time had arrived, which was marked out by the patriarch Jacob for the coming of the Messiah. It was equally easy to count the seventy weeks of Daniel, and to see that it was now the time when they should come to an end. Let us adore the providence of God, His sovereign wisdom, and His faithfulness in keeping His promises.

2. *Let us consider the character of Zacharias and Elisabeth.* They were of noble descent, and both *of the seed of Aaron*, from which for more than 1500 years both the office of high priest in the Sanctuary, and of priests at the altar had been supplied: but they were living without show or display. Nobility adds lustre and influence to virtue: but without virtue, of what value is nobility? *They were both righteous before God*, serving Him with an upright and sincere heart, without human respect as without hypocrisy: righteous, according to the law, and faithful in their observance of all the precepts which it prescribed: righteous, as regarded their neighbour, giving him neither cause for reproach, nor occasion of scandal. Although righteous and virtuous, they were not without their trials, but they were submissive to the Will of God: they had no children, but they did not murmur; it was no longer even the object of their hopes, nor the motive of their prayers: they had turned all their longings towards the birth of the Saviour. How happy are those marriages, where equality of position and oneness of mind are to be found combined with virtue as real and solid!

3. *Let us observe the circumstance of the place and time in which the appearance of the angel to Zacharias took place.* It was in the temple at the moment of burning incense, and of offering up the prayers appointed by the rites of the Jewish nation; it was at the time that the people were praying without, as usual at the

time of incense, and when they were waiting for the blessing of the priest on his return. What happier moment to obtain from Heaven the most signal favours! Let us frequent the House of God; let us be diligent in frequenting public prayer, and the services of the Church, and above all, let us specially be present at the time when the true Oblation is offered up to God, even Jesus Christ Himself! What advantages may we not derive, especially if we worship there with the outward and inward reverence which this divine Sacrifice demands of us! But if we are called upon, in our office of priests, ourselves to celebrate this holy Eucharist, with what attention and decorum ought we not to observe the due order and observances which are appointed! With what recollectedness of mind and purity of heart, with what fervour, what love and gratitude ought we not to minister at this holy ordinance!

SECOND POINT.

The circumstances which occur during this appearance.

Three objects suggest themselves here for our consideration.

1. *The angel of God.* Let us remark his visible presence near the altar. *There appeared unto him an angel of the Lord, standing on the right side of the altar of incense. And when Zacharias saw him, he was troubled, and fear fell upon him.* Millions of angels surround the Altars of our Churches. If their presence is only visible to the eye of faith, are we therefore to shew them less respect, love, and trust? Let us admire, in the second place, the goodness of this celestial being. *But the angel said unto him, Fear not, Zacharias; for thy prayer is heard, and thy wife Elisabeth shall bear thee a son, and thou shalt call his name John.* It is the work of good angels to reassure us, and all the feelings they inspire us with are those of peace of mind, and confidence in God. Let

us observe, in the next place, the name, dignity, employment, and might of the angel. *Zacharias said unto the angel, Whereby shall I know this? for I am an old man, and my wife well stricken in years.* Zacharias shews here some mistrust as to the accomplishment of that which this heavenly messenger announces to him. *And the angel answering said unto him, I am Gabriel that stand in the presence of God and am sent to speak unto thee, and to shew thee these glad tidings.* It is not without reason that the angel here declares his name. *Gabriel* signifies *the power of God.* It is the same angel, who revealed and explained to Daniel the prophecy of the 70 weeks, and is soon about to announce to Mary, the birth of the Saviour. The name of *Gabriel*, by recalling to Zacharias the famous prophecies of Daniel, ought to have made him feel the injustice of his question, and how blameable his doubts had made him. Do we look upon the good thoughts and inspirations which God sends to us, as His messengers, and do we follow them obediently? The occupation of the archangel Gabriel is to carry forth the commands of God, but without ever withdrawing from His Presence. So those, who are commissioned on earth to publish to the world the Will of God, must be always united to Him. Lastly, what we should remark in the Angel Gabriel, is the severity which he exercises. After having made himself known to Zacharias, he adds, *And behold thou shalt be dumb and not able to speak, until the day that these things shall be performed, because thou believest not my words, which shall be fulfilled in their season.* For one careless word, nine months of silence? We should soon be cured of our faults, if we punished them as severely. When God speaks, man must be silent, listen, believe, and obey. If we judge by this rule, how few there are who are true believers?

2. *Let us consider S. John, and continue the words of the angel. Thy wife Elisabeth,* he said to Zacharias, *shall bear thee a son, and thou shalt call his name John. And thou shalt have joy and gladness: and*

THE ANGEL APPEARS TO ZACHARIAS. 13

many shall rejoice at his birth. For he shall be great in the sight of the Lord, and shall drink neither wine nor strong drink, and he shall be filled with the Holy Ghost, even from his mother's womb. And many of the children of Israel shall he turn to the Lord their God. And he shall go before Him in the spirit and power of Elias, to turn the hearts of the fathers to the children, and the disobedient to the wisdom of the just; to make ready a people prepared for the Lord. S. John, says the Angel, shall be great in the sight of the Lord, not on account of the nobility of his origin, but because of the wonders which the Lord was about to work at his birth, the gifts of the Holy Spirit with which he should be filled, the innocency of his conduct, the austerity of his life, and lastly, by the ardour, the purity, the constancy, of his labours, and the success of his zeal. How well the angel knew, in what consists true greatness! He knew no less perfectly also the heart of man. What could be more fitting in truth to make ready a people prepared for the Lord, than to set before sinners, that it is their God and their Saviour whom they have forsaken; before heretics, that it is the ancient law which they are destroying, and that they are degenerating from the simplicity and uprightness of heart of their fathers: before unbelievers, that they are neglecting the first principles of common prudence, in matters of the greatest importance, and in which there is no other part for them to take, than that to which the example of true believers invites them.

3. *Let us take notice of Zacharias. Remark first his fear. He was troubled,* the Gospel says, *and fear fell upon him.* If a friend of God is frightened at the sight of an angel, the minister of God's services, what will be the terror of sinners, when they shall see Jesus Christ, surrounded by all His Angels, the ministers of His vengeance! Consider in the second place his prayer. *Thy prayer is heard,* the angel said to him. He had formerly asked for a son: but for a long while, he had desired only to see the Messiah, the Expectation of the

c

whole nation, Whose coming, according to the prophets, could not be far distant. His prayer was heard in both ways, and in a manner far surpassing his hopes. When we seek the furtherance of God's interests, God interests Himself in ours. When God does not answer our prayers, or delays to answer them, it is always for our good. Let us examine in the third place what was Zacharias' fault. On the one side, it was a great one; for the authority of God was a reason for belief against all the appearances of reason, and in spite of every obstacle of nature. Moreover his office of priest required of him a more perfect obedience, and a faith which might serve as an example to the people. On the other side, his fault appears excusable, for it was but momentary, and caused by trouble and sudden fear. But how shall we find an excuse for our continual and cherished distrust, the scruples which we affect or adopt upon reflection, our want of submission, our shameful incredulity? Observe lastly, the punishment of Zacharias, when he said to the angel, *Whereby shall I know this?* Doubtless, he desired to have a sign, a miracle which should confirm to him the truth of the things which were told to him. That sign was given to him, he became dumb. Such was the involuntary result of his request, which proved at the same time, the punishment of his guilt, and the assurance to him of God's goodness towards him. He accepted this punishment with submission and gratitude. God often answers our prayers, in order to punish us for an indiscreet request; but His chastisements in this world are, in the order of His grace, always tokens of His favour.

THIRD POINT.

Of the circumstances which follow the vision.

Three objects present themselves also here for our consideration.

1. *Zacharias. And the people waited for Zacharias, and marvelled that he tarried so long in the temple.*

THE ANGEL APPEARS TO ZACHARIAS.

And when he came out, he could not speak unto them; and they perceived that he had seen a vision in the temple: for he beckoned unto them, and remained speechless. And it came to pass, that, as soon as the days of his ministration were accomplished, he departed to his own house. What fervour! Zacharias does not excuse himself from completing his time of service notwithstanding his infirmity, and his anxiety to communicate to Elisabeth the happiness that had been promised them. What humility! he does not fear to shew himself to the people, and he submits with resignation to the humiliations of his state. What love of retirement! he does not tarry, after his sacred functions are concluded, he returns to his own house as soon as his ministry is no longer needed. What lessons does his conduct convey to us!

2. *The people deserve our admiration.* What piety! they do not murmur at the length of the sacrifice, but wait in prayer until he comes out to them. What discretion! they do not exult in the disgrace that has befallen a minister of the altar. What charity! they do not accuse or suspect him of any crime. What respect! they assume only that Zacharias had seen a heavenly vision, and the infirmity which they perceive in him makes him only the more worthy of respect. Thus should we reverence those who are afflicted, interpret every thing in good part, never suspect evil in any one, least of all in the ministers of the Lord.

3. *Consider Elisabeth. And after those days, his wife Elisabeth conceived, and hid herself five months, saying, Thus hath the Lord looked upon me, to take away my reproach among men.* What faith in this holy woman! Zacharias makes known to her no doubt by writing the mercies of the Lord: immediately she believed, and her faith was rewarded. What humility! having conceived, according to the promise of the angel, she does not seek to show herself in the world, and to publish her happiness. Thus souls, which are specially favoured by God, should hide the graces, which He bestows upon them,

or only speak of them, when obliged to do so, by obedience or necessity. What gratitude! she did not cease to thank God, and admire His Providence. God afflicts and consoles us, as it pleases Him, according to the designs of His sovereign wisdom. Why then should we disquiet ourselves, since we are in the Hands of God Who is Almighty, Who governs every thing, and Who loves us? Let us thank Him for every thing, and every thing He does will turn to our advantage.

Prayer. Yea, O my Saviour, I will give Thee thanks at all times, but especially when it pleases Thee to try me. Blessed beyond measure shall I be, if in order to gain Thee, Thou shouldest grant to me to suffer as much as sinners suffer only to lose Thee! It is to bring me back to Thee, Lord, it is to save me from eternal torments that Thou thus afflictest me in this present time; and the blessings which Thou, in the order of Thy Providence, deniest me, Thy grace will repay me with usury in Heaven. Strike then, O merciful justice of my God. Prune, cut away here below, provided that Thou spare me in eternity. Amen.

Meditation III.

THE ANNUNCIATION.

1. The angel Gabriel is sent to Mary—2. This angel converses with Mary—3. He leaves her: three circumstances worthy of reflection.—S. Luke i. 26-38.

FIRST POINT.

The Angel Gabriel is sent to Mary.

And in the sixth month, the angel Gabriel was sent from God, unto a city of Galilee, named Nazareth, to a virgin espoused to a man whose name was Joseph, of the house of David; and the virgin's name was Mary.

1. *Consider the solemnity of this embassy.* It is God, Who sends a heavenly messenger to the earth; it is *an*

angel, of the highest order; it is *Gabriel*, the strength of God, who is sent: it is the entire celestial court who are attentive to this great event: let these introductory circumstances imbue us with a religious awe.

2. *Meditate on the subject of this embassy.* The Incarnation of the Word in the chaste womb of a virgin concerns the restoration of the whole human race. Let us then here bring before our minds the most Holy Trinity, who in the presence of all the blessed spirits, are saying, not as formerly '*Let us make man in our Image*,' but let us make the God-Man, Who shall reconcile Heaven and earth, restore fallen man, raise him up to Us, and make him worthy to occupy the place, of which the rebel angels rendered themselves unworthy. Let us accomplish our design and send down the long-waited-for Messiah. It is thus that the Three Persons of the Holy Trinity worked together specially in the accomplishment of this prodigy of Divine Love. The Father gives His Son to mankind, the Word consents to His own Incarnation, and the Holy Spirit offers Himself to bring about this great Mystery. Let us prostrate ourselves with reverence and gratitude at the sight of such a signal favour; of love, so boundless.

3. *Examine the terms of this Embassy;* it is not to great cities, to the palaces of princes, to the daughters of kings, clothed in purple and covered with gold and jewels, that the Angel is sent; it is to Nazareth, a small city of Galilee; it is to a virgin named Mary, espoused to Joseph. It is true they were both of the royal house of David; but their family had long since lost its splendour, and Mary is, in the eyes of the world, only the future wife of an artizan. It is nevertheless to her that God sends forth His Embassador; it is in her that God wills to work the greatest marvel of His Almighty Power. But He will not work it without His creature's will. It is neither birth, nor the rarest gifts of nature which attract the notice of God: true merit, in His eyes, consists in modesty, humility, innocency of life, love of purity. Mary is not forewarned of

the designs of God on her behalf nor of the celestial Embassy which is approaching her: how will she receive it? how will she respond to it? Our first parents, clothed with original innocence, were commanded to transmit it to us: it only required of them one single act of obedience; but they failed even in that, and, at the first attack of the wicked spirit, they yielded. Eve allowed herself to be seduced by vanity, and Adam, by too easy compliance. Zacharias, warned by the same Angel, who to-day is sent to Mary, of the future birth of a Son and of His greatness, was so troubled and overcome, that his fear led him into unbelief, and brought upon him a signal punishment. Now, how will the Blessed Virgin bear the weight of the unexpected greatness which is about to be announced to her? She will conduct herself in a manner to excite the admiration of all succeeding generations. "Behold, from henceforth all generations shall call her blessed."

SECOND POINT.

The Angel converses with the Blessed Virgin. Compare the sublime favours, which the heavenly spirit announces to Mary, with the candour, the noble simplicity, and the excellence of the virtues of this holy Virgin, and we shall have before us in the promises of the Angel, the highest gift that Heaven can bestow, and, in the answers of Mary, the holiest that earth can produce.

1. *The Angel salutes Mary, and Mary is troubled. The Angel came in unto her, and said, Hail, thou that art highly favoured, the Lord is with thee. Blessed art thou among women.* Gabriel breaks in upon the solitude of Mary; he enters the place, where she was offering to the Lord, ever present in the sanctuary of her soul, the sacrifice of her prayers. Thereupon he addresses her, and whilst sublime praise is expressed in the terms of her salutation, he gives her three titles of incomparable greatness.

The first, with regard to herself. *Hail, thou that art highly favoured.* As if he would say, You are of all created beings the holiest; you are a treasure of virtue by the innocency of your conduct and the purity of your life. The second, with regard to God. *The Lord is with thee.* As if to say, You are cherished, protected, and indwelt by Him. He is in you, He is with you, you are governed in everything by His Spirit. The third, with regard to mankind. *Blessed art thou among women.* That is to say, distinguished, raised above other women. Never before had an Angel spoken to a mortal in terms so respectful and so wondrous! *When she saw him, she was troubled at his saying, and cast in her mind what manner of salutation this should be.* Mary's only reply was her silence: but what virtues are implied by this silence! 1. What humility! her heart rejects entirely the praises which are given to her; she appropriates none of them; she takes no part in them, but refers all the glory to God. 2. What modesty! even praise distresses, disturbs and alarms her. 3. What prudence! she considers, what is this salutation which is given to her, whence it comes, and whither it leads: she is cautious, and keeps herself on her guard. If the praises of an Angel, who only speaks as the messenger of God, caused Mary to be troubled, how much more ought we to fear the praises of men, which have mostly, only for their subject, the natural and dangerous gifts of birth or mind, talents or beauty! We ought then to call to mind the example of Mary; but how on the contrary, and to our own hurt, do we not oppose to these virtues three contrary vices! 1. A deeply rooted pride. We accept praise, and imagine it to be our due, and the secret estimation, in which we hold ourselves, often goes beyond that which others award to us. 2. A hypocritical modesty. Far from being troubled by the praise of others, we take pleasure in it: we allow our hearts to be satiated by it, and only appear to reject that which is offered us, in order to elicit fresh praise. 3. A fatal security and imprudence. Far from being on our guard, and holding ourselves aloof, flattery captivates our confidence and disarms it. Is it not alas! by these artifices, that the spirit of error and the spirit of impurity have seduced a multitude of souls, and have gained the victory, perhaps, over ourselves?

2. *The Angel reveals to Mary the great mystery of the Incarnation, and Mary sets forth her difficulties to him.* The Angel, perceiving her trouble and her disquietude, says to her, *Fear not, Mary: for thou hast found favour with God. And, behold, thou shalt conceive in thy womb, and bring forth a son, and shalt call His name* JESUS. *He shall be great, and shall be called the Son of the Highest; and the Lord God shall give unto Him the throne of His father David: and He shall reign over the house of Jacob for ever; and of His Kingdom there shall be no end.* In order to quiet the distress of the Blessed Virgin, the Angel calls her by her name, and after having confirmed to her what he had already made known to her respecting her present dignity, he announces to her her future greatness: he reveals to her that she is about to become the Mother of the Messiah, that she will have for her Son, the Son of the Most High; that this Son will reign, and that His reign will have no end. O Blessed Virgin! what greatness for you! what blessings to mankind! what glory for your Divine Son! what joy to the world! Hasten then to attain to the greatness to which your God calls you. But no, she pauses; Mary is in accordance with the will of God; she loves God, and Him only; she is a virgin, and desires to remain so; she knows that it is pleasing to Him, Who is holiness itself; and yet she is to become a Mother. She waits to know whether all this greatness is compatible with the virginity which she professes, and which she knows to be well-pleasing to the Lord. *Then Mary said unto the Angel, How shall this be, seeing I know not a man?* I am a virgin, and God has inspired me with a desire to remain such. Of all the thoughts which occupied the soul of Mary at that moment, she gives utterance to but one, and that one

serves us as a witness to her extreme love of virgin purity. Here we have the first utterance which the announcement of so much greatness has drawn forth from her lips, an utterance which has echoed throughout the universe, which has developed, and will develope, to the end of the world, an infinite number of spouses of Christ, and which has gained for the Blessed Virgin the glorious title of Queen of virgins. O, blessed Virgin! O, mother of purity! how conformable is the disposition of your heart to the design which God has in store for you!

3. *The angel Gabriel explains the ineffable mystery, and Mary acquiesces.* Faith does not extinguish reason by bringing it into submission: it does not forbid in a believer, the desire of gaining knowledge, and of receiving instruction; such was the position of Mary. There was neither doubt nor distrust in her respect. She does not ask, like Zacharias, for a sign in order to believe, or a convincing proof which should captivate the mind: but, disposed to believe whatever is told, she asks only to be instructed. Her words bear the impress of a wise reason, of a pious soul, of a pure heart, and at the same time, of a mind, attentive to profit by the revelations of the angel, and ready to acquiesce in the designs of God. Therefore Gabriel makes it his duty, 1. to explain to her, even to the least detail, the manner in which the great mystery was to be brought about. *The Holy Ghost shall come upon thee, and the power of the Highest shall overshadow thee: therefore also that holy thing which shall be born of thee shall be called the Son of God.* O adorable mystery! O sanctifying Spirit, descend to-day into my soul, and by the divine operation of Thy grace, cause that Jesus Christ shall be born there! 2. The angel reveals to Mary what had happened to S. Elisabeth. Nothing is to be hidden from the humble, pure, and teachable Mary; thus does God reward faithful and submissive souls. *And behold thy cousin Elisabeth, she hath also conceived a son in her old age: and this is the sixth month with her who was called barren.* Mary did not doubt: she did not need

to have her faith strengthened by the example of the still recent miracle of the conception of the saintly forerunner; but the Angel willed to fill her with a double cause for rejoicing, and adding to a miracle, the account of another miracle, he would thereby teach her, that whether it be a woman, who conceives in her old age, or a virgin, who shall have a Son without losing her virginity, the one was not more difficult than the other to Him, Who can do every thing in Heaven and in earth. Thus he adds, *For with God nothing is impossible.* It is doubtless for our sakes, much more than for her's, that the angel Gabriel thus explains himself, in order to teach us that this mystery, as well as all the other mysteries belonging to the God-Man, are founded on the Almighty power of Him, Who has created all things out of nothing. Consequently, let us put far from us all frivolous reasonings of the human mind. *With God nothing is impossible.* Here is the answer to all the objections made by unbelievers against religion, and to all the difficulties which could, at any time, present themselves to our minds, to disturb our faith. I believe then, O my God! I believe with a firm unshaken faith all that Thou hast revealed in Thy holy Word, because *with God nothing is impossible:* and since it is not in my power to conceive the wonders which Thou canst bring into operation, I believe, because Thou hast said it. I do not reason, because *with Thee nothing is impossible.* After these explanations, Mary in few words, expresses the most lively faith, the deepest humility, the tenderest love, the most submissive obedience, the simplest acquiescence, the most ardent desire to co-operate with the designs of God, in short, the most perfect abandonment to His divine will. *Mary then said, Behold the handmaid of the Lord: be it unto me according to Thy word.* Then was restored the happiness of mankind, the mystery of the Incarnation consummated, prophecies fulfilled, and the disobedience of our first parents repaired. Let us not fail, when meditating upon this mystery, to cherish in our hearts the love of Jesus, the Author of our salvation.

THIRD POINT.

The Angel departs from the Blessed Virgin.

And the angel departed from her. Then was accomplished the ineffable mystery of the Incarnation of the Word—it is for pure hearts to contemplate it in silence.

1. *On the part of God.* God the Father gives us His Son, Who, at this moment, is made Man in the chaste womb of the Blessed Virgin, by the operation of the Holy Ghost. Behold the chiefest work of God's Almighty power, the end and perfection of all His works, by which His infinite Goodness communicated Itself in a manner the noblest, the most intimate, the most complete, and the most worthy of Himself.

2. *On the part of Jesus Christ.* At this moment, the Son of God is Man, and a man is the Son of God: the same Person is God and Man, God eternal and eternally begotten, existing in the bosom of His Father, and a Child hidden in the bosom of His Mother. This moment so long foretold has at length arrived; from this moment mankind has a Saviour, a man like themselves, Who offers up Himself to accomplish for them all the will of God His Father, to submit to the doom of death pronounced against the first man and all his descendants: from this moment man yields to God a homage worthy of Him, equal to Him, and which He cannot refuse to accept. The Messiah promised to mankind is already conceived in the chaste womb of Mary; and Who is He, —this divine Messiah? What will He be? *He is the Son of the Highest:* and as such He will have all power in Heaven and earth; He shall be called JESUS, which signifies Saviour. He fulfils already, and shall fulfil, to the end, all that is implied in that great Name. He shall have *the throne of His Father David,* and that Heavenly throne, of which that of David was only the figure. *He shall reign over the house of Jacob,* over the true

Israelites, the heirs of the faith of Abraham. He shall reign with them in glory after their death, and *of His kingdom there shall be no end.*

3. *On the part of Mary.* As soon as the Angel departed from her, then took place in her, that which he had told her. From the pure blood of this spotless Virgin, the Holy Ghost formed a Body, into which He breathed a perfect Soul, and at the same moment, the Word of God became united substantially, and in oneness of Person, to this Body and this Soul. Then Mary, from being the handmaid of the Lord, became His Mother, and truly Mother of God, since the Child which she had conceived, and which was of her blood in her chaste womb, was truly God. O blessed obedience, upon which the Almighty Creator of Heaven and earth descended into the womb of Mary!

Prayer. Oh King! alone worthy of all our homage, and of all our love; it is Thee alone whom I desire to follow, Thee alone whom I would serve. O loving Saviour, the desire of all nations, the joy of mankind, our Redeemer and our Master! behold Thee at length! Thou art, Thou dost exist in the midst of us! Receive my earliest homage! suffer me to study all Thy actions, to follow Thy steps on earth, and to contemplate the wonders which mark every instant of Thine earthly life. With what feelings was the heart of Thy Mother penetrated, at this adorable moment of Thine Incarnation! This ineffable goodness, which united her so intimately to God and brought her so near to Him, was granted to her humility, purity, faith and submission. How far removed am I from the possession of these virtues! Grant them to me, Thou Who becamest Incarnate for our sanctification. Prepare my heart by Thy grace and love, and form Thyself in it by Thy Spirit, so that I may only live by Thee, in Thee, and for Thee, that it may be no longer I that live, but Thou Who livest in me. Amen.

Meditation IV.

MARY VISITS ELISABETH.

1. The departure of Mary—2. Her arrival at the house of Elisabeth—3. The visit which she makes her, and her return to Nazareth.—S. Luke i. 39-56.

FIRST POINT.

The departure of Mary.

And Mary arose in those days, and went into the hill country with haste, into a city of Juda. Consider, 1. the motives which determined Mary to take this journey. 2. the virtues which she practises in taking it.

1. *Three motives determine Mary upon taking this journey.* First, and foremost, obedience to divine inspiration. She does not visit Elisabeth merely to assure herself of the truth of what the angel had said to her: her faith is perfect: neither is it in order to make known to her relation the mystery which had been accomplished in her, which she hides even from her espoused husband, to whom so many reasons would seem to prompt her to reveal it; but attentive and obedient to the motions of the Holy Spirit, whose guidance she follows in every thing, she yields simply to the impulse which moves her to visit Elisabeth, in the belief that the Lord had thereby some purpose to be fulfilled. And so in truth it was; He willed to sanctify the forerunner, to shew forth His Glory and the power of His Son from the first moment of His conception, and filling the two mothers with a fresh abundance of His graces, to make them taste the sweetest consolation. In the good dispositions with which God inspires our hearts, He has often special designs for the manifestation of His Glory, for the profit of our neighbour, and for our own perfection and consolation. How often do we lose many precious advantages by our resistance of His grace, or our distractions.

2. *Friendship is a motive, which determines Mary on taking this journey.* Mary and Elisabeth were relations; both had become mothers by a miracle, although of a very different nature; each bore in her womb, the one the Messiah, the other the forerunner. What sweeter bonds could there be to form a tender union between these two happy mothers? Saints are not insensible to the charms of a friendship founded upon virtue, upon the similarity of graces received, or the resemblance of some vocation, and its offices; they are on the contrary, more capable of tasting its sweetnesses, and more exact in fulfilling its duties.

3. *Charity urges Mary to pay this visit.* Elisabeth was in years, and in an advanced state of pregnancy: and in this state, and in the situation in which her husband was, she needed some one to be with her in whom she could place confidence, and who could help and comfort her; and it is for this purpose, that Mary undertakes her journey. Till then, the love of God, the spirit of humility, and fervour in prayer had kept her at home; but charity to her neighbour makes her leave home; this alone guides her, animates her, and not that love of seeing and being seen, that curiosity or that ostentation which are so often, to say nothing further, the motives of the visits which we pay.

2. *Mary departs;* but how many virtues does she not exercise on her journey?

1. *A deep humility,* which nothing shakes, and which does not permit her to indulge in any comparisons between herself, the height of her dignity, and the infinite difference which existed between the Son, Whom she was about to bring forth, and that of Elisabeth. The change which had come over her, does not alter the simplicity of her conduct. The handmaid of the Lord is not swayed by those capricious laws, which society and good manners have established, which the vanity of this world carries out with so much exactness, and which the petty jealousies of mankind have rendered indispensable: she ignores those distinctions of rank, those claims

which self-love has originated and introduced, and which it exacts with so much punctiliousness. Far from her, was that pride which so often hinders us from fulfilling our duties to our neighbour.

2. *Mary shews an heroic courage, of which nothing cools the ardour;* neither the hardship of the journey, nor the difficulties of the way, neither her state of health, nor her youth, nor the delicacy of her sex, are reasons for dispensing herself from performing God's work, and setting forth at the call of duty. Charity, when it reigns in the heart, disposes it to render to a neighbour, all the services of which it is capable, not to save itself any trouble, or pains, and above all, to join to the good offices which friendship requires of us, noble and elevated ideas of faith and religion.

3. *Mary exercises an admirable diligence in her journey and allows nothing to retard her.* Neither curiosity can turn her on one side, nor fatigue incline her to take repose; nothing can moderate her fervour, her activity. When it is a question of our own pleasure, or of our own satisfaction, we do not make any difficulty, we throw ourselves into it with ardour and zeal; but if it be a matter of doing good to others, what difficulties, what inability, what want of courage, what dilatoriness! Let us reform ourselves by the example of the Blessed Virgin.

SECOND POINT.

The arrival of Mary at the house of Elisabeth.

Let us observe, 1. the salutation which Mary makes to Elisabeth, and the effects which it produces. 2. the answer which Elisabeth makes to the salutation of Mary, and the glorious titles which she gives her.

1. *Mary entered into the house of Zacharias, and saluted Elisabeth.* Those, who are favoured of the Lord, are always prompt to make it known to others. Mary goes to meet her cousin, and what the angel revealed unto her, that she makes known to Elisabeth. True charity

goes forth to embrace the whole world, and looks for no return. If God's love had not prevented us, and did not prevent us every day, should we ever have known Him? should we think of offering Him our homage? *And it came to pass that when Elisabeth heard the salutation of Mary, the babe leaped in her womb: and Elisabeth was filled with the Holy Ghost.* The Gospel does not tell us, in what terms Mary offered her salutation to Elisabeth; but it does make known to us the wonderful effects which it produced. 1. On S. John. As soon as Elisabeth had heard the voice of Mary, by the greatest of all miracles and the most singular favour, Jesus, from His mother's womb, acts upon S. John. He sanctifies his soul, according to the promise of the angel to Zacharias. He makes Himself known to him, and makes known to him the ministry of forerunner which he was destined to exercise; He makes him already exercise this ministry by means of his mother; and finally, fills him with a heavenly delight which makes him leap for joy. Thus the presence of Jesus Christ, in the august Sacrament of our altars, works the most wonderful effects on those who receive it in true faith: but they receive more or less grace according to their state of preparation. 2. The salutation of Mary has a miraculous effect upon Elisabeth. This holy woman, filled with the Spirit of God, and enlightened from on high, knows and announces the sublime mysteries which have been accomplished in Mary; the Incarnation of the Word, and the divine Motherhood. Interpreter of the feelings of the son whom she bears in her womb, she executes for him the office of forerunner, and sets forth the greatness of Jesus, and of His Mother.

2. *Elisabeth, filled with the Holy Ghost, spake out with a loud voice and said, Blessed art thou among women, and Blessed is the fruit of thy womb. And whence is this to me, that the mother of my Lord should come to me? For lo, as soon as the voice of thy salutation sounded in mine ears, the babe leaped in my womb for joy: and blessed is she that believed:*

for there shall be a performance of those things which were told her from the Lord. Let us consider the titles and the praises which Elisabeth gives to Mary.

1. She calls her *Blessed among women.* The Angel had already given her that title, and Elisabeth adds, *and Blessed is the fruit of thy womb,*" as if she had said, How blessed must thou be, O holy Virgin, who bearest in thy bosom the Author and the Source of all blessing.

2. Elisabeth continues. *Whence is this to me, that the mother of my Lord should come to me?* What great truths and what divine knowledge does not the Presence of Jesus Christ spread abroad in the heart of Elisabeth. She appears to be penetrated with the same feelings of modesty and humility so abundantly shewn forth in Mary. The holy Virgin took upon her the rank of the handmaid of the Lord, even when she became His Mother. Elisabeth acknowledges the greatness of the Son of Mary, and calls Him her Lord, even when He comes to visit her. Have we the same feelings towards Jesus Christ, when He comes to us? Does His divine Presence and His Grace impress us with the same transports and the same joy in the adorable Sacrament of His Body and Blood? If we have the faith and piety, the humility and the gratitude of Elisabeth, how shall we then express our admiration, our respect and our love, and how shall we exclaim, *And whence is this to me that my Lord and my God condescends to visit me?*

3. Elisabeth says to Mary. *And blessed is she that believed.* She congratulates Mary only on the precious gifts of grace and faith which she had received from Heaven; and in truth, is there any other real and lasting happiness? We hear daily in the world a girl spoken of as happy, who secures a good position by her marriage: and another pitied, whose generous and devoted faith has led her to renounce all earthly hopes, and to seek by devoting herself to a religious life to secure the rewards promised to His disciples. Could we not however apply to this Christian virgin the words, *Blessed*

is she that believed the promises of the Saviour; thou shalt see the entire accomplishment of them in the hundredfold which thou shalt receive here below, and in the heavenly place which is reserved for thee hereafter.

THIRD POINT.

The visit of Mary to Elisabeth, and her return to Nazareth.

And Mary abode with her about three months, and returned to her own house. Consider, 1. the advantages which her remaining in the house of Zacharias brought about; and 2. the motives for her return to Nazareth, before the birth of S. John the Baptist.

1. *Under the appearance of ordinary services, what advantage did not the presence of Mary procure for the house of Zacharias.* If her first appearance, if her first words produced such wonders, what abundance of graces, consolations, and benedictions, did not her residence there during nearly three months bring with it! She bore in her heart and her bosom the most excellent gifts; in her heart, the fulness of grace, and in her bosom, Jesus Christ, the Author and Source of all grace. Oh happy house, to be found worthy to possess for so long a time so great a blessing. This precious advantage communicated itself to all those who frequented the house of Zacharias. Although they were ignorant of the mystery of a God-made-Man in the womb of the Blessed Virgin, yet they could not fail, in speaking and listening to her, to be impressed with respect for her, and filled with love to God.

2. Observe the motives which led Mary to return to Nazareth before the birth of S. John. Elisabeth was already in her sixth month, when Mary arrived at her house. It was then near the time of the birth of her child, when this holy Virgin, always attentive and obedient to the guidance of the Holy Spirit, returned to Nazareth. We may imagine three reasons for her not

remaining for the birth of S. John (if she did not do so, as many commentators have said, and as the Gospel itself appears to imply). 1. on the part of Mary, the greatness of her purity. However holy Elisabeth was, and however holy the fruit of her womb, she was not exempt from the law of nature; and therefore it was not befitting for the Virgin, Mother of God, to be present at the birth of her cousin's child. The estate of virginity requires that certain acts of decorum should be observed, in order to avoid giving scandal to our neighbour, and putting one's self into danger. 2. On the part of Elisabeth. The perplexity of her situation, which needed the help of others, and prevented her from offering to Mary the attentions which she required. True charity makes us always thoughtful and considerate towards others. 3. on the part of S. John. The glory of his birth, the marvels which were about to take place at it, could not fail to draw down upon him all the attention of those around him, and render him the object of their wonder; which could not have been, at least with decency, in the Presence of Him from Whom he drew all his greatness. Jesus Christ therefore withdraws in order to leave to His forerunner, in his turn, all the glory of that day; the time would come, when the Forerunner, in his turn, would withdraw, in order to leave the glory to his Master. Let reason, prudence, and the will of God always be the guide of our actions, and each thing will have its turn. Providence disposes everything with wisdom; it is for us after the example of Mary, to carry out His intentions, and not to disturb the wise economy of His designs by our impetuosity or haste. Let us learn also from this holy Virgin, who, as soon as Elisabeth no longer needs her services, hastens to return to her own home; let us learn only to employ the necessary time in our visits; and not to multiply indefinitely imaginary necessities; and let us learn also to carry with us thither a spirit of piety in accordance with the mind of God. If the dispositions of those whom we visit, do not permit of our holding edifying conversations with them, at least, let us make up for their deficiencies, by the modesty of our own behaviour, the moderation of our sentiments, and by maintaining a certain reserve, or rather charity, which often has more effect upon the minds of others than the most pious discourses.

Prayer. Pour down then upon me, O my God! this loving and fervent charity; kindle me with that sacred fire with which Thou didst fill the heart of Mary, and through her, that of Elisabeth; that I may apply myself more than hitherto to all that may procure Thy glory, my own salvation, and that of my brethren. Be Thou Alone the End of my friendships, the bond of companionship, the object of my visits, and the principle of my conversations. Let Thy Spirit be the author, Thy glory the bond, and Thy Love the fruit of them. Let the example of the Blessed Virgin serve as our model in all the visits we pay, which, far from being acts of charity, means of increasing the union of our hearts, fitting opportunities for edifying our neighbour or of receiving edification from him, are, on the contrary, only too often an intercourse of vanity and frivolity, of worldliness and distractions, vices and passions, communicated by us, and received from others. Amen.

Meditation V.

HYMN OF MARY.

Elisabeth inspired by the Holy Spirit, having spoken to Mary, that Holy Virgin, filled with the same Spirit, answers her in that magnificent hymn which the Church repeats daily, and which is the first in the New Testament. Mary praises God in it, 1. for that which He has done in her; 2. for that which He has done against the oppressors of His people; 3. for that which He does on behalf of His Church.—S. Luke i. 46-55.

FIRST POINT.

Mary praises God for that which He has done in her.

My soul, she cries out, *doth magnify the Lord, and*

my spirit hath rejoiced in God my Saviour. For He hath regarded the low estate of His handmaiden: for behold, from henceforth all generations shall call me blessed. For He that is mighty hath done to me great things; and holy is His name. And His mercy is on them that fear Him, from generation to generation. These first words of the hymn of Mary contain

1. *The expression of her gratitude.* My soul, she says, is filled with admiration, my heart is transported with love. I no longer belong to myself, the Saviour fills all the powers of my soul. How great He is, this God of goodness. He has laden me with favours which my mouth cannot sufficiently magnify, because my heart cannot comprehend all its happiness. I was the most ignorant and unlearned of His handmaidens, and He has vouchsafed to look upon me. What gratitude! What love! Thus does a soul express itself, when it is truly humble and faithful to the graces of its God, and always penetrated by His mercies to it: whether it speaks of them to God Himself, or converses with others of them, it feels nothing but rapture and love; and such is the spirit which animates Mary. Her soul, as it were, steeped in the power and goodness of her God, acknowledges His gifts, adores His mercies, proclaims His powers, but all absorbed as she is in her happiness, it is not in herself, nor for herself, that Mary rejoices; it is in God, the sole Author of her salvation. Far from glorifying herself for her own merits, she sees nothing in herself but her own nothingness. The goodness of God only makes her yet more humble. Let us seek to form in ourselves these sentiments, and to enter into these dispositions. If we are tempted by the false appearance of human greatness, let us say to ourselves, O my soul, I have nothing great except the Lord, I admire only Him, all must be referred to His Glory: if by the seductions of pleasure, let us say, 'There is no solid joy, no pure and lasting pleasure except in God; my spirit will desire none other: my heart will desire none besides: if by the poison of praise or the mazes of self-love, let us turn to the

thought of our own nothingness, and recall to our hearts the humiliating remembrance of our sins.

2. *The words of Mary contain a prophecy.* Here am I, she says, become an object of wonder to all ages: He that is mighty hath magnified me: from age to age my name will be exalted amongst men, and I shall be known amongst them as the most blessed of women. If she had not been inspired from on high, would she have known for certain that her name would be held in honour, and that all generations would call her blessed? Let us join in the words of the Magnificat, and, filled with the remembrance of the virtues, greatness, and happiness of this Blessed Virgin, let us contribute as much as in us lies, to the honour which has been bestowed upon her name.

3. *The words of Mary contain a perfect tribute of praise to the attributes of God.* Elisabeth had said to her; Thou art blessed in having believed in the words of the angel, wishing thereby to set forth, that it was her faith which was the cause of her happiness. Mary adds to this truth by saying, My happiness is great, I acknowledge it, but I owe it to a favour freely granted me by the Lord. His good pleasure alone is the source of the honour and of the favour which it has pleased Him to bestow upon me. He has chosen me by an act of His goodness; this it is which makes all my greatness; this it is which penetrates my soul, and makes me overflow with love. Yes, it is the sovereign Master, Whose Name is Holy, and Whose power is without bounds, Who hath done in me such great things: His mercy is infinite. Ah! if men would not cease to adore and to fear Him, they would see His greatness descend from the fathers to the children, and continue from one generation to another. Here Mary specially praises the three attributes which characterise all the works of the Lord, and teaches us that all the mysteries, and even the Gospel itself are founded on the power, the wisdom, and the mercy of God. Can there be a greater motive of faith to an upright soul? But the proud mind rejects the mysteries of power which

it cannot comprehend; the corrupt heart resists the mysteries of holiness which it cannot enter into; and sinful man abuses the mysteries of mercy, of which he extends or narrows the compass, according to the inclination of his passions. Let us avoid such fearful evils; let us thank God, for that which He accomplished in the Blessed Virgin; let us, in the words of Mary herself, acknowledge with thankfulness what He accomplishes in us, whenever He enters into our hearts in the Sacrament of His Love, that ineffable Sacrament of His Power, His Holiness, and His Mercy.

SECOND POINT.

Mary praises God for that which He has done against the oppressors of His people.

He hath showed, said she, *strength with His arm; He hath scattered the proud in the imagination of their hearts. He hath put down the mighty from their seats, and exalted them of low degree. He hath filled the hungry with good things, and the rich He hath sent empty away.*

1. *Mary recalls here the past.* God, she seems to say, has brought to nought at all times the machinations which the wicked have formed against His people. Sennacherib, Holofernes, Antiochus have felt the power of His strong arm: but never has He more signally displayed His might than in the time of Pharaoh, the first persecutor of Israel; He overthrew him from his throne, and cast him, with all his army, into the depths of the sea. The Hebrews, on the contrary, despised, trodden under foot, without arms, without defence, without any resources, and destitute of all help, have come forth from their bondage, victorious, and full of glory. The sovereign Master of all earthly possessions has spoiled their rich oppressors: and their victims, destitute of even the necessaries of life, have found themselves enriched by the spoils and the treasures of Egypt. The

might of the tyrant has been overthrown, and the weakness of Israel has triumphed. Let us admire with Mary this supreme greatness. Who of us would not set his confidence in Him, Who can thus, with so small an exercise of His power, put down the mighty, and Who delights Himself in thus bountifully exalting the humble of heart?

2. *Mary prophesies of the future.* That which she utters with regard to Pharaoh in particular, is still, in her mouth, a prophecy of that which should come to pass, whether as regards the Jews, who, after having crucified the God of lowliness, Who set Himself to oppose their pride, have seen in their shameful dispersion, their vain projects fall to the ground: or as regards the heathen, who having raised themselves up with fury against Christ and His religion, have seen the proud wishes of their hearts crushed down, or have become themselves the heritage and the conquest of Christ, Whose Empire has spread over all the countries of the world. Christianity has suffered, on the part of tyrants, a persecution far greater, more prolonged, and bloodier than the children of Israel experienced in Egypt. But have these tyrants fared better than Pharaoh? And under the protection of the same God, have not Christians triumphed in a manner still more glorious than the Hebrews did? Who does not see in all this, the literal accomplishment of the prophecy of Mary, and her words exactly verified? The persecutors of religion have been overthrown from their thrones, and the Christian religion reigns in their stead. Let us join with the holy Virgin, in blessing the Lord, for the justice which He exercises upon the enemies of His Name.

3. *Mary gives us instruction for our present use.* Does she not seem to say to each one of us, Let him amongst you, who finds himself in any position of honour, power, or wealth, take care not to employ them against the weak, or the indigent; let him fear the just and powerful avenger of the innocent and oppressed: and let him, on the other hand, who groans under the oppression of

the unjust, humble himself, and put his trust in the Lord, and let him rest assured, that, even through submission, he will reap a glorious victory.

THIRD POINT.

Mary praises God for that which He has done on behalf of His Church.

He hath holpen His servant Israel, she continues, *in remembrance of His mercy: as He spake to our fathers, to Abraham and to his seed for ever.* In order rightly to understand these words, we must distinguish here three times, or seasons.

1. *The time of the promises.* The Israel of old, or the Church of the Old Testament, had its promises. By faith in the promises, the Jew honoured God, gained His protection, and obtained salvation. The great promise made to Abraham, and confirmed to the other patriarchs, was that, of his seed should be born a Son, in Whom all the nations of the earth shall be blessed. Nothing can be more clear than this prediction. Thus the Jews awaited this promised Son, the Messiah, the Christ, the Anointed of the Lord, with an entire oneness of desire and longing. Happy for them if they had acknowledged Him with an equal fidelity! But, at the same time, it is a matter of consolation for us to see that that which was thus accomplished, had been foretold so clearly, and so long a time before its accomplishment.

2. *We must distinguish the time of the accomplishment of the promises.* The time has come, and the new Israel, the Church of Jesus Christ, rejoices in it. The Son of Blessing has come: a virgin bears Him in her womb; soon He will appear. He will make Himself known, He will accomplish all that has been foretold of Him. It is Mary herself who announces it to us; she teaches us that the Incarnation of the Son of God, and the Advent of the Messiah are the ending of the pro-

mises of the law, and the beginning of the promises of the Gospel. We see with our eyes the execution of this prophecy. The nations of the earth have been enlightened with the light of the Gospel, and they have renounced the worship of idols, in order to worship the true God alone; but as for ourselves, we see something more striking still.

3. *The duration of the accomplishment.* The promise is *for ever*, says Mary, that is to say, it extends to all generations, to the end of this world. The religion of Christ has not been in reality a passing brilliancy, which has dazzled men during some generations; we see it endure for nearly two thousand years, notwithstanding the different characters of the nations who profess it, and the revolutions which have taken place, and in spite of persecutions, heresies, schisms, abuses and scandals. Every day fresh nations are brought to embrace the faith, and to participate in the promised blessings.

Prayer. We have been partakers ourselves, O Lord, in these abundant blessings, although we were amongst the number of these idolatrous nations. Withdraw them not from us, O God, because of our unfaithfulness and our continual backslidings. Do Thou continue them to us, and rather increase them to us, yet more than before, for the sake of Thy faithful ones who dwell in the midst of us. May we abuse them no more, but transmit them faithfully to our descendants! May the perfect accordance, which we behold between Thy promises and their fulfilment, animate and confirm our faith, and fill us with gratitude and love! May Thy mercy especially rest upon our country, and dwell with it for ever. Amen.

Meditation VI.

COMMENCEMENT OF S. JOHN BAPTIST'S CAREER.

His birth, his circumcision, and his retreat into the desert.
S. Luke i. 57-80.

FIRST POINT.

Birth of S. John.

Now Elisabeth's full time came, that she should be delivered; and she brought forth a son. And her neighbours and her cousins heard how the Lord had shewed great mercy upon her: and they rejoiced with her. To rejoice with those whom God favours, and wish them joy of the advantages which He bestows upon them, is—

1. *A duty of humanity, which we ought to fulfil with exactitude.* The joy which we express to our neighbour at any good fortune which befalls him, not only increases his happiness, but makes our own; and our neglect in the performance of this duty often becomes an offence.

2. *A duty of charity, which should be fulfilled with sincerity.* Far be it from us then to hide, under the words of congratulation or cordiality, an envious, or spiteful spirit, an angry and jealous heart.

3. *A duty of religion, which we ought to fulfil in a pious spirit; that is to say, by referring every thing to God.* It is God Who gives us our talents, our worldly good, our successes: let us applaud the distribution which He makes of His favours; let us honour His gifts and those on whom He bestows them, if we wish to have any share in His benefits ourselves. The company of the faithful is but one body, the advantages of each member are common to the whole body, and all the members ought to take part in them. It is equally

the duty of humanity, charity, and religion to share the afflictions which befall our neighbour, and to weep with those that weep; but how shall we fulfil these duties?

SECOND POINT.

Circumcision of S. John Baptist.

And it came to pass, that on the eighth day they came to circumcise the child:

1. Examine in this ceremony, the person of S. John. Although he had been set apart from his mother's womb, he is not thereby exempted from fulfilling the law of circumcision. Extraordinary graces do not dispense with the observance of a law common to all.

2. Observe the relations of S. John. *And they called him Zacharias after the name of his father.* This name was dear to the family of S. John, and had in esteem amongst the people, since he to whom it belonged was distinguished by all the virtues, which render a man holy in the eyes of God, and honoured in the eyes of men. It was but a natural impulse, and a feeling common to all parents, who desire to live on in their children, and who do not wish their name to fall into oblivion. Would to God that our Christian names were simply made use of to distinguish us from each other, and not to flatter our vanity, and foment our pride! Would to God that our names served to set forth and nourish our faith, and not merely to mark the spirit and character of the feeling which too often prompted the parents in their choice!

3. Consider Elisabeth. She would, doubtless, have specially rejoiced to see the name of her husband carried on in her son: but she knew that her son was not to live for this world, that he was destined for an employment of a heavenly nature, that he was born of special grace, and born to announce to men the God of grace: that he was therefore to bear a name, which should owe nothing to flesh and blood, a name conformable to the

privileges of his birth, and the greatness of his destiny. Thus, without saying that she had been instructed as to the name of the child by a special revelation or by some writing of her husband, she steadily opposed the wishes of her relations. *And his mother answered and said, Not so: but he shall be called John.* John, in Hebrew, signifies God, and grace. The names which men give either signify nothing, or if they have any signification, are generally but ill carried out by those who bear them.

The relations of Elisabeth answered her: *There is none of thy kindred that is called by this name;* but she continued firm: and, faithful to the command of Heaven, to the light of faith, to the spirit of the Gospel, and the motions of the Grace, of which her son was to be the preacher and minister, she constantly affirmed that he should be called John. Happy those mothers, who, having recognized the calling of Heaven with regard to their children, know, like Elisabeth, how to sacrifice the inclinations of a maternal tenderness to the supreme direction of the will of God, and to despise the indiscreet murmurs and importunate representations of friends and relations, who only regard the matter from a worldly point of view.

4. Consider Zacharias. *And they made signs to his father, what he would have him called. And he asked for a writing-table, and wrote, saying, His name is John. And they marvelled all. And his mouth was opened immediately, and his tongue loosed, and he spake, and praised God.—And his father Zacharias was filled with the Holy Ghost, and prophesied.* Let us admire here in Zacharias his faithfulness in obeying the commands given him from Heaven, in confirming to his son the name of John; his sudden cure, the recompense of his faithfulness and patience; his gratitude to God in the first use he makes of the faculty of speech thus restored to him; lastly, the fresh power bestowed upon him by God in filling him with His Spirit, and inspiring him with the gift of prophecy. How good and merciful is the Lord! He never sets bounds to His liberality.

How are we then our own enemies, when we shew ourselves unfaithful and ungrateful towards Him!

5. Contemplate the people. *And fear came on all that dwelt round about them; and all these sayings were noised abroad throughout all the hill country of Judæa: and all they that heard them laid them up in their hearts, saying, What manner of child shall this be! And the hand of the Lord was with him.* Observe, in this people, their feelings of admiration, respect and religion, at the sight of all the wonders which took place; their zeal in publishing the marvels of which they had been the witnesses; their faithfulness in preserving the remembrance of them in their hearts, in occupying themselves with them, and in pondering over them. Let us also admire all these wonders; let us thank God for them; let us regard S. John with a feeling of the highest reverence, and let us pray that we may obtain the grace to prepare ourselves to receive Him, Whom S. John already announces by the striking miracles of his birth.

THIRD POINT.

The retreat of S. John Baptist in the desert.

And the child grew, and waxed strong in spirit, and was in the deserts till the day of his shewing unto Israel. Hardly had S. John grown out of childhood, than he retired into the desert, and remained there hidden from the world until the age of thirty years. This child, consecrated from his mother's womb, flies from the contaminations of the age; this innocent soul sacrifices itself to the rigours of a life of penitence; this unusually gifted man awaits the usual age to enter upon his public functions: this prophet, enlightened with a heavenly light before he had seen the light of day, keeps himself hidden; this voice of the Eternal Word maintains a silence for thirty years, before he makes himself heard. What a pledge of future success in his preachings do not these antecedents and these preparations give! He can speak effectually of repentance, who has constantly practised it. What lessons, what examples does not S. John here offer for all ages, and all stations of life!

1. *To youth.* He teaches it to grow in innocence, and to fortify itself in the true spirit of religion and of piety. Happy he who, after having thus passed his earliest years, feels himself called of God, and retires from the world to meditate in retirement on the law of the Lord, and to practise it in its fulness. What fruits will he not bring forth, when it shall please God to call him to serve Him in the world!

2. *What an example does not S. John set to those who are living separate from the world.* Let him, who lives alone, consecrate his solitude by study, and meditation on holy books, prayer, and self-denial.

3. *What a lesson, finally, does the conduct of S. John give to those living in the world.* Let him who lives in the world make for himself therein a solitude, wherein he can practise, according to his station in life, the exercises of religion, and work out his own salvation.

Prayer. Grant, O God, that by keeping in mind that sanctifying retirement, in which S. John practised the austerities of a life of penitence, in which he was admitted to an intimate communion with Thee, I may, according to his example, fulfil with faithfulness the duties of my calling, that I may carry them on in a spirit of continual union with Thee, and that I may embrace and cherish the crosses which it may please Thy adorable providence to lay upon me. Amen.

Meditation VII.

HYMN OF ZACHARIAS.

This hymn has three parts. In the first, Zacharias addresses himself to God in thanksgiving for the gift of a Saviour: in the second he speaks of the joy, which that Saviour is about to procure for us: in the third, he addresses himself to S. John, and makes known his high destiny: in the fourth, he returns to the enumeration of the blessings which we receive from a divine Saviour, born amongst us.—S. Luke i. 68-79.

FIRST POINT.

Of the Saviour which God gives us.

Blessed be the Lord God of Israel, for He hath visited and redeemed His people, and hath raised up a horn of salvation (that is to say, He hath raised up a powerful deliverer) *for us in the house of His servant David, as He spake by the mouth of His holy prophets, which have been since the world began, That we should be saved from our enemies and from the hand of all that hate us, to perform the mercy promised to our fathers, and to remember His holy covenant, the oath which He sware to our father Abraham that He would grant unto us.* In these first words, Zacharias considers the Lord,

1. As present, that is to say, as having lately come down from Heaven, and actually dwelling on earth, in the house of David, as if he had said, Blessed be the name of the Lord God Whom Israel adores, because He has come down from the highest Heaven to visit His people, and to redeem them from slavery. It is of the blood of David His servant, that the Messiah-God is conceived in the womb of a virgin; the Child who is about to be born of her will be the Saviour, Whom we look for. This holy man had had the happiness to welcome beneath his roof this Blessed Virgin, daughter of David, who bore in her womb this mighty and powerful Saviour; but he had not had the consolation of speaking to her: and he makes up for it by a burst of praise. He and his wife

were the sole possessors of this great secret. Zacharias publishes it, but he contents himself with naming the family of the Saviour, without naming His mother. For us, who have the blessing of having had this revealed to us, let us praise the blessed Virgin Mother, and let us bless God, with Zacharias, for the great benefit of our redemption already commenced. The expression of the horn of our salvation of which this holy priest makes use to denominate the Saviour, signifies strength and power, corner-stone and angle, and lastly, ray of light. We know in what sense these three significations apply appropriately to our Lord. Jesus is the mighty Power of God, because He has made the world. Jesus is the chief Corner-Stone of the building. Jesus is the true Light which lighteneth every one that cometh into the world, the Brightness of His Father's glory, and the express Image of His Person.

2. *Zacharias sets forth the Saviour, as announced by the prophets.* Thus, he says, God had promised Him from generation to generation by the mouth of His holy prophets, whom He has made the guardians of His mysteries, and the depositories of His oracles. The holiness, the continuance, and the uniformity of the witness which the prophets bear, is a divine proof, which will for ever condemn the incredulity of the Jews and unbelievers, and the weakness of the faith of many Christians.

3. *Zacharias contemplates the Saviour as victor over our enemies.* He had pledged himself, continues he, to protect us from the fury of our enemies, and to hide us from the persecution of those that hate us. The carnal-minded Jews, only expecting a temporal advantage from the advent of the Messiah, have always misapplied those expressions of the prophets which foretold the defeat of their enemies. Our real enemies are the devil, the world, and the flesh, sin, and death. United to our Saviour, we have nothing more to fear on their part: grace is sufficient for us to overcome their attacks; let us then ask earnestly for it, and be faithful in acting up to it.

4. *Zacharias considers the Saviour as promised to the patriarchs.* God, continues he, sware to perform the mercies promised to our fathers, and to remember the holy covenant, upon which He had entered with them. He had sworn to Abraham, His servant and our forefather, that, in the course of time, (and that time was now come,) He would come Himself, and deliver us from the hands of our persecutors. Our Saviour ought to be so much the more endeared to us, as He has been solemnly promised, and long expected. The accomplishment of the promise which has been made to us has been the crowning point of His mercy, and the result of His faithfulness. *Blessed* for ever *be the Lord God of Israel.*

SECOND POINT.

Of the happiness, which that Saviour has procured for us.

That we, being delivered out of the hands of our enemies, might serve Him without fear, in holiness and righteousness before Him all the days of our life. The happiness, for which we are indebted to our Saviour, is, that, by the aid of His grace and without any enemy having the power to hinder us,

1. *We may live in righteousness and holiness,* that is to say, in the exercise of every virtue, and in the fulfilment of all our duties towards God and our neighbour.

2. *That we can also practise these virtues before Him,* in the presence of God. Alas! how many are there who only bring virtue into practise, when it is seen of men and has their approbation.

3. *That we have it in our power to live thus all the days of our life,* that is to say, at all periods, and under all the circumstances of our life, and, if we will, that we may persevere unto death. Let us here then bewail so many days, so many years spent in following the inclinations of our own evil passions, in the service of the world,

without thought of God our Saviour, and let us, at length, begin to live holily and *before God*, with a firm resolution, by the help of His holy grace, to continue thus *all the days of our life.*

THIRD POINT.

Of the high destiny of S. John.

And thou, child, shalt be called the Prophet of the Highest : for thou shalt go before the face of the Lord, to prepare His ways : to give knowledge of salvation unto His people, by the remission of their sins, through the tender mercy of our God.

1. *Zacharias announces here the dignity of S. John ;* he calls him the prophet of the Highest, prophet from the womb of his mother, prophet in his birth, in his name, in all his person ; the greatest of the prophets, the last of the prophets of the old dispensation, and the first of those of the new: and lastly, according to the judgment pronounced on him by his Master, *more than a prophet.* Let this high dignity raise up our thoughts of this great saint.

2. *Zacharias declares the occupation of this great saint.* Happy child, he seems to say, the fruit of mercy and of blessing, *thou shalt be called the Prophet of the Highest,* and thou shalt carry out the glorious ministry, to which thou art called as such. *Thou shalt go before the face of the Lord,* the Messiah, our Saviour and our God, thou shalt *prepare His ways,* thou shalt dispose the Israelites, thy brethren, to acknowledge and follow the Heavenly Teacher, Who is about to follow in thy steps, to enlighten and instruct them. There is hardly any one in the world, who has not some share in this divine employment of S. John the Baptist: not only the Apostles, and pastors in regard to their people, but even parents towards their children, heads of families towards their servants, teachers towards their disciples, all are enjoined *to prepare the way of the Lord.* With

what zeal, following the example of S. John, ought not each to acquit himself of this duty!

3. Zacharias bears witness to the doctrine of this great forerunner: he calls it, *the knowledge of salvation*, knowledge which alone is the true one. What doth it avail us in reality, if all other knowledge is brought to perfection amongst us, if this is neglected. Happy the people, who, ignorant of all other knowledge, should posssess this! but woe to him, who is ignorant of this knowledge, even if he should possess all other besides? Most miserable are these men, who, excelling in all other knowledge, with talents to teach the way of salvation, teach instead the way of perdition by discourses or writings which breathe forth only impurity, heresy, or irreligion! Sublime geniuses, polished writers of this century, what glory, what a reward, what consolation even to yourselves, might you not gain, if you made use of your intellect, and the charms of your writing to make our Creator, our Saviour, religion and virtue known and loved of others!

4. Zacharias foretells the fruit of the mission of S. John. O divine child! he continues, you will give to the people of the earth *the knowledge of salvation.* Moved by your discourses, they will hasten to repent, and they will obtain *the remission of their sins.* It will be through your ministry, that will be showered down upon us the fruits of *the tender mercy of our God,* Who is just come down from Heaven *to visit us,* and to receive us into the bowels of *His tender mercy.* Oh how great and infinite is this mercy of God! We have sinned against Him, and yet He it is, Who comes to bring us, to offer to us, the pardon of our sins, and we refuse Him. He entreats us, this God of goodness, by the bowels of *His tender mercy,* because He knows what we owe to His justice. Ah, if we did but rightly understand, with what ardour and with what gratitude should we not accept His offers, and make use of this tender and divine mercy! Oh ineffable mercy! which I have so often experienced! Shall I be so miserable, as to return again

to the sins which I detest, and which Thou hast forgiven?

FOURTH POINT.

Of the benefits which we receive from our Saviour.

Through the tender mercy of our God; whereby the Dayspring from on high hath visited us, to give light to them that sit in darkness and in the shadow of death, to guide our feet into the way of peace. Zacharias concludes his hymn by a fresh enumeration, yet more detailed, of the benefits which our Saviour bestows upon us.

1. He celebrates the visit which He makes to us. What hope, he seems to say, do not the first rays of the Sun of Righteousness make to shine in our eyes, Which now begins to rise above our heads! It is from the height of Heaven, from the bosom of His Father, that this Divine Saviour comes down to earth to visit us, to make Himself man, to live with us, to give Himself up for us, and to die for us. What a height, what a depth, what a visit, what mercy! But that which Jesus Christ has done once in His Incarnation, that He does daily for us still in the Holy Eucharist. It is there, that His tender mercy is most specially manifested. What prodigies of love are hidden there!

2. One of the benefits of our Saviour's Birth is, says S. John, the light which He spreads around. In what an abyss of confusion, in what a fearful chaos was the world plunged, when the Sun of Righteousness, the Light of truth appeared. Iniquity prevailed on all sides, all minds were led astray, the law of God was either ignored or violated, the public worship was only hypocrisy, the sacrifices but abomination; the temple and altar, a rock of offence. By dint of giving themselves up to follow their own passions, men had lost even the will to restrain them, and to bring them into submission. Having thus shamefully become the slaves of vice, they neither knew the high dignity from which they had fallen, nor the true happiness they had lost. By not knowing God, they had lost the knowledge of themselves. The soul had lost

the knowledge of its own nature; its immortality appeared to it only a matter of opinion. Man thought himself like unto the brute beast, because he allowed himself to live like one. There was no longer any solid virtue; no longer any true feelings of religion. Mankind accustomed to walk *in the* thick *darkness* of crime and corruption, were no longer amazed at the most shameful disorders. Vice had no longer any thing repugnant in it; iniquity was committed without scruple; such was *the shadow of death* in which they were sitting, or rather such was the gulf which had swallowed up the whole human race, when Christ came to draw them out thence; and He did so, by becoming the Way, the Truth, and the Life. He has shewn the way of the kingdom of God by the purity of His doctrine, by the holiness of His Life; and the paths of righteousness have been regained and followed. All was falsehood and error in man, and all has become light and truth in Christ: all mankind was corrupt and dead, and all have been washed, purified, brought to life in Christ: His Gospel has enlightened the world, has brought it out of its ignorance, its superstitions and its vices. When Zacharias spoke, this Sun of righteousness was hardly risen, and did not yet shine; but now that we have seen its brilliant course, that we are surrounded by His Light and His warmth, what misery for us, if we continue to walk on *in* the *shadows* of sin and of error, in the ways of perdition, and of eternal death.

3. The last of the blessings which Zacharias acknowledges as derived from the Saviour's birth, is the peace which He gives us. Peace with God, peace with our neighbour, peace with ourselves, peace on earth, and peace and eternal rest in Heaven.

Prayer. O God, notwithstanding the many blessings which we have received from Thy divine and adorable Incarnation, how many amongst us, who have been so specially made partakers of them, languish in a sinful ignorance of the intentions of Thy mercy, of the favours of Thy goodness, and the laws of Thy wisdom! Am I, who have been carefully taught, more faithful in responding to Thy grace? May this divine Fire which Thou camest upon earth to kindle, embrace and warm my heart, that all my desires may become regulated, my indignations chastened, and my actions purified; that henceforth without alarms and without fear, assured of Thy help, and tranquil under Thy protection, I may pass my days in zeal for Thy service, may walk *before Thee in holiness and righteousness*, and all my steps may lead me to the goal of a happy peace, in the bosom of Thy tender mercy. Amen.

Meditation VIII.

GENEALOGY OF JESUS CHRIST ON THE SIDE OF S. JOSEPH.

In this genealogy, the Wisdom, Goodness, and Providence of God are plainly set forth. S. Matt. i. 1-17.

FIRST POINT.

The Wisdom of God.

The generation of Jesus Christ, the son of David, the son of Abraham, proves beyond all question the coming of the Messiah. This proof gains strength each day, and will confound for ever the obstinacy of the Jews. For the longer they wait for the Messiah, the less will they be in a condition to prove His descent on the side of David, all the families which descended from him, having become long since intermingled. Let us adore Christ, the true Messiah, Who has come at the time, and in the manner, which God had promised; let us adore the divine wisdom, which disposes of all events, in the manner the most fitting for the accomplishment of His divine purposes.

2. This wisdom is manifested in the fulfilment and combination of two prophecies which appear mutually to negative one another. The first of these prophecies was to the effect that the Messiah should be born of a virgin, and the other, that He should inherit the throne of David, to which a woman could neither succeed herself, nor could she consequently transmit her rights to it to her offspring: but the marriage with Joseph did away with the difficulty. Joseph being the head of the eldest branch of the royal family of David, Jesus, Who was born of the lawful wife of Joseph, is necessarily the only and lawful heir of Joseph. The supernatural and miraculous order of the conception of Jesus in the womb of the Virgin, far from taking away from Him the right of succession, could only confirm it to Him.

3. The wisdom of God appears again visibly in the other advantages which are brought about by the marriage of Joseph and the Blessed Virgin. By that means, God kept hidden for a time, from the evil spirits and from men, the wonders of His divine operation; the honour of Mary was thereby protected, and a support and consolation provided for her, and the happiness of Joseph secured. Let us praise the Lord for these acts of His wisdom; let us rejoice with Joseph and the Virgin Mary; and let us pray for the conversion of unbelievers.

SECOND POINT.

The Goodness of God.

The goodness of God is set forth, not only in that He hath given us His only Son, and that this Son, Whose generation is from everlasting and ineffab'e, willed to have a human generation and genealogy: but still more in the choice which He made of the patriarchs, from whom He willed to be descended. Amongst these, 1. He gives us Saints to excite our courage; Abraham, distinguished by his faith; Isaac, by his obedience; Jacob, by his goodness, and constancy, etc. 2. He gives us penitent sinners to animate our confidence; David,

Manasses, etc. 3. Sinners, of whose repentance we know nothing, that we may take heed lest we fall. Who would not tremble at the thought of an idolatrous Solomon, of whose conversion we read no account? Amongst the four women, named in the genealogy of Christ, two are not of the Jewish race, Rahab and Ruth, that we might understand, that, though strangers to the Jewish nation, and sinners, we are not excluded from that redemption, which is for all mankind. Let not the Jews glorify themselves then any more, in that they are the true children of Abraham, Isaac, and Jacob; we are their true children, and heirs of the promises, since we belong to Jesus Christ, the Son of David, and of Abraham. Judah and his brethren, who were the chiefs of the twelve tribes, are the figures of the twelve Apostles, fathers of all the Christian Churches. What a consolation to see that God thought of us in the midst of the favours which He bestowed upon the Jews, and that He thought of us in such a way, that the goodness He shewed to them was but the shadow and figure of those blessings which He was preparing for us! Let us thank God, and profit by so great a privilege! Our greatest glory is doubtless to belong to God, made Man; but this glory will not be real or efficacious to us, unless we live in a manner worthy of our divine adoption.

THIRD POINT.

The Providence of God.

1. This providence shews itself in the different stages of the history of the chosen people; but all these changes made no difference in the designs of the Most High. In every event of life, men make their plans; but those of God alone never fail of their fulfilment. Let us adore here the sovereignty of Him Who made Heaven and earth. Let us acknowledge and make known that He hath done what seemeth Him good, that He ordereth all things according to the counsels of His wisdom, that He maketh every thing serve to His glory, by following the in-

violable laws of His justice, and the feelings of His goodness towards us.

2. This divine providence shews itself in the revolutions which the privileged family, whence Christ was to be born, underwent. We see it somewhile on the throne, again in captivity, and lastly, in the obscurity of a laborious and humble life. Who would not have thought again and again, that the designs of God were overthrown? But that which appears to bring them to nought is exactly that which hastens their fulfilment. It had been resolved in the Eternal Counsels, that, at a time foretold, the Uncreated Word, the Son of the Eternal Father, and Consubstantial with God His Father, should take a body in the womb, and of the most pure flesh, of a virgin; that from this adorable Union of the Word with our human nature should be born the God-Man, a Mediator between God and men, the Head of all Christians, the Author and Principle of a new dispensation; that this God-Man, the only Son of God, should be the Son of Abraham, Isaac, and Jacob; that He should descend from David and Solomon; that He should unite in His person all the claims of the royal family of Judah. But how many obstacles were there not to the fulfilment of these prophecies! How many revolutions during the course of 2000 years! It matters not. Nothing can hinder the execution of the promise, neither the age of Abraham, who was a hundred years old, when Isaac was promised to him, nor the barrenness of Sarah, nor the ill-will of Ishmael against Isaac, nor the oppression of the Israelites, whilst dwelling in the land of Egypt, nor the apparent mes-alliance of Booz, nor the adulterous connection of David, nor the idolatry of Solomon, nor the infidelity of the greater part of his descendants, nor the captivity of Babylon, nor the poverty to which the family of David were reduced, nor the rule of the Romans, nor the impiety of Herod, king of the Jews. The day of the Lord arrives, and in the course of events which had been fixed, and at the appointed time, Jesus Christ is about to be born, that is to say, our Saviour, the Christ, the Anointed

of the Lord, who will make us partakers of His divine Unction; the son of David, whom the Jews waited for, as He that should re-establish the kingdom of His fathers; the son of Abraham, in whom all the nations of the world should be blessed, and Who, in virtue of being the only Son of God, and first-born of the children of men, will be first their Surety and their Victim, to become afterwards their high priest, their Judge, and their King.

3. The divine Providence shines forth in the circumstances which Jesus Christ chose for His birth. He was to be born of the royal family; but the race of David is no longer on the throne, the sceptre of Judah is departed, its sovereignty is abolished, its glory and wealth are annihilated; there is nought left to them but their good name, and this is, as it were, the signal of the near approach of the Deliverer. The temporal throne of David was only the figure of the spiritual throne of the Messiah. This was one of the signs, by which He was to be known: but if He had possessed its human glory, it would have been too difficult to distinguish the temporal from the spiritual royalty; and those who would have followed Christ might have deceived themselves on this point. Could Christ have condemned the vanities of the world, if He had been born in the midst of its pomps? How could He preach the ways of Heaven, and follow those of earth? How establish by His doctrines, the contempt of things of this life, if His Birth, His Life, His example had contradicted His doctrine? Hence the cause of the decay of those who immediately preceded the time of the Messiah; hence the example and the law which He left to His posterity, namely to all Christians, and to each one of us in particular. Let us learn thence, what we ought to esteem and seek for! Let us adore this divine Providence, which governs all things. Let us preserve peace of heart in all the events of life; and whether God exalts us or humbles us, let us receive with submission and gratitude the ordering of His Adorable Will. Whether we be the

children of kings or of peasants, let Jesus be our model: He has Himself been both.

Prayer. Yea, O Lord, every thing is determined in the designs of Thy Providence: every thing therein is ordered, every thing is regulated; the career which I am to follow is all marked out for me; I will therefore think only how to discharge those duties which are required of me. O Jesus, make me faithful to my duties, and conformable to Thy Will. O my divine Pattern, I will shun that which Thou didst shun; I will seek only that which Thou hast sought; I will seek, as Thou didst, the glory which cometh of God only; I will avoid the glory which cometh of men. Far be it from me to pride myself on the birth and titles of my ancestors, or to praise anything in them, but what Thou hast seen worthy of reward! Far be it from me to conceal an origin, which has been humble or obscure, under supposed names or fabulous greatness! What weakness would it be in a heart made for Thee, O my God! How unworthy of me, who am a Christian, that is to say, an inheritor of the joys of Heaven, and called to possess a throne, a crown, immortal glory, if I make any other greatness than these of my heavenly birth, my celestial family, my high and supernatural dignity of child of God, the object of my thoughts! Grant, Lord, that in whatever state I am, I may respond to Thy wisdom, by fulfilling Thy intentions for me; Thy goodness by serving Thee with affection; Thy Providence by conforming myself to Thy Will. Grant me to make a right use of prosperity and adversity, and of all the events of life by which Thou willest to save me. Amen.

Meditation IX.

AN ANGEL ANNOUNCES THE INCARNATION TO S. JOSEPH.

The Gospel teaches us here successively what concerns the Blessed Virgin, Joseph, and our Saviour. S. Matt. i. 18-25.

FIRST POINT.

That which concerns the Blessed Virgin.

Now the birth of Jesus Christ was on this wise: When as His mother Mary was espoused to Joseph, before they came together, she was found with child of the Holy Ghost. These few words point out to us for our admiration in the Blessed Virgin, 1. her exaltation, 2. her silence in her exaltation, 3. her confidence in God under the most trying circumstances.

1. Her exaltation. By the mystery of the Incarnation, since the Son of God, when He took upon Himself to deliver man did not abhor the Virgin's womb. She became really and truly the mother of Him, Who in His Divine Nature and Personality, was God. For she bears Him in her womb; and He, Who in His Godhead is the only Son of God, is in His Manhood, the only Son of the Virgin Mary. Through the divine operation of the Holy Spirit alone, the Blessed Virgin conceived, and remaining a Virgin, becomes a Mother. Her Son, Who in His eternal generation has only God for His Father without any mother, has, in His earthly generation, only the Virgin Mary, for a Mother, without any father! Ah! who can ever conceive the greatness thus bestowed upon her? For ever blessed and exalted let her be amongst all people on earth, and all the inhabitants of Heaven, this

Virgin so highly exalted, this blessed Mother of Him who was God.

2. *Silence of Mary in her exaltation.* Silence full of humility! she utters not a word of the great things which God hath done in her; she neither confides in her father Joachim, nor in the holy S. Anne, her mother, although she knew the interest which they would have felt. Silence, full of resignation! Mary needed not to fear, it is true, either the reflections of the public, or the reproaches of her family; her betrothal to Joseph was known; but could she also rest calm, as regards him to whom she was espoused! Could she doubt but that the knowledge of her situation must most cruelly distress and agitate him? Must not the needful care of her own good name oblige her to confide this mystery to him? Nevertheless she takes no steps in the matter, but leaves it to the wisdom of God to reveal it to him.

3. *Her confidence in God.* In this critical situation, Mary doubts not that God will do for her that which she cannot undertake for herself. She had before her the example of Elisabeth, her cousin, to whom God had revealed the Incarnation of the Word; why should she not hope that He would do as much in behalf of her husband; this second revelation appearing to be yet more needful than the first? Ought she not to believe that the mystery of her conception must be revealed from Heaven itself, being of such a nature as not to be believed from the lips and on the assurance of the person most concerned in it? She continues to hope and to hold her peace, persuaded that God will not fail her. She does not believe herself called upon to reveal to mankind the secret which had been made known to her. The Lord knows the time, and the manner in which to make it known, when, and to whom it may please Him. Mary rests herself upon Him, and thinks only of His mercies, adores the mysterious obscurity of His designs for her, and gives herself up entirely to the care of His Providence. Ah! how worthy is she of our respect, and our imitation.

SECOND POINT.

That which concerns S. Joseph.

Then Joseph her husband, being a just man, and not willing to make her a public example, was minded to put her away privily. But while he thought on these things, behold, the angel of the Lord appeared unto him in a dream, saying, Joseph, thou son of David, fear not to take unto thee Mary, thy wife; for that which is conceived in her is of the Holy Ghost. And she shall bring forth a son, and thou shalt call His Name Jesus: for He shall save His people from their sins. Then Joseph being raised from sleep, did as the angel of the Lord had bidden him, and took unto him his wife.* Consider first the disquietude of Joseph, then his consolation, and finally his obedience to the commands of God.

1. The disquietude of Joseph. What a trial, what perplexity for this just man! he sees the condition in which Mary is; but he knows her piety; he is persuaded of the purity of her heart, of the holiness of her life: her irreproachable conduct assures him of her faithfulness towards himself, but her condition witnesses against her. And even her silence seems to accuse her. He does not see on what grounds to free her from blame, and yet he dares not condemn her. To be a witness of what one knows not how to believe, what a trial, what a perplexity! Thus dost Thou, O my God, put Thy servants to the most cruel tests, in order to strengthen their virtue. Joseph, in order to satisfy, at the same time, the law which forbids him to hold any intercourse with an adultress, and his own desire not to bring Mary to public shame, forms the resolution to leave her secretly. In the ignorance, in the cruel alternative in which this just man finds himself placed, what wiser or more moderate course could he take? Would that this example, so conformable to the spirit of the Gospel, might serve us as a rule, lead us, if our own honour is attacked, even by good

men, our brethren and our neighbours, to hold our peace, to utter our sighs before God, to refer to Him the justice of our cause, or, at least, not to seek to vindicate ourselves in an angry spirit! Would that it might teach us, when we see the honour of others attacked, to suspend our judgment, to keep silence, to refer ourselves to God, that He may enlighten the minds of others, that He may calm those, whose hearts are embittered or prejudiced!

2. The consolation of Joseph. How honourable and abundant it is! He is visited by an angel, who is sent to him from God. He is admitted into the secret of a mystery, which was unknown to every one else, he is recognized as the husband of Mary, by the express command of God Himself. He is constituted as head of the Holy Family, with all the rights of a father over the Son of God; and it is as such, that he is commanded to give Him His Name of Jesus. How good the Lord is! He wipes away Himself the tears of those whom He loves, after having tried them; and He consoles them, in proportion to that which they have suffered. He would rather work a miracle than forsake His servants in their need, and He is always faithful in regarding those, who, in their troubles, think only of fulfilling His commands and pleasing Him.

3. The obedience of Joseph to the commands of God, and the service which is entrusted to him. He believes without hesitation in the mystery which the angel had revealed to him. He obeys, without delay, the commands of the Lord, and takes unto him his wife. This holy virgin had been an object of suspicion to him, but now she becomes worthy of respect: he had judged her to be unworthy of him, but now he only regards himself as far inferior to her; he understands how far he should not only cherish her, but honour her. He is instructed by the messenger of God in the secret of the Incarnation of the Word; and, from that time, he learns that his union with her has nothing in common with ordinary alliances: that he is the husband of the Virgin in the eyes of men, but that in the order of Providence, she has

no other claims upon him save those of companionship, support, and consolation. With what zeal, and faithfulness will he not fulfil this holy service! He responded to the respect, confidence, and attachment which Mary placed in him, by the feeling of a veneration which made him regard her more as his sovereign than as his wife. As a virgin did she enter his house, and as a virgin she remained there. But, although a virgin, she bore in her womb the Son of God. Joseph fails in none of the care, in none of the attentions, which the claims of the mother and the dignity of the Son call for from him. Why are we not also as obedient to the voice of God, when He speaks to us in the depth of our hearts by His grace, as Joseph was to the voice of the angel?

THIRD POINT.

That which concerns Jesus.

Now all this was done, that it might be fulfilled which was spoken of the Lord by the prophet, saying, Behold a virgin shall be with child, and shall bring forth a son, and they shall call His Name Emmanuel; which being interpreted, is, God with us.

1. Observe how Christ accomplishes prophecy. Not only is He Himself the fulfilment of the law and the prophets, but moreover it is He, Who, as God, inspired the prophets with what they were to write. It is He who ordered beforehand, and caused to be published, all that He willed to be done upon earth, and He willed to foretell it in detail, that He may set a seal upon His religion, which falsehood should never be able to withstand. It is He, Who willed to be born of a pure and holy virgin-Mother, who should be filled with grace: it is He Who chose all the circumstances of His Birth, His Life and Death, that we might not forget when we read of them, that all has thus taken place in order to fulfil prophecy. But when the prophecies relate to the sins of mankind, they are the effect, not of the choice of

God, but of His Foreknowledge and of His Providence. Adore then the Son of Mary, Son of God, the absolute Master of time and of all events, faithful in the accomplishment of His promises, and the fulfilment of His word foretold by the prophets.

2. Examine what is the name given to Christ in prophecy. He is called *Emmanuel*, that is to say *God with us;* but *with us* in how many different ways! *God with us,* by His Incarnation; God united to our humanity; God-man, Man and God; *God with us* by His Birth, and during the whole course of His mortal life: *God with us,* by His grace, and by His adoption of us; *God with us,* by His perpetual protection; *God with us* in the Eucharistic sacrifice, and in every Communion: *God with us,* in meditation and in prayer, in temptation and in suffering, in death, and in eternity. What favours, what mercy! And if God is thus willing to be *with us* in so many ways, can it be possible that we should refuse to be with Him?

3. Consider what is the name given to this God-Man in the Gospel. His name is *Jesus,* that is to say, Saviour; Sacred Name, which explains that of *Emmanuel,* and which explains to us why God wills to be *God with us,* and wherefore He comes to us. He does not come to judge us, to condemn us, to punish us: He comes to comfort, support, defend, deliver and save us. A great name only dishonours a person, when it is obtained without being deserved, when it is borne without being carried out in the life. Jesus fulfils all that is contained in the name of Saviour, and bears out its meaning even at the price of His Blood. Name, full of grace and of truth, which points out not only the Person, but the power and the ministry of this redeeming God! He comes to *save His people,* that is to say, the Jews and all those who, by the rejection of the Jews and with a disposition contrary to theirs, shall enter into their rights. All are called to salvation. All who will acknowledge Jesus Christ, believe in Him, and obey Him, shall be washed from their sins, delivered from the slavery of the

Evil one, saved from hell, and shall enjoy the fruition of life eternal. Can there be found yet any among us who prefer their sins to their Saviour, slavery to liberty, their ruin to their salvation, the devil to God, hell to Heaven?

Prayer. Jesus, Name full of greatness and of power, full of sweetness and of delight! By thy power, confound my enemies, by Thy sweetness penetrate my heart. O Precious Name and full of love! May It be imprinted on my tongue and graven in my memory, may It be without ceasing in my mouth, and the last word which my dying lips shall utter! Amen.

Meditation X.

THE BIRTH OF OUR SAVIOUR.

The Gospel sets before us in the details of this mystery, 1. how ineffable God is in His providence, 2. how worthy of admiration are S. Joseph and the Blessed Virgin in their virtues, 3. how worthy of adoration Jesus is in the manger. S. Luke ii. 1-7.

FIRST POINT.

God ineffable in His Providence.

And it came to pass in those days, that there went out a decree from Cæsar Augustus that all the world should be taxed. And this taxing was first made when Cyrenius was governor of Syria. And all went to be taxed, every one into his own city.

We see here first of all how certainly God brings about His ends by the means which He ordains, however distant or impossible they may appear at the time. Mary was at home in the house of her husband, and nevertheless it was preordained that her Son was to be born in a stable; how should that be brought to pass? Mary is settled at Nazareth: the time of the birth of her Son is drawing near, without her having the least thought of leaving that city, and yet nevertheless, according to the prophet, the Saviour was to be born at Bethlehem; how should that be accomplished? Mary was of a humble class in life, the wife of a carpenter in a small town in Galilee; and yet her Son must be acknowledged as the Messiah. It must be shewn to the world, that He is of the royal Family of David: how shall that be done? Nevertheless it is all brought about. The Roman Emperor was concerned only about matters of human policy, to gratify his own vanity, by ascertaining the strength and the riches of the Roman Empire. He puts forth an edict to this end: God overrules it to His own.

2. We see here how universal is the providence of God in the means it employs, however disproportioned they may appear! Everything here below is subordinate to this supreme power which subjects every thing to itself, and makes every thing serve to the manifestation of His Glory. The edict of the Emperor brings the blessed Virgin to Bethlehem; and the concourse of strangers, who like herself, had come there in obedience to the edict, make it impossible for her to find a lodging. The greatest, like the smallest events, vices as well as virtues, the vanity of Augustus as much as the obedience of Mary, everything has its place in the designs of Providence, and concurs together in carrying out His will. Man cannot conceive what are the means which God has preordained, and which He employs to execute that which He has resolved upon; it is the part of piety to adore them without seeking to penetrate them.

3. We see here how deep is the Providence of God in His designs, however hidden they may be by the veil of chance. Jesus is born at Bethlehem in order to fulfil the prophecy which had marked the place of His birth. He is inscribed authentically in the public registers of the Empire, that it may be manifest to the nations of the world what were the time and place of His birth, and that He was the son of Abraham, and the descendant of David. Jesus was born in a stable, He was laid in a manger, in order to be the Founder of an Eternal Empire, which was to bring all the other empires and monarchs of the world under the laws of humility and self-renunciation. All this appears here to the eyes

of flesh to be the effect of chance; but what is chance but an empty and chimerical name? All is ordered and arranged by the ordering of Thy Providence, O my God. How holy and adorable is Thy Providence! How blind are men in their judgments and in their projects! As for me, O Lord, in whatever place or situation I find myself, I will only recognize Thy hand which governs the universe, and I will adore with submission the holy and wondrous dispositions of Thy Providence.

SECOND POINT.

S. Joseph and the Blessed Virgin worthy of admiration in their virtues.

And Joseph also went up from Galilee, out of the city of Nazareth, into Judæa unto the city of David, which is called Bethlehem, (because he was of the house and lineage of David,) to be taxed with Mary, his espoused wife, being great with child. And so it was, that while they were there, the days were accomplished that she should be delivered. And she brought forth her first-born son, and wrapped Him in swaddling-clothes and laid Him in a manger; because there was no room for them in the inn.

1. Admire here, in them, their obedience to the orders of the Emperor. They obey without seeking any pretext for exemption from them, either in the nobility of their origin, for they were of royal blood: or in the holy mystery, of which they were the ministers and co-workers, for Mary bore in her womb the Son of God: or in the fatigue of the journey, for it was long and difficult: or in the risks which this holy Virgin might run, for she was in her ninth month, and it was the depth of winter; or in the character of the Emperor, who had issued the edict, who was an idolater. Let us learn to submit ourselves to all earthly powers, however rigorous their commands may be, so long as they are not manifestly opposed to the will of God. The true believer recognizes the commands of God in those of the

sovereign to whom he is subject. Whether he is just or unjust, heathen or idolatrous, heretical or Catholic, he pays him his homage, and renders him the lawful tribute of his obedience.

2. Let us admire the patience of S. Joseph and the Blessed Virgin in the rebuffs, which they were called upon to suffer. Let us picture to ourselves what must have happened to them under the circumstances. Arrived at the end of their journey, when they might have hoped to find some rest, they only experience still greater fatigues. They seek, on their arrival at Bethlehem, a lodging, and they find none: they advance farther into the town, they search the streets: every place is filled: they retrace their steps, they beg, they entreat: all their search and all their enquiries are in vain: friends, relations, acquaintances, all turn a deaf ear; they only meet with rebuffs, contempt, insults; the cold, the night, the tumult, the bustle of a crowd of strangers, the public throng, all increase their fatigue and their perplexity. In what a state does not Mary find herself! In what distress is not Joseph plunged! But their patience is not to be exhausted. There does not escape from them one word, nor one expression of complaint or murmuring. Better instructed than others in the secrets of God's conduct, they are not ignorant that those whom He employs in His greatest works, must be prepared for the severest tests.

3. Admire their resignation in the part they are obliged to take. Unable to find a lodging in any house, in consequence of the throng of people, they retire to a stable. It is thither that God conducts the two persons on earth, whom He most closely cherishes, S. Mary and S. Joseph. They do not misunderstand the guidance of the Lord that leads them; they adore it with love and resignation; to reward their faith the Saviour showers down on them His most signal favours, and grants them the consolation of being themselves the first to behold the Word made Flesh. It was then in this place of refuge, so suitable to the birth of a Child destined to die upon the Cross, that one Saturday, the 25th of Decem-

THE BIRTH OF OUR SAVIOUR. 67

ber, in the year of Rome 753, towards the middle of the night, Mary, without suffering any loss of her virginity, gave birth to her Son, the heir, the Prince, and the firstborn, according to the flesh, of the house of David. She laid Him in the manger, which was to Him instead of a cradle, and wrapped Him in swaddling-clothes. There with her husband Joseph she offered to Him the first and the purest adoration, which earth has ever rendered to Him. Let us rejoice with this divine Mother and S. Joseph and join our praises to theirs, seeking above all, to imitate their resignation, their patience, submission and faith.

THIRD POINT.

Jesus worthy of adoration in His manger-bed.

But who is then this Jesus, Who is thus born in a manger-bed? It is our God, our Mediator, our Example.

1. It is our God. It is the Son of God, Equal to His Father as touching His Godhead, and like unto us by virtue of His Humanity. It is our God, but as Isaiah calls Him, the God "that hideth Himself." What a wonder! The Eternal One, an Infant of a day, the Word of God, a child without speech, the Almighty, a feeble babe! O great God! however hidden Thou mayest be, faith reveals Thee to my heart, and I pay Thee my deepest homage. If Thou hidest the splendour of Thy Majesty under the garb of infancy, Thou art only the more to be loved! What, the Son of God, even before He is born, obedient to an earthly Prince! The Messiah so long expected, so ardently desired, experiences only rebuffs on the part of men! The King of Israel, King of Heaven and earth is born in a stable, is laid upon straw! Ah! I understand it; Thy kingdom is not of this world, Thy reign is the reign of holiness upon earth, and of glory in Heaven.

2. Jesus is our Mediator. On the one hand burning with love to God His Father, and filled with zeal for His glory; already in the Cradle He renders to Him adoration worthy of Him, and offers Himself to accomplish all

His will: He is also beloved of His Father with a sovereign love, and the Object of His tenderest good pleasure. On the other hand, burning with love for men, and filled with zeal for their salvation, He joins them with Himself, He makes Himself their Head, and offers Himself to make a complete satisfaction for them: how much therefore ought He not to be loved by them.

3. *Jesus is our Example.* If He gives us precepts as to obedience, humility, patience, mortification, detachment from things of earth, and poverty, from His earliest days, does He not Himself set before us an Example of these virtues? He is born in a stable, laid in a manger, of which He has the use only as a loan. Let this stable, this manger speak to us eloquently, to teach us to cherish the virtues which Jesus sets before us, and to bring us to a generous and real contempt of all that the world esteems, and to the esteem of all which it despises!

Prayer. Come, O Saviour, and vouchsafe to be born in my heart. Grant to me that, taught by Thy example, and strengthened by Thy Grace, I may be poor in spirit, humble in heart, as a stranger upon earth, mortified and obedient, as Thou art in Thy manger-bed. Thou hast become a child, O my Saviour, only that I might become a perfect man. Thou didst suffer Thyself to be wrapped in swaddling-clothes only to free me from all the bands of sin. Thou hast willed to be born in a stable, only to admit me to Thine altar here below, and to make me partaker of Thy Glory hereafter. Thou didst come down to earth, only to raise me to Heaven, and the rebuffs which Thou didst experience, when Thou wast refused room in the inn, have secured to me a place in Paradise. Lastly, Thou didst make Thyself weak, only to strengthen me: poor, to make me rich. Grant, O Lord, that such graces may not become, by their disuse, so many grounds of condemnation against me, but rather grant me to make the best use I can of them, that so they may lead me to Thy Glory in Heaven. Amen.

Meditation XI.

THE ADORATION OF THE SHEPHERDS.

The Gospel distinguishes in this event, three different periods, 1. that when the shepherds were told by the angels of the birth of a Saviour, 2. that of their departure, their arrival, and their sojourn in Bethlehem, 3. that of their return home. S. Luke ii. 8-20.

FIRST POINT.

The shepherds are informed by the angels of the birth of the Saviour.

And there were in the same country shepherds abiding in the field, keeping watch over their flock by night. And lo, the angel of the Lord came upon them, and the glory of the Lord shone round about them, and they were sore afraid. And the angel said unto them; Fear not: for behold I bring you good tidings of great joy, which shall be to all people. For unto you is born this day, in the city of David, a Saviour which is Christ the Lord. And this shall be a sign unto you, ye shall find the babe wrapped in swaddling clothes, lying in a manger. And suddenly there was with the angel a multitude of the heavenly host, praising God, and saying, Glory to God in the highest, and on earth peace, good will towards men.

1. Who were these shepherds? They were of a poor and obscure condition. The Saviour, in calling them the first to His cradle, shews that He does not reject any one; let us then go to Him with confidence. They were laborious and watchful; they led an innocent, simple life, conformable to their station. Idleness, luxuriousness, or dangerous occupations are the sources of sin which separate us from God and His favours. They were *shepherds;* it is under this title that our Saviour often represents Himself, as being the chief Shepherd of

our souls, and He loved in these shepherds, the image of the pastors of His Church. They had an upright and teachable heart; they waited for the Messiah in the state of life in which God willed to manifest Him to them, without reasoning either as to what He should be, or what He should do. The Word of God Who comes to instruct us, has no need of our intellect, nor of our power of reasoning. It is with simplicity of faith that we should adore Him in the Manger, and in the Holy Eucharist, if we desire to have any share in the fruits of these divine mysteries.

2. What was the conduct of the angels? Suddenly, these shepherds are surrounded by a bright light which pierces through the darkness of the night. By the help of this miraculous light, they perceive near them a heavenly angel, and at first, they are sore afraid. Their fear is great, but it does not last: their consolation is greater still, and it will continue to increase, and will only end with their lives. The angel speaks to them, but they do not answer, however surprising the tidings which he announces to them are. Also their faith merits to be rewarded, and supported by new wonders. *A multitude of the heavenly host* joins the first messenger of Heaven, and all sing in concert the praises of God. What happiness for these shepherds to become, as it were, the witnesses of the joy, which constitutes in Heaven the portion of Saints and angels, whose entire occupation is to bless and praise the Lord, in transports of eternal joy. But what new impression must not the disappearance of these blessed spirits have made upon these shepherds, as they rose together, and in a visible manner went away from them into Heaven, to continue there their heavenly songs! What a sight for their eyes! what raptures for their hearts!

3. What did these Heavenly messengers say? The first amongst them announces the Saviour, points Him out to them by tokens equally surprising as remarkable, and one and all celebrate His birth. *Fear not*, said the heavenly being to them, *for behold I bring unto you*

good tidings of great joy, which shall be to you and to all people. Israel awaits the Messiah: today, this very night, but a few moments ago, this Child, the Desire of all nations was born at *Bethlehem, the city of* which *David* was the founder. This Child is the *Saviour* not of angels, but of yourselves: He is a *Saviour,* not like some of these whom God has often sent unto you and who were only the type of this one: but He is the Saviour of Saviours, the Saviour of all men; such is His office, and the boundlessness of His love. He is the *Lord* of the universe, of angels and of men, the author of nature and of grace, the absolute Master of all; such is His greatness and His power. What shame for us! The angels take part in a mystery of which the fruits are not for them: and we, for whom a Saviour is born, who give ourselves up so readily to false and debasing joys, are perhaps indifferent, insensible to the greatness and reality of this. But by what *sign,* continues the angel, will *you find* your Saviour so merciful, so powerful, and so long foretold? *Ye shall find the babe wrapped in swaddling clothes lying in a manger.* And in this child, behold the Messiah, Him in Whom "dwelleth all the riches" of the Wisdom of God; in the swaddling clothes, behold the signs of His greatness and the vesture of His power: in the manger, behold the tokens, nay the very throne of His glory! Pride of man, come and annihilate thyself before this cradle; proud man, acknowledge that the humility of thy Saviour is the only way by which thou canst be restored to those blessings which thy pride has caused thee to lose, and that it is in self renunciation and in poverty that the God-Man comes to thee, Who wills to deliver thee from the slavery of sin, and the tyranny of thy passions! Hardly had the first of these celestial spirits announced the Messiah, than *a multitude of the heavenly host* joined him and sang this heavenly song, *Glory,* that is honour and thanks be given *to God in the highest;* let *peace* come down to day, in the name of the Lord God of Israel, to men of *good will,* disposed to believe His Word, to observe His laws, and to profit by His mercy! *In the highest* Heavens, *glory to God* Who is the Author of this great mystery, in which His goodness, wisdom and power shine forth; to God, Who is the end of this mystery, by which He receives an obedience, a satisfaction, and a homage worthy of Him! *on earth peace to men,* peace brought among them by love, peace with God by a perfect reconciliation, peace with themselves, peace of mind, peace of conscience, peace, the most delicious and most precious of all possessions, peace towards men of *good will*, that is to say to men, obedient to God, submissive to His laws, and who yield to Him the homage of their good will!

SECOND POINT.

Of the departure of the angels, their arrival at Bethlehem, and their sojourn there.

And it came to pass, as the angels were gone away from them into Heaven, the shepherds said one to another, Let us now go even to Bethlehem, and see this thing which is come to pass which the Lord hath made known unto us.

1. What is that which inspires the shepherds to go and see the wonders which have been announced to them? Firstly it is example. They stir *one another* up and encourage each other to respond to the grace which God has shewn to them, and soon they are all of one mind, one soul, one will: the same thoughts, the same words, the same feelings incline them to go to Jesus Christ, the Author of their salvation. Thus should friendships, societies, families, and believers, endeavour mutually to urge one another continually to the exercise of virtue, patience, repentance, and other good works. Thus should we encourage one another to piety by the example of so many saints, who have gone before us, of so many earnest and holy men who live in our day, or who, scat-

tered throughout the Church, entreat us to join our praises and thanksgivings, and acts of adoration to theirs. The shepherds also encourage themselves by the thought of the place whither they are bound, and the object which awaits them there. *Let us go even now to Bethlehem and see this thing which is come to pass.* The place is *Bethlehem;* the object of their journey is God, their new born Saviour. And whither are we being urged to go? Is it not to our God, and to our Saviour? is it not to Bethlehem, which means house of bread; is it not to the Bread which came down from Heaven, which is the spiritual Food of our souls? Lastly, the shepherds encourage one another by the thought that this knowledge and that their instructions proceed from the Lord, *which the Lord hath made known to us.* Does not the Lord equally call us? Shall the Christian education we have received, and so many warnings, good inspirations, and teachings be of no avail?

2. How did the shepherds go to Bethlehem? They went to the stable *with haste*, with all the promptness and eagerness which the tidings they had received could inspire them with. They do not even wait for daylight, they depart the same night, they hasten with confidence, and leave their flocks without anxiety to the care of Him who calls them. How far are we from the fervour of these pious shepherds! Let us then go forward with promptness, and without delay. He who desires to attain to the perfection to which God calls him, ought to labour at it unceasingly, and zealously: let us then advance and run without delay and fearlessly in the way which Heaven points out to us. Strengthened by the counsels of God's good angels, and the advice of wise and holy friends, let us not fear that prayer will hinder our occupations, or almsgiving injure our fortune, or piety, our reputation, or zeal, our health.

3. What do the shepherds find at Bethlehem? They *find* there Jesus, *Mary and Joseph.* An air of innocence and modesty distinguishes the divine Mother. Goodness and gentleness mark out him, who appears to be the

father. Weakness and helplessness, poverty and indigence shew the Messiah, the Saviour so long expected. No ray of light shines on His countenance, no mark of Divinity makes itself felt across the shadows which surround Him; but God has spoken: these shepherds do not reason either as to the Object of revelation, nor the suitableness of the mystery; they contemplate at their leisure the divine Child; they admire Him, they adore Him, and offer Him the first-fruits of their worship, they receive the first favours, and are enkindled with His love. O happy lot! Oh touching sight, worthy of envy! But, without envying their lot, let us make good use of our own, which is not subservient to theirs, 1. In the Object of their faith. They only see with their bodily eyes a feeble and helpless child. If, in this child, they see their God and their Saviour, it is only with the eyes of faith; now, by faith do we not also see Him, the same God and the same Saviour in His Sacrament, and cannot we there pay Him the same adoration, and obtain from Him the like favours? 2. In the motives of faith. They had been instructed by the angels, Who this child was. The message of the angels was to them the word of God, it is true; but we have also the message of the Angels, and we have besides the Word of God Himself, and the teaching of His Church, which reveal to us the mystery of the Holy Eucharist, and tell us that it is the Bread of life. 3. In the supports of faith. They saw the Humanity of Christ; but though it is true that we have not this consolation, yet if our faith is exercised to a greater degree than theirs, it only yields more abundant glory to God, and is more profitable to ourselves. If instead of the form of a child lying in a manger, we see only the outward tokens of bread, and instead of the stable and the manger-bed, the Churches and the altars which have been erected to do honour to Him throughout the world. Alas! nothing is wanting to the evidences of our faith; let us make use of them, and nothing shall be wanting to our happiness.

THIRD POINT.

Of the return of the shepherds.

And all they that heard it wondered at those things which were told them by the shepherds. But Mary kept all these things in her heart. And the shepherds returned, glorifying and praising God for all the things, that they had heard and seen, as it was told unto them.

1. Consider here the astonishment of the multitude. Many had heard of all that had happened during the night; some had learnt it from the shepherds themselves, others from those to whom the *shepherds* had related it; all were exceedingly amazed, and nothing in reality was more fitted to excite a universal wonderment. The birth of the Saviour of Israel in a stable, an apparition made to some poor shepherds, a song of praise sung in their presence by the multitude of the heavenly host, all these circumstances joined together, and made known abroad by those unlearned men, whom no one could suspect of interested motives, must needs throw the Jews in the neighbourhood of Bethlehem into a strange state of amazement. Nevertheless, notwithstanding their surprise, the Jews contented themselves with reasonings and conjectures, which each made at the moment according to the inclination of his own mind. But of what use is a barren admiration? Ought they not to have hastened to the stable, and there worshipped their Saviour? Ought they not to have striven for the honour of lodging Him and receiving Him into their own houses? Alas! what will it profit us to have admired the mysteries of God and His law, or the sermons which we hear on those subjects, if this admiration remains unfruitful and without effect? Will it not rather be a subject of condemnation against us?

2. Consider Mary. But if the carnal and sensual Jews took so little part in marvels so worthy of their attention, Mary, that holy virgin, so attentive and full of

faith, did not regard them with the same culpable indifference. The shepherds had related to her all the circumstances of the angelic vision which had led them to Bethlehem, she rejoices with them in the Lord; let us rejoice with her. Each new event retraced vividly in her memory those which had preceded it. The words which the angel had spoken to her, that which she had heard from the lips of Elisabeth, her maternity, the miracles of her conception, and the way in which God had dispersed the fears of Joseph, what she had heard the shepherds relate, all led to the same conclusion, all confirmed in her the Divinity of her Son, and made Him more and more beloved, precious, and worthy of admiration to her. She did not cease to compare together and meditate on the Divine character of all these events; *She kept all these things and pondered them in her heart;* she nourished her faith with them, and thus grew in love; let us also imitate her example. It is from her, as it is believed, that S. Luke learned all these details, and all that concerned our Blessed Saviour up to the time of His public ministry; let us feel grateful to God for them.

3. Consider the shepherds. *They returned glorifying and praising God,* singing the praises of the Saviour, and blessing Him for all His mercies. That which *they had heard* from the mouth of the angels, that which *they had seen* with their own eyes; the conformity of the event with that which had been announced to them, the distinction which the Lord had shewed them in admitting them to His Divine confidence, were henceforth the consolation of their estate, and the subject of their conversation. With what zeal did they not publish, on their return, the wonders of God, and make them known to others! Is it thus that we return from God's House to our own house, that we come from prayer, Divine worship or Communion? Is it with the same gratitude and the same satisfaction that we consider in our holy religion, the infallible proofs of its truth, the relation which its dogmas bear to the present state of mankind,

the agreement of prophecy with the events which take place, the harmony between what we see in our days, and what passes under our eyes, with what we read of the past? whilst, on the contrary, all the systems of religion invented by men are equally discordant to the past and to the present.

Prayer. How worthy of adoration, O my Saviour, art Thou in Thy sacred manger! I unite myself in heart and spirit with those pious shepherds, who adore Thee there, and the angels, who glorify Thee in Heaven. What shall I render to Thee for having thus given Thyself to me? Ah, I give myself to Thee; I consecrate myself wholly to Thee, O Divine Jesus! to live only in Thee, and by Thee, Thy spirit, and Thy love. Grant, Lord, that I may not content myself here with a barren and outward adoration, but may, like Mary, keep all Thy words in my heart, and nourish my soul with them; and that, studying at the foot of Thy manger-bed, the virtues of Thy Divine Infancy, Thy humble, mortified, hidden and recollected Life, I may render myself conformable to it, in order that hereafter I may become partaker of Thy glory. Amen.

Meditation XII.

THE CIRCUMCISION OF OUR SAVIOUR.

When eight days were accomplished for the circumcising of the child, His name was called JESUS, *which was so named of the angel before He was conceived in the womb.* In this single verse three subjects present themselves for our meditation, 1. the circumcision, 2. the Name of Jesus, 3. the renewal of the year. S. Luke ii. 21.

FIRST POINT.

The Circumcision.

1. This ceremony was ordained by God Himself. He had appointed it first to Abraham and then to Moses, in order to mark out His people by a distinguishing sign.

Jesus, in submitting to it, although He was above the law, since He was Himself the Author and the End of it, gives us the example of the obedience which we owe to the laws of God, and condemns those dispensations, reserves, and relaxations which we allow ourselves so readily.

2. Circumcision was a humiliating act. Jesus, in submitting to it, although the King of saints, takes His lot with sinners, and receives the mark of infamy, and the penalty of sin; an example utterly opposed to our pride. We are covered with iniquities, and we assume the appearance of innocence: we claim even the privileges of sinlessness, in that we will neither suffer the punishment of sin, nor the remedy for it. How little conformable are we to our Divine Model!

3. Circumcision laid a burden on those who received it, to keep the whole law of Moses, and Jesus bore the yoke in order to deliver us from it. But let us take care. He has substituted baptism for circumcision, and in exempting us from legal circumcision, He has bound us to spiritual circumcision, that is, the cutting away of all the evil and premeditated thoughts of our minds, of all the unregulated and voluntary affections of our heart, of all the idle or sinful words of our mouth, in short, of all which displeases Him in our conduct, and bears the mark of our original evil nature, and is contrary to the obligations of our baptism.

4. Circumcision was painful. Jesus, being only eight day old, submits His tender and innocent flesh to the knife of circumcision; He feels the sharp pain, His Blood flows. He offers the first-fruits of His Blood to His Father for our salvation, and He will one day shed It to the very last drop. O Jesus, in order to save me, Thou didst shed Thy Blood, and I am not willing to suffer any thing, in order to ensure my own salvation. That Divine Blood already sufficed for the redemption of men, if God had willed to be thereunto content. How Thou dost hasten, O my Saviour, to shed for me Thy Blood! and shall I delay yet to give Thee my heart?

O God, Whom I have so deeply offended, accept this precious Blood as the atonement for my sins. O Divine Saviour, apply the merit and the virtue of It to me, that, at least, I may never more offend Thee. Let one drop of this adorable Blood fall upon my heart to soften its hardness. Alas, I receive so often this precious Blood, in the Holy Communion; how is it that I am not enkindled, consumed with Thy Divine Love?

SECOND POINT.

Of the Name of Jesus.

And His name was called Jesus.

1. Name, full of majesty and greatness. At this adorable Name, every knee should bow of things in Heaven, and things in earth, and things under the earth. At this Name, Heaven recognizes its King, earth, its Deliverer, and hell, its Conqueror. The Church pronounces it always with a special token of reverence; how do we utter it?

2. Name, full of strength and power. Name, given unto men, whereby they may be saved. This Name alone has opened Heaven and closed hell, bound the devil, overthrown idols, and banished idolatry. Nothing is refused, which is asked in the Name of Jesus; the sick are healed, the dead brought to life, and devils put to flight: let us then invoke this Holy Name often, and with perfect confidence.

3. Name, full of purity and holiness. It is from Heaven that it came; it was an angel who brought It. It puts to flight impure thoughts, and inspires only pure desires. It has no enemies, save foul spirits and sensual souls. Let us then strive to attain to perfect purity, that we may be worthy of the graces which this Holy Name brings with It.

4. Name, full of sweetness and tenderness. The Name of Jesus, or of Saviour, speaks to us only of the goodness of Him Who bears it, and promises nothing

less to those, who love it, than the remission of their sins, deliverance from hell, and the possession of Heaven. What favours, what hopes, what eternal blessings! What heart could resist the sweetness of that Name? Let the Name of Jesus be then without ceasing in my heart, and on my lips!

THIRD POINT.

Of the first day of the year.

When eight days were accomplished for the circumcising of the child. These words recall to us the shortness of time, its employment, and its end.

1. The shortness of time. The longest course of time, when it has passed, is no longer any thing. What is the year which has just expired? What is all the time which we have lived? What is all the time which the world has lasted? It has all passed; and in past time, a century, a year, a week, a day are all the same thing. The time to come is of the same kind; the year which is beginning, the time which yet remains to us of our lives, the time which the world will last, will pass away, and when it is past, it will be no longer any thing; but eternity will never be past. Oh fools that we are to attach ourselves to the things of time which last for so short a time, and not to sigh after eternal things!

2. The uncertainty of time. How many there are, of all ages, of all conditions, of all classes, who have seen the beginning of last year, but have not seen the end of it! It will be the same with this one: perhaps we shall be of the number of those who will not see its end; we cannot be sure of one day, of one moment. Let us then begin it, as if it were to be our last.

3. The employment of time. The manner in which we shall have employed our time will decide our fate in eternity. Let us examine, how we have spent the year which has just closed. If we have not fallen into the greatest sins, let us thank God for it; but at least, let

us confess, what sluggishness in the service of God, what distractions in prayer, what neglect of the services of the Church, how much has been amiss in all our actions. How many faults we might have avoided, how many good works we might have done, what occasions of the practice of virtue, of the exercise of charity, patience, zeal, humility, self-mortification, have we not lost? Let us weep bitterly, that we have thus wasted our opportunities, and beg of God for His forgiveness. Here is a new year which He gives us, in which to repair our losses. Ah! if He were to grant the same to lost souls, how would they employ it!

4. *The end of time.* At the end of time, there remains nothing of the sufferings and the pleasures which we have had in time. The penitent and the voluptuary, when they come to their last hour, find themselves in the same position, in that the mortifications of the one, and the enjoyments of the other, have equally vanished away: there remain to them only their works, that is to say, their merits or their demerits. What regret for the one! what consolation for the other! What satisfaction should we not feel to-day, if we had passed the last year in holiness and in earnestness! There would remain nothing of the trouble, which it had cost us; and what remains to us of the pleasures, which have turned away our hearts from God? Let us grieve that a time so precious has been so ill employed. Let us thank God, that He has preserved us till this moment, and that the end of time has not yet come to us, but let us remember that we are drawing near to it. What will then be our feelings? That which we would have done with it no longer rests with us; but we have it in our own power now; let us therefore be wise, and profit by a warning which may perhaps be the last which we shall receive.

Prayer. I have resolved, O my God! no longer will I delay. Ah! I perceive the danger, the folly of it. This day, this moment shall become for me the date of an unchanging conversion. I will make use of the time that remains to me, and seek to recover by the earnestness of my love that which I have misused or wasted. I come with confidence and with tears, Oh adorable Victim; Thou who didst shed in Thy circumcision the first drops of Thy blood, and Who dost promise me that Thou wilist pour forth for me all that yet remains; at the sight of Thy obedience to a law to which Thou wert not bound, I bind myself without reserve to the eternal submission which I owe Thee; at the sight of these first sufferings, which divine justice exacts from Thee for the appearance only of sin, which Thou hast taken upon Thyself, I conceive what ought to be my horror of sin; and the gulf between me and it, however venial it be, shall be boundless. Thy legal circumcision, oh divine Saviour, shall be for me a powerful and ever-renewed motive for mortifying my senses, crucifying the flesh, and circumcising my heart: I will strive to cut off all that flatters my evil nature, to flee from all that enervates the heart, to keep far from all which strengthens my passions, and to separate myself from the pomps and vanities and pleasures, which I renounced at my baptism, to die at length to the world and to myself, that I may live only in Thee, oh my Saviour! Such are my resolutions; but shall I keep them faithfully? I need but Thy Name, O Jesus, to support and strengthen my weakness; and that Name, so dreaded of hell, of which It has humbled the power, I will employ with success against the enemy of my salvation. Amen.

Meditation XIII.

THE ADORATION OF THE MAGI.

Consider with the sacred historian, 1. the departure of the Wise Men from the East, 2. their arrival at Jerusalem, and their proceedings there, 3. their conduct at Bethlehem, 4. their return to their own country. S. Matt. ii. 1-12.

FIRST POINT.

The Magi set off from the East.

Now when Jesus was born in Bethlehem of Judea, in the days of Herod the king, behold there came wise men from the east to Jerusalem, saying, Where is he that is born King of the Jews? for we have seen his star in the east, and are come to worship him.

1. Remark in these wise men, their attention in considering the new star, and in discovering its hidden meaning. How many beheld it without understanding the mystery it sets forth! How many events in life would be guiding stars to us, if our continual distraction did not prevent us from giving attention to them!

2. Consider their reflections on that which this new phenomenon required of them. They understood well, that it was not to satisfy their curiosity, that heaven announced to them the birth of the King of the Jews, but in order that they might seek Him and adore Him. The light which God gives us, will turn to our condemnation, if we do not bring it to bear upon His service and our salvation.

3. Examine their determination to go and inquire at Jerusalem, where the place was, where the new-born King was to be found. God does not always teach us everything Himself; but He gives us those who are the depositories of His Word and Sacraments and interpreters of their real meaning. Our duty is, when we

find ourselves in doubt or difficulty, to seek for help from His appointed ministers.

4. Meditate on their fidelity in obeying what God lays upon them, and appears to require of them. Prompt and courageous obedience, which fears neither the fatigues nor the dangers of a long and tedious journey, nor the railleries, nor the opinions of men. Is it thus we obey God? The wise men leave their country at the guiding of a star; and we, who have God's word, His strength, His commands, His light, which has so long shone before our eyes, will not make the slightest sacrifice for Christ. These strangers set forth at the least sign; and we, whom the Lord is constantly calling to Him, remain unmoved, notwithstanding His warnings, His inspirations, and His commands. What keeps us back? Ah! let us fear, lest the piety, the obedience, and faithfulness of these Magi should rise up one day in judgment against us, and accuse us of our indifference, our slothfulness, and our want of submission.

SECOND POINT.

The Magi at Jerusalem.

When Herod the king had heard these things, he was troubled, and all Jerusalem with him. And when he had gathered all the chief priests and scribes of the people together, he demanded of them, where Christ should be born. And they said unto him, In Bethlehem of Judæa: for thus it is written by the prophet; and thou, Bethlehem in the land of Juda, art not the least among the princes of Juda: for out of thee shall come a Governor, that shall rule My people Israel. Then Herod, when he had privily called the wise men, inquired of them diligently, what time the star appeared. And he sent them to Bethlehem; and said, Go and search diligently for the young Child: and when ye have found Him, bring me word again, that I may come and worship Him also. When they had heard the king, they departed; and lo, the star, which they saw in the east, went before them, till it came and stood over, where the young Child was. When they saw the star, they rejoiced with exceeding great joy. Four sorts of persons are here proposed for our consideration. Herod, the chief priests and the scribes of the Jews, the people of Jerusalem, and the Magi.

1. Observe Herod. His trouble: a child makes him tremble. The wicked are never at ease, even on the throne. His cruelty; from this moment, this usurper and foreigner has resolved upon the death of the child; but God sets at nought the projects of the wicked. His anxious curiosity: which serves only to torment him, to set forth the glory of the newly born Infant, and to instruct these who are seeking for Him. His dissimulation and hypocrisy: but soon he will appear in his true colours and become for ever the execration of men. Such is the end of hypocrites.

2. Consider the chief priests and scribes of the Jews. How great is their blindness! They seek for the Messiah in the Holy Scriptures, they find Him, they point Him out to others, they mark the place of His birth, but they will not worship Him themselves; sad presage of the long continued blindness in which we see them remain to this day; lesson of warning to those who shew the way to others, and wilfully stray from it themselves. But whatever may be their errors, let believers, taught by the example of the Magi, profit by their experience.

3. Examine the people of Jerusalem. Their frivolity! They are troubled without knowing wherefore, and merely because Herod was troubled. Those in a high position inspire their feelings and passions into those even who hate and censure them. Their folly! They are troubled at that which ought to fill them with joy, at the fulfilment of that which has been the object of their longing and desire, now about to draw near: a fatal disposition of mind, which already shews what that hardened people will do one day. How many amongst Christians shrink from the approach of solemn seasons of the Church, lest they

should be called upon to fulfil those religious duties which are the delight of true believers!

4. Observe in the Magi. 1. Their courage in asking for the new-born King, in publishing what they had seen in the Heavens, and in declaring that they were seeking Him on earth to worship Him, without troubling themselves whether they were thus offending the ambition of him, who was then reigning over the Jews. 2. Their perseverance in not allowing themselves to be discouraged by the difficulties delays and oppositions, which they must meet with, till they received the tidings they sought for. 3. Their patience in bearing the questionings, perhaps, the derisions of the court as also of the town. 4. Their trials and temptations: they were doubtless surprised that, in the capital of Judea, nothing should be known of the birth of the Messiah; that they should be sent to Bethlehem, an unknown and insignificant place, and that, lastly, although they had made known so important a fact, no one should leave Jerusalem to follow them. 5. Lastly, their joy, their happiness, when, on leaving this ungrateful city, they see once more the star, and that not only does this star appear to them in the East, but that it goes before them, and shews them the way. Ah: how good the Lord is, how He hastens to comfort those who suffer for His sake, and how abundant are His consolations! God's Holy Spirit does not forsake teachable souls. If He seem sometimes to leave them for awhile in darkness, He soon shews Himself to them again; oh! how sweet and comforting are such moments. Let us adore, with fear as well as gratitude, the justice of God and His mercy. The Jews are already beginning to blind themselves, and unbelievers and strangers, the Gentiles, of whom the Magi are, as it were, the first fruits, begin to see the true Light.

THIRD POINT.

The Magi at Bethlehem.

And when they were come into the house, they saw the young Child with Mary His mother, and fell down and worshipped Him: and when they had opened their treasures, they presented unto Him gifts of gold, and frankincense, and myrrh.

1. Examine the idea which the wise men conceived of the Child Jesus, and let us judge of them by their conduct. They arrive at Bethlehem; the star, which guided them, came and stood over where the young child was, as if to make them understand that it is there that they were themselves to stay; and then it disappears. At this signal, they enter the house that has been thus pointed out to them, and there they find a Child in His Mother's arms. The simplicity of the place where they are, and the poverty which surrounds them does not discourage them; they fall at His feet; and worship Him not only as the king of the Jews, but as God and the Saviour of mankind. What are the raptures of these first worshippers of the King of kings! In what sublime contemplation are they not wrapt on beholding Him! What idea do they form of Him! What a sincere offering of themselves, an offering by which they submit to Him not only their prostrate bodies, and their humbled heads, but spirits and hearts wholly lost in admiration. Jesus Christ fills them inwardly with the unction of His grace, the fire of His love; and that celestial unction and that sacred fire shew themselves without, by the sweet and abundant tears which they shed. Who would not be moved at such a sight? How these Magi ought to rejoice that they had undertaken this journey, and that they found themselves so well rewarded for their pains, and their fatigues! Alas! it is the same God, Whom we have present on our altars! why have

we not the same faith, the same feelings? why do we not present to Him the same offerings?

2. Observe what is the thought which this mystery ought to give us of the Infant Jesus. Ought we not to say to ourselves, Who is then this Child, Who causes Himself to be thus announced by a star in the Heaven, and by prophets on earth, Who, from His cradle, calls the wise men from the East, that they may worship Him, Who blinds the proud guardians of the law in the midst of their light, troubles the wicked even on his throne, and amidst all the paraphernalia of his majesty? Ah! happy then those who have believed in Him, and have worshipped Him, whilst yet hidden under the veil of His Flesh! But what will become of those who shall have refused to own Him, who shall have despised Him, reviled Him, and persecuted Him?

3. Consider the nature of the presents which the Magi offer to the Child Jesus. They offer Him gold, incense and myrrh. It was, doubtless, on their part, a sign of respect to the king, who had been announced to them in the choice of these presents; but this choice was overruled by God. There is no doubt, that there is a mystery here: and the Church has always interpreted it as such. They offered Him gold as to their king, incense as to their God, and myrrh as to a man. Let us acknowledge Jesus Christ under these three characters. Let us adore Him as our God, follow Him as our King, and love Him as our Saviour. Let us offer to God the gold of a charity, pure and fervent towards God, and active as regards our neighbour; the incense of an assiduous and fervent prayer, and the myrrh of a real, and persevering self-denial. We have various ways in which we may substitute the practice of different works of piety for the presents of the Magi. To assist the building of Churches, the beautifying of His Altars, the accessories of divine service, this is to offer incense to Jesus; to comfort the poor in their needs, this is to offer Him gold; to provide for the burial of those who have died in His faith, to procure the prayers of the Church for the sick

and dying, this is to offer Him myrrh. Do not the three presents of the Magi also seem to be the natural symbols of the threefold profession of those who enter on a religious life? the present of gold, the symbol of the vow of poverty, which strips a person of all their wealth, and all personal possessions; the gift of incense, the symbol of the vow of obedience, the works of which are more pleasing to God than burnt sacrifice and incense; the present of myrrh, the symbol of the vow of chastity, which makes us, as it were, dead to the flesh, and the carrying out of which requires the exercise of a continual self-denial.

FOURTH POINT.

The Magi return to their own country.

And being warned of God in a dream that they should not return to Herod, they departed into their own country another way. Let us observe here in the Magi,

1. Their progress in divine illumination. A star had warned them to go, the Scriptures had revealed to them the place whither they were to go, and now God Himself undertakes the ordering of their return. See them now admitted to the most intimate and the most extraordinary communications from God, a just reward of their faithfulness in following Jesus. If our spiritual knowledge does not increase, it is because we do not respond sufficiently to the light which God gives us.

2. The devotedness of their obedience. They put in practice that precept so important, and often so difficult to carry out, that it is better to obey God than man. How often does not human respect cause us to transgress! Let us learn to mistrust a world, which would entice us to return to it, after our devotional exercises are ended, under pretence that it wishes to worship Jesus Christ with us; but which only seeks in reality to take Him from us, and to stifle Him in our heart.

3. The change of their road. They returned by ano-

ther way; but as for us, is it not always the same way which we take, the same negligence, the same lukewarmness, the same dissipation, the same weariness of prayer, the same self-love, and self-seeking?

4. *Their return to their own country.* Our country is Heaven. We have strayed away from it by sin, we can only return to it by repentance, and the practice of all those virtues of which our Saviour has given us an example.

Prayer. The Magi prostrated at Thy feet, O my Saviour, are the first-fruits of the Gentiles. I render Thee thanks for their call, which is a pledge of mine; but am I as faithful in answering to it, as were these first apostles of the Christian religion, my true examples, and my fathers in the faith? Ah, Lord, awaken anew in me the spirit of this divine call, of this precious grace, of which the adoration of the Magi recalls to me the remembrance, of that inestimable grace with which Thou hast favoured me by a special predilection, notwithstanding my unworthiness, and which, since I received it, I have only too often deserved to lose. Let the remembrance of my Christian calling be henceforth, O God, the spring of my liveliest gratitude; and may the maxims and obligations which it lays upon me be the single rule of my conduct. Amen.

Meditation XIV.

PURIFICATION OF THE BLESSED VIRGIN MARY.

In this holy ceremony, the sacred text sets before us three objects for consideration, the Holy Family, the aged Simeon, and Anna the prophetess, which will form the subject of the three following meditations. S. Luke ii. 22-24.

As regards the Holy Family,

We have here three things to meditate upon; the Purification of the Blessed Virgin Mary, the Presentation of Jesus in the Temple, and the presence of S. Joseph.

FIRST POINT.

The Purification of the Blessed Virgin Mary.

And when the days of her purification, according to the law of Moses, were accomplished, they brought him to Jerusalem, to present him to the Lord: (as it is written in the law of the Lord, Every male that openeth the womb shall be called holy to the Lord:) and to offer a sacrifice according to that which is said in the law of the Lord, A pair of turtle doves, or two young pigeons.

1. Remark in Mary her obedience. She obeys a law in which the terms in their proper sense seem expressly to except her, since they state distinctly, " If a woman have conceived seed, then she shall be unclean seven days." (Lev. xii. 2.) But out of love for the law of God, and in order to avoid giving scandal to others, who were ignorant of the great mystery of her conception, wrought in her favour, Mary does not avail herself of the exception from this law, which she could have pleaded. On the contrary, she observes the precepts of the law, and fulfils all its ordinances to the minutest detail. Is it with the same love, the same fervour, and punctuality that we obey God? Alas! we either transgress His law entirely, or else we observe it but imperfectly.

2. Consider in Mary her humility. She conceals from the eyes of men the glory of her virginity, which she had been so jealous in guarding in the eyes of the angel and before God. She enters the outer court of the temple, as if she were unclean, and needed to be purified. This holy Virgin knows that God knows her purity, and that suffices to her: she is but little disquieted by human judgments. How different are we! We are but slightly disturbed at our defilements in the sight of God, and care only to appear pure in the eyes of men.

3. Admire in Mary her spirit of poverty. Accord-

MEDITATION XIV.

ing to the law, the mother was bound to offer a lamb and a turtle dove, or if she was not able to bring these, she might offer two turtle-doves, or two young pigeons in their stead. Mary places herself in the last category, as being more suited to her present condition. She is not ashamed to appear poor in the eyes of the world, and in God's House. Alas! is it not often in this holy place that we seek, most of all, to display our worldliness with so much ostentation and excess?

SECOND POINT.

The Presentation of Jesus Christ in the Temple.

Jesus Christ is brought to the temple, He is offered up there, and He is there redeemed.

1. Jesus Christ is brought to the Temple. *They brought Him to Jerusalem.* Consider this tender lamb brought from the stable to the Altar, as a victim destined to be sacrificed. Contemplate this divine Child, now in the arms of Mary, now in those of Joseph. O sweet Burden, Who dost give strength to those who bear Thee, and Who bearest Thyself the universe in Thy Hands! With what care, with what attention, with what tenderness do not Thy parents hold Thee in their arms! Alas! is it not thus O Divine Jesus, that I should myself bear Thee, when I have the happiness to receive Thee in holy communion?

2. Jesus Christ is offered in the Temple. The law commanded that all the first-born, if males, should be offered to God, as being specially dedicated to Him, in memory of His having, in order to deliver His people, slain all the first-born of the Egyptians, and spared those of the Israelites. Jesus, although the giver of the Law, seeks no exception from it, but wills to fulfil it in all its details. Mary, being then purified, she and S. Joseph carry Jesus into the second court of the Temple, to present Him to the Lord. It was then that God received in His Temple an Offering worthy of Himself, and equal to Himself, the First-born of all creatures; Him,

Who fulfilled all which the offerings of the Old Testament had foreshadowed, and Who was to be the perpetual Offering of the New Testament, and to raise to a divine dignity all which should be offered in His Name, and united to His Sacrifice. What a sight was this holy Oblation for Heaven! What an honour for Joseph and Mary, by whose hands It was offered! What honour for the earth, for whom this august Victim offered Himself! Let us unite ourselves to this divine Sacrifice: let us consecrate ourselves, in union with Jesus Christ, to God without ceasing, wholly and unreservedly, for life and for death, for time and for eternity.

3. Jesus is redeemed from the Temple-service. The first-born, who were dedicated to the Lord, should have remained in the service of the Temple; but God having destined the entire tribe of Levi for this purpose, the law ordained that all the first-born of other tribes should be redeemed at the price of five shekels. Jesus was not destined to serve in the temple; He was Himself the living Temple, Which was to be destroyed and rebuilt in three days. The temple and the sacrifices were to be done away with for ever. A new altar, new sacrifices were to follow, and last to the end of the world. It was then at this price of five shekels, that He was redeemed, Who was to redeem us from hell at the price of His Blood, Which was to flow forth from the five wounds of His Sacred Body. O my divine Saviour! by these adorable Wounds, and by this Precious Blood which Thou sheddest for me, suffer not that the price of my redemption should be shed in vain for me.

THIRD POINT.

The presence of S. Joseph.

Joseph appears here as the head of the family, as the husband of Mary, and as the father of Jesus.

1. As head of the family, he arranges for the performance of the ceremony, provides what is needful, and takes care that the requirements of the law should be

fully carried out. Thus the head of every family should provide, that the law of God should be minutely observed in his house. He should commend to God's care and protection, all who are dependent upon him, and in particular, offer to Him his children, dedicate them to His ministry when God calls them, and yet not force them to consecrate themselves to it, when God does not call them.

2. As husband of Mary, Joseph takes part in her offering, in her fervour, in her poverty, in her privations, and in her virtues. The husband of a pious wife, far from hindering her in her religious observances, should seek to encourage her, to help, to support, and love her.

3. As the (supposed) father of Jesus, Joseph has the happiness of presenting Him to God in company with Mary, His Mother. He was not his real father; but he had the glory of bearing that name, and of fulfilling the office. The Gospel gives him that name, whether he is mentioned in conjunction with Mary, or whether he is named separately; it is the name which men gave to him during his life, and doubtless our Saviour also Himself addressed him by it.

Prayer. O divine Saviour! Who didst offer Thyself up to Thy eternal Father, as the only Victim capable of making atonement for us, I offer myself to Thee with all my imperfections, and with the entire self-surrender which is befitting a sinful victim; offer me up as a sacrifice to Thy glory, by the mortifications which it may please Thee to lay upon me: consume the imperfections of my soul by the fire of Thy love, that I may one day be presented to Thee with a pure heart in the Temple of Thy glory. Amen.

Meditation XV.

CONTINUATION OF THE PURIFICATION OF THE BLESSED VIRGIN.

OF THE AGED SAINT SIMEON.

Meditate, 1. on his faith, 2. his hymn, 3. his prophecy.
S. Luke ii. 25-35.

FIRST POINT.

The faith of Simeon.

And, behold, there was a man in Jerusalem, whose name was Simeon: and the same man was just and devout, waiting for the consolation of Israel: and the Holy Ghost was upon him. And it was revealed unto him by the Holy Ghost, that he should not see death before he had seen the Lord's Christ. And he came by the Spirit into the temple; and when the parents brought in the child Jesus, to do for Him after the custom of the law, then took he Him up in his arms, and blessed God.

1. Admire in the aged saint, his faith in the promises of the law and of the prophets. Simeon was waiting for the promised Redeemer, he longed without ceasing for that happy moment which was to bring about both the happiness and the consolation of the people of God. In this hope, in this expectation of the Messiah, he lived a life of uprightness in the fear of the Lord, and the Holy Ghost was upon him. If we had a real faith in the promises of the Gospel, if we were really waiting for the blessings which are promised to us in it, we should not find any difficulty in living in holiness, and in retaining the Holy Spirit within our hearts: but a too feeble faith, a life of worldliness, or of carelessness and sin, deprives us of the consolation of God, extinguishes all hope in us, and makes us look only with fear upon the next life, and the second coming of Christ.

2. Observe the faith of Simeon in the revelation of the Holy Spirit. The Holy Ghost had revealed to him that he should not die till he had seen the Messiah; he longed for that happy moment to come; nevertheless, he was only to see Him in the infirmity of His mortal flesh, and was to die soon after. But we, on the contrary, are to see Him after our death, in the splendour of His Glory, when all our troubles shall be ended, and we shall reign for ever in Heaven with Him; and yet this thought alarms and frightens us. O holy Spirit come into my heart, in order to detach it from all earthly things, and do Thou cause me to long for the happy moment of my deliverance and of my true happiness.

3. Consider how great was the faith of Simeon in the presence of Jesus, the Saviour. Led by the Spirit of God, he came to the temple, just as this Divine Child was brought in, to be presented to the Lord. He sees Him, he contemplates Him, and inwardly adores Him. The ceremony being concluded, he can no longer restrain himself; he approaches Him, takes Him in his arms, and blesses God, and gives utterance to the transports of his joy, gratitude and love. If we had a lively faith, should we not know that we have the same Jesus in the Sacrament of the Holy Eucharist, and should we not receive Him with the feelings of Simeon? But alas! is it not often the spirit of vanity, or curiosity, self-interest, or custom, or even human respect, or some other sinful or unworthy motive, which brings us to God's House or to His Altar?

SECOND POINT.

The Hymn of Simeon.

The aged saint, bearing Jesus Christ in his arms, gives himself up to the transport of joy which fills his heart, and blessing God with a loud voice, bursts forth in the wondrous words of the Nunc Dimittis, in which he sets forth the greatness of Jesus, and draws down upon himself the wonder of Joseph and of the Blessed Virgin.

1. He gives utterance to the joy which fills his heart. *Lord, he cries, now lettest Thou Thy servant depart in peace; for mine eyes have seen Thy Salvation.* Yea, O God, I am now about to leave this world, and I feel that Thou dost call me to Thyself. I leave it without regret. What should I do here below any longer, since, according to Thy promise, Thou hast fulfilled all my desires? I have seen with mine eyes Him Whom I waited for; the Messiah, Whom Thou hast sent to be the Saviour of the world. How sweet will death be to me, after such happiness! Thou didst promise me Thy Salvation, Lord, and I possess Him. How true art Thou in Thy promises! How blessed it is to serve Thee, and to trust faithfully in Thee! Would that we, after each Communion, and in the hour of death, might taste a like peace, and a like desire to die in the Lord!

2. Simeon set forth the greatness of Jesus. *Which Thou hast prepared before the face of all people: a Light to lighten the Gentiles, and the Glory of Thy people Israel.* It is He, Whom all nations should look upon as the Author of grace, and the End of their salvation. This Sun of righteousness shall clear away the darkness of their ignorance: He shall be the special glory of Israel, of that chosen people, amongst whom He has been born, and who will have the happiness of being the witnesses of His miracles. And in truth, is not Jesus, the Salvation which God has given to men, and is it not by Him alone that they can be reconciled to God? It is in vain, that an impure and proud philosophy seeks its salvation elsewhere. Jesus is the Salvation offered and presented in the eyes of all people: promised at the beginning of the world, granted in the midst of time, and announced throughout the world. Jesus is the *Light of the Gentiles;* by Him the Gentiles have come out of the darkness of idolatry, and have had their eyes opened to the light of the Gospel. Do we

K

thank God that He has caused us to be born in the midst of this glorious Light? Do we walk in the light which shines upon us? Do we not still follow the maxims and practise the works of darkness? Jesus is the *glory of Israel;* it is by Him, that this people has been acknowledged by the Gentiles as the people of God. Happy would it be, if the greater part of that nation had not, by an obstinate blindness, which we can neither understand nor sufficiently deplore, drawn down upon themselves the misfortunes foretold by the prophets! But a new Israel has taken their place, and that new people are ourselves; let us then glory only in knowing Jesus Christ, in following Him, and loving Him!

3. The language of this aged saint fills Joseph and Mary with amazement. *And Joseph and his mother marvelled at these things which were spoken of Him.* The wrapt discourse of Simeon was a complete compendium, and contained within it the substance of all the teaching of the patriarchs and prophets. However sublime its expressions were, they could have had nothing in them new or surprising to Joseph and His Mother; nevertheless, they marvelled at these things which were spoken of Him. Such is the character of a lively, tender, and respectful love. We never think ourselves sufficiently instructed in that which concerns a person whose fame affects us; we are glad to hear things repeated of him which we knew already, and such are specially the feelings of those who love Jesus. Although they knew it, they rejoice to hear the recital of His greatness; they find always something in it wherewith to fill their hearts, and the things which interest them are ever new, and never fail to be worthy of their deepest admiration. However well instructed we may be in the mysteries of our religion, let us listen and profit by the teaching of God's ministers, and be attentive to put into practice the examples which the faith, piety and charity of our neighbour gives us.

THIRD POINT.

The prophecy of Simeon.

The aged saint, having given back to His parents the Child Jesus, Whom he had till then held in his arms, wishes them the graces proportionate to the happiness which they enjoyed, and *blessed them;* that is to say, that he addressed to God his prayers and wishes for them. Then turning to Mary, the mother of Jesus, distinguishing her from Joseph, who was not His father, he addresses her in particular, and expresses himself in terms which were prophecies equally with regard to Jesus her Son, herself, and mankind in general.

1. As regards Jesus. The Child which you have brought into the world, *Behold this Child,* he says, *is set for the fall and rising again of many in Israel; and for a sign which shall be spoken against.* He came into the world only to be its Saviour, and He will be, in truth, a source of salvation to many, whom their faith in His word, and their correspondence to His grace will render partakers of the fruits of His redemption; but to how many others, who are unbelievers in His words and rebellious to His calls, will He not become, against His intentions, and in spite of His earnest desire, a stone of stumbling and an occasion of falling! A day will come, that He will give Himself up to the most shameful death for the people of Israel, and for all mankind. In this state of weakness and suffering, He will be for many a sign which shall be *spoken* against. Here is the third prophecy of the Gospel, of which we see the fulfilment. Jesus Christ has been spoken against, and is so still; let us neither be surprised, nor let our faith be shaken by it; it has been foretold. Those who speak against Him bring upon themselves their own condemnation; those who follow Him make sure of their eternal salvation; what happiness for these, what misery for the others! To which do we belong? Do not let us deceive ourselves; we speak against Christ by not sub-

mitting ourselves to His Holy Spirit, to the doctrines taught by His Church, and by not ruling our lives according to His commandments and precepts. Alas! is not my whole life a continual contradiction to the Gospel? Shall I then always live after this manner?

2. As regards Mary. Simeon prophesies to her the sorrows which she would have to suffer. *Yea, a sword, he tells her, shall pierce through thy own soul also.* Mary was to see the heart of her Son pierced with a spear, and was to have her own heart pierced with the sword of grief. O great God! was it not enough that Thy Blessed Mother was destined to this bitter suffering? Must it be foretold her thus thirty years beforehand? Nourish with care, this beloved Son, O holy Virgin Mother! your sufferings will grow with His growth; and your anguish will last as long as His life, and will increase in proportion as this tender Lamb draws near to the time appointed for His sacrifice. May my life be passed, as her's was, in retirement, in grief, and in tears, at the thought of the sufferings of my Saviour, and of her's.

3. As regards mankind—*that*, adds Simeon, *the thoughts of many hearts may be revealed.* The sword of persecution reveals the secrets of hearts, and makes known their most hidden thoughts. The mask falls then, the veil is torn away, and no one can then conceal either from themselves or others, their true feelings. Let us examine here our love for God, our attachment to religion; let us sound our hearts; are they proof against the loss of property, rest, reputation, or even life? Alas! perhaps they cannot stand even the test of some pleasure, or self-interest, or the raillery of others, or the slightest contradiction.

Prayer. Attach firmly to Thyself, O God, this weak heart of mine, suffer it not to lead me astray, and let me not yield to its rebellions against Thee. Grant rather that I may be spoken against by the world, and pierced for Thy love's sake with a sword of suffering. Grant that I may be pierced with grief at the sight of my sins, and that this suffering, by purifying me, may make me worthy to have a share in Thy glory. Suffer me not to speak against the precepts, the examples, the doctrine, and the teaching of Thy Divine Son; but give me that constant and courageous faith which may make me confess myself His disciple before men, so that at the last day He may not deny me before Thee. Amen.

Meditation XVI.

CONCLUSION OF THE PURIFICATION OF THE BLESSED VIRGIN.

OF THE SAINTLY ANNE, THE PROPHETESS.

Observe with the Gospel, 1. the character of the prophetess, 2. her presence in the temple, 3. the return of the holy family to Nazareth. S. Luke ii. 36-39.

FIRST POINT.

The character of the prophetess.

1. S. Luke speaks to us of the nobility of her family. *And there was one Anna, a prophetess, a daughter of Phanuel, of the tribe of Aser.* The Evangelist names as an honour the father and the tribe of the prophetess, and tells us that she was not of unknown parentage, but of a family, known and distinguished, to shew us that birth lends weight to the testimony of a good life. And in truth, a person of distinction who joins to nobility of blood the practice of virtue, can do much in the cause of religion; but on the other hand, what harm does it not cause, and how sinful it is, when superiority of rank only serves to lend a helping hand to error, to encourage vice, and to depreciate virtue!

2. The Gospel praises the widowhood of S. Anne. *She was of a great age, and had lived with an husband seven years from her virginity: and she was a widow*

of about fourscore and four years. Married as soon as she was of sufficient age, her husband only lived seven years, and from his death to the age of fourscore and four years, which was her age at the time of the Purification of the Blessed Virgin, she had formed no new ties. A widowhood, so faithfully persevered in, deserved the praise of the Holy Ghost. And in truth, happy is that state, which, after that of virgins who follow the Lamb whithersoever He goeth, is the most conformable to the inclinations of the heart of Christ, and most fit to receive His Divine communications.

3. The Holy Scriptures praise the piety of the prophetess. *She departed not from the temple, but served God with fastings and prayers night and day.* This holy widow, the true model of those who are either free or separated from the cares of the world, had made for herself a plan of life, regulated with a view to the perfection of her estate. All her days were sanctified by fastings, and all the hours of the day, as well as the night, were divided amongst her various religious exercises. The temple was her most accustomed abode. She passed her life in mortification and prayer, without fearing that so austere a life might injure her health, or shorten her days. What delights has a life of purity, spent in self-denial and prayer, and how would these delights be sought after, if they were better known! Prayer, self-denial and purity are united by the most indissoluble and closest bonds. Without prayer, mortification would be intolerable; without self-denial, prayer is lifeless; without prayer and self-denial, purity is fragile, and in danger of being lost.

SECOND POINT.

Of the presence of the sainted prophetess.

1. Admire her piety. *And she coming in that instant, gave thanks likewise unto the Lord.* Whilst Jesus, Mary and Joseph were still in the temple, the holy widow arrived there. How sad it would have been

for her to have missed a moment so precious! It was that in which the aged Simeon, still holding Jesus in his arms, was foretelling what would befall the Son and the mother. How the piety of the virtuous Israelite deserved the happiness! She sees the Divine Child, contemplates Him, and penetrates the mystery hidden under the ordinary exterior of His adorable person. What were her joy, her respect, and her love! She burst forth into thanksgivings, and blessing, and gave herself up to transports of joy, and publicly gave glory to God and bore witness to His Son. If this gifted prophetess had been absent from the temple at this hour, she would have lost an ineffable blessing. God bestows His graces at certain moments, on certain occasions; let us watch for these precious moments, and let none escape us. The very religious duty, the very devotional exercise which we have neglected, might perhaps have been the occasion which God has chosen to bestow upon us some special favour. Let us imitate the love of this holy woman for the worship of God. With what feelings and with what reverence ought we not to worship God in His House of Prayer! But alas! is not the way in which we often behave ourselves when there, the greatest insult we can offer Him? Does it not witness against us, does it not shew our want of faith in His divine Presence?

2. Observe the zeal of this holy woman. *And spoke of Him to all them that looked for redemption in Jerusalem.* Already she performs the work of an apostle. Penetrated with the consolation of having seen the Messiah, she makes Him known to all whom she knew in Jerusalem amongst the faithful Israelites. She speaks to them with that prophetic and inspired tone which so effectually persuades men, and with that apostolic fire which enkindles all hearts. If the love of Jesus reigned within our souls, His greatness and His goodness would be the subject of our conversations; not content to love and know Him ourselves, we should seek to make Him known and loved by others.

3. Remark her discretion. To whom does she shew forth Jesus Christ? *To all them that looked for redemption in Jerusalem.* All the Jews awaited the promised Redeemer, but some with false ideas of a worldly greatness and temporal deliverance, and others with the utmost indifference. A small number only waited for His coming with longing desire, and in the spirit which was befitting true Israelites. It is only to such that the sainted widow brings the words of salvation, and relates what she has seen, and what the Holy Spirit has made known to her. There would have been imprudence and even risk in speaking of Him indifferently to every one, especially in a town where a wicked king was on the throne, who was the most cruel enemy of the Saviour. Amongst ourselves, all call themselves Christians, and profess to belong to His Church: but how few are there who really care for the spread of Christianity, or who sincerely desire the establishment of God's kingdom and the true redemption of Israel! How few are there with whom one could speak of the eternal Redemption which we wait for, and of the means which we must take to attain to it!

THIRD POINT.

Of the return of the Holy Family.

And when they had performed all things according to the law of the Lord, they returned into Galilee, to their own city Nazareth.

1. They returned without undue haste. They do not leave the temple, until they have perfectly fulfilled all which the law prescribed, until they have heard all that God willed to make known to them by the mouth, of Simeon and Anna. The haste with which we leave Church immediately after divine service, or the Holy Communion, or any other act of public worship, and our anxiety to be freed from our religious duties, often deprives us of all the good effects which we might gain from them. Let us then end all our acts of devotion

by some time given to recollection, that we may take away with us and carry home some good resolution.

2. They withdraw reverently and in a profound silence. The silence of Mary and Joseph during the whole time of this ceremony, appears very surprising. S. Luke does not even say of them, as he did of the shepherds, that they returned praising God. How deep is this silence, how worthy of admiration! Have we not sometimes tasted its sweetness in prayer or in Communion? Have we never experienced that blessed state of silence in which the soul is overwhelmed before the Majesty of God, at the thought of His benefits? This gift of God is as rare, doubtless as it is precious; but it is ordinarily the reward of the perfect observance of the law, and it requires always the greatest faithfulness to preserve it.

3. They did not linger when the service of God was concluded. They do not tarry at Jerusalem to rest themselves there, or to enjoy the admiration which all the wonders had drawn down upon them. They return to their own home without losing a moment, in order to occupy themselves there with their ordinary occupations. A striking example to parents, whose life should be divided between their domestic duties and their religious duties, and who, in order to preserve the feelings of piety which have been inspired in them by the service of God's House, ought not to let themselves be hindered by vain amusements, or frivolous conversations but should return from the House of God to their own houses, to fulfil there the duties of their station, and exercise themselves successively in the fulfilment of their various duties.

Prayer. Alas! Lord, the time is short, and what use have I made of it till now in working out my salvation? Make me know this day what its true importance is, in order that I may consecrate it entirely to the one thing needful, and after the example of the holy Anna, occupied day and night, with my salvation, may not depart from Thy temple, that is, from Thy House of Prayer and from Thy Divine Presence. Ah! how

I regret the time of which the world has deprived me!
I will then carefully use, O my God, all the moments
which Thou shalt give me: I will make the best use
I can of the days which Thou shalt grant me, and I
will henceforth fear nothing, save, lest, when they are
ended, they should be found to be unworthy of Thy Heavenly rewards. Amen.

Meditation XVII.

OF THE PERSECUTION OF HEROD.

The Gospel presents to us here three objects for our consideration, 1. the flight of the Holy Family into Egypt, 2. their abode in Egypt, 3. their return thence. S. Matt. ii. 13-23.

FIRST POINT.

The flight of the Holy Family into Egypt.

Behold the angel of the Lord appeareth to Joseph in a dream, saying, Arise and take the young Child and His mother, and flee into Egypt, and be thou there until I bring thee word; for Herod will seek the young Child, to destroy Him. When he arose he took the young Child and his mother, by night, and departed into Egypt; And was there until the death of Herod, that it might be fulfilled which was spoken of the Lord by the prophet, saying, Out of Egypt have I called my son. God gives here a command for the preservation of His Son.

1. Examine what this command was. It is a source of humiliation to Jesus Christ. It is an order of flight, of flight from His own country, of flight into Egypt, of flight before Herod, of flight in the character and with the name of Saviour. Should a God flee from the wrath of a man? Is such a command suitable to the greatness of the Sovereign Master of all? No, doubtless, according to worldly ideas; miracles, prodigies, brilliant achievements would be much more to our taste. Let us learn

to reform our ideas to those of God. This command, however humiliating it may appear to us, is infinitely glorious to God, because His greatness cannot be more honoured than by the humiliations of His Son, humiliations such as had been foretold by the prophet. This command, is not only glorious to God, but advantageous to man, who can find, by meditating thereupon, matter for instruction in the ways of salvation, for comfort in humiliations, and for edification in the persecutions which are never wanting in the Church, to His members and His elect.

2. To whom is this command addressed ? To Joseph. What an honour for this truly just man ! He is entrusted with the secrets of God, is constituted the man of His right hand and the instrument of His authority; he is in communication with these blessed spirits who are commissioned to announce to him the will of the Lord on earth; he holds the place of God the Father: he is the head of the Holy Family, the guardian of Mary, and of our Blessed Saviour, and thus has the right to command their obedience; what an honour, but above all was there ever such a holy, elevated, important office ? How great is that of God's priest, to whom Jesus Christ is given and entrusted for the nourishment of the true children of Israel, and to whom the faithful are entrusted by God Himself.

3. How is the command of God carried out ? First on the part of Jesus. Penetrate with faith into His inward feelings: with what faithfulness and love does He not submit to the commands of His Heavenly Father ! Secondly on the part of Mary. Let us sound her heart; the position of Mother of God does not make her forget that she is the wife of Joseph, and with what eagerness does she not obey his commands ! Thirdly on the part of Joseph. What submission ! what blind and unanswering obedience, prompt and without delay, exact and without omission, constant and without any limitation as to time ! Let us admire how S. Joseph and the Blessed virgin prepare themselves for this flight, without trouble

and without undue haste, without anxiety, as to the dangers and fatigues of the journey, without reply, without reasoning, without complaint or murmuring, either against the rigour of so humiliating and so irksome a command, or against the circumstances of the time, which was by night; or of the place, which is Egypt, an idolatrous country; or against Herod himself, that unjust persecutor. These holy spouses leave it all to the Lord to do as He sees fit; think only of obeying Him, and are only anxious to take care of the Divine Child, Whom they are desired to take out of the way of persecution. How truly worthy they are of one another, and how worthy of Jesus! When shall I strive to render myself worthy of Him by the imitation of their virtues, that is to say, by a blind obedience, a firm faith which is proof against all trials, an unshaken patience, and a perfect confidence?

SECOND POINT.

The abode of the Holy Family in Egypt.

Not only does the sacred historian relate to us here, what took place in Egypt, but also what happened at Bethlehem and at Jerusalem.

1. What took place in Egypt. The holy family live there poor, obscure, unknown, but precious in the eyes of God, and the objects of His tender favour. They live in the midst of idolatry, but continue to offer to God the purest worship and the most perfect homage; they live there in the midst of all kinds of crime and wickedness, but are bright examples of every virtue. Wherever we may be, in whatever station of life, with whomsoever we may live, let us keep ourselves hidden, humble, and recollected with our Divine Saviour; let us stand firm against evil, and let us be every where the good odour of Jesus Christ, and the edification of our neighbour. But what would it be, if in the House of God itself, if, in the midst of Christianity and of true religion, or still more

in the sacred ministry, if in the midst of good examples, we should be ourselves a subject of offence.

2. What took place at Bethlehem. *Then Herod, when he saw that he was mocked of the wise men, was exceeding wroth, and sent forth, and slew all the children that were in Bethlehem, and in all the coasts thereof, from two years old and under, according to the time which he had diligently enquired of the wise men. Then was fulfilled that which was spoken by Jeremy the prophet, saying, In Rama was there a voice heard, lamentation, and weeping, and great mourning, Rachel weeping for her children, and would not be comforted, because they are not.* Here then is human power, which, armed against weak children, employs all its force, exercises all its fury, and fills the place with blood and massacre. But God, without appearing to interfere, overthrows all the projects of men, and makes every thing work together for the execution of His own designs. O human prudence, how vain art thou against the wisdom of God! Herod caused a multitude of children to be slain, in order that one single child, the object of his fury, should perish: and this child whom he fears, alone escapes him. The prophecies are fulfilled, the Birth of the Messiah is announced throughout the world, the cries of the mothers and the blood of the children are a voice which echoes even to the hills of Rome, to the ears of Augustus. The holy Innocents gain an eternal life, and God receives in these tender victims the first-fruits of the precious Blood, by which the earth will soon be watered and purified. Such has been and such will always be the effect of all the persecutions against Jesus Christ and His Church; they will show the impotence of the powers of the earth, they will fulfil prophecy, they will extend the knowledge of the truth; they will bring about the eternal happiness of those who are the victims of them. How worthy of envy is the lot of these children, who were sacrificed for Jesus Christ, and of those who die after baptism! What a happiness to be thus saved, before having had the use of free

will! But if we make a good use of our will, it may be still more blessed and more glorious in the sight of God. Far from complaining, let us thank the Lord that He has preserved us to enjoy so great a blessing. Let us watch and pray, that we lose it not through our own fault.

3. *What takes place at Jerusalem.* Consider there an usurper on the throne, abandoned to his evil passions, and plunged in every kind of crime; impious, ambitious, dishonest, cruel, having no religion except his policy, feeding himself upon the tears of his subjects, making a sport of shedding blood, not sparing that of his own children: a criminal tormented by his own evil deeds, a prey to grief, to spite, and anger; tossed about by suspicions, fears, disquietudes; hated by his people, and become the execration of the universe; a blasphemer struck down by God, eaten of worms, infecting his own palace, insupportable even to himself, dying in his impiety, and dictating even, when expiring, the edicts of a cruelty, no longer to be dreaded. Lastly, consider Herod dead, as he had lived, an enemy of God, and having God for his enemy: become the eternal victim of the wrath of God, and cast down into the abyss which burneth with fire and brimstone. See then in what have ended all the intrigues, and all the glory of this monarch. The world has left him the surname of great, but how different are the judgements of God from those of the world! Of what use is it to any one to be great in the eyes of the world, if he is an abomination in the sight of God?

THIRD POINT.

The return from Egypt of the Holy Family.

But when Herod was dead, behold, an angel of the Lord appeareth in a dream to Joseph in Egypt, saying, Arise, and take the young child and his mother, and go into the land of Israel: for they are dead which sought the young child's life. And he arose, and took the young child and His mother, and came into the land of Israel. But when he heard that Archelaus did reign in the room of his father Herod, he was afraid to go thither; notwithstanding, being warned of God in a dream, he turned aside into the parts of Galilee. And he came and dwelt in a city called Nazareth that it might be fulfilled which was spoken by the prophets; He shall be called a Nazarene. Observe, upon what event this return takes place; in what manner it is made; and what is the place to which the holy family return.

1. Upon what event this return takes place. Upon the death of Herod. God overrules all events, and He wills that we should await them with patience and submission, without anxiety and without murmuring, and that we should make a wise use of them. The power of men, their favour, or their anger, last but for a time, as also their life. Every thing dies, but Jesus Christ alone dies not. Let us fear Him then only, let us love Him only, let us fix our affections on Him alone. All the persecutors have died, and the martyrs alone live and reign for ever with Jesus Christ.

2. In what manner is this return made? By the command of God, always addressed to S. Joseph, who, in his conduct, gives us a fresh reason to admire his obedience, his prudence, and his authority. His obedience: he takes no step except by the command of God, and therein he is the true model of souls who desire to lead a holy life, who should listen without ceasing to the voice of God, Who speaks to them, whether by the duties and obligations of their station which they should endeavour to learn and to fulfil; or by those who are set over them, to whom they should render a ready obedience; or by holy thoughts, or good desires, which they ought to follow. His prudence: he fears to return to Bethlehem, where Mary had given birth to the Saviour, because Archelaus, the successor of Herod his father in the kingdom of Judæa, was already known for his cruelty. God wills that we should make use of our reason, when His will is not revealed to us, and that we should learn to fear, to doubt, and to seek His help, because then He

will not fail to enlighten us. If we wish to keep Jesus within our hearts, let us imitate the prudence and the wise precautions of S. Joseph. Let us give heed to what places we direct our steps; what sort of persons are to be met with there; and who have the predominating influences there. Lastly, his authority: we see that every thing depends upon Joseph. Mary and the Child keep silence, and yield to his guidance; they observe the most minute subordination. Under what pretence then do we seek to withdraw ourselves from subjection to those powers, to whom God's ordinances have placed us in obedience?

3. What place is the destination of the Holy Family on their return? It is Nazareth, a small town of Galilee, in order *that it might be fulfilled which was spoken by the prophets, that Jesus Christ should be called a Nazarene.* This name has three meanings; 1st. it signifies consecrated or sanctified. Such is Jesus, such is every Christian by his baptism; are we such in our lives? 2ndly. It signifies flower, or off-shoot. Jesus is this flower or off-shoot of the branch of Jesse, and of David, of whom the prophets speak, and especially Isaiah. It is on Him that we have been grafted, it is by Him that we have been adopted. Let us live in a manner worthy of this adoption. 3rdly. It signifies inhabitant of Nazareth. It was a tradition received from the prophets, that the Messiah, was, in this sense, to be called a Nazarene. Jesus has permitted Himself to be called by the Jews, idolaters and unbelievers in contempt, sometimes a Nazarene, from the name of His City, sometimes a Galilean, from the name of His province, to teach His servants to bear with joy, the opprobrious names which are given them, and by which men seek to render them odious and despicable. Happy he who, for love of Him, knows how to practise this lesson of humility!

Prayer. The just man is not without trial; but Thou dost not forsake him, O my God! Persecutors and persecution pass away; but the fruit of persecution patiently endured does not pass away. Thou hast experienced it

Thyself, O divine Jesus! in that state of humiliation and dependence to which Thy love for me has reduced Thee. Could I with such an example, or with such incentives, complain of the trials which I undergo, or which await me? Ah, Lord, let me never forget that, in order to share in Thy glory, I must share in Thy sufferings, and that I shall be so much the more closely united to Thee in Heaven, as I have had the greater share in them here below. Amen.

Meditation XVIII.

OF THE CHILDHOOD OF JESUS CHRIST UP TO THE AGE OF TWELVE YEARS.

The Holy Spirit does not teach us any thing more of the hidden life of Jesus, save, 1. That He was brought up at Nazareth, 2. that He grew and waxed stronger there, being filled with wisdom, 3. that He took part in the public services of religion. Let us meditate with care and with good effect on such precious truths. S. Luke ii. 39-41.

FIRST POINT.

The Child Jesus brought up at Nazareth.

They returned into Galilee, to their own city Nazareth. What a source of humiliation for Jesus Christ was this place of residence!

1. It drew down upon Him continual contempt. Nazareth was a place which was despised, both for itself, and on account of its being situated in the province of Galilee. This city seemed to communicate its obscurity, and the contempt in which it stood, to the dwellers in it, and this contempt was reflected upon Jesus Christ in many of the circumstances of His life. Jesus preaches humility to us in every act of His life; and we avoid it every where; we make every thing an occasion of vanity. Is the place of our birth of any note, we make it a ground for our own exaltation, and for holding others in con-

tempt; if we are born in a place little known or of small repute, we feel ashamed of our birth-place, we leave it, and seek a more brilliant sphere, without fearing even the perils to which our vanity exposes us. Let us give ourselves up to the guidance of Providence, and be contented with our station; and if any thing is left to our choice, let us prefer, from inclination and for the love of God, that which is the lowliest and most despised in the eyes of men.

2. The abode of Jesus Christ at Nazareth gave rise to injurious prejudices against Him. The most sincere perhaps of His disciples, when he heard Him spoken of as the Messiah, asked, *Can any good thing come out of Nazareth ?* This, even the Galileans thought; what then would the people of Judæa think, to whom all Galilee was an object of contempt ? The prejudices of men against places, provinces and nations, have in them a contempt very absurd and very unjust. Let us bear this injustice, if it is our lot. Let it not trouble the peace of our heart, nor hinder us from reaching on to perfection.

3. Their abode at Nazareth brought insults and outrages upon Jesus Christ. How often was He called in mockery, Nazarene, Galilean! The first of these two names was put in the writing of accusation that was fastened to His Cross, and the second was that by which Julian the Apostate called Him in derision. But the Apostles and Christians made use of them also in reverence, to heal the sick and to drive away devils. Let us desire to be humbled, despised, and mocked with Christ, that with Him, we may be exalted, glorified, and crowned.

SECOND POINT.

The child Jesus growing up in His father's house.

And the child grew, and waxed strong in spirit : filled with wisdom, and the grace of God was upon Him.

1. Jesus *grew* and *waxed strong* in body. Alas! it was a Victim, Who was growing, in order to be offered up for His Father's glory, and our salvation, Who was waxing

strong that He might bear the weight of our sins, and of the penalty which was due to them; and we grow and wax strong, only in order to multiply our sins, far from growing only to God's glory, and increasing in strength, only that we may serve Him better. Jesus increased in wisdom. He was *filled* with it, because He was Wisdom Itself, the Eternal Wisdom of God: but He did not shew forth more than was proportionate to His years, that He might be an example to all ages; an example, which all parents should unceasingly set before their children. Jesus Christ at Nazareth, unknown in the humble home of S. Joseph, but distinguishing Himself in it by His gentle, submissive, docile and prudent behaviour, which rendered Him well-pleasing in the eyes of God and of men; such is the divine spectacle which He sets before them.

2. Jesus grew in grace. *The grace of God was upon Him.* An outward grace from the charms of His person, as the Psalmist says, "fairer than the children of men." There was manifest in His appearance, in His behaviour, in His discourses, a surpassing modesty and dignity; an inward grace, of which He Himself was the Source and the Author, and which He came to communicate to us, but only manifested by degrees. Parents often lavish their attentions to procure for their children those exterior graces which render them pleasing in the eyes of men; but have they the same care to preserve and cultivate in them the grace of God? Alas! it too often happens, that children lose their innocency before they have barely attained to the age of reason; and before they have ceased to be children, have already acquired habits of sin, which time, instead of weakening, only strengthens.

THIRD POINT.

The Child Jesus, taken to the public worship of the Temple.

Now His parents went to Jerusalem, every year at the feast of the Passover. The law of Moses ordered that every man and every male child should go three times a year to Jerusalem to offer their vows and their sacrifices to the Lord, that is to say, at the feast of Pentecost, the feast of Tabernacles, and the great Paschal Feast. It appears as if the Holy Virgin and S. Joseph went there regularly with the Child Jesus on these appointed days, although S. Luke only speaks here of the Passover, on account of the event which he is about to relate, and which took place at this feast.

1. Consider the assiduity, with which Jesus was taken to Jerusalem at this solemn feast. If the fear of Archelaus, says S. Augustine, prevented the holy family from dwelling in that great city, the fear of God also prevented them from keeping away from that city to solemnize this great feast. It is an essential duty of parents to accustom their children to take part modestly and fervently in the services of the Church, not only by setting them an example of devotion, but by taking their children thither themselves, and inspiring them with that spirit of reverence, attention and prayer, which is due to the presence of God in His Holy House.

2. Observe, in what spirit Jesus went to the Temple. He went with joy, behaved Himself there with reverence and offered there with love His prayers to God His Father; He celebrated there specially the Passover, He being Himself the true Paschal Sacrifice which should take the place of the former Passover: He offered Himself to His Father, as being the true Lamb, Which was soon to be offered up, and which should fulfil the figures of those ancient sacrifices, and establish a new, perfect, sufficient, and perpetual Sacrifice. It is also a duty of parents to instruct their children as regards the greatness of the Sacrifice which the Church commemorates, and of the feasts which she celebrates.

3. Examine in what spirit we ourselves take part in this holy Sacrifice, and celebrate the solemnities of the Church. Do we not often miss attending at the divine services, at Prayer, at Communion? Do we not often make excuses on this point, and thus cast ourselves off from the Communion of Saints? Or if we appear

in the assemblies of the faithful, is it not with an air of constraint, of impatience, and distraction, with an assiduity purely external and Judaical, which justifies but too well what the apostle says, that there can be no concord between Christ and Belial, between the spirit of God, and the spirit of the world.

Prayer. Alas! how far removed am I from Thy tender piety, O my divine Saviour! How have I strayed from Thine example, O my blessed Pattern! In proportion as Thou didst grow in age and in strength, Thou didst appear to increase in wisdom, in knowledge and in virtue; I advance each day in age, and each day I am farther from Thy divine Wisdom, and follow and care only for the vanities of this world. The longer I live, the more ungrateful is my conduct, giving no thought whence I came, nor whither I go, nor what use I ought to make of time, nor of eternity, and of the destiny which awaits me there. O uncreated Wisdom, hidden under the garb of childhood, enlighten me, guide me. Grant that I may become again a child, by humility, by innocency and by obedience to Thy holy laws, O divine Jesus! By the holiness of Thy childhood, forgive me all the sins and infirmities of my childhood, and of my whole life. O adorable Child! May my love for Thee grow, and wax stronger continually till the last day of my life. Amen.

Meditation XIX.
JESUS, AT TWELVE YEARS OF AGE, ASKS QUESTIONS OF THE DOCTORS.

Three circumstances, in this event related in Holy Scripture, deserve our attention, 1. S. Mary and Joseph lose Jesus, 2. they find Him, 3. they speak to Him. S. Luke ii. 42-50.

FIRST POINT.
S. Mary and S. Joseph lose Jesus.

And when He was twelve years old, they went up to Jerusalem after the custom of the feast. And when they had fulfilled the days, as they returned, the child Jesus tarried behind in Jerusalem; and Joseph and His mother knew not of it. But they, supposing Him to have been in the company, went a day's journey; and they sought Him among their kinsfolk and acquaintance. And when they found Him not they turned back again to Jerusalem, seeking Him.

1. These words tell us how Mary and Joseph lost Jesus. It was certainly not through their fault, but by an intentional act of the divine Wisdom. If Jesus remained, unknown to them, in the temple at Jerusalem, His object was, on the one hand, to prepare the Jews to acknowledge in Him a supernatural and wholly divine wisdom; and, on the other, to re-awaken in Joseph and Mary the thought of His divinity, and to render them an example, and a consolation to those souls who are tried by inward desolation. Jesus sometimes hides Himself from the most devout souls, in order to instruct them and to perfect them, that they may understand that the sensible delights of devotion are God's gift, and not their desert, that they may give proofs of their fidelity and love, and accustom themselves to serve God for Himself and not for His gifts. These trials are generally neither prolonged nor frequent, and are always helpful when we make a good use of them; but it happens only too often that we lose the sweetness of Christ's Presence, through our own fault, our distraction and our sins.

2. What was the grief of Joseph and Mary, when they had lost Jesus. They went a day's journey without any suspicion of the absence of their Son, never doubting that He had joined Himself to some of the inhabitants of Nazareth, their relations or friends, and that they should see Him in the evening; but when evening comes, and it is a matter of each family re-assembling, and joining together to pass the night, Jesus does not appear; they begin to fear and to be alarmed, they seek Him, but no one has seen Him. What must then have been the anxiety of His parents! What the

excess of their grief! How did they pass that cruel night? What fears, what reflections, what self-reproaches must they not have made to themselves. The wrath of Herod, the perils of Egypt, had not caused them such grief. For then Jesus was with them, but now they enjoy His Presence no longer. He is not with them. What must have been the agony of His Blessed Mother, to lose thus the divine Light, the Life of her soul, Him Whom she loved a thousand times more than herself. Where is He? What has become of Him? Where shall He be sought? Where found? A soul, who in the absence of Jesus, does not experience the like distress, does not truly love Him; and what danger there is that she may never find Him! Alas! how often have I lost Thee, O Jesus! without grieving over it! And what would have become of me, if Thou, by Thy divine goodness, hadst not been the first to seek me!

3. How great was their ardour in seeking Jesus. After having sought in vain all the evening, the next day, as soon as it was daylight, they set out to *turn back again to Jerusalem*, enquiring for Him, wherever they came, without being able to learn any tidings of Him. Whatever haste they made, they could not arrive at Jerusalem till towards the evening. At once and without taking any rest, they seek Jesus, and without success. The next day, they made new enquiries, which were equally useless. When Jesus is sought, He must be sought with zeal, with confidence. This divine Saviour sees the emotions and desires of our hearts; He knows the moment, when to calm and speak comfort to them.

SECOND POINT.

S. Mary and S. Joseph find Jesus.

And it came to pass that, after three days, they found Him in the temple, sitting in the midst of the doctors, both hearing them, and asking them questions. And all that heard Him were astonished at His understanding and answers. And when they saw Him, they were amazed. They find Him, but after how long a time, in what place, and under what circumstances?

1. After how long a time? It was the third day after having lost Him, as if Jesus would thereby set forth the mystery of His Resurrection. It is not for us to regulate the time of trial. God shortens or prolongs it according to the designs of His wisdom, always with relation to our needs and our spiritual advancement.

2. In what place? In the temple, and not in the midst of His relations. It is not in tumult, and in the midst of the world, but in His own House, His Church, and in prayer that we must seek Jesus. Whatever may be the gifts and powers of those, to whose instructions we listen in Church, it is always God's Word, which we hear there. When we listen in this frame of mind, we always receive some benefit, and often there needs but a word to touch the most hardened heart, to bring back peace of mind to the most desolate, and enable it to recover the good which it had lost.

3. Under what circumstances do S. Mary and S. Joseph find Jesus? Attending the public instructions, where He prepares, for their tender love, a sight which enraptures their hearts. It was an ancient custom at Jerusalem that the doctors should repair on certain days to some of the outer courts of the temple. There, seated on raised benches, they formed a sort of semicircle, in the centre of which a numerous assembly was arranged to listen to their discourses. It was in this assembly that Jesus was. O what joy for S. Mary and S. Joseph, when they discovered there this well-beloved Son, Whose absence had caused their grief! How well repaid they were for their fatigues by the joy which His presence procured them! But what was their astonishment, when they heard Him asking thoughtful questions, answering with enlightenment to those which were put to Him, explaining passages of Holy Scripture, and drawing out their real meaning with precision; replying to the remarks of the doctors with an air so modest, and a manner so sublime, that the assembly were in amaze-

ment. What increase of consolation, when they heard Him making use of the freedom which was allowed in this instruction to ask questions of the teachers, and to propose to them difficult passages? This vast audience and the masters in Israel were equally surprised to see a child of twelve years old, joining to the beauty of His person, the modesty of His age, the sweetness of His voice, so much wisdom, learning and knowledge. Every one wished to see this marvellous Child: every one enquired His name, His family, His country, and His bringing up. As they left the assembly, the wonders which they had witnessed were the only subject of conversation. What must have been the feelings of S. Mary and S. Joseph on this occasion! They knew well that Jesus was Uncreated Wisdom; and all which they saw could add nothing to the idea which they had already of His Perfections: but what doubtless surprised them was to see Him shew Himself forth so soon to the eyes of men; He, Who, till now, had lived a life of obedience to them, of silence and retirement. O Jesus! Teacher of our souls, cause Thy voice to be heard in my heart, so that I may listen to none but Thee, admire and relish Thee only.

THIRD POINT.

S. Mary and S. Joseph speak to Jesus.

His mother said unto Him, Son, why hast Thou thus dealt with us? behold, Thy father and I have sought Thee sorrowing. And He said unto them, How is it that ye sought Me? wist ye not that I must be about My Father's business? And they understood not the saying which He spake unto them.

1. Remark the complaint of S. Mary. The public instruction being ended, S. Joseph and S. Mary draw near to Jesus. His Mother, having, as it were, more right to speak to Him, addresses herself to Him, and reproaches Him with a respectful tenderness for His absence, for the secret which He had made of His inten-

tions, and for the anxiety which He had caused them. If, in our troubles, we knew how to carry our anxieties and our complaints to the feet of Jesus, we should find in Him the consolations which those, to whom we are wont to utter them, so seldom can give us.

2. Observe the answer of Jesus to His Mother. Wherefore afflict yourself, and seek for Me? said He to her; ought you not to have remembered, that, being God, as I am, and sent by My Father to do His works, I must occupy Myself with My Mission? These are the first words of Jesus, which the Gospel records to us. These words are the declaration of the mystery of the Incarnation, of the end of this mystery, and of the dedication of Jesus to the glory of His Father, and our salvation. These words are for the instruction of every Christian, who ought often to say to himself, and if needs be, to others, I am in this world only to serve God, and to work out my own salvation.

3. Meditate on the acquiescence of His parents in the words of Jesus. The holy Virgin, speaking to the Divine Saviour, had called Joseph His father: but Jesus Christ, answering to them both, speaks to them of His true Father, Who was God. He raises their minds above that which they saw in Him, by pointing out to them that they must accustom themselves, although He was, according to human ideas, still in His childhood, to see Him act for the interests of God His Father. It is then probable that they understood well of what Father He spoke; but they did not understand what were these things, which concerned the service of His Heavenly Father, with which He must occupy Himself, nor how and when He was to be employed in them. Nevertheless they carried their questionings and their curiosity no further. Let us also receive with respect the word of God, although we do not understand all the mysteries which it contains. Let us content ourselves with the lights which God gives us, without desiring such as, far from being useful to our souls, would perhaps only be hurtful to them: let us perform faith-

fully these duties which God requires of us at the moment, without seeking to penetrate into the future, or to unravel the designs of Providence, which we ought only to admire.

Prayer. O divine Jesus! grant that I may profit by the advantages which Thou bestowest on me with submission, that I may gather up Thy graces with faithfulness, and admire Thy wisdom, so that if I ever should have the misery to lose Thee, I may have the joy of finding Thee again for ever. May my eyes be fixed without ceasing upon Thee, so that I may fulfil Thy commands at the first intimation of Thy will, and when it shall be a question of Thy service, let nothing hinder me from obeying Thee, even unto death. Make Thyself master of my will and of my heart, that there may be nothing in me, which is not subservient to Thy glory and to the fulfilment of Thy will. Amen.

Meditation XX.

THE HIDDEN LIFE OF JESUS.

The Hidden Life of Jesus from the age of twelve years to that of thirty. S. Luke ii. 51-52.

A pious curiosity would desire a long and minute detail of the words and actions of the Saviour, up to the age, when He began to preach His Gospel openly: but the God-Man, Who was to instruct the world by His doctrine, and to save it by the price of His death, when the time should be come for Him to speak and to suffer, willed, first of all, only to edify it by the retirement of His Hidden Life, and by the example of His domestic virtues. His holy Mother, who entered perfectly into His designs, repeated nothing further to the sacred historian who had the happiness to compile the account of His Life, save the few words, that on His return from

Jerusalem at the age of twelve years, *He went down with them and came to Nazareth, and was subject unto them;* and that *His Mother kept all these sayings in her heart;* and that *Jesus increased in wisdom and stature, and in favour with God and man.* However brief these words are, they teach us nevertheless, if we will fathom their depth, 1. what was the humility, 2. the obedience, 3. the progress, and, 4. the duration of the hidden life of Christ.

FIRST POINT.

The humility of the Hidden Life of Jesus.

1. His condition at Nazareth. He passes for the son of a carpenter. He accepts the position, and does not seek to be acknowledged as ought else. He is content to call Joseph, father: and to conduct himself towards him as a son.

2. His home was that of a working man, and suitable to his profession, consequently it was poor and confined, with but few comforts, and bare of all luxuries, and even of many necessaries. The same would apply also to His food and clothing.

3. His occupations. They were conformable to the condition of him who passed as His father, and His divine Hands, which uphold Heaven and earth, were occupied in providing for the needs of men by tedious labours, and an employment purely mechanical. O God! O uncreated Wisdom! Couldest Thou have given us a more touching lesson of humility? How can it be, O divine Jesus! that we, being Thy disciples, should still be proud and vain, that we should seek for glory and distinction, and desire to appear better than we really are, and think ourselves so constantly above our station, and condition?

SECOND POINT.

The obedience of the Hidden Life of Jesus.

How did Jesus Christ employ His time from the age of twelve years to that of thirty? The Gospel teaches us in one short sentence, *He was subject to them.* He was subject to His parents, He obeyed their commands; and is not that all that God requires of us? Obedience alone ought to fix the sum of all our actions, and the example of Jesus leaves us no excuse for dispensing with our obligations in this respect, especially if we ask ourselves,

1. Who is it that obeys? It is the only Son of God, the Eternal Wisdom, the Creator and Maker of the world, the Saviour of men.

2. Whom does He obey? His own creatures, those whom He infinitely surpasses, and that beyond all comparison, in greatness, in wisdom, and in power.

3. In what does He obey? In the simplest, the most ordinary, and the most wearisome things, such as would be met with in the home of a working man.

4. How does He obey? By looking upon the will of His earthly parents as the will of God His Father, giving unction to His obedience by the inward love, respect, and submission of His heart, and rendering it outwardly edifying by the promptitude and exactness of His obedience.

5. Wherefore does He obey? In order to satisfy the Majesty of His Father, which had been offended by the disobedience of our first parents, to give us an example, and to restore us to the ways of that obedience which we owe to God, by obeying the will of men for love of Him; and in order to consecrate and raise in His person our obedience. What a lesson! What an example! Let us obey our superiors, as Jesus obeyed His parents; let us command our inferiors, as they commanded Jesus.

THIRD POINT.

The progress of the Hidden Life of Jesus.

In proportion as He grew in years, so did He draw down upon Him the favour of God His Father, by the fulness of wisdom, and the gifts of grace. 1. He grew in wisdom and favour with men; 2. with God; 3. He grew in both by the practice of the most ordinary duties.

1. Jesus grew in wisdom and favour with men in proportion as He advanced in years, that is to say, He proportioned to His years that which He allowed to appear in Him of wisdom. In the same manner as the sun, which, although always equally luminous in himself, nevertheless shines upon us, and gives us light in proportion as he rises upon our horizon, so Jesus Christ, the Sun of Righteousness, hidden under the form of a Child, casts His rays of Light farther, and renders the greatness of His wisdom and His holiness more piercing and more brilliant, according to the different periods of His strength and His age. A Divine Model, which should unceasingly be set before the eyes of youth, that with Jesus Christ they might grow, at the same time, in years, and in wisdom.

2. Jesus grew in favour with God, that is to say, that the virtues which shone forth in Him were sincere and true in the sight of God. Of what avail is it to us to regulate our external conduct, and to appear righteous in the sight of men, if in God's sight our sins increase and multiply unceasingly, if our virtues are only apparent, feigned and hypocritical?

3. Jesus increased in wisdom and in favour by the practice of the most ordinary duties. Our progress in virtue does not depend upon our actions themselves, but upon the spirit which animates them. Do not let us then complain, that we are not in a position to do great things for God. Jesus sets us an example of a holiness which is within our reach, and which is none the less sure and precious, because it is hidden; let us only give heed, whilst drawing continually near to the end, never to say, We have done enough. Let us always be hungering and thirsting after righteousness; so that if we were to live for ever, we might compel ourselves, according to our power, to become continually more holy; for we do not belong to the service of God only for a

limited time, like mere mercenaries, but we are dedicated to it for ever.

FOURTH POINT.

The duration of the Hidden Life of Jesus.

Jesus was about thirty years of age, when He began to shew Himself in public. Wherefore, having to pass thirty three years on earth, does He spend thirty in a hidden obscure life, and only gives three to the public duties of His mission?

1. He did so, in order to conform to the customs of the Jews, according to which no one could enter upon his public duties, till he was thirty years old. If only we were animated with the spirit of Christ, we should not so often seek to excuse ourselves from the performance of our religious duties, on account of our age.

2. It was to make us understand the advantages of a hidden life, and to teach us to love such a life. When it is a question of our learning to do great things, and even suffering much in the eyes of others, who are attentive to our struggles, and the spectators of our victories, it might be said that grace and even nature support us easily; but in order to make us adorn an obscure life and an unknown retirement with gifts and graces, for that we need a Divine Model. Alas! Do not thirty years of the life of Jesus, spent in such an estate, suffice to restrain the ardour of our self-love, which we often disguise under the name of zeal; or to make us relish humility, self-renunciation, abnegation, those virtues so opposed to our pride, our vanity, our ambition?

3. It is to teach those who enter upon the ministry of the Gospel, not to undertake so divine an office, till they have exercised themselves for many years in the acquirement of zeal and hidden virtues, till they have subdued pride and self-love, which easily disguise themselves under the semblance of piety, fervour, and charity, and seek only their own gratification in the exercise of the apostolic functions.

Prayer. O Divine Jesus! Who didst grow, or rather appear to grow in wisdom, and in stature, and in favour with God and with men, alas! how different has it been with me! In proportion as I have grown in years, I have grown in evil; in measure as Thou hast multiplied my days and Thy blessings, I have multiplied my sins and my ingratitude. All the good which Thy liberal hand has bestowed upon me, wherewith to serve Thee, I have turned into evil and outraged Thee therewith by using it against Thyself. My body, my mind, my health, talents, fortune, all these blessings have been turned in my hands into instruments of iniquity. Give me grace, O Lord, that, at least for the future, they may be made the instruments of righteousness and repentance. May I follow the example of Thy blessed Mother, who kept all Thy sayings so carefully in her heart! Amen.

Meditation XXI.

THE PREACHING OF S. JOHN THE BAPTIST.

Commencement of the preaching of the Gospel by S. John the Baptist. S. Matt. iii. 1-3. S. Mark i. 1-4. S. Luke iii. 1-6.

The beginning of the preaching of S. John is also, as S. Mark calls it, *the beginning of the Gospel of Jesus Christ, the Son of God. John did baptize in the wilderness, and preach the baptism of repentance for the remission of sins.* The baptism which he administered was a pledge of repentance, and prepared men to receive the forgiveness of sin; but this baptism only prepared the way for another, which was effectually to remit our sins. John said; *Repent ye: for the kingdom of heaven is at hand.* By these expressions he announced the coming of the Messiah, the Son of God, Who was to preach the Gospel, found His Church, form for Himself a new people, reconcile God with mankind, and make Him reign in their hearts. We find then here 1. motives for the strengthening of our faith; and 2. grounds of self-humiliation in examining our conduct.

FIRST POINT.

Motives for the strengthening of our faith.

1. First motive: the facts of the Gospel confirmed by their date and their publicity. Christianity is not a religion founded on a philosophical system, but on historical facts; it is a mode of instructing mankind, which is at once worthy of the greatness of God, and most suitable to man's feebleness. The Christian religion is not one of those popular traditions which have no origin, or which are lost in an unknown and fabulous antiquity; it is not one of those Pagan, or Mahometan fables which have no facts to attest them. The Christian religion has had a beginning, and it dates from that which has been most noble, most universal, and most enlightened. See how S. Luke marks the period. *Now in the fifteenth year of the reign of Tiberius Cæsar, Pontius Pilate being governor of Judæa, and Herod*[a] *being tetrarch of Galilee, and his brother Philip, tetrarch of Ituræa and of the region of Trachonitis, and Lysanias, the tetrarch of Abilene: Annas and Caiaphas*[b] *being the high priests: the word of God came unto John, the son of Zacharias, in the wilderness, and he came into all the country about Jordan, preaching the baptism of repentance for the remission of sins.* We see here in this date, the persons, the places, the time marked with the greatest exactitude. It is then under the first

---

[a] This Herod was the son of the Herod who put the Innocents to death, and he it was who caused the head of S. John the Baptist to be cut off, and to whom Pilate sent our Lord. He is sometimes called king; but he was properly only tetrarch, that is to say governor of a fourth part of the country.

[b] There were two high priests at that time, who exercised the office of high priest in turn every year.

Cæsars that the preaching of the Gospel began, and that all the acts of the Gospel took place upon which the whole of Christianity is founded. It is in the most enlightened and the best known country; it is in Judæa, before the eyes of a Roman governor, so to say before the eyes of the Emperor and the whole Roman Empire, and of the whole universe. Can there be any thing better authenticated and more public? Is it by a word of scorn or of mockery that facts of this kind are to be destroyed, which bear so palpable a character of greatness and of truth?

2. Second motive for the strengthening of our faith. The facts of the Gospel established by their agreement with the prophetical books. The prophetical books were neither invented nor changed by the Christians, since they are far more ancient than Christianity, and that, by a singular Providence, they were in the hands of Jews, the declared enemies of the Christian name. The prophetic books are divine, because they have announced in so minute a detail, and with so much certainty, events which were only to take place several centuries after they were foretold. Lastly, the facts of the Gospel are divine; and the Christian religion founded upon these facts, is divine, since these facts have been foretold by the prophetic books. From the beginning of the preaching of the Gospel, the prophecies began to be accomplished, and this is what the four evangelists all point out carefully. S. John appears by the banks of the Jordan, [c]*as it is written, in the book of the words of Esaias the prophet saying, The voice of one crying in the wilderness, Prepare ye the way of the Lord, make His paths straight;* [d] *as it is written in the prophets, Behold I send my messenger before Thy face, which shall prepare Thy way before Thee.* From this first step, the Gospel is found to agree with prophecy: but also from this first step, all the false prophets who have appeared have been in fault. None of them have been preceded by this voice crying in the wilderness.

[c] S. Luke iii. 4.   [d] S. Mark i. 2.

They and their false dogmas have stood alone, have held to nothing, have been bound up with nothing, and are far from being able to trace their origin to that which is the first beginning of the world, which is that of true religion. It is because it belongs only to God to give to His works that close and extended connection, which unites together every part from the creation of centuries to their ending. Blessed for ever be Thine ineffable wisdom, O God: Who hast put this wonderful agreement between Thy two Testaments, and hast thus sealed them with the inviolable seal of Thy divine authority. There is none but Thou, O great God! Who art thus the sovereign master of time and events, Who canst cause to be foretold what shall come to pass, and also bring to pass that which has been foretold; the prudence or the malice of men cannot accomplish thus much. The majesty, the power of Thy word make themselves felt here; and neither evil spirits nor men can undo them.

3. Third motive for encouraging ourselves in our faith. The facts of the Gospel are established by their importance, and the faith which has been placed in them. There are some facts which can be believed easily, because they are of no consequence, and are the cause of no change, nor is there any object in searching them out. I call important facts those, which could not be believed but by the change of all a person's ideas, and his ways of thought, by renouncing the worship in which he had been brought up, in order to embrace a new religion, by the reforming of his habits, and the contradiction of his own inclinations, and by exposing himself to the loss of honour and reputation, his goods, and even life itself. Such have been the facts of the Gospel. These facts are believed now a days throughout the world; they have been believed from the beginning, without which belief, these facts would not have been handed down to us. If they have been believed from the beginning, they are true, because they could not have been believed without being examined and without an assur-

ance of their importance, and of the consequences which they should have, and, because in examining them there was no possibility of a mistake, on account of their authenticity, their publicity, and the stir which they excited. I believe then, O God, and it is with this perfect conviction that I receive Thy Gospel, and that I desire to meditate on it, and to practise it, in the hope of finding there the remission of my sins, and the eternal rewards which Thou dost promise us in it.

4. Fourth and last motive for conforming ourselves in our faith. The facts of the Gospel established by the holiness of those who have announced them, and of those who have believed them. Who were the first preachers, the first historians, the first partakers of the Gospel, and the first Apostles who transmitted it to us? Holy men, eminent in all kinds of virtue, men brought up in repentance and the solitudes of the wilderness, sent and authorised by God, filled with His Spirit, gifted with the most precious gifts of Heaven, often even with that of miracles. And who are the Apostles whom modern philosophy sends to us? Philosophers filled with their own importance, solely occupied with the spread of their own renown, and always disputing amongst themselves for the honour which cometh of man: composers of romances, verse-makers, writers of farces, comedies; authors who allow themselves every possible license; moralists who only preach pleasures and sensual indulgences: these are they who present themselves to us, not as coming forth from the wilderness, but from the theatre, or from places devoted to iniquity, in order to throw dust in our eyes, and warn us that Christianity is only fanaticism and prejudice? What days have we then reached, O God, and how great is now-a-days the blindness of men? Books are read with admiration, which our fathers would have rejected with horror, and men are listened to as enlightened teachers, whom they would not have judged worthy of ought but contempt. Fatal teachableness! May it at least point out to us that which we owe to our true masters in the faith!

SECOND POINT.

Grounds of self-humiliation in examining our conduct.

The Gospel offers us four subjects for our consideration.

1. The repentance which S. John preaches to us. Now what reason have we not to humble ourselves! For what is our repentance? What proportion does it bear to our sins? What earnestness do we shew in it? How do we practise the fasts, the abstinences which the Church enjoins us? How do we accept the crosses and afflictions which God sends us? Ah! let us bethink ourselves that the fruit of repentance is *the remission of sins*, and let us understand what is the price of such a gift; the damned know it; but there is no further remission for them.

2. The approach of the kingdom of Heaven, which S. John announces to us, is a new subject for our self-humiliation. *Repent ye*, saith he, *for the kingdom of Heaven is at hand*. The Kingdom of Heaven of the Church militant has already come to us; we are members of it, so to say, subjects born of this holy kingdom: but the kingdom of Heaven, of the Church triumphant is drawing near. The moment which will decide whether we shall be admitted into this kingdom, or whether we shall be rejected, is not far off; perhaps we are drawing close to it. Are we ready, or, at least, are we preparing ourselves for it? Do we not know that it may come at any hour, and come when we least expect it?

3. *The way of the Lord*, which S. John warns us to *prepare*, is another subject of humiliation. *The voice of one crying in the wilderness, Prepare ye the way of the Lord, make His paths straight.* Thus we see that what is done to prepare the road, by which a king, or a powerful prince is to pass, is the allegory, under which the prophet commands us to prepare the way of the Lord. *Every valley* must first *be filled*, all the hollows

or ditches of the roads must be filled up and raised. These valleys are the figures of the blanks which are found in our life, and in the omission of our duties. Let us then employ our time usefully, and fulfil our obligations towards our neighbour and towards God; let us perform punctually our religious duties, and those which belong to our station, and we shall have filled up every valley. Then *every mountain and every hill must be brought low*, that is, all pride of intellect, pride of heart, pride shewn in our manner, in our pretentions, in our conversation. But especially in our repentance must we bring down all pride, every mountain and every hill, and not dissemble any thing which may serve to humble us. In the third place, *the crooked places* must *be made straight*, the whole road must be made plain. God comes to us when we seek Him with a single intention, when we only act so as to please Him, and offer up to Him all we do; whatever other intentions we mingle with this, are like so many bye paths which lead us away from the straight road, and make the way crooked. In following these bye paths, we walk for a long time, and weary ourselves much, but do not advance a step, till often the night surprises us before we have reached our journey's end. Lastly, *the rough places* must *be made smooth*. What inequalities there are in our temper, in our conduct, and even in our devotions! How much asperity and hardness in our manner, in our words, and even in our zeal! How difficult we are to deal with! Let us make plain, smooth, soften all these, if we would prepare the way of the Lord, if we desire that He should come to us.

4. Lastly, the sight of the Saviour which S. John announces to all the world, is the final motive for our self-humiliation; *And all flesh shall see the salvation of God.* The Saviour, sent by God, has visited the whole race of mankind, and has been announced to all the world, nevertheless all have not received Him, nor followed Him; but a day will come when all will behold Him as their Judge. Woe to those who have not chosen

to look upon Him on earth as their Saviour! How do we regard Him? With what teachableness do we receive His commandments? With what submission do we obey His Church? With what faith do we adore Him in the Holy Sacrament of His Body and Blood, and in His Sacrifice of Himself on the Cross? With what eagerness, with what purity of heart do we receive Him? With what love do we thank Him for His benefits? With what ardour do we await His promises?

Prayer. Purify Thou my heart, O God! And make it more attentive to Thy voice, which warns me without ceasing of my wanderings, and which cries to me to prepare the ways by which Thou willest Thyself to come to me. Hasten Thy manifestation, O divine Saviour; and, in order to make me worthy to profit by it, enlighten me as to all that might make me to be defiled in Thy sight; or rather do Thou create in me a new heart. O Jesus, repress my inclinations, plane down my irregularities, break down my pride, humble my self-love, cut off and prune, so that Thou mayest find all the avenues of my soul prepared for Thee to come and reign over my heart, and possess it for ever. Amen.

Meditation XXII.

PREACHING OF S. JOHN BAPTIST.

The Gospel treats here, 1. of the person of S. John the Baptist, 2. of the subject of his preaching, 3. of his feelings with regard to Jesus Christ. S. Matt. iii. 4-12. S. Mark i. 5-8. S. Luke iii. 7-20.

FIRST POINT.

Of the person of S. John the Baptist.

1. What was his preparation for the sacred ministry? In the first place, it was holiness. He had been sanctified from his mother's womb. He who has never been stained by sin, has great advantages in fighting against

it. Secondly, it was solitude. He had spent nearly thirty years in the wilderness. Before we begin to speak, we ought to have meditated for a long time in silence. Thirdly, it was a vocation. He did not leave his solitude, till God's voice commanded him to do so: but as soon as he heard it, he did not delay for a moment. Fourthly, the knowledge of the written and moral law of men: a knowledge which must be acquired in retirement and study, and without which we could not say to each what befits his station. Lastly, repentance. *And the same John,* says the sacred text, *had his raiment of camel's hair, and a leathern girdle about his loins; and his meat was locusts and wild honey.* The repentance which he practised was much more severe than that which he preached; and both condemn our laxity, our luxurious and self-indulgent life, and our worldly and dissipated surroundings.

2. What was the zeal of S. John in the exercise of his ministry? In the first place, it was a zeal full of vigour against sectarians, who were filled with pride and presumption. *But when he saw many of the Pharisees and Sadducees come to his baptism, he said unto them, O generation of vipers, who hath warned you to flee from the wrath to come?* You who infect every thing with the poison of your doctrine and of your false interpretations, wicked sons of wicked fathers, in what frame of mind do you come to me? Are you frightened and pricked by my words? Let it be seen by your works, that you sincerely detest your former sins. If you are penitents in good earnest, *shew forth worthy fruits of repentance.* Thus S. John spoke also to the people, when he failed to see in them any better dispositions than in the Pharisees and Sadducees: he threatened them with much fervour, he sought to turn their hearts by humbling their spirits, and his conclusion was always, *Repent;* leave the ways of iniquity, turn away God's anger by good works, for the time of His vengeance is at hand. His zeal was full of gentleness for humbled sinners, who only sought to know what they should do to

appease the anger of the Lord. He suited his addresses to the condition of these true Israelites; he entered into their personal dispositions. He did not say to them; you are unworthy of mercy, or, in order to gain mercy, you must live like me in the wilderness; but he treated them with that kind compassion, which does not fail to gain in private those who have been touched by public preaching. He only exacted from them justice, almsgiving, and the exact observance of the duties of their station in life. *And the people asked him, saying, What shall we do then? He answereth and saith unto them; He that hath two coats, let him impart to him that hath none: and he that hath meat, let him do likewise. Then came also publicans to be baptized and said unto him, Master, what shall we do? And he said unto them, Exact no more than that which is appointed you. And the soldiers likewise demanded of him saying, And what shall we do? And he said unto them, Do violence to no man, neither accuse any falsely, and be content with your wages.* Lastly, his zeal was indefatigable. This saintly dweller in the wilderness did not appear wearied with the multiplicity of his labours, he shewed no distaste at the bluntness of those who came to propose to him numerous questions; he answered all; he satisfied every one. But it would be too long to relate all his instructions. *Many other things*, says S. Luke, *in his exhortation preached he unto the people.*

3. How great was his humility in the success of his ministry? *There went out unto him all the land of Judæa, and they of Jerusalem, and they of Jordan, confessing their sins.* What an edifying and delightful sight, this concourse of people who, converted and contented, returned thence blessing God! Even the enemies of truth dared not separate themselves from the multitude, and had allowed themselves to be carried away with the rest, and if they were not converted, their jealousy and their spite was the punishment of their hardness of heart. But little was wanting to cause matters to go too far, and that the esteem, in which his

auditors had held S. John, should undergo a change. *The people were in expectation, and all men mused in their heart of John, whether he were the Christ, or not; John answered, saying unto them all, I indeed baptize you with water; but One mightier than I cometh;* that is to say, I am not the Messiah Whom you are expecting: it is true that I baptize you with water in exhorting you to repentance, but here my ministry comes to an end; I am only sent to prepare the way of another; He, Who cometh after me, and Whom you will soon see in the midst of you, is clothed with an authority infinitely superior to mine. Thus, as soon as S. John perceived he was the object of their thoughts, he spoke of Jesus, he exalted His greatness, and seized every opportunity of bearing witness to Him. A zeal so enlightened, so courageous, so humble, merited the glory of martyrdom, with which he was so soon to be crowned.

SECOND POINT.

The subject of the preaching of S. John Baptist.

All his discourses seem to reduce themselves to these three thoughts: we must repent; we must repent truly; and we must not delay our repentance.

1. We must repent; and for this he alleged three motives. First, the anger of God. *Who hath warned you,* he asks, *to flee from the wrath to come?* Alas! We have offended God; but we do not know whether we have appeased His anger, and, what is still more deplorable, we know that we have done nothing to appease it. Can there be a more fearful state, than to live in a state of enmity to God? How then can I have lived in such a state myself? O holy penitence! Who will teach me to have recourse to thee? Happy those who know thee and give themselves up to thy efficacious restraints. The second motive of repentance which S. John Baptist set forth, was the severity of Christ's judgment. *Whose fan is in His Hand,* he says, *and He will purge His floor, and gather His wheat into the*

garner: but He will burn up the chaff with unquenchable fire. That is to say, like a careful labourer, He will appear with His fan in His hand, and will cleanse His granary: He will gather together the wheat into His barns; He will receive believers into His Church, and thence, if they persevere, they will pass into the abode of everlasting happiness. As for the straw, the figure of thoughtless or unbelieving men, He will burn them in a fire which shall never be extinguished. Terrible day, on which this division of evil and good, of punishments and rewards, by our Blessed Lord will take place! Then nothing will escape from His eyes, nothing will divert His justice, nothing resist His power. Happy he, whom repentance will reassure at that great day, and who will be found worthy to have a place in Heaven to reign there eternally! Lastly, the rigour and eternity of the torrents of hell, is the final motive which S. John makes use of to lead men to repentance. The fire of hell is *a fire unquenchable.* To him who meditates earnestly, on what this fearful punishment of hell fire is, what act of penitence would appear too hard? To him who meditates earnestly on what eternity really is, what repentance would appear too long? When eternity is concerned, can one take too many precautions? And in order to reassure yourselves against your alarms, *begin not to say,* continues S. John, *within yourselves, We have Abraham to our father;* that in consideration of His servant, God will deliver us: *For I say unto you, That God is able of these stones to raise up children unto Abraham:* that is, the Almighty, Who formed Adam out of the dust of the ground, can destroy you all, and change the stones which you see in this wilderness into new men, who, through obedience and faith, shall have a better title to be called children of Abraham than yourselves. In vain does the philosopher boast that he knows God, if he does not acknowledge Him Whom God has sent to save mankind, Jesus Christ His Son; in vain does the Jew call himself a child of Abraham, if he does not believe in

Jesus Christ, the Son of that promise, in Whom Abraham believed, and by Whom he was justified; in vain does the Christian call himself a disciple of Jesus Christ, if he corrupts His doctrines with heresy: in vain do God's priests, and those who are dedicated to a religious life, reckon upon the holiness of their profession, if their conduct is not conformable to it. And do not say that God has only made us, in order to let us perish; assuredly no, since He offers us repentance. Why do we not embrace His offer? Do not let us say, that if this is so, the whole world will be condemned. No, no, for in spite of our sinfulness, Jesus Christ has and always will have a great number of faithful followers. Why should we not add to the number? But if, in the place where we are, wickedness should prevail, know we that God can raise up for Himself obedient children in countries the least civilized, and in lands the most uncultivated, children whose salvation shall make up for our fall, and whose zeal shall condemn our rebellions and our apostacy.

2. We must then heartily shew forth the repentance which our sins demand of us. *Bring forth then*, says S. John, *worthy fruits of repentance.* Now in order to bring forth these worthy fruits, we must first detest the past, that is to say, examine carefully our sins, weep for them bitterly, detest them sincerely, and confess them minutely; but how do we acquit ourselves of this first part of our repentance? We must then examine into the present, that is, look carefully what is our present state, whether in relation to God, or to the world. Are we in the true faith, in the true religion, in the Catholic and Apostolic Church? If we are not, we must not rest easy, we must not blind ourselves; for our salvation is in our membership with Christ's Church. If we are, then let us cling closer to it, and ask of God the grace to remain faithful to it. Then let us examine our state with regard to the world. Are our relations to it such as are sanctioned by God's law? Is there nothing opposed to it? How do we fulfil our duties? Do not we take unfair advantages and amass more profits or gain than

we lawfully ought? Do we not allow ourselves more
leisure, more repose, than the duties of our station permit? Do we not follow maxims, or practices which are
contrary to justice? Do we injure our neighbour in any
way? Lastly, we must regulate the future, with relation
to God, our neighbour, and ourselves. With regard to
God, let us practise our religious exercises, prayer and
meditation with more fervour: let us pay more reverence to God's House, and shew more zeal in frequenting the services which are performed there: let us draw
near to the Blessed Sacrament oftener, and with more
earnest preparation. As regards our neighbour, let us
exercise works of mercy, and give alms according to our
power. As regards ourselves, let us exercise a holy
self-denial, banishing idleness, self-indulgence and luxuriousness from our lives; let us observe the fasts and
days of abstinence appointed by the Church, not as a
matter of habit, but in the spirit of repentance. Let us
suffer patiently the difficulties of our position, whatever
they may be, the afflictions which God sends us, the trials
which others cause us, the sufferings of illness, and the
terrors of death. Let us mortify our senses, by self-
denials more proportioned to our sins, following therein
the motions of the Holy Spirit, and the counsels of a
wise teacher.

3. We must not delay to repent for four reasons.
The first, because time is short, and death is at hand.
*And now also the axe is laid at the root of the trees;
every tree, therefore, which bringeth not forth good
fruit, is hewn down, and cast into the fire.* A general
warning for entire nations, whom God rejects as He rejected the Jews; a special and daily warning for sinners,
whom God takes out of this world, and condemns to
eternal fire. The weakness and infirmities of old age
announce to some the approach to death; whilst health,
strength, and the vigour of manhood do not assure to
others a long life. Let us then make use of the short
time that remains, to bring forth good fruits and to do
good works.

The second reason for repenting without delay is, that, the sooner we begin it, the easier we shall find it; the joy of not having put it off to the last will encourage us, the habit of doing right will help us on, and the peace of a good conscience will satisfy us. Ah! Is not such a life a thousand times sweeter than one which is passed in sin, in remorse, and in continual fears? Why then delay to embrace it?

The third reason to hasten our repentance is, that the longer we put it off, the more difficult we shall find it. The longer we enjoy forbidden pleasures, the more do we thirst after them, and the more unquenchable is our desire for them: the more we yield to our passions, the weaker we become to resist them; the longer we put off our conversion, the longer do we desire to defer it. The habit of doing evil, and that of delaying to do right strengthen equally. Old age, which takes away our strength, does not take away our vices, nor change our hearts.

Lastly the fourth reason for not putting off our repentance is, that in deferring it, one runs a risk of never repenting at all. Ah! how many have deceived themselves thereby! That unfruitful tree has been cut down: that impenitent sinner is dead; and what is his lot? O useless regrets! O vain despair! Shall this fate be mine? Suffer it not, O my Saviour! From this day I will begin a new life. O Saintly forerunner of Jesus Christ, teacher and true pattern of repentance, may I have grace to follow thy teaching and example, and to be faithful to my resolutions. Amen.

THIRD POINT.

Feelings of S. John the Baptist with regard to Jesus.

These feelings regard the person, baptism, and the last judgement of Jesus Christ.

1. The person of Jesus Christ. *I indeed baptize you,* says S. John, *with water unto repentance: but He that cometh after me is mightier than I, whose shoes I am not*

worthy to bear: He shall baptize you with the Holy Ghost and with fire. By these words, S. John sets forth the divinity of Jesus Christ; for since the Holy Spirit is God, and Jesus imparts Him by His Baptism, He must needs be God Himself. He points out, moreover, His power; Jesus Christ, as the Ruler of nature, could change the laws of nature at His will, and work therein unheard of miracles; S. John was not to work any miracle, and if he had done any wonderful work, it would only have been by the power of Jesus Christ. In a word, S. John was only a man, and Jesus is God-Man. Jesus Christ is the Lord, the Christ, the Divine Saviour: and S. John, however holy he might be, was only the forerunner and servant; thus, after having acknowledged in Jesus a power infinitely superior to his own, he adds that he is not worthy to fall down at His feet, *to stoop down and unloose the latchet of His shoes.* Now, we, sinners, of what are we worthy? And yet, nevertheless, when He permits us to draw near to Him and His holy Altar, how do we present ourselves? With what inward feelings do we appear there? In what frame of mind do we keep ourselves in His presence?

2. What did S. John think of Jesus Christ, as regards His Baptism? *I indeed have baptized you with water,* he said to the Jews: but He that cometh after me, by the Baptism which He will establish as a messenger of God, will pour the Holy Spirit into the souls of those who shall believe in Him, and will purify them, as things are purified which are passed through the fire. The baptism of S. John was only a baptism of water, which betokened repentance, and urged men to it: but the baptism of Jesus Christ, under the outward sign of water, communicates the Holy Spirit, Who is a Divine fire, the Spirit of purity, Who, like a devouring fire, purifies the soul, and burns away all its defilements: the Spirit of love, which, like a beneficent fire, penetrates the heart with a gentle heat, warms it, softens it, and makes it glow with the purest flame: the Spirit of light, which, like a bright fire, enlightens our understanding, persuades, confirms, makes

us know and taste the Mystery of God, the designs of
His providence, instructs us in our duties, in the nothingness of things here below, the importance of our salvation, and the durability of eternal things. How privileged
are we to have received holy Baptism: how miserable
to have lost our innocence! How we should be to be
pitied, if Jesus had not prepared for us a second baptism,
the baptism of repentance, through which, by the virtue
of His Blood, our sins are washed away, and our losses
can be repaired! Let us then believe firmly in the remission of our sins; let us cultivate the needful dispositions, and continually seek after them, and preserve carefully the fruits which true repentance brings forth in us.

3. What were the feelings of S. John the Baptist, as
regards the last judgement of Jesus Christ? In making
known the Messiah, he set Him forth as the dispenser of
good and evil, the awarder of rewards and blessings, to
Whom God has given all power to judge all men. A judgement figured by the wheat which He will store up in His
granary, and the chaff which He will cast into eternal fire:
an effectual judgement, because Jesus Christ exercises it
as the Sovereign Ruler of the world. The earth and
its inhabitants belong to Him by right of creation and
by right of conquest: it is His granary where are found
gathered together, the good and the bad, these who receive the faith in a teachable spirit, and those who obstinately reject it. An equitable judgement, because to
every one will be rendered according to the state in
which they shall then be found, the chaff to be burnt,
the wheat to be preserved, the wicked to be punished,
the good to be rewarded; because it will be given according to the use which each one shall have made of the
time and of the advantages which have been given to him:
the wicked, having had it in their power to become
good, and the good, having had opportunities of becoming wicked; because it will be rendered in particular according to the proportion of the good and evil which
each shall have done, so that the guiltier a man is, so
much the greater will be the torments which he will

have to suffer, and the holier he is, so much greater will be the rewards bestowed upon him, the punishment of the one and the reward of the other being equally eternal. Lastly, the judgement will be effectual, inasmuch as no appeal can suspend it, no artifice can elude it, no present can bribe the Judge, no prayer can move Him to pity them, and no power can resist it. Alas! what resistance can straw make to the reaper? Let us await in peace this judgement, and prepare ourselves for it. Do not let us usurp the right of judgement by judging those whom we have no claim to judge. Let us comfort ourselves under the wrong judgements of men, because they will soon be rectified.

Prayer. Thy words, O august forerunner, and still more thine example, teach me to avoid the rigour of the judgement of Jesus Christ by the practice of repentance. May I have the strength and courage to bring forth the worthy fruits of repentance, that is to say, to live in a sincere love of God and my neighbour, in an extreme terror of sin, in an ardent thirst after righteousness, in a life of self-denial, humility, and earnestness, in the fulfilment of the duties of my station, that I may at length find myself at my death among the good wheat which the Lord will store up in His barns for all eternity. Amen.

Meditation XXIII.
JESUS BAPTISED BY S. JOHN BAPTIST.

Let us apply ourselves to draw out with the sacred text, all the circumstances of this event, 1. Jesus presents Himself to be baptized, 2. Jesus receives Baptism, 3. Jesus comes forth out of the waters of baptism. S. Matt. iii. 13-17. S. Mark i. 9-11. S. Luke iii. 21, 23. S. John i. 31-33.

FIRST POINT.

1. Consider the ardent desire which S. John had to see Jesus. He longed with a holy impatience for the moment of that glorious visit which had been promised

to him. He had in the womb of Elisabeth, felt the presence of Jesus, still hidden in that of Mary; but since they had been born, they had not seen each other, and S. John did not know the Lord under His human form. Nevertheless God, in sending him to baptize, had promised him, that in the course of his ministry he should see Him, and had taught him by what sign he was to recognize Him. "Go," He said to him, "establish a baptism of water, in order to bring My people to repentance; but know that this baptism is nothing in comparison with that of My Son. *He shall baptize you with the Holy Ghost, and with fire;* when He shall present Himself to you, in order that you may be able to distinguish Him from the rest, and to point Him out to your disciples, *Upon Whom thou shalt see the Spirit descending, and remaining on him, the same is He that baptizeth with the Holy Ghost.* Do not hesitate at that moment, but say to the Jews assembled around you, 'Behold the Son of God, behold Him Whose baptism confers the gift of the Holy Spirit.'" Thus instructed, the Sainted forerunner was looking forward to behold soon *the Desire of all nations* and of his own heart. This sweet hope kept alive his courage, and supported him in his labours. With what ardour did he desire this blessed day! Such is the longing which we ought to have for the blessed Sacrament of His Body and Blood and in order to fit ourselves for such a happiness, we ought to spare no pains, nothing ought to appear hard or wearisome to us.

2. What was the joy of S. John on beholding Jesus? His hope was neither deceived, nor delayed. *Then cometh Jesus from Galilee to Jordan unto John to be baptized of him.* S. John had no difficulty in distinguishing Jesus from the crowd. He recognized him by the sign which God had given him. What was then the bliss of the holy man, the sole witness of this wonder! With what attention, and reverence, and inward joy did he behold the sight with which Heaven favoured Him, did he contemplate this Incarnate Word, this divine

Messiah, Whose presence alone had made him leap in his mother's womb! What will be our happiness when we shall see Him in Heaven! Let us feed our hearts on so sweet a hope.

3. What was the surprise of S. John, when he saw Jesus approach to receive baptism from him! *Then cometh Jesus unto John to be baptized of him; but John forbade Him, saying, I have need to be baptized of Thee, and comest Thou to me? And Jesus answering said unto him, Suffer it to be so now; for thus it becometh us to fulfil all righteousness. Then he suffered Him.* Should not our astonishment be still greater, when we see Jesus draw nigh to be our spiritual food and nourishment? *Comest Thou to me, Lord?* we ought to say to Him. Let us draw back then with the feeling of our unworthiness, but let us also draw near with that of obedience; let us yield ourselves up to the exceeding greatness of His love, and since He commands us, let us receive Him, but let it be with the same self-abasement and humility with which S. John baptized Him.

SECOND POINT.

Jesus receives baptism.

And Jesus was baptized of John in Jordan. Wherefore did our Lord will to be baptized of S. John? We may consider three reasons for His doing so.

1. In order to do honour to the baptism of His forerunner, and to confirm his act. First of all, to honour it, as instituted by the command of God His Father. The written law came from God, and announced the law of grace. The baptism of John held a sort of middle place between the one law and the other, and announced the latter in a clearer and closer manner. Jesus, Who willed to submit to all the ordinances of the ancient law before substituting for it the new law, willed in the same way to receive the baptism of John before establishing His own

in order to fulfil all righteousness. He willed thus to accredit it as instituted for the sake of public utility, and to contribute by His example to the fervour and edification of the people, willing thereby also to accomplish *all righteousness*. It is thus that a thoughtful Christian gladly joins those religious associations, which have been instituted for the purpose of maintaining piety amongst the people, and thus preserving them in the spirit of their original intention.

2. Jesus willed to be baptized by S. John, in order to prepare and sanctify water to become the outward element employed in the divine Baptism, which He was about to leave us, by consecrating it and making it capable, through the contact with His Spotless Flesh, to purify our souls. Thus Jesus was occupied in all His actions, in furthering the glory of His Father and our salvation. How great should be our gratitude for all His benefits!

3. The design of Jesus Christ, in receiving the baptism of S. John, was to give us a striking lesson in this great example of humility with which He willed to conclude His life of privacy, and to begin His public life, and thus it is, He *fulfils all righteousness*. Jesus, in the midst of sinners, receives, like them, the baptism of repentance; and we, filled with pride, are ashamed to seek the remedy for our sins, when we have not been ashamed to commit them. Jesus, clothed with our infirmity, and laden with our sins, receives the baptism of repentance, in order that, in the Sacraments which He should institute, we might be clothed upon with Him, His righteousness, His strength, and His holiness.

THIRD POINT.

Jesus comes forth out of the waters of baptism.

What wonders take place at the moment, when Jesus comes up out of the water! He passes through the multitude, and goes to a distance in order to pray.

Then the Heavens were opened to His sight; the Holy Spirit descends upon Him in the shape of a dove; the Heavenly voice of the Father makes itself heard, and the Baptism of the new Covenant is distinctly marked by these wonders.

1. *Jesus,* having been baptized, prays. Prayer should precede, accompany, and follow all our religious acts. It is in prayer that God bestows His favours; but He never communicates them in greater abundance, than when prayer has been preceded by some great act of virtue.

2. Hardly had Jesus betaken Himself to prayer, than *the Heaven was opened.* Oh enrapturing sight! O worthy object of our desires! Alas! the Heavens have been closed for a long time. Thou alone, O Jesus, hast merited, that they should be opened. Behold Thine inheritance, behold the reward of Thy labours, behold the recompense which Thou dost destine for Thy faithful servants. Who could refuse to serve Thee at such a price?

3. *And the Holy Ghost descended in a bodily shape like a dove upon Him.* Jesus receives in a visible manner the Holy Spirit, as the Chief among men, in order to communicate Him to His members, and to sanctify them; as the teacher and ruler of men, to instruct and enlighten them. The dove is the symbol of gentleness, simplicity, purity, and tender longing; let us then ask the Holy Spirit for these virtues, of which He is the Author and the Giver.

4. *And a voice came from Heaven, which said, Thou art My Beloved Son; in Thee I am well-pleased.* This voice was the voice of the Heavenly Father, addressed to His only Son, the Object of His love. This voice is addressed to all the world, to all created beings, to all mankind, to all ages, to teach them, that no one is accepted of God, save His Son, and those who are in Him, and with Him.

5. The baptism of the New Testament was clearly pointed out by the baptism which Jesus received from

S. John. Then, for the first time, God shewed Himself in all His Majesty; and the Three Persons of the Holy Trinity made their presence felt, the Father by His Voice; the Son by His Humanity; and the Holy Spirit, by the dove. Jesus receiving, in the water, the baptism of John, set apart and sanctified water as the outward sign or form of Baptism. In His prayer, He has set us an example, and given us a form of prayer to make use of. By the Presence of the Three Persons of the Holy Trinity, He has shewn us what are the effects of it, since by Baptism the Heavens are opened, the Holy Spirit is given to us, we become the members, the brethren of Jesus Christ, the heirs and adopted children of His Father, that is to say, His well-beloved and cherished children.

Prayer. Blessed wilderness, which resounded to the voice of the Heavenly Father, and witnessed so many wonders, which took place at the baptism of Jesus! Why cannot I spend my life in thy retreats, to meditate there at leisure, far from the distractions and tumult of the world, on the goodness of my God, the glory of my adoption, and the greatness of my hopes! But at least, I may form for myself a solitude in the midst of my heart, where I may never lose sight of these great truths, and may seek to render myself acceptable to the Heavenly Father, Who can love me through and in Jesus alone. O Son of God! The only Object of the affections of Thy divine Father, how shalt Thou not be the sole Object of mine? Where can I find Thy equal in power, goodness, riches? Who should be worthier of my heart or more capable to render it happy? O most tender Saviour, unite Thyself to me; present me to Thy Father, that He may see Thee in me, and see me only in Thee, that by Thee I may be made worthy to be loved by Him, and to love Him eternally. Amen.

Meditation XXIV.

GENEALOGY OF JESUS CHRIST.

Genealogy of Jesus Christ on the side of the Virgin Mary.
S. Luke iii. 33-38.

It is easy to make the genealogy recorded by S. Luke agree with that of S. Matthew. Amongst several ways of doing so, we will take here the simplest and easiest. We can verify it, if we will give ourselves the trouble, by confronting the two genealogies with what we are about to say. S. Matthew, in bringing down the descent from Abraham to S. Joseph, the husband of Mary, speaks of the descent, properly so called, and by way of generation. *Abraham begat Isaac, and Isaac begat Jacob*, etc. But S. Luke, going back from Jesus up to God Himself, speaks of descent, either direct or indirect, and for that purpose makes use of an indefinite expression, saying, *which was*. *And Jesus Himself began to be about thirty years of age, being (as was supposed) the son of Joseph, which was the son of Heli, which was etc.* That S. Luke does not always speak of direct descent by way of generation, appears at once in the first and last which he mentions; for Jesus was only the reputed son of Joseph, since Joseph was the husband of the Virgin Mary, the mother of Jesus, and Adam was only son of God by creation. After this observation, we must remark, that in the genealogy of S. Luke, there are two instances mentioned of indirect lineages, in which sons-in-law are put in the place of sons. As the Jews did not allow the names of women to appear in their genealogies, when a race came to an end with a daughter, instead of mentioning her name in the descent, the name of the son-in-law was put in instead. The two sons in law whom S. Luke mentions are *Joseph*, son-in-law of *Heli*, and *Salathiel*, son-in-law of *Neri*. This single simple explanation suffices to raise every difficulty. Joseph, the son of Jacob, as S. Matthew calls him, was the son-in-law of Heli, as S. Luke calls him, and Salathiel, son of Jechonias, as S. Matthew calls him, was son-in-law of Neri, as S. Luke calls him. All the rest agrees perfectly. S. Mary was then a daughter of *Heli*, thus called by abbreviation for Eliakim, which is the same name in Hebrew, as Joachim. *Joseph*, son of *Jacob*, and *Mary*, daughter of *Heli*, had a common origin. Joseph, by *Abiud* the elder, and Mary, by *Resah* the younger. By this, both descended from the two branches which sprang from David, namely, from the royal branch, of which *Solomon* was the head, and from the other branch, of which *Nathan* was the head. By *Salathiel*, the father of *Zerubbabel* and son of *Jechonias*, Joseph and Mary descended from *Solomon*, the son and heir of David; and by the wife of *Salathiel*, the mother of *Zerubbabel* and daughter of *Neri*, whose son-in-law *Salathiel* was, Joseph and Mary descended from *Nathan*, another son of *David*, so that *Jesus*, Son of *Mary*, reunited in Himself all the blood of David. S. Matthew only traces the genealogy of Jesus up to Abraham; it was the promise of the Messiah, made to the Jews; but S. Luke traces this genealogy to *Adam*, which was the promise of the Messiah made to all mankind; and this will form the subject of our meditation: a meditation, in which we will consider Jesus Christ, as the Son of Adam, promised to the first man, and to his posterity; Jesus Christ, as resembling Adam, being subject to the sentence of death pronounced against the first man and his posterity: lastly, Jesus Christ, as a new Adam, repairer of the evils, which the first man had brought down upon himself, and his posterity.

FIRST POINT.

Jesus Christ, son of Adam, promised to the first man and his posterity.

1. A promise, made in a manner worthy of God; worthy of His goodness; it had been given from the

beginning of the world, that it might be the consolation of Adam and his descendants. It was a promise worthy of His wisdom: which was renewed to the chief of the ancestors of this Divine Messiah. Amongst the children of Adam and of Noah, *Abraham* was the first who was chosen, and made the father of the faithful; then *Isaac* and *Jacob, Judah,* and lastly, *David,* that there might be no misapprehension as to the person of the Messiah, nor the pre-eminence of His character. Lastly, it was a promise worthy of the greatness of God; it was announced and delayed for about five thousand years, in order to exercise the faith of men, in order to make them understand, that such a Messiah was a blessing which deserved to be long desired, and earnestly prayed for. Let us adore and thank God, the Ruler of time, and the Sovereign arbiter of destiny.

2. A promise, fulfilled with faithfulness. Jesus, the Son of Mary, re-unites in Himself alone all the blood of *David,* and this traces His descent up to *Adam* by the way which God had pointed out in the Holy Scriptures, and which none other but He could do. This genealogy of Jesus, inscribed in public documents, was acknowledged to be true by those who lived at the time and in those places; and the enemies of Jesus Christ, and persecutors of His disciples, have never dared to attack it as false, and it is for this reason that Jesus calls Himself so often *Son of Man,* which is the same thing as *Son of Adam.* In reality, this name bears its own proof with it. Son of Adam, means the son promised to Adam, and descended from Adam by a lineage marked out and foretold. Who other than God could have accomplished a promise of this nature? Let us acknowledge, and adore our divine Saviour, and give ourselves up entirely to His service.

3. A promise of Jesus Christ, unveiled to our eyes by a special blessing from God. Son of Adam, as well as all mankind, behold Thee now, O Saviour, on the earth. God had marked out in the decrees of His wisdom, through what generations, at what time, and in what

circumstances Thou shouldest come into the world. It matters little, what rank our family hold: but what we ought to thank God for is, that we have been born in the midst of Christianity, in membership with the Catholic Church, at a time when we see, not only the accomplishment of the prophecies respecting the Messiah, but also of the prophecies which He Himself spake concerning the establishment of the Church, her duration, her struggles and her victories: at a time, when we can enjoy all the fruits of the Messiah's merits, and of the gifts which He has given to men, and all the adorable benefits of His love. What happiness for us, if we know how to profit by them, but what misery, if we allow all this to become useless to us!

SECOND POINT.

Jesus Christ, as resembling Adam, being subject to the sentence of death, pronounced against the first man and his posterity.

A sentence which all who have preceded us have undergone, to which we ourselves must submit ere long, and which Jesus Christ Himself endured.

1. A sentence, which all who preceded us have undergone. What has, in truth, become of all those nations whose history we learn, all those men of whom we read here the names, and of all who lived at the same time with them? They have been. *Who were*, that is all we can say of them. What remains of their works, of their projects, their wars, their victories? All thereof has been, and is no more.

2. A sentence which all must submit to, who are, or shall be born, and which we ourselves must undergo ere long. All which comes to an end is of short duration. Adam and several others have lived 900 years: that is past. The time of the Messiah, expected during so many centuries, has at length arrived; it has already passed, nearly two thousand years ago. It is thus that the end of the world, and its whole duration will appear

only to be a moment. Do we after this strive for the things of this world, care about and occupy ourselves with them? Ah! Rather let us think of eternity, flee from sin, and prepare for death!

3. A sentence, which Jesus Christ suffered Himself. He willed thereby to satisfy the justice of God, which should make us understand, how great an evil sin is. He willed also thereby to sanctify our death, and to soften its bitterness: and also to encourage us, and teach us how to die well. Should death appear hard to us sinners, when Jesus, Who was Innocency itself, willed to submit to it?

THIRD POINT.

Jesus Christ, as a new Adam, repairer of the evils which the first man had brought down upon himself, and his posterity.

Jesus Christ repairs all these evils, in that He is 1. the Conqueror of death. 2. The author of a new generation. 3. The source of a new life.

1. The Conqueror of death. Jesus submitted to death, like all the descendants of Adam; but He submitted to it by overcoming it; as Son of man, He went down into the tomb, but, as Son of God, He rose from it again on the third day. It was not for Himself, that He conquered death; it was for us, and for all men, and for all who believe in Him and abide in His grace. It can never be said of Jesus Christ that *He was*, that *He has been*. He *is yesterday, to-day, and for ever*. It is the same with those who die in His faith and love. Let us then cling closely to Him Who dieth not, and through Whom alone we cannot die eternally.

2. Jesus is the Author of a new generation. Children of Adam, by generation, we are born in a state of wrath, in original sin, and are despoiled of the blessings which the goodness of the Creator had originally destined for us: but regenerate by Jesus Christ, and sanctified in the waters of Baptism, our condition becomes infinitely superior to what it would have been. Adopted in Jesus

Christ, we become children of God, and heirs, brethren, members of Christ, and co-heirs with Him. What happiness! Let us then forget what we are in Adam, in order to remember only what we are in Jesus Christ.

3. This divine Saviour repairs all our evils, in that He is the source of a new life, a life sanctified by His righteousness; supernatural, through His grace; divine, by the gift of His Spirit, and the heavenly Food of His Body and Blood; lastly, a life immortal in the bosom of our God through our participation in His merits.

Prayer. By what act of love, O Jesus! could I ever sufficiently shew my gratitude to Thee! It shall be by putting off the old man, with its vices and its corrupt inclinations, and clothing myself anew with the new man, that it is to say, with Thy truth, Thy righteousness, and Thy holiness. O my divine Saviour! Thou dost make Thyself like to us, to make us like to Thee. Thou didst take our human nature, in order to communicate to us Thy divine nature. Thou didst share our evils, that we might be made partakers of Thy holiness. I will then follow Thy commandments; I resolve to imitate Thine example, that I may attain to Thy glory. Amen.

Meditation XXV.

ON THE INCARNATION OF THE WORD.

The Apostle S. John begins his Gospel by teaching us, 1. what are the mysteries of the Word, considered with regard to Himself; 2. what are the mysteries of the Incarnate Word, considered with regard to mankind; 3. what is the foundation of our faith with regard to these mysteries; and, 4. what has been, and still is, the unbelief of men with regard to these same mysteries. S. John i. 1-18.

FIRST POINT.

Of the mysteries of the Word, considered with regard to Himself.

1. The Gospel of S. John sets forth to us the Word as God. And first of all, His eternity; *At the begin-*

ning was the Word. When the world was created, the Word was already. If He was already at the beginning, He has had no beginning, He is eternal. In the second place, His substance or His distinct Person: *And the Word was in God.* In God the Father, of Whom He was begotten, and brought forth by way of understanding or knowledge. God the Father, Who is the First Person in the Divine Nature, knows Himself and forms by His knowledge a perfect Image of His substance. It is then His Word, His Son, and a Person really distinct from Himself. It is the same with the Holy Spirit, of Whom the Gospel does not here speak, because its object in this place was only to make Jesus Christ known. The Father and the Son love each other with an infinite love; this love is the Holy Spirit, Who proceeds from the Father and the Son by way of inspiration, or love, and forms the Third Person of the adorable Trinity. Thirdly, His Divinity. *And the Word was God.* For there is nothing eternal and nothing in God, which is not God. The Father, the Word, and the Holy Spirit are three Persons, Who have only One and the same Nature, One and the same Divinity. If the nature of man is incomprehensible to man, how should not the nature of God be so also? Let us prostrate ourselves in reverence before this infinite and incomprehensible mystery: let us adore these Three Persons, Who are but One only God, and hope, that it may be granted to us as a reward to our faith, to have the bliss of beholding Them one day face to face.

2. S. John sets before us the Word in the creation of the world. *All things were made by Him; and without Him was not any thing made that was made.* Every thing was created and made by the Word. The Gospel does not thereby exclude the other Persons of the Holy Trinity, but only seeks to set forth more and more the Divinity of the Word. All which God works out of Himself, is equally the work of the Three Persons. When we consider the Might in a work of God, we are accustomed, according to the language of Holy Scripture,

to attribute it specially to the Father; when we consider the Wisdom, we attribute it to the Son; when we consider the Holiness, and Love, we attribute it to the Holy Spirit, but all Three Persons join equally therein. With what feelings towards God ought not the Creation of the world to inspire us! Feelings of admiration. What power, what magnificence, what grandeur! what a multiplicity of objects, what variety, what fruitfulness, what wisdom, order, proportion, solidity, duration, providence! Feelings of gratitude. God has made every thing. He has made me: it is from Him that I hold all the blessings which surround me. Feelings of submission and dependence. I do not belong to myself, but to Him Who has made me; I must not therefore employ myself, make any use of myself, but in accordance with His Holy Will. As regards other creatures, I must abstain from those which are forbidden me; I may make use of those which are permitted to me, with moderation, temperance, and sobriety. If some things are kept back from me, or cause me pain or grief, I must not murmur. Feelings of love. O senseless beings, who worship creatures without acknowledging their Author! O still more senseless, who, knowing the Creator, place their happiness in created things, fix their hearts upon them, place their affections in them! Do they persuade themselves, that the pleasure which is found in the love of creatures is not also to be found in the love of the Creator? Do they believe that the preference which they should give to the Creator over the creatures would remain unrecompensed, or that the unworthy preference which they give to the creatures over the Creator will remain unpunished?

3. S. John sets before us the Incarnate Word: *And the Word was made flesh, and dwelt among us.* The Word was made Man, like unto us. He took a body and a soul such as ours; so that Jesus Christ, this Man Who dwelt among men, and conversed with them, is the Second Person of the Holy Trinity, the Incarnate Word of God, the Son of God, God and Man both to-

gether, the Creator of the universe and Saviour of men. In Jesus Christ, one single Person, which is that of the Word, and two Natures, the divine and the human nature. Adorable and incomprehensible mystery, which is daily renewed in a measure upon our Altars, where Jesus Christ comes down, to dwell still amongst us, to dwell even in us and in our hearts! O Love of our God! By what love could we ever respond to it? What wondrous depths there are in the Christian religion! This is the summing up; Before time was, the Word was in God: at the beginning of time, the Word became Incarnate; at the end of time, the Incarnate Word, Jesus Christ, God and Man, will judge the world, and there will only remain eternity. Woe to him whom these truths disquiet or find insensible, instead of enrapturing him, and making him to glow with love!

SECOND POINT.

Of the mysteries of the Incarnate Word, considered with regard to mankind.

1. Mystery of life and of light. *In Him was life: and the life was the light of men. There was a man sent from God, whose name was John. The same came for a witness, to bear witness of the Light, that all men through him might believe. He was not that light, but was sent to bear witness of that Light. That was the true Light, which lighteth every man that cometh into the world.* In being born again by Baptism, we receive a new and inward life, by which we live to God, through the life of Jesus Christ, the life of continual love which the Holy Spirit sheds abroad in our hearts: we receive a new and inward life in which we live, by which we believe and hope, by the help of which we direct our steps, we distinguish objects, we see things such as they really are, the shortness of time and the importance of eternity, the beauty of virtue, and the enormity of sin, what pleases God, and what is displeas-

ing to Him. Our actions, thoughts, desires, and our most secret intentions, regulated by this light, form a pure and holy life, a life of light which seeks not darkness, which fears not the light of day. Jesus Christ is this essence of Light, this Sun of Righteousness, which enlightens us inwardly by His grace, and outwardly by His doctrine, His examples and His miracles. Is my life, alas! a life of light or a life of darkness? It is He moreover, Who is the Creator of the earthly light which meets our eyes: it is He, lastly, Who enlightens the understandings of all, in the natural as well as in the supernatural order of things. O Jesus, my Life, my Light! may I know Thee only, and live only by Thee!

2. The mystery of the Incarnate Word is for us a mystery of regeneration and of new birth. *But as many as receive Him, to them gave He power to become the sons of God, even to them that believe on His Name; which were born, not of blood, nor of the will of the flesh, nor of the will of man, but of God.* By the faith and Baptism of Jesus Christ, we are regenerated and made children of God, and inheritors of His Kingdom. Flesh and blood have no part in this regeneration, but only faith and the application of the merits of Jesus Christ. Have we the noble and elevated feelings, which such a glorious birth ought to inspire us with, or have we the low and earthly feelings of our original birth?

3. The Word, by His Incarnation, works in our behalf, a mystery of grace and truth. *And we beheld His glory, the glory as of the Only-Begotten of the Father, full of grace and truth. John bare witness of Him, and cried, saying, This is He of Whom I spake. He that cometh after me is preferred before me; for He was before me.* We are now too well taught, that it should come into our minds to compare Jesus Christ to S. John Baptist or to Moses. He came after them, but He is before them. He is come to exercise a ministry infinitely superior to theirs. All that we have of spiritual blessings, comes to us from the Incarnate Word, we

have received it of the fulness of Jesus Christ. From Him we have received grace, *grace for grace*, that is to say, grace, as grace, which is purely a free gift, which is in no way due to us, and which is differently distributed according to the will of God, and the designs of His Wisdom. Grace of the same nature as that of Jesus Christ, supernatural and divine; grace, nevertheless different from that of Jesus Christ, according to the difference which there is between a creature and the God-Man. In Him, grace of Natural Sonship, full grace, incommunicable grace; in us, grace of adoption, grace given by measure, grace which we have the power to reject when it is offered to us, and which we can lose through our own fault after having received it. It is from Jesus Christ alone that we have received the truth. The world is but a lie; philosophy is but vanity, the various sects which prevail are but error, the law of Moses only a figure; Jesus Christ alone has given us grace and truth. Truth in His mysteries, in His Sacraments, His doctrine, His promises. What there was of grace and truth before Him came equally from Him, and His future and anticipated merits. With what gratitude, respect, and love ought we not to follow this divine Head, and to unite ourselves to Him!

THIRD POINT.

Foundation of our faith with regard to these mysteries.

We only believe, in accepting these mysteries, that which has been seen and witnessed, 1. by Christ, Who has beheld the invisible mysteries of God; 2. by the apostles, who have seen the visible mysteries of Christ; 3. By Christians, who have seen the mysteries of the Church.

1. Jesus Christ has beheld the invisible mysteries of God. The mysteries of the faith are of two sorts, the one, spiritual, inward, invisible, such as these of which we have just spoken; the others, consisting in pal-

pable and visible facts. *No man hath seen God at any time:* saith S. John; *the Only-Begotten Son, which is in the bosom of the Father, He hath declared Him.* If we are asked, whence we know the invisible mysteries of God, our answer is an easy one, from Jesus Christ. And Who else could teach us such holy and deep mysteries? What mortal has ever seen God, and fathomed the depths of that Incomprehensible Being? We hold them then, these mysteries, from the Word of God Himself, from the only Son of God, Who has willed to reveal them to us.

2. The apostles have seen the visible mysteries of Jesus Christ. If we are asked from whom we hold the palpable and visible mysteries, we will reply, we hold them from those who have been eye-witnesses of them. Without speaking of Moses, whose whole law is a figure of Jesus Christ, without speaking of the prophets who announced Him, and of S. John Baptist, who pointed Him out, who set forth His divinity by declaring that He Who came after him was before him, and existed before him, we have for witnesses the apostles, disciples, the first Christians who *have beheld His glory, the glory as of the Only-Begotten of the Father, full of grace and truth;* His glory in His miracles, in His transfiguration, His resurrection, His ascension, and the visible pouring down of His Spirit: and these witnesses have sealed their testimony with their blood.

3. All Christians have seen, and we see ourselves the mysteries of the Church. Amongst the early Christians, some saw the miracles of the Apostles and their martyrdom. They saw the Church formed, and maintained according to the promises and predictions of Jesus Christ. Some saw the power of miracles granted to the early Church, and the apostolic spirit, and the spirit of martyrdom continued in her, and the Church increasing amidst heresies and persecutions. We ourselves see this Church, continuing on to our own times; we see idolatry destroyed, and the name of Christ adored throughout all the world; we see books which con-

tain the beginning, the progress and consummation of this great work, and the history of this prodigious change which has taken place in all parts of the world; the history of a hundred different nations, who have, at different periods, embraced Christianity, and every where we see the same spirit of holiness, and willingness to suffer for the faith. O holy city, how firm are thy foundations! How irreproachable and worthy of belief are Thy witnesses, O Lord! Let me in turn question the libertine! When an unbeliever, under the name of philosopher, seeks to assure me, that God, after having created mankind, after having endowed them with reason and intelligence, regards them no longer: that every thing ends with this present life; that there is no life but the present, and consequently no reward for virtue, no hell for vice, I ask him, Whence do you know this? Who told it you? You wish it to be so, I believe that; but still that is not a proof. By dint of wishing it, you have persuaded yourself that it is so. Well! but still this is no proof. What can you shew besides? Some metaphysical reasonings, in which you lose yourself. Ah! in mysteries so sublime, in an affair of this importance, and in order to destroy proofs of facts, something more is needed than human reasonings; ideas purely arbitrary cannot shake our religion: it is founded upon too firm a foundation.

FOURTH POINT.

The unbelief of men with regard to these mysteries.

This unbelief shewed itself at the time of the coming of Christ, before the coming of Christ, and shews itself only too plainly since His coming.

1. At the time of the coming of Jesus Christ. *And the light,* says S. John, *shined in darkness; and the darkness comprehended it not.* The light shines in the darkness, and disperses it; but wilful darkness, which is sin and the love of sin, have resisted the light. Men,

who loved their sins, would not receive life, holiness, Jesus Christ. *He was in the world, and the world was made by Him, and the world knew Him not.* This true Light appeared in the world, in order to lighten every one, and the world, which was His work, far from knowing Him, persecuted Him. *He came unto His own and His own received Him not.* Jesus Christ preached to the nation amongst whom He willed to be born; and His own nation, far from receiving Him, required His death. Ungrateful and perfidious men, is it then God Whom ye will reproach for your faithlessness? Is it the light which has failed you, or you who have failed to the light?

2. Before the coming of Jesus Christ, men were faithless to His light. The Incarnate Word has always been *the Light which lighteth every man that cometh into the world.* He has spoken by the voice of the patriarchs, who took care to instruct their children therein; but the greater number of these, rejecting their salutary instructions, after having been bad sons, became bad fathers who produced children still worse than themselves. He spoke by the inward voice of conscience, but men took pains to stifle the voice. God has spoken by the silent voice of nature and of the entire world; but by a deplorable reversal, the creature has been loved to adoration, and the Creator has been rejected and persecuted. He has spoken by the voice of example. For some time after the deluge, there were a few righteous persons spread over the earth; then a numerous nation was formed, professing to worship God and to wait for the Redeemer: her prophets, a thousand miracles wrought in her favour, her temple, the admiration of the universe, all this, instead of touching sinners, only served to kindle their jealous fury against this nation; and what was still more deplorable, more than once idolatry penetrated even into this privileged nation to persecute their prophets and their just men.

3. Since the coming of Jesus Christ, how many un-

believers remain still in darkness! The Apostles have been sent to all nations to carry thither the light, and what has been the cause that all nations have not been enlightened? The apostles were put to death, their disciples were persecuted, and it is only by a miracle of the Almighty that the light has been preserved. The successors of the Apostles find every where the same resistance, and the same dangers. There remain still heretics and schismatics who receive the name of Jesus Christ but who reject the teaching of His Church, as if Jesus Christ had not founded her to be the pillar and ground of the truth. They prefer the human opinions of some particular teachers to the unchangeable dogmas of faith which the Church has always held. Their own experience might disabuse them; but their darkness is so much the denser the more wilful it is. The unbelief of a nation may, little by little, be cleared away; but a nation, once plunged in schism or heresy, knows no return. Lastly, there remain still unbelievers and infidels. These latter, more guilty than the others, see nothing in the midst of light. They glorify themselves in their own darkness, they sink into it as deep as they can, and far from seeking light, they hate it, they flee from it, when sometimes in spite of themselves, it shines before their eyes. O inconceivable blindness!

Prayer. Alas! my Saviour! If my sins have not led me into a like abyss, I owe it to Thy mercy alone. Miserable sin, how I ought to fear thee, how I should fear the darkness which thou dost spread around thee. O Jesus! enlighten me, preserve me: may I direct my life according to the light of Thy Gospel; and in order to render myself worthy of those blessings, of which the law had only the shadow and the figure, grant that I may offer Thee a worship wholly spiritual and worthy of Thee, and grant that I may live only by Thee. Amen.

Meditation XXVI.

THE TEMPTATION OF OUR LORD.

In the temptation which Christ underwent, we see, 1. the manner in which we ought to prepare ourselves for temptations, 2. the manner in which we ought to fight against them, 3. the motives we have for overcoming them. S. Matt. iv. 1-11. S. Mark i. 12-13. S. Luke iv. 1-13.

FIRST POINT.

The manner in which we ought to prepare ourselves for temptations.

How ought we to prepare ourselves for temptations? The example of Christ teaches us.

1. By retirement from the world. *Then was Jesus led up of the Spirit into the wilderness to be tempted of the devil.* Jesus, after having received the Holy Spirit, always filled with His power, and guided by His inspiration, left the Jordan, and withdrew into the wilderness. Happy those, into whom the Holy Spirit has inspired the generous resolution to renounce the world entirely, and who, faithful to their vocation, close the entrance of their heart to all the false maxims of this world, and to all the vices which prevail in it. If we have not been called to this happiness, let us seek at least each year, to suspend our intercourse with the world for at least a retreat of some days, or to give ourselves a retreat of one day in a month. But an habitual and indispensable wilderness for us is, such a separation from the world, that we should live in it as it were only of necessity; that we should despise its pomps, keep aloof from its vanities, detest its maxims. It is, in the next place, that we should avoid all occasions which we know to be dangerous to ourselves, and finally, it is inward recollection, by which we should keep a continual guard over our senses, and watch over all the motives of our hearts. Do not let us hope to be able, without these precautions, to resist the temptations of the enemy. We shall fall blindly into all his snares, and even be

conquered, without being aware that we have been tempted. Alas! How often has not the Holy Spirit led us towards this wilderness, and by how many misfortunes has not our resistance been followed!

2. We must prepare ourselves for the battle of temptation, by the practices of the wilderness. *And when He had fasted forty days and forty nights, He was afterward an hungred.* The first practice of the wilderness, is fasting and self-denial. Our Lord fasted forty days and forty nights, without taking any food, by a miracle which had never been before worked, save in the person of Moses, the promulgator of the law, and in that of Elias, the chief of the prophets, a miracle which He had yet greater reason to work, Who came to fulfil the law and the prophets. It is in order to honour this fast of our Blessed Lord, that the Church celebrates the holy season of Lent. Besides the exact observances of the fasts and days of abstinence which are commanded, a Christian ought to avoid all luxury and self-indulgence in food, clothing, and sleep; he should keep under his body, and only feed it sparingly, treating it like a slave, who only gains strength, in order to rebel against us and ruin us, who, during this life, is always on an understanding with our enemies, and who will never be really subservient to our interests, until it has undergone a change in the bosom of the earth, and has been raised again. The second practice of the wilderness, is prayer and meditation. It is in these holy practices that our Lord passed forty days. But alas! we flee solitude and become wearied in it, because we do not love prayer. We have no courage to weaken our body by mortification, because we do not take pains to nourish our soul by prayer. The third practice of the wilderness, is the study of religion and of the Holy Scripture, according to our ability and condition, the study of the maxims of piety and the examples of holiness, which the saints have given us, and finally, the study of the duties of our station, which we must learn in order to fulfil them exactly, not allowing ourselves to study any thing,

but pious and instructive books, the study of which we can offer up to God.

3. The expectation of a struggle is a preparation to triumph over temptation. Our Lord entered into the wilderness, in order *to be tempted* there. We only come into the world in order to be tried by temptation, and to offer to God the trials of our faithfulness. We must then expect to be tried, 1. In all places, In the wilderness and in retired places, in God's House, and in the ministry, and still more violently on the mountain and in the great world. 2. At all times. If the devil, when he was overcome, left our Lord, it was but for a season, in order to return afterwards with greater fury. 3. Lastly, in all sorts of ways; by stratagem, by force, and the inward suggestions of this spirit of malice, and by the external influences of others, by ourselves, and the objects which surround us, by health and by sickness, by prosperity and adversity, by joy and by sadness, by presumption and by fear, by hatred and by love, by knowledge and by ignorance. How, oh my God, can we hope to withstand so many attacks, if Thou, taking upon Thyself our weakness, hadst not promised us, the succour of Thy strength? It is in this Divine succour, O Jesus, that we put our confidence; it is by this, that we will rekindle our courage.

SECOND POINT.

The manner in which we ought to fight against temptation.

There are temptations of the heart, the mind, and the senses; let us learn of Christ, how we ought to resist them.

1. There are temptations of the heart, which attack us by flattering our inclinations, and which lead us, by slight beginnings, to the greatest sins. Our Lord, at the end of forty days, having willed to experience hunger, the devil, in order to tempt Him, presents himself to Him under a human form: seeing Him exhausted, he pro-

poses to Him a speedy means of providing for His needs. You are suffering, he says to Him, and this arid desert can offer you nothing, but you know what God can do, and you know what you are. *If Thou be the Son of God, command that these stones be made bread.* It is thus that the devil, taking advantage of our situation, of our infirmities and our needs, examining our character, our inclinations, our governing passion, excites us to satisfy our own evil desires. He appears at first only to propose to us a necessary relief of our wants, an allowable indulgence, or a lawful pleasure; but how many have fallen, little by little, and by degrees into the most fearful crimes, from having listened to this first suggestion? The devil makes use of his knowledge and his intelligence to attack the Saviour, and the Saviour makes use of God's Word to defend Himself. *It is written,* Jesus answers him: *man shall not live by bread alone, but by every word that proceedeth out of the mouth of God,* that is to say, it is not so much the food which he takes which makes man live, as the will of God which he ought to follow. According to Christ's example, let us without disquieting ourselves, answer the tempter from the Scriptures, and with the words of salvation. Does he seek to lead us into sensual pleasures? Oh, crafty devil, is there no joy except in satisfying one's passions? is there no joy but in the tumult of the world? no contentment save in a luxurious and sensual life? Ah! in the word of God and in love and obedience to God's commandments, in victory over our passions, in the Holy Communion, there is far greater happiness to be found than in all the most flattering visions which thou dost suggest to me.

2. There are temptations of the mind which attack us by flattering our pride, and which lead us into error and presumption. The devil, disconcerted by the wise answer which Jesus had just made to him, could not conceal himself any longer. Throwing aside his borrowed character, and using the power which God had granted him, he takes possession of Jesus by an unheard-

of outrage, and bears Him through the air *to the holy city, and setteth Him on a pinnacle of the temple*. Jesus had answered him by the Scriptures; this father of lies dares to employ this word of truth and holiness, in order to teach error and persuade to sin. *If thou be the Son of God*, he said to Jesus Christ, *cast thyself down; for it is written, He shall give His angels charge concerning thee, and in their hands they shall bear thee up, lest at any time thou dash thy foot against a stone*. The devil can bring us to the edge of the precipice; but he cannot throw us down it. He can suggest to us extraordinary ways which flatter our pride, particular courses which make us remarkable; woe to us, if we forsake the common roads of humility, and of the obedience which is due to our superiors and to the authority of the Church! In them alone is our safety, and it is there God has pledged Himself to keep us from error; beyond them, there is nought but a precipice. Our Lord, without waiting to point out that the malicious spirit had misquoted the passage of Holy Scripture, and omitted the words at the end, *in all thy ways*, answered him by this well-known passage, taken also from Holy Writ: *Thou shalt not tempt the Lord thy God*. Let us leave to those who are learned in the study of the Scriptures, the care of proving the abuse which the evil one and heretics make of the texts of Scripture and of the writings of the Fathers: let us content ourselves by opposing to seductive arguments the simplest and most ordinary truths of the goodness of God, and of His equity towards men. Let us keep ourselves within the bounds of humility, which faith and our station in life require of us; let us not tempt God by seeking to dive into mysteries, and to enter upon questions which are above our comprehension, still less let us seek to gain credit by despising or condemning those who have authority in the Church.

3. There are temptations of the senses which attack us, by flattering us with the highest hopes; and which lead us to the basest and most shameful actions. *Again*,

the devil taketh Him up into an exceeding high mountain, and sheweth Him all the kingdoms of the world, and the glory of them, and saith unto Him, All these things will I give Thee, if Thou wilt fall down and worship me. The devil, rendered more furious by the resistance of Him whom he was attacking, carries Him up to a high mountain. There, in a moment, he sets before His eyes a dazzling image of all the kingdoms of the world, and makes Him see the greatness, glory, and magnificence of them. All this belongs to me, he adds; it belongs to me to dispose of them, and I will give them up to you, if you will worship me. What horrible blasphemy! what imposture! what perfidy! what a proposal! It is thus, by vain phantoms, by delusive hopes, and deceptive illusions, that the devil moves our imagination and disturbs all our senses. What promises does he not then make us! Riches, power, authority, pleasures, perfect happiness, all our desires shall be satisfied, if we will once give ourselves up to him, if we will shake off the yoke of God! Ah! if we are miserable enough to believe him, how soon we discover how heavy his yoke is, how shameful it is, and how trifling are his promises! He sees us, with contempt, cringing at his feet, dishonouring ourselves by numberless acts of baseness, and groaning under the weight of the chains with which he loads us; his perfidy triumphs then over our credulity, his pride rejoices in our humiliation, and his hatred feeds itself on our unhappiness. Our Lord answers him first by one word of indignation. *Get thee hence, Satan.* It is thus that violent temptations should be forcibly repulsed if we do not wish to let ourselves be dazzled by their attractions. Our Lord added; *It is written, Thou shalt worship the Lord thy God, and Him only shalt thou serve;* words truly worthy to be graven on our hearts in ineffaceable characters: it is in the service and love of God that greatness, glory, and perfect happiness are to be found. Let us examine ourselves then, whether it is God alone, Whom we worship and serve: let us know that to serve the world and our passions, to desire only the possessions, riches, greatness, and pleasures of the world, is to worship the devil at the expense of the worship and love which we owe to God alone.

THIRD POINT.

The motives which we have for overcoming temptations.

These motives may be considered either with regard to Jesus Christ, to the temptation itself, the tempter, or our own interests therein.

1. Motives for overcoming temptation, considered with regard to Jesus Christ. His example should console us in our temptations. Do not let us believe that all is lost because we are tempted, and because our temptations are severe, frequent, or connected with repugnant objects, since our Lord has willed, for our consolation, to suffer the like temptations. Nothing but our own consent, freely given to temptation, can make us guilty. The strength of Christ ought to be our support. He is our Head; He has overcome, that He might obtain for us the power to overcome; shall we be cowardly enough not to conquer with Him? Shall we offer Him this affront, shall we deprive Him of this glory?

2. Motives for overcoming temptation, considered as regards the temptation itself. It is not insurmountable. God does not allow us to be tempted above our strength. Let us then make use of the strength which grace gives us, and ask for that which we need. Temptation also is not lasting. If we resist the devil, he wearies at length, and withdraws; he is even afraid of us, and leaves us at least an interval and time to breathe. *And when the devil had ended all the temptation, he departed from Him for a season.* Lastly, temptation does not last for ever; it ends with life; perhaps we are near the close of our life; let this reanimate us. Yet but a while, and behold, we are conquerors for ever.

3. Motives for overcoming temptation, considered as

regards the tempter. The devil is a deceiver, who seeks only to throw dust in our eyes: hardly have we fallen into the snare which he sets for us, than we perceive that we have been his dupes; he will insult us by disclaiming us, and, had we but resisted, we might have treated him with scorn and contempt. The tempter is our enemy, he only seeks to ruin us; whether we are happy or unhappy on earth, disquiets him not; but that we should not possess the heaven which he has lost, but that we should be partakers of his revolt, and companions in his punishment, this is the only aim which he proposes to himself. Lastly, he is the enemy of God; shall we range ourselves under his banner, to fight against our Creator, and our Saviour?

4. Motives for overcoming temptation, considered as regards our own interests. 1. Motives as regards our spiritual advancement. Temptation, resisted with perseverance, purifies and adds to our virtue, by making us bring forth many and fervent acts of piety. It teaches us our own corruption, and makes us grow in humility; it joins us more closely to God, and obtains for us greater graces. 2. Motives as regards our present happiness. When our Lord had resisted all the temptations, *then the devil leaveth Him, and behold, angels came and ministered unto Him,* that is to say, they provided Him with food. There is no food so delicious as the consolation which is felt by a soul, which has fully resisted temptation. With what confidence does it not then approach to the food of angels, to the Holy Eucharist! What strength, what sweetness does it not find there! Could it desire, having drawn near to it, any of the false happiness which temptation offers to it? 3. Motives as regards our eternal lot, which depends upon the manner in which we shall have resisted temptation. To reign with Christ and the angels in Heaven, or to burn in hell with the devils; the one will be the punishment of our cowardice, or the other the reward of our victory.

Prayer. Grant, O Lord, that I may avoid the one

and gain the other, or rather be Thou Thyself, O Jesus, my strength in temptation. May humility keep me in fear and in a prudent circumspection! May Thy grace keep me in Thy ways, and by making me triumph over my visible and invisible enemies, conduct me to the aim to which I aspire, namely the Temple of Thy glory. Amen.

Meditation XXVII.

PREACHING OF JESUS CHRIST IN GALILEE.

1. The place where Jesus Christ began to preach, 2. The manner in which He preached, 3. The first successes of His preaching. S. Matt. iv. 12. S. Mark i. 14. S. Luke iv. 14-15.

FIRST POINT.

Of the place where Jesus Christ began to preach.

1. It was neither at Jerusalem, nor even in Judæa. *Now when Jesus had heard that John was cast into prison, He departed into Galilee.* Jesus, under the Divine guidance, deferred to a less disturbed season His first appearance in Judæa, in order to render His labours more profitable. The persecution excited at Jerusalem against S. John Baptist, and the recent stir which had taken place there on his account, determined the Saviour to return to Galilee. He willed thereby to teach ministers of the Gospel not to aggravate persecution by their presence, but rather to carry further the words of salvation, which they are commissioned to publish. The evangelists do not tell us, in what this persecution which was raised against S. John consisted; they only say that S. John was cast into prison, delivered up doubtless to the high priests by the Scribes and Pharisees, who, wearied with hearing him so freely and so often preach against public disorders, and specially against the scandals of which they themselves were

guilty, summoned him before the council of the high priest, where he had the glory of enduring the greatest outrages for his Master's sake. It appears that these affronts and punishments, which were intended to discourage this saintly forerunner by the fear of still greater severity, were to him, as they are to all the true ministers of Christ, only the food of the fire of Divine love, which consumed him. Convinced that it was necessary to obey God, notwithstanding the opposition of men, he did not relinquish his ministry when it abated: he only left the wilderness of Judæa, crossed to Jordan, and went to expose himself to new dangers by preaching repentance, and announcing the coming of the Messiah to the Jews settled on the other side of the stream. He chose a place suitable for his baptism, which was the territory called Bethany, in the Greek *Bethabara*, that is to say, the passage: a very different place from the village of the same name, much further from Jerusalem. His zeal had the greatest success, and gained for him in the time to come the esteem of those who had previously plotted his death.

2. It was to Galilee that Christ withdrew Himself, in order to give there His first teachings, to shew forth His example, and to lavish His miracles. This portion of the Holy Land became afterwards His usual place of residence, and, as it were, the centre of His mission. Unfortunate Jerusalem! ill-fated Judæa! which by persecuting the forerunner, dost lose the presence of thy Saviour! Happy Galilee! if thou didst but know how to profit by thy blessings! It is thus that the unbelief of some turns to the advantage of others. Unhappy that I am, how might I not have advanced in the ways of perfection, if I had been faithful to all the graces which I have received! Shall I always continue to let others benefit by the blessings which have been offered to me?

3. It was *in the power of the Spirit* that Jesus *returned into Galilee*. The Holy Spirit, Who is the Spirit of Jesus, had led Him into the wilderness to be

tempted there, and He now leads Him into Galilee, there to begin His preaching. It belongs to the Holy Spirit to appoint the times and places for us, to teach us when we should flee from persecution or meet it, hide ourselves in the wilderness, or appear in public, speak or hold our tongues. What great things we should do for the glory of God, for our own salvation, or that of our neighbour, if we were but resolute in forming no plans for ourselves, except by the inward call of the Holy Spirit, and in obedience to those set over us! But what almost always influences us, is either our own self-love, or the love of repose, pleasure, vanity, ambition, or self-interest. What a loss to ourselves and to others, for which we shall have to answer to God!

SECOND POINT.

Of the manner in which Jesus Christ preached.

Jesus Christ, returning to Galilee, does not at first confine Himself to any one place. Alone, after the manner of the prophets, and having as yet no disciples, He went over the villages and towns, *teaching in their synagogues, and preaching the Gospel of the kingdom.* The scribes and doctors of the law were wont to instruct the people in the synagogues; and to these assemblies did He repair, in all the places through which He passed, and every where and at all times He taught *in the power of the* Holy *Spirit*, that is to say, that He preached with simplicity, Himself giving an example, and working miracles.

1. With simplicity: without adorning His discourses with the flowers of a worldly rhetoric. He spoke the language of the Holy Spirit, a language which is so much the more powerful, as it is the simplest, which He joined to a touching simplicity, adorned with much nobleness and grandeur. The books of devotion, which bear such a character, ought to commend themselves to us in preference to others, and we should choose such for our own use.

2. *Himself giving an example.* Jesus Christ taught *in the power of* the Spirit, that is, He preached by example, setting forth in Himself the union of all those virtues, which the Holy Spirit, inspires into the heart, and of which He recommended the practice to others, giving no room for any suspicion that He was animated by any other motive, than that of zeal for the glory of God and for the salvation of souls. Is it thus that we instruct, reprove, or correct?

3. *By working miracles.* Jesus Christ taught *in the power of the Spirit*, that is to say, by the power of miracles. He confirmed the truth of His word by the works of the power of the Holy Spirit, by a countless number of miracles, and miraculous cures. Although no special miracle is specified here, the passages which follow will prove to us that a great number took place, specially in Capernaum and its neighbourhood. O Jesus! Divine Zealot of souls, speak to my heart *in the power of the Spirit,* work the miracle of my conversion, and engrave on it the truths which Thou didst teach.

THIRD POINT.

Of the first successes of the preaching of Christ.

'And His fame went throughout all the regions round about. And He taught in their synagogues, being glorified of all.

1. *Praise, well merited by Jesus Christ.* It is not wonderful that the reputation of a Man so simple and yet so majestic in His language, so grave and so affecting in His discourses, so noble in His sentiments, so august in His person, so mighty in His works, should spread so rapidly in the surrounding neighbourhood of all the places which He honoured with His Presence. Let us join ourselves to this multitude, in order to render praise to our Saviour, that He willed thus to begin the work of salvation. Let us inspire others with the same feelings, and seek with all our power to extend more and more the glory of His Holy Name.

2. *Praise, referred by Jesus Christ to His Father.* All praise, which, by reason of its object, cannot be referred to God by him who gives it, is false, frivolous, and even sinful: all praise, which is not referred to God by him who receives it, is poisonous to him, is an usurpation of God's glory, and generally, one of the greatest obstacles to conversion, or to spiritual advancement. Let us examine ourselves as to the praise which we give, and which we receive.

3. *Praise, reproved by Jesus Christ, when it remains barren, and is followed by no fruit.* We praise a book of devotion, which we read, or a Christian preacher, whom we listen to: but if we do not profit by them, if we do not become better, our praise turns into a witness against ourselves. Do not let us content ourselves with empty praise, but let us act.

Prayer. O Jesus! Praise is a dangerous temptation. How shall we resist it without Thy succour? Give me then, Thyself, a humble soul, a modest spirit, but as we need to be entirely dead not to be sensible of the odour of the incense which is burnt around us, make me die to myself by a complete and perfect detachment, by the most humiliating trials, that I may be able to resist the attraction of flattery, and the delusions of self-love. Amen.

Meditation XXVIII.

JESUS IS PRESENT IN THE SYNAGOGUE OF THE NAZARENES.

He commands their admiration, confounds their injustice, and escapes from their fury. S. Luke iv. 16-30.

FIRST POINT.

Jesus commands the admiration of the Nazarenes.

1. *By the greatness of His reputation.* The mighty wonders which He had wrought, since His Baptism,

throughout Galilee, and in particular, at Capernaum, were known at Nazareth. S. Joseph was dead: and it appears as if, when Jesus went into Judæa to be baptised there, that the holy Virgin left her abode at Nazareth to establish herself elsewhere, perhaps at Cana, a city of Galilee. However that may be, Jesus did not forget in the course of His mission, His own country. *He came to Nazareth, where He had been brought up: and as His custom was, He went into the synagogue on the sabbath day.* All the people were charmed doubtless to see Jesus in their assembly, and they doubted not that they were about to have the pleasure of hearing this Man speak, of whom already so many wonders had been related. Is it with a like eagerness and the same hope that we resort to all places where Jesus Christ is to be found, and specially to these assemblies of Christians where devotion is sustained and nourished by good example, and where prayer is more efficacious by the agreement and union of those who pray?

2. Jesus Christ commands the admiration of the Nazarenes by the attractions of His Person, and the gravity of His discourses. When the time for giving instruction was come, He went to present Himself to the chief of the assembly, in order to expound, according to custom, some passage of the Scriptures: *He stood up for to read, and there was delivered unto Him the book of the prophet Esaias. And when He had opened the book, He found the place where it was written, The Spirit of the Lord is upon Me, because He hath anointed Me to preach the Gospel to the poor; He hath sent Me to heal the brokenhearted, to preach deliverance to the captives, and recovery of sight to the blind, to set at liberty them that are bruised, to preach the acceptable year of the Lord. And He closed the book, and He gave it again to the minister,* or chief of the assembly, *and sat down. And the eyes of all them that were in the synagogue were fastened on Him.* Never had the curiosity of this audience been so keenly

excited. A young prophet in the flower of His age, with the air of nobility, of gentleness, and modesty which shone through His whole Person, could not fail to enrapture all hearts. The voice so full of charms, the majestic authority and the expression of humility with which He had just read the divine oracles, made them desire with eagerness that He should explain the passage to them. Ah, if we knew how to fix all our looks upon Jesus, without letting them turn away to a thousand frivolous objects which distract us, His voice would make itself heard in our heart, and what sweetness, what delights, what knowledge would It not bring therewith It!

3. Jesus draws down upon Him the admiration of the Nazarenes by His explanation of the Scriptures. He began by saying to them, *This day is the Scripture fulfilled in your ears.* This Divine Teacher, in order to explain His text, needed only to lead the Nazarenes to compare the words of Isaiah which they had just heard read, with that which they had already heard published of Him. The resemblance was palpable, and the accomplishment of the prophecy evident and manifest. The Holy Spirit had descended in a visible form upon Jesus, and from that time Jesus had accomplished all which the prophet had foretold. It was not easy to oppose so convincing a proof: the Nazarenes felt it, *and all bare Him witness* that what they had heard of Him was exactly what they had just read in the prophet; and this is the testimony which every reasonable mind would render, who should compare in good faith the Evangelists with the prophets. Unbelievers affect often to oppose to the proofs of Christianity, the proof, which they allow to false religions, but here all parallel ceases. Christianity alone is marked by the seal of prophecy, a divine seal which no force can wrest from it, and no cunning can imitate. Would that I could, O my Saviour! make amends to Thee by the readiness of my faith, and the sincerity of my witness, for so many unbelieving discourses, and impious libels!

The Nazarenes could not refuse their admiration to Jesus. All *wondered at the gracious words which proceeded out of His mouth.* But ought they to have been content with that? Did they not owe the deepest respect, the sincerest attachment, the tenderest and most self-denying love, to the character of holiness, of power and goodness which the prophet had drawn of Him, and which He fulfilled so well. Thou art, O my Saviour, Holiness itself! Thou hast received the fulness of the Holy Spirit, and the unction of Divinity, and Thou dost come amongst us, who are poor, miserable, and unworthy of Thee, and Thou dost come only to heal our evils, and fill us with Thy good, to announce to us the mercies of God, and to prepare us for the day of His justice! O charitable Physician, mighty Redeemer, just Rewarder, is it enough to admire Thee, can I thank Thee and love Thee enough? Finish Thy work in me, O my God! instruct me, comfort me, deliver me, enlighten me, heal me, sanctify me.

SECOND POINT.

Jesus confounds the injustice of the Nazarenes.

1. He confounds their contempt by His silence, 2. their murmurs by the Scriptures, 3. their anger by His patience.

1. Their contempt, by His silence. The beauty of the discourses of Jesus Christ, the solidity of His instructions, the noise of the wonderful events related of Him, did not protect Him from an unhappy prejudice. Contempt succeeded in a few moments to the raptures with which the Nazarenes appeared to have been penetrated. The Saviour had not left off speaking, before they said one to the other, *Is not this Joseph's son?* O fools that ye are! What matters it whose Son He is, and how lowly His birth may be, if His works are so great? Rather, on the contrary, His birth, according to you, being lowly, should make what you see in Him appear supernatural and divine. How can you pass thus rapidly

R

from a just admiration to the most unjust contempt? Do you believe in His works, notwithstanding the apparent obscurity of His birth? Soon you will know that He, Whom you believe to be the son of Joseph, is the Son of the Most High, and has no other Father than God Himself. But no, a capricious reasoning, a false ridicule obscures for the unbeliever the splendour of the brightest light: every thing serves to confirm men in their unbelief, whom pride and passion have fore-determined to disbelieve. Thus, in all times, the humility of Jesus Christ has been a stumbling block to proud and frivolous minds, whilst the greatness of His works, and the manifestation of His glory have not been able to overcome their unjust prejudices. In our days still, and in the midst of Christianity, we have heard Him called the carpenter's son, in a blasphemy, over which we cannot sufficiently mourn, and for which we should seek to make amends by our deepest homages.

2. Jesus confounds their murmurs by the Scriptures. If this divine Saviour answered nothing to the contempt which these Nazarenes testified by their words, He let it be seen that He was more than the son of Joseph, by answering to the unuttered murmurs to which they did not give vent. Jesus penetrated their thoughts; He forestalled their words, by saying to them, *Ye will surely say unto Me this proverb, Physician, heal thyself:* and you will say to Me, *Whatsoever we have heard done in Capernaum, do also here in Thy country.* Such were in reality the thoughts which the Nazarenes were turning over in their minds. Blind that ye are! If you believe the miracles done at Capernaum, do you need other miracles? And if you do not believe them on the authority of so many irreproachable witnesses who have seen them, do you deserve that Jesus should work any miracles before you? In vain, do the unbelievers of our time hold the same language as the Nazarenes. Miracles are not to be obtained with an insulting air, and in a spirit of unbelief. Jesus opposed to the proverb of the Nazarenes a sentence, the truth of which is

proved at all times. He added then, *Verily, I say unto you, No prophet is accepted in his own country,* which He proved by two examples drawn from the Old Testament. *But I tell you of a truth, many widows were in Israel in the days of Elias, when the heaven was shut up three years and six months, and great famine was throughout all the land; but unto none of them was Elias sent, save unto Sarepta, a city of Sidon, unto a woman that was a widow. And many lepers were in Israel in the time of Eliseus the prophet; and none of them was cleansed, saving Naaman the Syrian.* The Nazarenes laid much stress upon its being His native country; they thought that in its favour, and to do it honour, Jesus ought to employ all His gifts and all His powers; but Jesus pointed out to them that God judged far otherwise; that these gifts were not dispensed according to the will of flesh and blood, that He sees the heart, and upon this knowledge refuses to the one the benefits He grants to the other; and that lastly, they were not to be surprised, that, as they saw in Him only the son of Joseph, while the people of Capernaum looked upon Him as one sent from God, He should do more for them than for the Nazarenes. He taught them that the country of a prophet is generally the place, where men were least disposed to profit by His instructions, and to deserve the succour of miracles, and that they were themselves a present witness of this. Let us then love our country by sanctifying ourselves therein, by striving to edify and to minister to it; let us love those who govern it, and never take part in plots formed against them, nor in any ill-feeling towards them.

3. Jesus confounds the anger of the Nazarenes by His patience. His discourse, full of power and of a holy freedom, and the knowledge which He shewed therein of the secrets of all hearts, shewed in Him doubtless the Messiah, as much as the miracles which they asked of Him could have done; but this simple and convincing reasoning was very far removed from the spirit of the synagogue; they were scandalised at the claim which a

man, whom they believed to be the son of an ordinary labourer, laid to the title of Messiah : they were offended to see themselves represented as unworthy of the blessings and miracles of Jesus Christ: especially the two examples which Jesus had quoted from the Holy Scripture appeared to them odious, and outrageous comparisons. *And all they in the synagogue, when they heard these things, were filled with wrath, and rose up, and thrust Him out of the city, and led Him unto the brow of the hill whereon their city was built.* The justice of a reproach is often most shewn by the manner in which it is received. The way in which the Nazarenes received the discourse of Jesus Christ only proved still more, and fully justified all which He had spoken to them of the evil dispositions of their hearts. These miserable men, blinded by their resentment, being unwilling either to know themselves, or be known of others, gave themselves up to their pride and their jealousy. Far from looking into their own hearts, and acknowledging themselves unworthy of God's blessings: far from admiring in Jesus the divine gift of searching hearts, and His wisdom and zeal; far from gathering up the precious truths which fell from His lips, they were indignant, and allowed themselves to be angry with the divine Physician, Who sought to heal them. Jesus opposes nought to the transports of their rage, save an invincible patience. He permits Himself to be led, driven forth, conducted, whithersoever they would, without the least resistance. They ask of Him miracles; behold a miracle of gentleness and patience; and if they do not yield themselves up to it, they will soon behold another, which they cannot avoid acknowledging. Happy if they do but know how to profit by it.

THIRD POINT.

Jesus escapes from their fury.

An extreme fury, an useless fury, a fury punished with rigour.

1. An extreme fury, which went the length of wishing to put to death by their own hands Him Who had been the object of their admiration. *They led Him unto the brow of the hill whereon their city was built, that they might cast Him down headlong,* and crush Him in His fall. What had He then done to deserve death? What is His crime? Of what is He accused? What! without any pretext, without observing any law, or any order of procedure, without any appeal to justice, they proceed thus to a tumult, and the Innocent is led forth to punishment! It is only against Thee O Jesus, and against Thy servants, that fury is so blind and precipitate; it is for the consolation of Thy disciples, that Thou hast willed to experience it Thyself.

2. An useless fury. *But He, passing through the midst of them went His way.* These madmen could not even intimidate Him whom they sought to kill. He passed through the midst of them, without their being able to stop Him. Whether He made Himself invisible to their eyes, or whether He made them motionless, and took from them all power to injure Him, whether His power acted upon their souls, and upon the passion with which they were possessed, He only leaves them the shame of having taken useless steps to bring about His death. Thus has it happened that martyrs also have escaped miraculously from the fury of tyrants; but when they have fallen victims to it, their victorious soul passed from their hands, to speed its flight to Heaven, where, thenceforth safe from all danger, it enjoys with Jesus Christ a happy immortality. Jesus Christ will always have disciples filled with His Spirit, incapable of fear, and zealous of the glory of matyrdom.

3. Fury rigorously punished. The least trouble which the failure of their attempt caused them was the confusion of discovering that they had merited from so great a prophet, their fellow-citizen, no other miracle than that which He had been obliged to work, in order to deliver himself from their bloody and parricidal hands. Another punishment infinitely greater was the loss to

their country which was caused by the withdrawal of Jesus from it; but the greatest punishment was the hardening of their hearts, which made them at last insensible to everything.

Prayer. Have I not also fallen, O Lord, into a like hardness of heart? My sins have but too much deserved it, and my insensibility to all which ought to touch me, gives me but too much ground to fear lest it be so. Nevertheless, O God, even the fear I feel makes me hope, that Thy mercies towards my soul have not yet come to an end. Do not Thou forsake me, O Jesus! If this fatal hardness has begun to find a place in my heart, do not suffer it to finish its work; disperse it and put it far from me, soften my heart, and make it alive to Thy goodness, and obedient to Thy teaching. Amen.

Meditation XXIX.

JESUS COMES FROM NAZARETH TO CAPERNAUM, WHICH HE MAKES THE CENTRE OF HIS MISSIONS.

Remark here with the sacred text, 1. the abode of Jesus at Capernaum, 2. the prophecy which announced His abode at Capernaum, 3. His preaching at Capernaum, and the surrounding villages. S. Matt. iv. 13-17. S. Mark i. 15.

FIRST POINT.

Of the abode of Jesus at Capernaum.

And leaving Nazareth, He came and dwelt in Capernaum, which is upon the sea coast, in the borders of Zebulon and Nephthalim. Here is again a substitution, and a transfer of God's favour. There is nothing more frequent in Scripture, and more terrible in the order of salvation, than this punishment of God, where we see some substituted for others, and the graces intended for the former passed on the latter, through the prevarication and unfaithfulness of those to whom they were first given. The Gospel furnishes us examples thereof, of four kinds.

1. From province to province. We have already seen our Lord leave Judæa, pass into Galilee, to begin there His divine ministry, and to carry thither the light of the Gospel, on account of the persecution which was raised against S. John Baptist. Woe to those who are in authority, if, by their connivance, their example or their violence, they contribute to the decay of faith, and to the corruption of morals.

2. From city to city. We see here Capernaum substituted for Nazareth, and we know by what excesses this latter city brought down upon it this severe punishment. Let us love in God, the city or the place, where we make our abode; let us pray for all those who dwell there with us; and let us contribute, according to our position and our power, to the preservation of faith, and the maintenance of good morals, piety, and wholesome doctrine there.

3. From one person to another. We shall soon see the apostleship of the traitor Judas pass into the hands of S. Matthias. How this example should make us tremble! How many others are there, which we do not know! We should be dismayed, if we could see the multitude of graces which we have lost through our own fault, and which have been given to others, who have profited by them. Yea, that tender devotion, that deep recollectedness, that love of prayer and of mortification, which I admire in such an one or in such another, were, it may be, graces which were destined for me. I do not murmur that they should enjoy them, for I have deserved indeed to be deprived of them; but, O Lord, the treasure of Thy mercy is infinite; take not away from me what yet remains. I will strive to use it so faithfully, that I may gain from Thee the restoration of those graces which my unfaithfulness has caused Thee to deprive me of.

4. From nation to nation. Nothing is more mani-

fest than the rejection of the Jews, and the calling of the Gentiles who have been substituted in their stead. Let us then serve the Lord with fear; let us fear the severity of His judgments; let us pray Him not to punish us in His anger by taking our faith from us: or, if we can not stay the course of His vengeance, if it is needful that faith should perish, let us perish with it, by remaining faithful to Him even unto death. Yes, Lord, such are my feelings: I trust that Thou wilt support me in them; or rather grant, O God, that I may never see this result of Thine indignation, and that Thy holy religion may be always honoured and cherished amongst us. Amen.

SECOND POINT.

Of the prophecy, which marked the abode of Jesus at Capernaum.

That it might be fulfilled which was spoken by Esaias the prophet, saying, The land of Zabulon, and the land of Nephthalim, by the way of the sea, beyond Jordan, Galilee of the Gentiles; the people which sat in darkness saw great light; and to them which sat in the region and shadow of death, light is sprung up. This prophecy pointed out, 1. the place where the Messiah was to begin to preach, 2. the condition of the Israelites of that country, 3. the state of the Gentiles of the same country, and that surrounding it, 4. the character of the Messiah.

1. The place where the Messiah was to begin His ministry. The town of Capernaum was situated on the confines of the tribes of Zabulon and Nephtali, near a great lake to which the name of sea was given, and which was sometimes called the lake of Gennesareth, and sometimes, sea of Tiberias or sea of Galilee. The prophecy comprises not only the town of Capernaum, but also the neighbouring places, where Jesus was about to preach the Gospel. This country was called Higher Galilee, or Galilee of the Gentiles, because the Gentiles possessed

several cities in it. Solomon had ceded twenty to Hiram, king of Tyre. Let us not cease to admire how the prophets had foretold all the proceedings of the Messiah, and how Jesus, following faithfully the course marked out for Him by His Father, does not take one step which is not a fulfilment of prophecy.

2. Isaiah had pointed out the condition of the Israelites of that country. They *sat in darkness*, not only because they were the most distant from Jerusalem and the Holy Temple, but still more because they lived in a profound ignorance of their religion and their duties, and that their conduct resembled much more that of the heathen who were around and in the midst of them, than that, which the children of Abraham and the worshippers of the true God ought to have maintained. Nevertheless, they are the first who had the benefit of seeing this great light, which comes to lighten the whole world, and it is amidst them that Jesus fixes His abode. Conceive what was their happiness, and consider also that it is but a feeble image of our own. .

3. Prophecy had marked out the state of the Gentiles of Capernaum, and its neighbouring towns. Could the prophet have better described the state of those idolaters, who had not the knowledge of the true God, and whose life was defiled with numberless abominations, than by saying that *they sat in the region and shadow of death ?* And nevertheless it was upon them that the divine light arose, which was sent to the children of Israel. They saw Jesus, they were witnesses of His miracles, and themselves, coming from Tyre and Sidon, received the cure of healing from Him. Alas! how often have I not perhaps myself been sitting in this dark region of death, leading, although a Christian, the life of a heathen, acknowledging no God except my own pleasure, following no law save that of my own passions, calm and without remorse in the abyss of sin and in a state of damnation! What would have become of me, if this divine Light were not come to enlighten me ? I should have remained in this fatal state until my death,

and from this shadow and region of death I should have passed, like many others, into the night and the torments of eternal death. Oh Divine Mercy, what can I ever do to acknowledge such a mark of Thy favour, so signal a benefit?

4. The prophet had drawn the character of the Messiah. He had called Him the great Light, and in that, he agrees perfectly with the Evangelist, who gives Him the name of *the true Light, which lighteth every man that cometh into the world.* Jesus is the true and great Light, which has dispersed the darkness, and which eclipses all other light. A perfect light, which has taught us all the truths necessary to our perfect happiness: a pure light, in which no shadow of doubt, error, or falsehood is intermingled: a free light, which was offered to us before we could either anticipate it or deserve that it should come to us: an eternal light, which only lightens us here below, in order to guide us to the full daylight of perfect light in eternity. O Jesus, be Thou my Light: may I know no other, and follow none but Thee!

THIRD POINT.

Of the preaching of Jesus at Capernaum, and the surrounding villages.

From that time Jesus began to preach, and to say, Repent: for the kingdom of Heaven is at hand. The time is fulfilled, repent ye, and believe the gospel. This preaching, short and simple, offers to us four important subjects for our meditation.

1. The fulfilment of the time. The time, which had been marked for the coming of the Messiah, is accomplished. The seventy weeks of the Prophet Daniel have expired. The sceptre, according to the prophecy of the patriarch Jacob, continues no longer in the house of Judah: it has passed into foreign hands. Let us then also say with regard to ourselves, *The time is fulfilled;* the time, in which God willed to place me on

the earth, has come; the time that He wills that I should remain there is already far advanced, and perhaps will soon be concluded. Alas! How have I employed it? Would that we could say also to ourselves: The time of folly and levity, of sin and dissipation, has passed with me: I have done with it. I begin a devout and Christian life, and I renounce for ever all which has kept me back from God and my salvation.

2. This preaching announces to us the approach of the kingdom of God: that is to say the institution of Christianity. And in truth, the establishment of the Gospel-law could not be nearer at hand. In a few days, we shall see Jesus associate His disciples in His work, and lay the foundations of His Church: and soon afterwards we shall hear Him Himself promulgate upon the mount the principal articles of His Gospel. For us, who have had the happiness to be born at a time, when this reign is established, when all is peaceful around us, how shall we profit by so great a benefit? Are we living members of this Church? Does God reign in us by His love, and by our exact practice of the law? Let us remember that there is for us another kingdom of God at hand, and that soon it will be decided, whether Jesus Christ shall give us a home in His kingdom, or condemn us to eternal punishment in hell.

3. This preaching sets forth to us the necessity of repentance. The forerunner of Jesus Christ had already preached it; but this Divine Saviour preaches it Himself, as a necessary means of preparation to receive the kingdom of heaven. Ah! how much more necessary it is for me, who, having been admitted into this kingdom of the Church, have conducted myself as a rebellious subject, who have so often violated all its laws, and profaned its holiness! It is no longer S. John Baptist: it is Jesus Himself, my Saviour and my Judge, Who exhorts me and urges me to repentance, because without it I can neither have a share in His redemption, nor escape from the rigour of His judgement. What a motive for me to bear the yoke of repentance!

4. Lastly, this preaching of Jesus leads us to believe the Gospel. We all fail in our faith; some, because they have none, others, because they have not enough, or because they do not stir up the little which they have. *Believe the Gospels,* Jesus Christ says to us all. Disciples of Moses, *believe the Gospel,* read it with attention; you will see there the types fulfilled, the prophecies accomplished, and the Messiah Whom ye look for, already come. Schismatics, heretics, sectarians, of whatever kind you are, *believe the Gospel:* you will see to what authority you ought to submit, and you will soon join yourselves to His Church. Deists, sceptics, philosophers of all sorts and of all names, *believe the Gospel:* and you will find the solution of your doubts, of your perplexities, of your disquietudes; and you will acknowledge that the Gospel alone has wherewithal to convince and to bring into subjection every reasonable mind. Sinners hardened by the habit of sin, *believe the Gospel:* meditate on it with attention, soon you will break your chains, and bless your Deliverer. Cowardly and slothful souls, *believe the Gospel:* search out its depths, make it the subject of your reflections, and soon nothing will be too much for you: you will walk with fervour and with joy along the most difficult paths of perfection. Poor, feeble, afflicted, persecuted, despairing, whoever you may be, *believe the Gospel:* you will find there your comfort and your consolation. It is your God, it is your Saviour Himself, Who exhorts you to it; *believe the Gospel.*

Prayer. I believe it; O divine Jesus! Support my faith. O true Light of the world, could I ever prefer darkness to Thee? May I never close my eyes, O God, to the rays of Thy grace, nor my heart to its attractions. O God of my life! Be also the God of my mind, that it may think only of Thee; the God of my heart, that it may only act for Thee; the God of my soul, that it may live only by Thee in time, that so it may live in Thee in glory. Amen.

Meditation XXX.

THE FIRST WITNESS WHICH S. JOHN BAPTIST BEARS OF JESUS TO THE DEPUTIES OF THE JEWS.

The sacred text teaches us here, 1. what were the motives of this deputation, 2. what were the questions put to S. John, and the answers he made to them, 3. what are the questions which we ought to put to ourselves. S. John i. 19-28.

FIRST POINT.

The motives of the deputation from the Jews to S. John Baptist.

Now, *this is the record of John, when the Jews sent Priests and Levites from Jerusalem to ask him, Who art thou?* This question, made under these circumstances signified, Art thou the Christ, the Messiah? and S. John answers it by taking it in this meaning. But wherefore this question? What were the motives of the deputation which was sent to put it to S. John? We may imagine four principal reasons.

1. Human respect. *These things were done in Bethabara beyond Jordan, where John was baptizing.* The chief council of Jerusalem had already ill-treated S. John Baptist. This holy forerunner had only changed his place of preaching without ceasing to exercise his office, and he continued to fulfil its duties with as much freedom, as if he had suffered nothing. The number of his audience and of his disciples increased every day. Even the people of Jerusalem looked upon him as a prophet, and this idea cast a slur upon the authors of the first persecution which he had undergone. It was, apparently, in order to clear themselves from this stain, that the council sent this solemn deputation to him, composed of Priests and Levites. It is thus that we sometimes see unbelievers retract, explain themselves, justify them-

selves, protest their reverence for religion, in order to free themselves, in the sight of men, from the blame of the impious doctrines which they have advanced.

2. Vanity. The priests were delighted to be able to shew by their deputation an appearance of zeal, to make known that they were attentive to all in which religion was concerned, and ready to acknowledge the Messiah as soon as He should appear. By this, moreover, they made it understood that to them alone belonged the right to decide who was the true Messiah; and that it belonged to them to set Him forth to the people, and that this same Messiah could not exact obedience till He had received their homage. But how opposed to these chimerical pretensions were the prophetic oracles!

3. Jealousy. S. John had not received his mission from them; he had not acknowledged their authority in the exercise of his ministry; that was apparently his first crime, and the pretext for the persecution which he had suffered. Moreover the ill-treatment on the part of the council had not taken away the reputation of this holy prophet from him. Perhaps also, they sought, under the appearance of an honourable deputation, an occasion of surprising him in his answers, and a more effectual means of making him lose the celebrity he had attained. Unhappy policy! Thy ways are only falsehood and artifice. He who does not seek God with an upright and simple heart is punished for it, in that he never finds Him, and recognizes Him nowhere.

4. The fear of finding the Messiah. The people had already suspected that S. John Baptist was the Messiah, and did not disguise their suspicions. The time at which the messenger of God was to come, agreed with the desire which prevailed for his coming; and all which was related of S. John, his appearance, his repentance, his preaching, his baptism, was very fitting to confirm it. It would have been grievous to the priests, that he whom they had ill-treated, and who acted with so much independence, should have been found to be, in reality, the Messiah. It was then one of the motives which in-

clined them to send him this deputation, in order to learn whether he were the Messiah, or rather to assure themselves that he was not. A painful situation, in which a person finds himself obliged to fear what is most to be wished for! How many persons resemble these Jews! How many only examine into religion in the fear of finding it true, and love to persuade themselves that it is false at the first difficulty which they meet with!

SECOND POINT.

The questions put to S. John Baptist, and his humility in the answers which he gives.

Four different questions are put to S. John Baptist.

1. They ask him who he is. *Who art thou?* Art thou the Christ, the Messiah? *And he confessed, and denied not; but confessed, I am not the Christ.* We feel in the repetition of these words, what the surprise and confusion must have been, in which S. John Baptist was thrown by this question, or rather the grief with which his heart was penetrated by perceiving that they could so grossly misunderstand the matter, and confound him with his Master. He rejected this proposition with energy, and directly and distinctly affirmed that he was not the Messiah. The truly humble man, when praises, titles, or qualities are assigned to him, which he does not deserve, feels indignant at them: but the falsely humble rejects them in such a way, as to make believe that they do belong to him, and that he has, by rejecting them, the merit of humility.

2. They inquire of S. John Baptist, whether he is Elias, or one of the prophets. *And they asked him, What then? Art thou Elias? And he saith, I am not. Art thou that prophet?* they add; *And he answered, No.* The truly humble man knows always how to find in praises, titles, and qualities, which he deserves, a sense in which he does not deserve them. S. John was Elias, according to the spirit; he was the Elias who

was to precede the first Coming of the Messiah: but he was not the ancient Elias, who was to precede His last coming. S. John was a prophet, and more than a prophet, since he foretold the arrival and the power of Him, to Whom all prophecies refer: but he was not a prophet in the sense of foretelling a distant event which he had not seen. To all these questions, S. John only answers by a word, since they delay him from speaking of Jesus. The truly humble man cuts short all that affects himself; he only seeks to turn the conversation, and let it fall on Him, Who is alone great, and alone worthy of all praise.

3. They question S. John as to what he thinks of himself. *Then said they unto him, Who art thou? that we may give an answer to them that sent us. What sayest thou of thyself?* He was then obliged to give an explanation. *He said, I am the voice of one crying in the wilderness, Make straight the way of the Lord, as said the prophet Esaias.* S. John could not say less; but he could also have said more, and have added that he was especially sent from God. Nevertheless he said enough to make it understood that his mission was authorised by prophecies, which were now beginning to be accomplished, and that this accomplishment announced the near coming of the Lord. If a really humble person is compelled to speak of himself he does so in terms the most concise, and the simplest, and always by referring all to the Author of all good.

4. Lastly they ask S. John Baptist, why he baptized. *And they which were sent were of the Pharisees*, that is to say, men enlightened, but haughty, disdainful, and criticisers; every thing must undergo their censorship; nothing in their ideas was useful, but what they did themselves, or what they authorised. They reproved or repressed the teaching, the most beneficial to the people of God, if he who offered it, did not place himself under their commands, or did not give himself out as one of their disciples or pupils. Lastly, the spirit of domination and pride, which was the distinguishing cha-

racteristic of this sect, persuaded them that nothing was lawful but that, which was done in accordance with their authority. It was with this imperious and contemptuous tone, which was so familiar to them, that *they asked him, and said unto him, Why baptizest thou then, if thou be not that Christ, nor Elias, neither that prophet?* But these deputies, being themselves priests and Levites, ought well to have understood from the last answer of S. John, that he was the forerunner of the Messiah, announced by Isaiah, and that, as such, he had more right to baptize than Elias, or any of the prophets; but he who is truly humble gives no answer to reproaches, and neither seeks to justify himself, nor to make good his rights. S. John only speaks of his baptism with modesty, and in but few words; but he enlarges gladly on the greatness of Jesus Christ. *John answered them saying, I baptize with water, but there standeth one among you Whom ye know not. He it is, who coming after me is preferred before me, Whose shoe's latchet I am not worthy to unloose.* So striking a witness on the part of a man such as S. John Baptist, and delivered under such circumstances, was well qualified to make an impression upon the deputies, and upon those who had sent them, if either had had only upright intentions; but they contented themselves with ascertaining the fact that S. John was not the Messiah, and they troubled themselves no more about a man, from whom they had nothing to fear. Thus the blindness of the Jews began to grow upon them, through the contempt they shewed for the first rays of light which shone upon them. Let us avoid this much to be dreaded blindness by a holy use of the light which surrounds us.

THIRD POINT.

The questions which we ought to put to ourselves.

1. Who are we? If Providence has placed us in a position of authority in the state, how do we employ

ourselves? How do we acquit ourselves of our duties? If we have been placed through grace in any office in His Church, how do we fulfil its duties? How are we, as regards the exercise of vices or of virtues? Are we given to anger, revengeful, evil-speakers, or charitable, compassionate, sober, chaste? In our spiritual life, are we indolent or fervent, recollected or distracted, mortified or sensual? Alas! Could we not say to ourselves with more truth than S. Bernard, "I am the wonder of my age, I am a monster in the world; I am an ecclesiastic, or a Christian by name, and yet I live a heathen life, or at least a worldly one? In my situation, in my condition, where all virtues should abound, I find in my conduct nought but vices."

2. What do we say of ourselves? And first, what do we say of ourselves to ourselves? Alas! What secret esteem of our own merits! What pride! What vanity! What do we say of ourselves to others? Do we not too often speak of ourselves? And is it not always in order to prove ourselves right, and to find others in the wrong, to praise ourselves, and to throw blame on our neighbour? Do we not dissimulate with ourselves in our self-examination, and seek to disguise the truth from ourselves? Do we strive to see ourselves as we really are? Do we not care to know more of others than of ourselves?

3. Why do we meddle with what does not concern us? *Why baptizest thou then, if thou be not that prophet?* You are neither a pastor, nor a teacher of the Church. Why then reason upon religion instead of practising it? You are neither a minister of state, nor a general of the army; why then criticise all that is done? You are not entrusted with the care of your neighbour: why then censure him, publish his faults, blame his conduct?

4. What is said, what is thought, what may be said of us? The criticism of public opinion may become a useful lesson to him who knows how to profit by it: but let us leave that point to our own special self-examination. Might not S. John here say to all in general,

Jesus Christ is in the midst of you, and you do not know Him; or if you do know Him, where is your respect, your love, your zeal for Him? Do you obey His law, do you imitate His virtues!

Prayer. O my God, how guilty I am! How many faults there are to be corrected in me! How many virtues to be acquired! How much cause for humiliation! Help me, Lord, to change my heart, to reform my conversation, and to regulate all my conduct. Do Thou confound for ever these thoughts of pride, which I have of myself. Recall to my mind continually the baseness of my origin, the shamefulness of my prevarications, and never suffer me to forget the state of nothingness whence Thou hast brought me, and that to which sin has reduced me; or if I am obliged to acknowledge that Thou hast wrought in me something good or great, let it be only to set forth the greatness of Thy power, the magnificence of Thy gifts, and that I may merit the reward which Thou in Thy glory dost award to true humility. Amen.

Meditation XXXI.

SECOND TESTIMONY GIVEN TO THE PEOPLE BY S. JOHN BAPTIST ON SEEING JESUS.

Nothing more complete, less suspected, and more authentic than this testimony.

FIRST POINT.

A complete testimony.

1. S. John Baptist announces, by this testimony, the Sacrifice and death of Christ for the sins of men. *The next day, John seeth Jesus coming unto him, and saith, Behold the Lamb of God which taketh away the*

sin of the world. It was the day after the embassy of the Jews, that Jesus, having arrived at Bethany from Capernaum, appeared on the banks of the Jordan. He remained there some moments, that He might be seen of S. John, and all his audience. The forerunner, seeing the Messiah, pointed Him out to them, saying, *Behold the Lamb of God;* as if he had said, Behold Him Who, far more efficaciously than our victims, is laden with the iniquities of the world, in order to blot them out by His Blood. The ancient sacrifices are about to be abolished. O Jesus! Thy sacrifice is daily renewed in Thy Church: I have the blessing of partaking of it; do I profit thereby?

2. S. John Baptist, by his testimony, announces the eternity of Christ in the bosom of God. Jesus, having only shewn Himself, and then again withdrawn Himself, S. John adds: *This is He of Whom I said, After me cometh a Man which is preferred before me; for He was before me.* Although, as Man, Jesus was six months younger than S. John, and had not begun His public ministry till after him, nevertheless, as God, Jesus was before S. John, and begotten of the Father from all eternity; and as Man and God, He was both by the Divinity of His person, and the greatness of His ministry, infinitely superior to S. John.

3. S. John Baptist predicts the excellence of the Baptism of Jesus Christ. *And I knew Him not; but He that sent me to baptize with water, the same said unto me, Upon whom thou shalt see the Spirit descending, and remaining on Him, the same is He which baptizeth with the Holy Ghost.* Ah! What happiness for me to have received the Baptism of Christ! I did not know what the happiness was, when I received it. Alas! How long have I been without knowing it! I know it now, O my Saviour, grant me grace to be more faithful to it than I have been hitherto.

4. S. John Baptist announces the Divine Sonship of Christ. *And I saw and bare record, that this is the Son of God.* Here is a distinct declaration of S. John, a

declaration which will also one day draw down upon S. Peter a commendation from Christ, and which will bring death upon Christ Himself from the hands of the Jews. Were it needful that I should suffer for Thee, even the most cruel death, O my divine Saviour, I have received Thy holy baptism. I will not give the lie to the promises made for me therein, and I will confess all my life, that Thou art the Son of God, Who hast come down from heaven, and hast died for us. Grant, O Jesus, that the purity of my life may answer to the sincerity of my resolutions.

SECOND POINT.

A testimony beyond suspicion.

1. There could be no suspicion of flattery, or natural friendship. *I knew Him not, but that He should be made manifest to Israel, therefore am I come baptizing with water;* that is to say, no human motive prepossessed me in His favour, nothing attached me to His Person, I had no connexion with Him, His face even was unknown to me when He presented Himself to receive my Baptism: I should have baptized Him without distinction, like an ordinary Israelite, if God, Who sent me to shew to the people of Israel that God-Man, their Saviour and their God, had not forewarned me with regard to Him, that I should see certain signs fulfilled on Him. In truth, S. John Baptist was still in his mother's womb, when he felt the presence of Jesus Christ; since that time, he had passed his life in the desert up to the age of thirty years, without ever having seen Jesus Christ. During the whole of his life, he had not spoken to Him more than once, and then only in a few words: and he only saw Him, in all, three times, of which this was the second. But if he had not the happiness of living in familiar intercourse with Him, he had that of thinking only of Him, speaking only of Him, and acting only for Him. How happy should I be, if I had the same faithfulness! Precious time, but irre-

parably lost has that been, in which I occupied myself in aught else but Thee, O my God! Ah! At least let me not lose that which Thou shalt yet grant me!

2. There was not in the testimony of S. John the Baptist any interested motive. His labours were continual, and were not lucrative. The austere life which he led enabled him easily to procure both food and clothing without the aid of those whom he taught. He expected nothing on earth from Him, to Whom he dedicated so many hardships and austerities, and what was he to receive as the reward of his faithfulness in his ministry? Sufferings, prison, and death.

3. There could not be in his testimony any motive of vain-glory. John only speaks of the Saviour in order to abase himself: he only exalts the virtue of the Baptism of Jesus Christ in order to diminish the virtue of his own: he only forms disciples for Jesus Christ: he only instructs people, in order to draw them closer to Jesus Christ: he had only been sent, he says, that He might be *made manifest to Israel*. How worthily he fulfils his mission! Do we thus fulfil the end, for which God sent us into the world, for which He made us Christians, for which He put us into the place we occupy? Is it with like purity, like disinterestedness, like humility, that we fulfil its duties?

4. The testimony of S. John the Baptist could not be suspected of collusion, or ambitious connivance. No one could, without a palpable absurdity, suppose that Jesus Christ and S. John had conspired together, and formed between them the plot which should make the one pass off the other for the Messiah and the Son of God. Besides the fact that they had never seen each other, that S. John had passed all his life in the desert, which every one knew well, as also that Jesus had passed all His life in the bosom of His family at Nazareth, and under the eyes of the world, what would moreover have been the result of such a plot, by which the one gave up everything to the other, and from which both could only gain labours, sufferings, and death? If ambition were

the mainspring of all this intrigue, it would have been for S. John to give himself out as the Messiah: his sacerdotal family was in higher consideration at that time than that of Jesus; he was in possession of the public esteem and admiration, before Jesus had yet appeared; the people thought that John was the Messiah; the synagogue had sent him deputies to ask him if he was so in reality; and this ambitious man humbles himself, abases himself in order to exalt Jesus, Whom no one as yet knew; these are not the proceedings of ambition. The testimony of S. John is then above all suspicion; humility and sincerity render themselves felt: and it is only the spirit of truth, which could have brought about this wonderful agreement between the forerunner and the Messiah. Let us thank God for the numberless proofs which His Providence gives us of the truth of religion.

THIRD POINT.

Authorised testimony.

1. By the descent of the Holy Spirit. *And John bare record, saying, I saw the Spirit descending from Heaven like a dove, and it abode upon Him.* It is then the Holy Spirit, Who, by the mouth of S. John, bears witness of Jesus Christ. S. John saw this dove, and he has been instructed as to the mystery, which was hidden therein: he only tells us what he has seen: ought I not then to believe him, rather than those frivolous men who only bring insipid railleries, in order to destroy facts?

2. Testimony of S. John authorised by the voice of God the Father. *And I knew Him not: but He that sent me to baptize with water, the same said unto me, Upon Whom thou shalt see the Spirit descending, and remaining on Him, the same is He which baptizeth with the Holy Ghost,* that is to say, you will see My only Son: He will come to present Himself to you, in order to receive the Baptism which I have commanded

you to establish: you will perceive the Holy Spirit descend, and remain on His Head under a visible form; then you will know, that He who humbles Himself before you is the Saviour of Israel, Who by the virtue of His Baptism, very different from your own, will communicate to you the grace and the gifts of the Holy Spirit. S. John only tells us what God Himself told him. Could S. John mistake this voice of the Father, Who spoke in him, and taught him? The testimony of S. John is then only the testimony of God Himself.

3. Testimony, authorised by the character of S. John himself. What a man was this holy forerunner! His conception, his birth, his solitary life, his public life, all is marvellous in him, and himself is a marvel! His words are oracles, his assertions are truths: his testimony is then a proof without contradiction.

4. Lastly, the testimony of S. John, authorised by the suffrages of the public. The people were within reach of knowing S. John, and they had so high an esteem of him, that no one would have dared to say a word against the reputation of this great man. Jesus Christ Himself bore witness to him, and his most infuriated enemies dared not reject him. This extraordinary and universal esteem, which S. John enjoyed, has been perpetuated from age to age, and has spread amongst all nations, amongst even the people, who have not the Christian law. How then could any throw doubt on what such a man assures us that he has seen? *And I saw and bare record that this is the Son of God.* Why should we rather believe idle babblers, who have seen nothing, and who only retail to us the reveries of their own imagining and the idle fancies of their corrupt hearts?

Prayer. I thank Thee, O Father eternal, that Thou hast made Thy truth thus plain to me. O Divine Saviour! O Lamb of God! Who takest away the sins of the world, Whom the desire of my salvation nailed to the Cross, Whom love offered up for me, and Whom charity sacrificed, grant that I may love Thee, and may be willing to die for Thy Name's sake and for

Thy glory. O Holy Spirit! Who art here set forth under the figure of a dove, Thou dost set forth to me under this loving symbol the gentleness, purity, and tenderness, which I ought to have to God. Make us, by Thy grace, gentle, pure, simple, peaceful, charitable, fervent, and zealous. Amen.

Meditation XXXII.

JESUS BEGINS TO GATHER DISCIPLES AROUND HIM.

The sacred historian here sets forth to us, 1. the call of two of the disciples of S. John Baptist, 2. the reception which Jesus Christ accorded them, 3. the zeal of those two disciples, who bring a third to Jesus Christ. S. John i. 35-42.

FIRST POINT.

The call of two of the disciples of S. John the Baptist.

1. Observe the fervour which keeps them with S. John. *The next day after, John stood and two of his disciples.* How was it that this saintly forerunner, who was wont to be surrounded with a great number of disciples, had, on this occasion, only two with him? It was that his day was in the decline, as we shall see hereafter. S. John had sent away the people, and his other disciples had taken the step of withdrawing with them: the fervour of these two had kept them still with their master, without their having any idea of the happiness which awaited them. Perseverance in attending the services of God's House and in the practice of our religious exercises is never without its reward. Singular gifts are generally for those who persevere. The constancy of these two disciples gained for them the grace of apostleship, and the glory of having been the two first disciples of Jesus Christ.

T

2. How great was their happiness in seeing Jesus! *And looking upon Jesus, as He walked, he saith, Behold the Lamb of God.* The Saviour willed to draw the two disciples of S. John the Baptist close to Himself, but it was needful that they should first begin by signalising their zeal and their fidelity. He contented Himself therefore by passing before their eyes, and giving them an opportunity of learning, that He Whom they beheld was the Lamb of God. What a happiness for these disciples! What grace! What a favourable opportunity! It is thus that Jesus shews Himself sometimes to us, as it were, in passing by, by a motion, a desire, a certain taste of holiness which makes itself felt in our souls, and which stirs them within us. An inward light seems to say to us then, Behold Jesus! Behold Him in Whom true happiness is to be found. Happy moments, if we did but know how to profit by them, and if we do not mistake this invitation to virtue for virtue itself.

3. Examine what was the fidelity of the two disciples in following Jesus. *And the two disciples heard him speak, and they followed Jesus.* They understood the thoughts of their Master, and the importance of this moment during which Jesus was passing by. They knew that on the preceding day this Divine Saviour had immediately disappeared; but what they did not know, was that He was not to shew Himself again in this manner, and that He was to return into Galilee. They set off at once then to follow Him, resolved not to lose this opportunity of speaking to Him, and of offering themselves to Him. Alas! How many, by cowardly delays, have missed their vocation, their perfection, their conversion, their salvation!

SECOND POINT.

The reception which Jesus accords to the two disciples of S. John.

1. He anticipates them, and speaks to them first. The two disciples of S. John were walking behind Jesus

with an impatient desire to speak to Him; but respect prevented them from accosting Him. How good Jesus is! How well He knows the dispositions of those who seek Him, and how those dispositions please Him, when they are accompanied by love, respect, and a desire to learn! Jesus anticipates their timidity. *Then Jesus turned, and saw them following, and saith unto them, What seek ye?* with an air full of gentleness and goodness. *Rabbi,* they answered Him, that is to say, *Master, where dwellest Thou?* They testified sufficiently by these short words, how much they desired to receive His instructions, and to profit by them. Here two important questions present themselves to our reflections, the one which Jesus makes to us, and the other which we ought to make to Him. That which He makes to us; *What seek ye?* That is to say, what are ye seeking in these places where ye go, in that company which you frequent, in these discourses which you hold, in that business about which you occupy yourselves, in the actions which you perform? Is it the glory of God, the kingdom of Heaven, the edification of your neighbour, your own sanctification, your salvation, or rather your own self-love, your own interests, your own pleasures? It is what you will one day have to answer for to Him. The question which we ought to put to Him is that of the two disciples. *Master, where dwellest Thou?* O Jesus, where is it that Thou dwellest? It is not in the tumult of the world's business, nor in worldly assemblies; it is in Heaven, it is in Thy temples, in retirement, in prayers, in self-recollection, in the practice of virtue that Thou art to be found. I know it, and I do not seek Thee there, converse with Thee there, listen to Thee there.

2. Jesus invites the two disciples to come, where He dwells. This Divine Saviour had taken a lodging in the neighbouring village, or in the neighbourhood. He says to them, *Come and see. Come,* word full of love, which fills these disciples with joy and consolation; word, which Jesus does not cease to say to us on earth, and which He will repeat at the last day, on behalf of those who

shall have listened to Him, and followed Him. Shall we then continue to resist so tender an invitation?

3. Jesus Christ keeps the two disciples with Him for the remainder of the day. *They came and saw where He dwelt, and abode with Him that day: for it was about the tenth hour.* That is to say, that there were two hours remaining of that day, which they spent with Jesus. Who can tell, what were the delights of that interview? How rapidly the moments passed! O ye who fear to follow Jesus, and to hold converse with Him, *come and see;* make experience of it, and prove for yourselves if there is not exceedingly greater sweetness to be found in following Him, and listening to Him than in living in distraction, in following and frequenting the world. O Jesus! Hold my heart close to Thee; favour it with some instants of Thy sweet intercourse, and thenceforth nothing else will satisfy it.

THIRD POINT.

Zeal of the two disciples, who bring a third to Jesus.

This third disciple was S. Peter; but who were the two first? One of the two was called Andrew. *And the two disciples heard John speak, and they followed Jesus. One of the two which heard John speak and followed him, was Andrew, Simon Peter's brother.* The other disciple is not named; but it is easy to understand that it was S. John the Evangelist, the same who wrote this account, and who conceals his own name out of modesty. The details which he has given us of that which happened to S. John the Baptist at Bethany, makes us plainly see that he was one of his disciples, and one of those who were most desirous to be with him. Andrew, having just left Jesus, *first findeth his own brother Simon, and saith unto him, We have found the Messias, which is being interpreted, the Christ, And he brought him to Jesus. And when Jesus beheld him, He said, Thou art Simon, the son of Jona, thou shalt be called Cephas, which is by interpretation, A stone.*

1. S. Peter is told, and brought to Jesus. The two

disciples were returning together, filled with consolation, when Andrew met his brother Simon. The faith with which he was penetrated, the zeal which devoured him, the desire of making disciples for his new Master, led him to say to his brother; *We have found the Messiah,* John the Baptist has pointed Him out to us, we have spoken to Him, we are just come out from His Presence. At these tidings, Simon, trembling with joy, and naturally of a quick and impetuous temperament, could not delay a moment. Andrew, equally impatient to make him a sharer in the blessing which he had found, and which he desired to make known to him, lost no time. *He brought him to Jesus.* It appears that the companion of Andrew, whom we suppose to be S. John, did not leave him, and that the three came together to find the Saviour. Nevertheless, it began to grow late, that is to say, it was, according to our manner of computation, six o'clock in the evening, for the feast of Passover was not far distant. But the disciples judged rightly that the Master would approve their ardour, and that His goodness would pardon their importunity. He who delays till the morrow is not really in earnest, and runs the risk of losing Jesus and His favours.

2. Jesus looks upon Peter. *Jesus beheld him.* Who can say what was the first glance of the Saviour upon a man, whom He destined to be the chief of His Apostles, the shepherd of His sheep, the guardian of His mysteries? How powerful must that look have been! With what love, with what ardour did He not enkindle the heart of the new disciple! What joy did He not pour down upon him! A day will come, when a similar look will overwhelm him with grief, and cause him to shed a torrent of tears, whose spring will never dry up. O Jesus, condescend to look upon me thus, in order to make me weep for my sins, and to consume me with Thy love.

3. Jesus changes the name Simon into that of Peter. I know you, He said to him, *Thou art Simon the son of Jona;* but a day shall come, and that at no great distance of time, that *thou shalt be called Cephas, which*

is by interpretation, A stone. The Saviour said much in few words to His new disciple; but neither he nor his two companions understood, at that time, the signification of his change of name. For us to whom it has been made known, let us, whilst we honour under this name the chief of the Apostles, remain inviolably attached to that Church, of which he was made, after Jesus Christ, one of the chief corner stones: to that Church, which can trace an uninterrupted succession of ministers up to the time of the Apostles, who received thus from Jesus Christ Himself, their authority to govern His Church.

Prayer. Woe to me if I separate myself from that Church, founded by S. Peter and the other Apostles. May I honour them in their successors, by yielding myself up to their authority. Grant, O Jesus, that firmly attached to the faith, the doctrines, and the mind of the Church, I may place all my happiness in believing what she teaches, in practising what she appoints, in loving what she loves, and by her means may thereby gain eternity. Amen.

Meditation XXXIII.

TWO OTHER DISCIPLES JOIN THEMSELVES TO THE THREE FIRST.

S. Philip gives us here the same example of faithfulness and zeal which S. Andrew has shewn us. He follows Jesus Christ from the moment that he first knows Him, and hastens to make Him known to Nathanael; but that which above all merits our special notice is, the praise which our Lord bestows upon this latter. Thus, 1. the call of Philip, 2. the call of Nathanael, 3. the conversation which Nathanael holds; such is the natural course of this meditation. S. John i. 43-51.

FIRST POINT.

The call of Philip.

1. Philip is called by Jesus. *The day following, Jesus would go forth into Galilee, and findeth Philip, and*

saith unto him, Follow Me. The Saviour was leaving Bethany, in order to return to Galilee with His three first disciples, Peter, Andrew, and John, all three Galileans like Himself, when He met Philip. *Follow Me,* He said, to him, and nothing more was needed to win him. Such is the power of the word of God over simple and faithful souls. How often has not Jesus spoken these words to us in the depths of our heart, these words so replete with love and sweetness: *Follow Me; follow Me,* and not the flesh; *Me,* and not the world; *Me,* and not your evil passions, your evil tempers, your covetousness, your ambition; *Me,* and not the multitude of things with which you occupy your minds so idly, which distract you, which corrupt you, which can never make you happy! Shall we for ever resist a command so authoritative, so loving?

2. Philip is animated by the example of his fellow countrymen. *Now Philip was of Bethsaida, the city of Andrew and Peter.* As they were all living together at Bethany, it is probable that they were all disciples of S. John. It would appear as if this had been the object which attracted our Saviour to this place, in order to gather together disciples who had been trained in the school of that great teacher. Philip had heard the two testimonies which S. John Baptist had already borne to Jesus Christ; he found his two fellow-countrymen in the company of the Saviour, and he heard Jesus Himself inviting him to follow Him. Could he refuse so loving an invitation? How many do we not know of our fellow countrymen, our neighbours, our friends, our relations, who have given themselves up to the service of God who serve Him faithfully and earnestly! If then we feel that the Lord calls us equally with them, let their example encourage us; otherwise we may fear that one day it will condemn us.

3. S. Philip follows Jesus. What obedience! The instant that Jesus calls him, he leaves all, and "follows in His train." In all that concerns our eternal salvation, everything depends upon our promptness in obey-

ing the calls of God. Let us experience for ourselves, the great advantages which this obedience brings with it. Come, and let us "taste and see how gracious the Lord is."

SECOND POINT.

The call of Nathanael.

1. In this call, let us consider the zeal of Philip. He has no sooner himself become a disciple of Jesus, than he becomes, after the example of S. Andrew, an apostle. He had a friend named Nathanael. He was one of those faithful souls, who were "waiting for the consolation of Israel." Philip hastened to make known to him his recent call. He sought him with all the eagerness of one who longs to make his friend partaker of a happiness, in which he feels him worthy to have a share. *We have found Him*, he says to him, *of Whom Moses in the law, and the prophets, did write, Jesus of Nazareth, the son of Joseph.* Have we the same earnest desire for the salvation of our friends? Worldlings and heretics are only too eager to seduce and to contaminate one another, and to make each other acquainted with whatever may help to strengthen them in sin and error: if we had but somewhat of their zeal! Let us admire here this ordering of God's Providence, which brings about that the one should become the instrument of the salvation of the other; teachers with regard to their disciples; pastors with regard to their flocks; parents with regard to their children; friends to their companions; and so on as regards others. And what a special bond of union to the souls of the redeemed in heaven will be the remembrance of this sacred influence formed here on earth below! But on the other hand, with what intensity of hatred will the hearts of the damned be filled one towards another, when they look back upon their earthly life, and see how they have, by evil friendships and influences, brought one another into this state of eternal damnation. May this thought rekindle our

zeal for the salvation of others, and make us watchful over our lives, that we may never be a cause of offence to any one, be it who it may.

2. Observe, what were the prejudices of Nathanael! At the bare mention of the name of Nazareth, he seemed to be repelled, and he exclaims: *Can there any good thing come out of Nazareth?* Such is mankind; Jerusalem despised every other city: Judea despised Galilee: in Galilee, Nazareth was of no repute; and in the city of Nazareth, the family of Joseph was looked down upon. The carnal mind is always prejudiced against Jesus: but it is the prejudice of darkness against light, of passion against virtue, of errors against the way, of falsehood against the truth, of death against life.

3. Meditate upon the answer of Philip to Nathanael. He was in haste and he replied only in these few words, *Come and see.* It is in truth the best means of overcoming prejudice. It is not prejudice to refuse to examine for one's self what the Church has condemned: this is docility: but independently of that, how much unjust prejudice is there not against the Church itself! Let us not judge by the conversation or the prejudices of others: and before we pass judgement, let us examine, prove and see. Thus did Nathanael, and as he had an upright heart, he was not obstinate in his prejudices, but followed Philip. Let us follow in the same way in a teachable spirit, the counsels of a wise friend or director, who only desires our salvation, and seeks to cure us of our prejudices.

THIRD POINT.

Conversation of Nathanael with Jesus.

1. In this conversation, Jesus shews that He knew the depths of all hearts. *Jesus saw Nathanael coming to Him and saith of him* to His three first disciples, *Behold an Israelite indeed, in whom is no guile!* What praise is contained in these few words! Does God behold this uprightness, this guilelessness, this simplicity, so

opposed to all artifice and all dissimulation, in my heart, in my words, in my conduct? Alas! What duplicity on the contrary, what dissimulation, what hypocrisy!

2. *Jesus shews that His eyes are in every place.* Nathanael, in drawing near to Jesus, heard what He was saying of him, and replying at once with that air of frankness which justified the character which the Saviour had just given of him, he said to Him, *Whence knewest Thou me?* Jesus replied to him graciously, *Before that Philip called thee, when thou wast under the fig tree, I saw thee.* At this reply Nathanael, seized with astonishment, exclaimed, *Rabbi, Thou art the Son of God: Thou art the King of Israel.* O great King! How sweet it is to serve Thee! Thou beholdest all which is done for Thee, and even what we would desire to do; and Thou dost reward even our unexpressed desires. Thou beholdest me in every place, and I cannot hide myself from Thee. Ah! How could I, even under Thy very eyes, have betrayed Thee, offended Thee, broken the oath of fidelity, which I had sworn unto Thee, and have served Thee with such faint-heartedness!

3. *Jesus shews us that He is the supreme Master over all.* Jesus answers him, *Because I said unto thee, I saw thee under the fig-tree, believest thou? thou shalt see greater things than these.* And then addressing Himself to His disciples, because what He was about to add concerned them, He said to them with the authority of a Master Who claimed their belief, *Verily verily, I say unto you, Hereafter ye shall see the Heaven open and the angels of God ascending and descending upon the Son of man.* And the angels did in truth come down to comfort Him in the garden of Olives; they were to be seen at His tomb, bearing witness to His resurrection, and they appeared again at His glorious Ascension. Can one not also add, that, during the time of our Saviour's preaching, and especially in the miracles which He ceased not to work, the apostles saw the Heavens, as it were, always open above Him? We

ourselves, at the last day shall see the Heavens open, and the angels and saints descend thence, and then reascend in the triumphal procession of their King. Shall we be of that number?

Prayer. It is by singleness of heart alone that I can hope, O divine Saviour! to be the witness of Thy glory, and to take part in it; but how can I gain this purity of heart, save from Thee, O Blessed Jesus, Who didst bestow it upon Nathanael? Cast also upon me the eyes of Thy mercy: create in me a pure heart, an upright mind, that I may follow after Thee, according to the example of Thy faithful disciple, and see Thee and praise Thee eternally with Thy angels in Heaven. Amen.

Meditation XXXIV.

OF THE MIRACLE WHICH JESUS WORKED AT THE MARRIAGE IN CANA.

This miracle ought, 1. to lead us to imitate the conduct of the bride, and the bridegroom of Cana, 2. to animate us to put our confidence in Jesus Christ, and, 3. to strengthen our faith in Him. S. John ii. 1-11.

FIRST POINT.

This miracle ought to lead us to imitate the conduct of the bride and bridegroom in Cana.

1. Observe their conduct before the feast. They invite Jesus thither. *And the third day, there was a marriage in Cana of Galilee, and the mother of Jesus was there; and both Jesus was called and His disciples to the marriage.* Jesus, accompanied by the five disciples whom He had chosen at Bethany, was on his way northwards, and journeying up the course of the Jordan, arrived on the third day at Cana in Galilee, beyond the lake of Genesaret. It was there that a resident in the

city, who was about to celebrate his marriage, invited Him to it. Jesus promises to be present, and goes there with his disciples. Let us imitate the pious conduct of this newly married couple, and let us invite Jesus Christ to be present with us in whatever we are engaged about. Before we undertake anything, and above all before we choose our vocation in life, let us pray Jesus to enlighten us, and to guide us in our choice.

2. Consider their conduct during the feast. Jesus was present there, as much to sanction the holy estate of marriage, which would one day be made the subject of attack by heretics, as to teach Christians to maintain in all festivities the rules of modesty and temperance. These newly married persons and their guests were in the presence of Jesus, and consequently all immodest dress must be banished thence, and purity might not be wounded by unseemly discourses, nor sobriety, by excess, nor charity, by slanderous words; the peace which reigned there must not be disturbed by quarrels or disputes, and thus a modest gaiety and a pure and innocent joy would pervade every thing. Jesus does not forbid us innocent pleasures: He does not refuse to take part in them with us, if only they are lawful and kept within due bounds. Let us then never take part in any, where He is not, and which are not according to His mind, and then they will be far more enjoyable to us, since not only will they be innocent amusements, but such as are sanctified by His presence.

3. Let us pay attention to what happened to them towards the end of the feast. They experienced the effects of the Almighty power of Jesus. What happiness must not the end of the feast have brought them, both at the sight of the wonderful miracle which then took place, and from the assurance which they had of a continual protection extended over them. It is not thus with the tumultuous pleasures, with which the world is intoxicated. The beginnings of them are attractive, bewitching, and full of delight; but by what bitterness and remorse, by what despair and shame, are they not fol-

lowed! And what will come of them, when they all come to an end with life! How must they have rejoiced that they had invited Jesus to be present at their marriage feast, and how happy would our marriages be, and what grace should we not find to overcome the difficulties which we must necessarily meet with in our married lives, if we did but enter upon them in company with Jesus, in a pure and Christian spirit, and not in a heathen or carnal spirit, for the sake of worldly profit or advantage.

SECOND POINT.

The miracle at the marriage in Cana ought to animate us to put our confidence in Jesus.

1. Confidence in Jesus, founded on His willingness to supply even our earthly needs. *And when they wanted wine, the mother of Jesus saith unto Him, They have no wine.* His mother perceives the need of wine apparently without its having been mentioned to her, and she speaks to her Son without waiting to be asked. She knew His power, and doubted not that He had but to will, in order to work a miracle, and she did not doubt that He would grant her prayer, and so she asks Him. Shall we not also ask in faith for the supply of our own needs, and those of others? She takes it for granted that her prayer will be heard. *She saith unto the servants, Whatsoever He saith unto you, do it.* And shall not the conduct of the Mother of Jesus Christ serve us as an example? Not only should we pray in faith, but we should also make use of the helps which God has placed within our reach.

2. Confidence in Jesus, founded on His Almighty power and willingness to grant our prayer. How many circumstances combine to prove this to us! It is nothing less than a miracle which His Mother solicits, and a miracle on an occasion which did not appear to call for a prodigy of His divine power. It was not a matter of giving back an only son to his widowed and desolate mother, nor of healing a sick man cruelly tormented,

nor of alleviating the sufferings of an unhappy being in his extreme necessity; but still she asks, and she obtains what she asks for. She draws near to her Son, she shows neither impatience nor distrust; but she simply says to Him, *They have no wine.* What need had she to say more? That petition, so respectfully veiled under the form of a narration of an event, sufficed. Jesus knew well what His mother desired. He answered her, *Woman, what have I to do with thee? Mine hour is not yet come.* His mother does not press the point. But the servants who did not know what was going on, were not long before they were enlightened. Jesus was only beginning to make His appearance with His disciples. He willed to teach them that flesh and blood had no claims, when the duties of the Apostolic ministry were concerned. Moreover He had set apart or foreordained the time, at which He willed to make His power shine forth before their eyes. This time was not yet come, and He willed to make this known. It was as though He had said to the Blessed Virgin, "Dost thou then fear that He that hath sent Me does not know when to mark out for Me the moment, at which His glory and Mine should be shewn forth?" Although the time, of which Jesus Christ speaks was at hand, He says nevertheless to the Blessed Virgin; The time is not yet come; which shows His religious attention to the times of grace, and the purity of His zeal for the glory of His Father. "He was waiting," says S. Augustine, "till all the guests should know that there was no more wine, and that the need for it should be manifest, in order that the power of the Son and the glory of the Father might be acknowledged. The hour was not yet come," says this Father, "when His Mother spoke to Him in behalf of the guests; but when He worked the miracle, the time had come." Moreover let us observe the *manner*, in which He grants His Mother's request. After His answer, which doubtless astonished the attendants, His Mother, far from being discouraged or surprised, remains so fully convinced that He would answer her petition, that she

OF THE MIRACLE WHICH JESUS WORKED AT CANA. 219

called the servants, and said unto them, *Whatsoever He saith unto you, do it.* Hardly had she uttered this command, than her request was granted. *And there were there six water-pots of stone after the manner of the purifying of the Jews, containing two or three firkins apiece ; Jesus saith unto them, Fill the water-pots with water. And they filled them up to the brim. And He saith unto them, Draw out now, and bear unto the governor of the feast. And they bare it. When the ruler of the feast had tasted the water that was made wine, and knew not whence it was; (but the servants which drew the water knew:) the governor of the feast called the bridegroom, and saith unto him, Every man at the beginning doth set forth good wine ; and when men have well drunk then that which is worse ; but thou hast kept the good wine until now.* We see then here how God rewards the faith of those, whose trust in Him standeth firm, even amidst apparent discouragements and trials. Though He tarry long, wait for Him.

3. Confidence in Jesus, founded on His glory, here beginning to be manifested forth. *This beginning of miracles did Jesus in Cana of Galilee, and manifested forth His glory: and His disciples believed on Him.* His glory is manifested here, in that this is the first of His public miracles, since He had associated His disciples with Him; and secondly, that He appears to have advanced the time in which to work His miracles at His Mother's intercession, and thus to have commenced, at this time, the functions of His public ministry; thirdly, it is on this occasion, that we first begin to know the glory of Jesus Christ, to believe truly in Him, and it is that on which His disciples themselves were confirmed in their faith. Should not all these considerations lead us to the knowledge and love of Jesus, our Saviour and our God?

THIRD POINT.

The miracle at the marriage in Cana ought to strengthen us in our faith in Jesus Christ.

1. This miracle is incontestable through the nature itself of the miracle. Water changed into wine is an unheard-of prodigy, which stands alone in its wonders. We perceive there the Creator of all things, the Master of the elements, and of all nature. There we see, revealed to us, the glory and power of the only Son of God. What a connection do we not find between this first public miracle of Christ, and the latest and ever-renewed miracle, in which He makes the Bread His Body, and the Wine His Blood? If we believe the first miracle, what difficulty can we find in believing the latter? I believe them both, O my Saviour, I believe them all. I adore Thy sovereign Power, I rejoice in Thy glory, and I render Thee thanks for Thy infinite goodness towards me.

2. This miracle is remarkable through the manner in which it was worked. It was without any external forms, without any preparation, and even without prayer, or invocation. Jesus, without moving from His place, says to the servants, *Fill the water-pots with water*, and they do it; He then adds, *Draw out now, and bear unto the governor of the feast*, who praises it as being a delicious wine. This change takes place through the hands of the servants, and so to say, through their ministry, without our Saviour's appearing to take any part in it. And in the same manner, the miracle wrought on the bread and wine in the Sacrament of the Body and Blood of Jesus Christ, which comes in reality alone through the operation of the Holy Ghost and by the power of Jesus Christ, is effected through the ministry of His priests, who have received for that purpose the power of Jesus Christ and the unction of His Spirit. How blind are those, who prefer to consult the testimony of their own senses, instead of humbling their wills to believe the mysteries which God has revealed to mankind in His Church!

3. This miracle is attested by the multitude of witnesses. That it was water, which had been put into these vessels is certain, beyond dispute: the servants of

the house had brought it there, those taking part in the ceremony had seen it there, and all were witnesses of it beyond suspicion. That it was wine, and that, the best, when it was drawn from the vessels, the master of the feast, the bride and bridegroom, the disciples of Jesus, and all the guests were the judges; and there was no means of practising deceit upon them. Let us consider how after that, the disciples must have looked upon their Master, or rather let us consider what our own thoughts of Him should be; what faith we ought to have in His power, what confidence in His goodness, what reverence for His Person, what desire to please Him, to cleave firmly to Him, and to serve Him all our lives.

Prayer. O divine Jesus! Shew forth Thy power and goodness in changing my heart, or rather in implanting there the power and joy of Thy Spirit, in the place of this weakness, this languor which rule there. Grant that, inflamed with the new wine of Thy love, it may have no longer any taste for the false pleasures of the world: cause the fire of Thy divine love, to take the place of the coldness which reigns in it. Grant that always obedient in following Thy commandments, and in doing every action, when and as Thou wilt, I may receive the reward of them in the day of judgement. Amen.

Meditation XXXV.

JESUS PREPARES TO GO TO JERUSALEM.

1. Jesus comes back to Capernaum, 2. He recalls Peter and Andrew, 3. He calls James and John to be His disciples. S. John ii. 12-13. S. Matt. iv. 18-22. S. Mark i. 16-20.

FIRST POINT.

Jesus comes back to Capernaum.

After this He went down to Capernaum, He and His Mother, and His brethren, and His disciples: and they continued there not many days. And the Jews' passover was at hand, and Jesus went up to Jerusalem.

1. Jesus left the town of Cana, although His glory had been manifested there by the miracle which He had wrought there. The reputation which we have gained in a place, the enjoyment we may find there, and whatever other temporal advantages may exist there, ought not to be to a minister of the Gospel, the motives which lead him to fix his place of abode; he ought only to regard those places to which the duties of his sacred office call him.

2. Mary, the mother of Jesus, follows Him to Capernaum, as also His brethren, that is to say, His relations and disciples. The zeal of a minister of the Gospel ought to lead him even to leave his family, rather than be wanting in the duties of his calling. He ought not to turn away from his ministry in order to go and live with his family: they must rather go and follow him thither where the call of duty has placed him.

3. Jesus remained only a short time at Capernaum, because the Passover was at hand, and He wished to keep it at Jerusalem, as He did in reality. It was therefore needful to arrange every thing so as to fulfil, during the time of that solemn feast, all the public duties of religion, and all that was required for the edification of a neighbour. Jesus was preparing Himself to go to Jerusalem, not only in order to keep the Passover as a private person, but in order to shew Himself forth there as the Messiah, to announce there His Gospel, and to persuade that great city, by His miracles and benefits, to believe in Him, and to receive the words of salvation which He was bringing to it. It is for this purpose, O Jesus, that, always filled with zeal for souls, Thou dost leave the city of Cana, and dost hasten to go forth from Capernaum, and dost seek to assemble around Thee faithful disciples, to be first the witnesses, and afterwards the imitators of Thy zeal. It is thus, that all Thy actions, all Thy designs tend to our salvation, whilst we neglect it, and occupy ourselves with every thing besides.

SECOND POINT.

Jesus recalls S. Peter and S. Andrew.

When Jesus had arrived at Capernaum, He allowed His disciples to retire to their own homes until He should call them. If Nathanael had not remained at Cana, the place of his abode, he returned thither: S. Philip, withdrew to Bethsaida, to which place he belonged; S. John came from Capernaum, S. Peter and S. Andrew, although originally from Bethsaida, lived also at Capernaum. Jesus, willing then to go to Jerusalem, accompanied by some disciples, called S. Peter and S. Andrew first to follow Him.

1. Examine here who are these whom Jesus calls. *And Jesus walking by the sea of Galilee, saw two brethren, Simon called Peter, and Andrew his brother, casting a net into the sea; for they were fishers.* They were fishermen, unlearned and ignorant men, without credentials, without authority, without any fortune except a boat and some nets, but moreover simple men, leading an innocent and laborious life, and occupied with the works of their station: such are those whom God prefers to the great, the rich, the wise, the sensual, idle, and self-indulgent.

2. Observe for what purpose Jesus calls them. *And He saith unto them, Follow me, and I will make you fishers of men.* It was often a habit with our Saviour to make these kind of allusions in His discourses, and thus to lead the minds of men naturally, by means of sensible objects, up to spiritual things. *Follow me*, He says then here to S. Peter and S. Andrew; you are fishermen, I am one also; you catch fish, I catch men; come with Me, and I will teach you this divine art. Doubtless they did not understand the full extent of these words. Who would ever have imagined that men of this kind, so simple and so uncultivated, should one day change the face of the universe, destroy idolatry and cause the crucified Jesus to be acknowledged as the only

Son of God? Let an apostate Julian, a Porphyry, a Celsus say otherwise, let the libertines and unbelievers of our day say still, if they choose, that the choice of Jesus was made out of policy, that He took simple and rude fishermen, because He could not persuade wise and learned men to follow Him. But we might answer them, Jesus willed only to be followed by simple and ignorant men, and these simple, these ignorant men have been followed by the most enlightened and wisest men in the world; they have converted the universe, cities, provinces, and even those nations amongst whom greater culture and knowledge existed than in the whole of the world besides. The ancient unbelievers have had nothing to oppose to this truth; and shall those of modern days ever be able to destroy it? Is it not here an authenticated fact that Jesus Christ announced, at a time when it appeared to be an impossibility, that of which the certainty has been handed down to us from generation to generation, and of which we behold the accomplishment?

3. Consider how Jesus calls S. Peter and S. Andrew by a word as He passes by them. *And they straightway left their nets and followed Him.* Woe be to him whom passion or distractions hinder from hearing that word! Woe be to him, who having heard it, does not wish to understand it, dissembles it to himself, puts a limit to it, or modifies it to suit his own inclination! Woe to him, who having understood it, rejects or defers to obey it, waits till it is repeated, stifles the remembrance of it, either in order not to respond to it, or to withdraw from his obedience basely, after having at first responded to it. How often has not Jesus called us to follow Him, to serve Him, to lead a holy and devoted life, and we have not deigned to respond to so gentle and heavenly an invitation! What might we not have become, if we had placed ourselves in the hands of this divine Saviour! saints, and perhaps instruments of which He might have made use for the salvation and sanctification of others. What a loss! what a misfortune! But do not

JESUS PREPARES TO GO TO JERUSALEM. 225

let us despair: He still calls us, let us listen to His voice. Let us begin to-day, although late, to follow this divine Master, and let us promise Him to follow Him henceforth with faithfulness and perseverance.

THIRD POINT.

Jesus calls S. James and S. John to follow Him.

And going on from thence, He saw other two brethren, James the son of Zebedee, and John his brother, in a ship with Zebedee their father, mending their nets, and He called them. And they left their father Zebedee in the ship with the hired servants, and went after Him.

1. S. James and S. John obey with alacrity. S. John had not left either his elder brother James, nor his father Zebedee, in ignorance of the miracle of which he had been a witness at Cana. They knew, as well as he did, what Jesus had done at Cana. This tender father was rejoiced that his youngest son should be already admitted amongst the number of the disciples of the Messiah, and the elder brother bore a holy envy of his brother, when Jesus called them both. What must have been the joy of these two brothers! What the happiness of the four friends when they found themselves reunited in the service of the same master! He who does not regard the call of God as a signal favour, begins to render himself unworthy of it, and runs a risk of soon becoming unfaithful to it. Zebedee, who saw himself thus deprived at once of his two sons, very far from lamenting it, thanked God that He had multiplied His benefits to him. Can a truly Christian parent regard otherwise the call of his son to devote himself to the ministry of God?

2. They obey with generosity. They separate themselves from a tenderly loved father; they do not even take leave of their mother, whose tenderness they nevertheless knew. They leave, as those two others had done, their boats and their nets, in the hands of those

who were hired by them, without knowing if they should ever regain them. Finally, they quit a mode of life to which they were accustomed, and occupations by which they earned their livelihood. But perhaps we may say that all that was not much. Alas! that which prevents us from following Jesus Christ with a full and entire faithfulness, that which God urges upon us to give up for the sake of His love, is surely something which in itself is still much less than this, and yet we cannot resolve to set ourselves loose from it.

3. They obey with promptitude. At once, immediately without delay, at the first sound of His voice, they leave all. Perfect model of religious obedience. Promptitude, sure index of fervour, forms the chief merit of obedience, which, in order to be worthy of God, ought not to be less prompt than that of inanimate creatures, who obey without delay the voice of their Creator. It ought to be similar to that, which, whether voluntarily, or against our will, we must yield to death, when it shall call us away from this world: an obedience which no worldly business we have entered upon, and no projects we have formed can retard one moment.

Prayer. O my God, so let it be: no attachment shall hold me back, no difficulty shall daunt me, when it is a question of serving Thee. I will rather renounce, if need be, that which I have, which is dearest to me; I will embrace that which is most difficult to me in order to obey Thy will, and to prove to Thee my obedience. Sustain these resolutions by Thy grace, O Lord, that I may be Thine in time and in eternity. Amen.

Meditation XXXVI.

FIRST JOURNEY OF JESUS TO JERUSALEM TO THE FEAST OF THE PASSOVER.

1. Jesus drives out those who were profaning the temple, 2. He answers the Jews who found fault with Him, 3. He reads the depths of their hearts. S. John ii. 13-25.

FIRST POINT.

Jesus drives out of the temple those who were profaning it.

And the Jews' passover was at hand, and Jesus went up to Jerusalem. It was the first Feast of the Passover since He had begun His public ministry. Since that time, He had not yet shewn Himself in the city. He was only known there by the testimony of His forerunner, and by the report of the miracles which He had already worked in Galilee. They would have been sufficient doubtless to have disposed that city to profit by His presence, and to prepossess it in favour of His doctrine, if its obstinacy had not been always insurmountable. Jesus entered it some days before the feast of the passover, followed by the four disciples whom He had called whilst passing along the coast of the sea of Tiberias, namely S. Peter, S. Andrew, S. James and S. John. Having arrived there, He went straight to the temple, where He willed to make Himself known by an act of authority, which should make a great noise, by driving from the house of God these profane persons who were dishonouring it, and whom the priests had suffered to continue there for a long time without troubling themselves to remedy the abuse.

1. Consider who these profane persons were. *And He found in the temple those that sold oxen and sheep and doves, and the changers of money sitting.* They were, on the one hand, self-interested Jews, who kept a

kind of market in the first court of the temple, sold there the things necessary for the sacrifices, and on the other hand, money changers, who, for the public accommodation, were making a very lucrative commerce, by giving, on condition of a certain profit, pieces of money in exchange for the gold or silver which was brought to them. Who are, alas! the profaners of our Churches, a thousand times more sacred than the Temple at Jerusalem, through the real and sacramental Presence of Jesus Christ? Those who come only to see and to be seen; who enter them, and even approach to the foot of the altar, with less respect and reserve than they would observe in the house of some great person; who appear there with all the splendour, the pride, the worldliness, the want of modesty, and the indecency, which are displayed in worldly assemblies; who converse there more freely than they would in the theatre, or a public hall; who even whilst they are appearing to be willing to render to God some homage, have their minds and hearts busied with useless or sinful objects; who leave, lastly, with yet more dissipation of mind, and with far more sin than when they entered it. Am I not myself of this number?

2. Observe how Jesus treats those profane persons. Their scandalous profanation had been tolerated, it was an established custom, and no further attention was paid to it: their money dealings were witnessed in the temple without any fault being found with them: but Jesus could not suffer this cause of offence to continue. He was indignant at it. The holy place, which was thus profaned with so little regard, was the abode of His Father: it was for Him to avenge Him: *when He had made a scourge of small cords, He drove them all out of the temple, and the sheep, and the oxen: and poured out the changer's money, and overthrew the tables; and said unto them that sold doves, Take these things hence: make not My Father's house an house of merchandise.* How many things which we pass over, or regard as of little importance, as even authorised or

excused by custom, or by the example of others are not thus regarded by Jesus Christ! The Church is the House of God: but we are the living temples of the Holy Ghost. See if there be nothing to purify in our hearts, nothing there which could offend the eyes of Jesus Christ, and draw down upon us the rigour of His punishments. Let us learn to regulate our conduct, and our judgements on this point, not by the customs of men, but by the holiness of the God Whom we serve.

3. Consider the zeal which Jesus shews on this occasion; a zeal which had been foretold, a devouring zeal. A zeal which had been foretold. The four disciples, who had been witnesses of what had just taken place, and who had never seen in Jesus Christ anything but gentleness and goodness, beheld with surprise the severity of this action. They called to mind the verse of the Psalm, which was often recited in their synagogues, "The zeal of Thine House, hath even eaten me up," and they saw that this prophecy was verified literally in the person of their Master. This oracle ought to find its fulfilment still, in all those whom Jesus has associated with Himself in His ministry, the zeal of Jesus, a devouring zeal, which has God only for its Author. This divine Saviour was penetrated by the Majesty of His Father, and He loved Him with a perfect love, whence sprung that lively and ardent zeal which animated Him. Ah! If we felt the same sentiments of respect and love for God, how ardent, wise, enlightened and efficacious would not our zeal be. Zeal which has no guiding principle save passion, which is only produced by an untamed and critical humour, by a restless and effervescing temperament, by anger, antipathy, and the hatred of our neighbour, by pride, and the desire to make ourselves of importance; such a zeal betrays itself, makes itself despised, and leads those who are guilty of it into rebellion; but the zeal which comes from God, is full of decorum in its movements, of holiness in its words, of gravity in its commands, and of authority and majesty in the person who

is filled with it. Nothing can resist, and every thing yields to such a zeal.

SECOND POINT.

Jesus answers the Jews who complain of His severity.

1. Examine the question which the Jews put to Him. *Then answered the Jews, and said unto Him, What sign shewest Thou unto us, seeing that Thou doest these things ?* The Jews had doubtless some authority in the temple, as the priests, the scribes, the Levites. Their question announces at least the existence of much animosity, envy, and unbelief in them. In order to remedy, say they, public abuses, it is necessary to have public authority, or an extraordinary mission from heaven: shew us then your power, and the proofs of a legitimate authority, which should justify that which you have just done: or if you are a prophet sent from God, give a proof of your mission by doing here some wonders: give us a sign of your mission by working some miracle. But was not the action which Jesus had just performed, in itself a sensible sign of His divine power, and a proof of His authority? Four unlearned Galileans, disciples of Jesus Christ, had but now acknowledged the fulfilment of a prophecy which regarded the Messiah: and these wise men at Jerusalem see nothing in it, but even take offence at it. But if they need another proof, another sign, it need not necessarily be a miracle. Did not the testimony of S. John Baptist, of whom they had heard speak, bear sufficient witness in favour of Jesus Christ? When they themselves sent messengers to the saintly forerunner, they were inclined, they said then, to believe in him, if he called himself the Messiah; now was not John still more worthy of belief, if he gave that title to another, and did not every one know that that other was Christ? Why then now require a miracle? But lastly, if needs be that there should be one, was not the success of the action, which Jesus had just performed, in itself, one! How should

a single man, unless he came with authority from God, not only undertake, but carry out a similar project, without, amongst so many persons interested in opposing themselves to it, any one daring to speak and defend himself? Why should all these sellers and these money changers suffer themselves to be thus treated, if they had not felt the impress of the Divinity which was in Jesus Christ? Was it not a great miracle, says S. Jerome, that a single Man, Who did not appear to be invested with any authority, should have performed without the least resistance what Jesus Christ had just accomplished. It must therefore have been, adds this father, that a Heavenly fire shone forth at that time from His eyes, and that the divine Majesty was visible on His forehead. But if they needed yet further miracles, were these Jews ignorant how many Jesus Christ had wrought in Galilee? Were not those who had witnessed them, at that moment at Jerusalem in order to keep the Passover? Had they not related them to them? Are they all madmen or knaves? But hardened as you are, Jesus will do the like at Jerusalem; you will see, and you will not believe. When the heart is carried away by passion, nothing suffices to it. According to unbelievers, it were necessary, that God should work a miracle for each one of them in particular, and that He should do it in the manner, and in the way in which they should prescribe for Him. Ah! It is not thus that we should deal with the Creator of the Universe. He cannot receive the commands of His creatures. His ways are higher, more majestic, more worthy of Himself, and more independent. He grants no miracles to those whom incredulity or malignity lead to ask them, because with such dispositions they are asked for, not in order that a person may become convinced, but in order that he may fight against them.

2. Observe what was the reply of Jesus, and in what sense the Jews received it. *Jesus answered and said unto them, Destroy this temple, and in three days I will raise it up. Then said the Jews, Forty and six*

years was this temple in building, and wilt Thou rear it up in three days? See what still are now a days, our freethinkers, our wits, who, in things which regard religion, take everything in a coarse and purely material meaning. What! Do Jews, who prided themselves upon their knowledge and who were accustomed to figures of speech, enigmas, parables, suspect nought similar hidden in the reply of Jesus! The more the matter appeared impossible to them, the more ought they to have felt that the words of the answer were not intended to be taken in their proper sense. They should then have asked of Him who gave the answer, in what sense He intended it, or if they dared not make such a demand of Him, they should have waited, as did the Apostles, till time should draw back the veil from the mystery, and give the explanation of it. Thus should we act on all occasions when we find any obscurity in Holy Scripture, in the mysteries of our holy Faith, in God's dealings with mankind. Let us not be less faithful to Jesus Christ, nor less submissive to His Church. God has His own appointed moments, and time will reveal all to us. But these learned men, proud of their wisdom, find the mode of action too humble for them. They begin by reasoning on the material temple, where they were, in calculating how much time had been spent in constructing it, and in putting it into the state in which it was, in deciding that the words of Jesus Christ contained a manifest contradiction, and finally, they withdraw, yet more incredulous than they had come. A just punishment for their pride, and wilful blindness. *But Jesus spake of the temple of His Body*, of that divine Body which the Jews would fasten to the Cross, which should afterwards be buried, and which was to rise again three days afterwards. O adorable Body! Thou art in reality the true Temple of God; it is in Thee that dwelleth all the fulness of Divinity, it is by Thee that we have access to God, that we are united to Him, by receiving Thee in the divine Sacrament of Thy Body and Blood.

3. Consider what effect the reply of Jesus produced in the time to come. This reply was a prediction by which the Saviour said to the Jews under a figure, As you sacrifice the Temple of My Father to your avarice, so you will sacrifice My Body to your envy. But what will happen? The same power which has just effected that which causes you scandal and confusion, will work hereafter a last wonder which you will not be able to understand, and under the weight of which you will be forced to succumb. This wonder is the Resurrection of My Body, which will take place in the three days which will follow the destruction which you will have accomplished; then I shall be the Conqueror of death, and My Resurrection will perfectly establish the truth of My mission. This prediction had its effect at the time appointed, that is to say, *when He was risen from the dead; His disciples remembered that He had said this unto them: and they believed the Scripture, and the word which Jesus had said.* It was thus that the same words blinded the unteachable Jews, and caused the death of Jesus, consoled the disciples of this divine Saviour, strengthened their faith, when they beheld its accomplishment, and converted the Gentiles, and convinced them of the Divinity of the Messiah. It is thus, O Divine Wisdom, that, by a single word, Thou dost punish Thine enemies, dost give Thyself up for us, dost form Thy Church, and comfort those who believe in Thee.

THIRD POINT.

Jesus reads the depths of their hearts.

1. He knows those who do not believe in Him. *Now when He was in Jerusalem at the passover, in the feast day, many believed in His Name, when they saw the miracles which He did.* Jesus does not refuse to give to this great concourse of people, who were then at Jerusalem this great proof of His mission; the Jews only demanded one miracle of Him, He works many and

such mighty ones, that many believed in Him. Alas! why do they not all believe? It was the effect alone of their obstinacy. Jesus knew them; He knows also now all those who do not believe in Him; He alone knows how far each of them is guilty, because He alone knows the measure of grace and of light to which each has resisted. But without examining how far they are guilty, a matter which does not concern us, let us content ourselves with pitying them, and praying for them, and let us consider how far we ourselves are guilty, if we have the misery of being of the number of those who do not believe.

2. Jesus knows those who believe in Him. *Many believed in His Name. But Jesus did not commit Himself unto them, because He knew all men.* In the hearts of these fickle and changeable Jews, whom the admiration of the miracles which Jesus had worked had drawn around Him, more than their love for truth or their respect for His Person, the Saviour read clearly that one day they would with loud voices require His Blood, and that there was not any safety for Him amongst them. He knew that those men, who appeared then so devoted to Him, and who believed in Him, were surrounded by those who were unbelievers, and that they had not, for the greater part, a faith sufficiently firm to resist the example, the authority, the artifices, or the calumnies of the latter; thus He resolved not to trust Himself to the affection which they were now shewing for Him, nor to the sudden admiration with which He beheld them possessed. We believe in Jesus, and in certain seasons we make professions of feelings of penitence which are edifying to others; but alas! can Jesus count upon us, can He trust in our promises? Does He see in us that generous determination to observe in all things His commandments, to surmount all difficulties, to overcome all temptations, to despise all human respect; to resist all evil examples, to avoid all that may give scandal, and to flee from all occasions of offence? Does He not see, on the contrary, in the

greater number amongst ourselves, believers without faith, hearts without piety, wills without actions, or at least a faith so feeble and so languishing, that sooner or later, it succumbs, and follows the stream, the multitude, the ways of the world?

3. Jesus knows man in Himself, and without the witness of any one. *And He needed not that any should testify of man; for He knew what was in man.* How blind the witness of men is! they can only think, judge, speak and bear witness of others by external appearances, and what more deceptive is there? These appearances moreover, which ought only to be turned into good by charity, are they not far oftener turned into evil through malice? Ah! do not let us judge our neighbours by the testimony of men; let us believe charitably what is said of them, and let us be edified by it; but do not let us lend any faith to the evil that is spoken of them. If it is our duty to make enquiries respecting any one, let us receive the witness of others only with the precautions which charity, prudence, and justice demand, and let us never judge others without seeking for enlightenment from Him Who alone needeth not that any should testify of man. Lastly, let us account the opinions and the words of others with regard to ourselves as of little importance. We ought neither to flatter ourselves with the favourable opinion which some entertain of us, nor disquiet ourselves with regard to what others may think or say against us; it is neither by the witness of our friends, nor that of our enemies that God knows and judges us. We ought to find in the good that is spoken of us, a subject for self-humiliation, and in the evil that is said of us, wherewithal to gain a better knowledge of ourselves. As to the rest, let us refer all to Him Who knows and sees what is in us, and do not let us seek to merit the approbation of any one save His.

Prayer. Alas! Lord, what have I done when I have sought the esteem of men? I have tried to mislead them, without remembering that I was misleading myself, and that I could not escape from the penetration and severity of Thy judgement. What have I done when I have distressed myself at the contempt of men? I have forgotten that I deserved Thine only, and that their contempt suffered for love of Thee, would serve to expiate my sins, and to purify me in Thine eyes. Be then, O Jesus! the only witness of my life, Whose contempt alone I fear, and Whose favour alone I seek for. Amen.

Meditation XXXVII.

CONVERSATION OF JESUS WITH NICODEMUS.

This conversation teaches us that there are obstacles to faith, which are difficult to overcome, over which Nicodemus triumphed: 1. obstacles on the part of the world, 2. obstacles on the part of the mind, 3. obstacles on the part of the heart. S. John iii. 1-22.

FIRST POINT.

Obstacles on the part of the world which Nicodemus overcame.

There was a man of the Pharisees, named Nicodemus, a ruler of the Jews: the same came to Jesus by night, and said unto Him, Rabbi, we know that Thou art a teacher come from God: for no man can do these miracles that Thou doest, except God be with him. How many obstacles to faith and piety are there not still to be met with in the world, over which Nicodemus triumphed?

1. His connection with an accredited party. Nicodemus was of the sect of the Pharisees. This sect made a profession of strict morality, and of a vigorous observance of the law: but, at the same time, they were superstitious, hypocritical, proud, and indocile; they had already shown their hatred to the forerunner, and did not seek to conceal the aversion they felt towards Jesus Christ. How needful it is to consider well with what class of persons we cast in our lot, and with whom we associate in our daily life!

2. *The elevation of distinguished rank.* Nicodemus was one of those who were called princes amongst the Jews, or heads of families, members of the sovereign council of the nation. The display and wealth which accompany noble birth, and the honours and dignities of the period, are difficult to reconcile with the humility, which forms the basis of Christianity. Placed in a high position, it is a great temptation to consider it an humiliation to think as do others in a lower station, to be affected by what affects them, to profess one common religion with them.

3. *The respect due to advanced years.* The age to which Nicodemus had attained made it difficult for him to listen to the instructions of one, who was not yet supposed to have reached the age of *forty years.* The greater the consideration and the authority which our age entitles us to, the more is our conduct observed, and our changes of opinion criticized, and the less have we often the moral courage to despise the judgements of men, and to overcome our own prejudices : let us then beware not to put off to a time so uncertain, and to advanced life, the execution of the good desires which are put into our minds from above. How difficult it is at that time of life, to begin to make ourselves acquainted with the doctrines and duties of our religion, and to undertake to change our hearts, and turn ourselves to a new life especially when our youth has been passed in license, and our minds have not been filled with aught else save doubts and insipid railleries on religion. Nicodemus was not one of such : but whilst studying the law he had not yet mastered the spirit of it. These obstacles of which we have just spoken were great, but Nicodemus overcame them nevertheless : he came to Jesus, but not without shewing some hesitation. He had an upright heart, and notwithstanding his prejudices, he had been impressed by the wonders which Jesus had worked. How difficult it was in truth, to prevent being impressed by them ! And how could the Jews of those days, and the unbelievers of to-day withstand the splendour of

those miracles, without falling at the feet of Jesus Christ? Nicodemus comes then to find the Saviour, but by night. O fear of the world! O human respect! How many conversions have you not hindered, how many souls have you not lost! Can it be, O Divine Wisdom, that any one dares not to speak to Thee openly, and declare himself publicly on Thy side! Shall one of the great men of this world think himself dishonoured, O King of Glory! if he is found conversing with Thee and receiving instruction from Thee? O Jerusalem, who dost thus lead captive thy inhabitants! What a flood of crimes and afterwards of shame and disgrace art thou not about to draw down upon thyself! Nicodemus shews still more weakness in his feelings than in his actions. *Rabbi,* he says in private to Jesus, *we know that Thou art a teacher come from God: for no man can do these miracles that Thou doest except God be with him.* Here are the beginnings of an acknowledgement which Nicodemus renders to the Divinity of Jesus, but it is not a decided avowal. How far greater was the faith of the first disciples of the Saviour before they had witnessed any miracle wrought by Him! Andrew says to his brother, *We have found the Messias.* Philip says to Nathanael: *We have found Him, of whom Moses in the law, and the prophets, did write, Jesus of Nazareth.* Nathanael, upon one word which Jesus speaks to him, cries out, *Rabbi, Thou art the Son of God.* To this, they were led by the witness of John, and the circumstances of the time which had been marked out by the prophets for the coming of the Messias; and yet this great man, this doctor of the law, this Pharisee, who ought to be so far better instructed than the disciples, and who, moreover had been witness of so many miracles, cannot attain to the same faith. But Jesus does not nevertheless discourage him: He has compassion on his weakness, He does not disdain his advances, He graciously approves his first efforts, He receives them with goodness, and even instructs him in the highest mysteries in a manner proportioned to his powers, but without sparing too much his prejudices and his weakness. Do not let us then despair, whatever obstacles we may find in the way of our salvation: let us hasten to Jesus; however feeble we may be, let us lay before Him our weakness, and let us make some efforts; He is Goodness itself, He will receive us, will strengthen us and will instruct us.

SECOND POINT.

Obstacles which arise on the part of the mind, and from which Nicodemus is set free.

1. First obstacle to faith; a strong minded spirit which materialises every thing, and believes nothing. *Jesus answered and said unto him, Verily, verily, I say unto thee, Except a man be born of water and of the Spirit, he cannot enter into the Kingdom of God. Nicodemus saith unto him, How can a man be born when he is old? Can he enter the second time into his mother's womb, and be born?* The Pharisee and doctor, taking the words of the Saviour in a literal and material sense, and without asking any explanation of them, began himself to explain what would be necessary in order to receive this second birth of which Jesus had spoken to him. According to him, it would have been necessary, that a man, formed and even old, should enter again into his mother's womb, and be born again a second time; whence he drew the conclusion, though without expressing it in words, but at the same time making it quite sufficiently evident, that the thing was impossible, and implied a contradiction. Such are your strong-minded men: they are filled with low and grovelling ideas, they have no ideas beyond those of matter, they see only prejudices, in virtue and vice; only policy, in the Church; only chance, in the order of the universe; only the present century, in the designs of Creation; whence they conclude that all that they are told of any thing nobler and more elevated, is repugnant to common sense, and is impossible. Jesus, Who beheld this error of Nicodemus, and Who willed to make use of it to lead

to his conversion, answered him: *Verily, verily, I say unto thee, Except a man be born of water and of the Spirit, he cannot enter into the Kingdom of God. That which is born of the flesh is flesh: and that which is born of the Spirit, is spirit. Marvel not that I said unto thee, Ye must be born again.* As if Jesus had said to him: Man must be born again, not from his mother's womb, but by water and by the Holy Spirit: and as the first birth, which comes of the flesh, is carnal and fleshly, so in the same way, the second birth, which comes of the Holy Spirit, gives a spiritual, holy, and divine life. Do not be astonished at that which I have told you, that a second birth is necessary in order to enter the kingdom of God: I speak to you of a new and spiritual regeneration, which raises you above the law of Moses, far more than that law raises you above that of nature. We have received it, that second birth of water and of the Holy Spirit, when we were admitted into Christ's Church, and were made children of God: let us thank the Lord for so great a blessing. We have in us two lives; the first, which we have received from the first Adam, an earthly life, and a life of sin; the second, which we have received from the second Adam, from Jesus Christ, by the operation of His Holy Spirit: a heavenly life, an inward life, a life of retirement and of self-mortification, a life of meditation and prayer, a life of union with God, a life of faith, of hope, and of love. Which of these two lives are we living? Alas! we hardly even know what the second life is.

2. Second obstacle to faith: a presumptuous spirit which demands a reason for everything, and which apprehends nothing. Nicodemus acknowledges his error, but yet many difficulties remain to him, and he is far removed from the perfect submission which faith requires. Jesus, in order to calm his mind as to the possibility of this second birth, and of this second life, although invisible, makes this comparison to him [a], and

---

[a] This comparison is so much the more forcible and energetic, in that in the original language, the same word signifies *wind* and *spirit*.

says to him: *the wind bloweth where it listeth;* the wind blows without any human power being able either to raise it, or to calm it, to direct it, or to stop it; *and thou hearest the sound thereof,* you feel the effects of it; you know that it exists; nevertheless, you do not see it; *thou canst not tell whence it cometh,* and where it began, nor *whither it goeth;* and whither it will end: *so is every one that is born of the Spirit.* As if He had said to him: This recognition of which I am speaking to you, which is effected by the operation of the Holy Spirit, is not seen by the eyes of man, but it is none the less real. This wind which is not seen, but of which the sound is heard, and of which the effects are seen, is an image of the Holy Spirit, Whose workings within the hearts of men are not seen, but Who bloweth where He wills, and as He wills; but Who does not act within, without the effects being visible without. Nothing could be better chosen than this figure, than this example. Amongst all the phenomena of nature, the wind, by its irregularity, its strength, and its invisibility, is one of the fittest to set forth the power of God, the incomprehensibility of His words, and to make men feel their weakness and their dependence. The example was unanswerable to any one who had desired only to believe: but Nicodemus wished to comprehend this mystery, and he answered, *How can these things be?* How? Why? These are the fatal shoals against which at all times presumption has dashed itself, and become shipwrecked. I cannot believe, says the infidel, that which I do not understand. Impostor, you believe well, without understanding them, the phenomena of nature, on the witness of your senses, and yet you can believe nothing on the witness of Him, Who has created nature, and endowed you with your powers of mind! You believe a thousand absurdities which your systems inculcate, and believe them on the authority of those who relate them to you, although they do not understand them any better than you do, and although they do not give you any proofs; and you will

not believe on the authority of the only Son of God,
Who has beheld that which He announces to you, and
Who has proved His mission by the most striking miracles!
Begin by believing; this path is the surest, the
most worthy of the greatness of your God, and the most
proportioned to your weakness. The philosopher even
believes the phenomenon which he endeavours to understand,
and into the principles and causes of which he
searches, and if sometimes God permits the truth of His
mysteries to become evident, and discloses the economy
of His dispensations, and their beauty, it is to the humble
and submissive heart, who believes in them, and not
to the presumptuous spirit, who, before believing in
them, requires an explanation of them.

3. Third obstacle to faith: an imperious spirit which
dogmatises over everything, and yet knows nothing.
There was besides in Nicodemus, yet the remains of pharasaical
pride which must needs be humiliated. Jesus
had led His disciple on to the point, when it was necessary
for him to suffer this process, that this dross might
be purged away. *Art thou a master in Israel*, He says
to him, *and knowest not these things? Verily, verily,
I say unto thee, We speak that we do know, and testify
that we have seen; and ye receive not our witness.
If I have told you earthly things, and ye believe not,
how shall ye believe if I tell you of heavenly things?*
Jesus does not reproach Nicodemus with not comprehending,
but with not knowing, and not believing. He
ought to have known that an upright spirit, and a renewed
spirit, is often spoken of in Holy Scripture: as
also of a sincere heart, created anew, and of pure water
which would wash away all the stains of our sin. We
cannot comprehend the mysteries of our faith, but we
ought to know them, to believe them, and to adore them
in silence. If the duty of instructing others falls to our
lot, we should moreover have a clear and distinct acquaintance
with them: we should study what are the expressions
which Holy Scripture makes use of respecting them,
in what terms the early Fathers speak of them, in what

sense the words of Holy Scriptures are to be taken, what errors respecting the mysteries have been condemned by the Councils of the Church. But pride oversteps all limits, and joins the extremity of daring to a profound ignorance. It speaks on all subjects, and is instructed in none. It is ignorant of even the first elements of Christian doctrine and decides even the most knotty questions. Are we not ourselves of that number? Do we never ignore that we are obliged to teach, or do we not mix ourselves up with teaching that which we ought not to know, or which we are in reality ignorant of? If the reproach made to Nicodemus was mortifying, it was salutary: the humbled Pharisee does not reply further: his silence was the proof of his teachableness, and by this teachableness he merited that Jesus should continue to reveal to him the sublimest mysteries, and that He should conclude the conversation by words of comfort and consolation.

THIRD POINT.

Obstacles on the part of the heart, from which Nicodemus was preserved.

Jesus Christ Himself points out here these obstacles, and sets forth that there are amongst men those who flee from the light, others who prefer darkness to light, and lastly others, who come to the light.

1. *There are those who flee from the light.* *And this is the condemnation,* says Christ, *that light is come into the world, and men loved darkness rather than light.* Jesus is the Light, Christianity is a religion of light, the Gospel is a law of light. The Catholic Faith teaches us what we have to fear or to hope for in the life to come, and what we have to flee from or to seek for in this life. All the other false religions, all other sects, all the systems of unbelievers are but darkness. Light is come into the world; it shines there still on all sides; if there are so few true believers, it is not for want of convincing proofs and of knowledge: the fault lies in the heart, and in the will. Men have loved

darkness better than light; they had freely preferred darkness to light, and this is the cause of their condemnation. Ah how sinful this preference is in the sight of God! How often have I not been guilty of it!

2. *There are some who prefer darkness to light; and why?* Because their deeds are evil. *For every one that doeth evil,* Jesus saith, *hateth the light, neither cometh to the light, lest his deeds should be reproved.* What is then the cause of so wrongful a preference? In the greater number, it is their deeds, their sins, and their predilection for iniquity, for shameful deeds, deeds of darkness. We hate, and put away from us an irksome light which reproaches us with them. Nature itself teaches us to hide them from the eyes of men: we seek to conceal them from ourselves, whether by excusing them, or by disowning the law which forbids them, or which requires of us a humble and sincere acknowledgement of them, and we imagine to ourselves, that by believing nothing, we shall hide them from the knowledge of God Himself, and escape from the rigour of His justice. Do not let us be surprised to see so many impious persons who reject the faith, so many deserters who abandon it: they are given up to deeds of darkness; therefore they flee from the light. In vain do unbelievers cry out against this judgement, which proceeds from the lips of truth itself, and notwithstanding their hypocritical discourses, the blasphemies with which their books are filled confirm it but too well. Let us then fear and flee from sin, which will at length, and by degrees, extinguish in us all the light of faith.

3. *There are those who come to the light. But he that doeth truth cometh to the light, that his deeds may be made manifest, that they are wrought in God.* Those who act according to the truth, that is to say, those who do what is right, or who repent and confess the evil which they have done, they love the light. He, whom vice has not corrupted, and who has followed the law of God, engraven in all our hearts, or who, having followed his passions, groans under the weight of his sins, and

expiates them as far as he can, receives with joy the light of the Gospel, because, being at peace with his conscience, he is so with God. Do we not feel this ourselves, when we draw near to God with confidence, when we have striven to follow holily His laws, obeyed His inspirations, resisted our passions, and kept our resolutions? But if, on the contrary, our conscience reproaches us, if we feel ourselves at a distance from God, do we not then find a difficulty in placing ourselves in His presence, and in performing our accustomed devotional exercises? In this state, let us return quickly into the paths of virtue, let us confess our faults, let us humble ourselves, let us seek the light which will make us know our faults, and we shall regain in our humiliation the peace and the confidence which we have lost. Nicodemus was not one of these corrupted souls, whose interest it is to hate and to flee from the light; he had the consolation of knowing himself to be one of those of whom our Saviour spoke, as coming to the light that their deeds might be made manifest. He rejoiced to have found the Saviour, and he remained constantly attached to Him. If he seemed to hold back in some measure during the life time of the Saviour, he came forward more boldly after His death, and after the descent of the Holy Ghost, when the profession of the faith became as necessary to salvation as faith itself.

Prayer. Suffer not, O Saviour, that through the multitude of my sins, I should fall into the unbelief of those impious men, which makes them love their darkness, and fear the light. Give me, oh my Saviour! that lively faith which makes men to hate darkness, to seek, to find, and to follow Thy light. I believe, oh my Lord! in Thy incomprehensible mysteries! I ask for no further guarantee than Thy word in order to believe them. Who am I that I should search out their depths? Increase my faith, Lord: give me grace to live according to my faith, in order that I may behold in Heaven, that which I can only believe and adore on earth. Amen.

Meditation XXXVIII.

OF THE OTHER MYSTERIES WHICH JESUS REVEALS TO NICODEMUS.

These mysteries are, 1. the divinity of Jesus Christ, the foundation of our faith, 2. the death of Jesus Christ, the principle of our hope, 3. the love of God towards men, the motive of our love toward Him. S. John iii. 13-18.

FIRST POINT.

Of the divinity of Jesus Christ, the foundation of our faith.

In order to complete the submission of the mind of Nicodemus, and to lead him to a perfect faith, Our Lord after having said; If you do not believe that which I have told you of the spiritual regeneration which takes place on earth, and of which I have given you a palpable example, how would you believe Me, if I should reveal to you that which takes place in the bosom of God, if I should discover to you the secrets of Heaven, with which earth has not yet been favoured? Jesus added: *And no man hath ascended up to Heaven, but He that came down from Heaven even the Son of man which is in Heaven,* as if He had said to him, And no one can teach you these heavenly truths, but the First-born among men: *for no man hath ascended up to Heaven* in order to search out there the depths of the things of God, *but He that came down from Heaven,* for the instruction and salvation of the world, and Who, whilst conversing and living on the earth, was yet at the same time actually also *in Heaven.*

1. By these words, the Saviour teaches us how He ascended up to Heaven. By the Heaven, which we regard as the throne of God, Jesus means the bosom itself of Divinity, that is to say the Three Divine Persons Who, really distinct amongst Themselves, have but

one and the same Nature, and are but One God. It is there, in the bosom of Divinity, where, as Son of man, Jesus ascended, when, by His Incarnation, His sacred humanity, conceived in the Womb of the Virgin by the operation of the Holy Ghost, was united to the Word of God in unity of Person. From that moment, in Jesus Christ, the only Son of God, man became God, and God became Man: from that moment the sacred Soul of Jesus Christ was admitted to the intuitive vision of God, and to all the counsels of His wisdom in a manner which has never been accorded to any other creature, and It received all the grace, all the knowledge, all the power which were suited to His dignity as Son of God, and to His rank as Master, Saviour, and Judge of the universe.

2. By these words, Jesus teaches us how He came down from heaven. He came down from thence by His Incarnation, when that Divine Word was made flesh, and, clothed with our flesh, dwelt among us. He came down from thence, because His sacred humanity, although substantially united to the Word, did not cease to be on the earth, to live there, to converse there with men, and that this Man Who was beheld on the earth, was none other than the Word of God, Who had become man by taking upon the earth a body and soul like ourselves.

3. By these words, Jesus teaches us how He is still in heaven. He was there when He was holding this discourse, and during all the time that He shewed Himself on the earth, because the Word in becoming man, had come forth from the bosom of the Father without leaving it, had come down from heaven without ceasing to be in heaven. He was there, because, although His sacred humanity was on the earth, It was always substantially and inseparably united to the Word, the second Person of the Holy Trinity, and His soul enjoyed unceasingly the clear vision of God. Such is therefore He, Who is the Author and Finisher of our faith. Do we err in believing on His word all that He has revealed to us,

and in placing our whole trust in Him? Ought we not to be ready, like the martyrs, to shed our blood for the truths which He has taught us? Let unbelievers, who delight to compare our mysteries and our rites to the fables and superstitions of idolaters, go then up to their source; let them enquire on what foundations their faith and their practices rest, and let them compare their answer with that which makes the foundation of our faith. Since His Ascension, Jesus Christ sitteth always at the Right Hand of God His Father, whence He will only come down again at the last day to judge the quick and the dead. We say in truth that He comes down upon our altars in the Divine Eucharist, but it is by multiplying His Presence there, and not by leaving heaven.

SECOND POINT.

Of the death of Jesus, the principle of our life.

1. Of the prophecy of His death. Jesus announces it. *And as Moses,* He says to Nicodemus, *lifted up the serpent in the wilderness, even so must the Son of man be lifted up.* I. The death of Jesus had been foretold, announced and prefigured by the law-giver of the Jewish nation. The Israelites, in the wilderness, having been bitten by a number of serpents, in punishment for their sins, Moses, by the command of God, set up a brazen serpent, and put it upon a pole, and when the children of Israel looked upon it, they were healed of their wounds. A type of Jesus Christ raised upon the Cross in order to deliver us from "the old serpent, called the Devil," (Rev. xii. 9.) and from sin. 2. The death of Jesus Christ had been predicted in its minutest detail by the prophets. Jesus, in His death as in His life, is the faithful and literal accomplishment of the law and the prophets. 3. This death of Jesus Christ was announced by His forerunner, when he said, *Behold the Lamb of God, Which takest away the sins of the world.* 4. Lastly, it was foretold by Jesus Christ Himself. From the first journey which He took to Jerusalem, He

announced His death in public, and in private, in the temple and in the house, by day and by night. It is this which He told the Jews who were assembled around Him in the temple, adding to it the prophecy of His resurrection after three days. He speaks of it also here, and points out minutely to Nicodemus the manner of His death, which should be the death on the Cross, for the salvation of men. He will foretell it again bye and bye, He will mark out the circumstances that will attend it, and He will name the authors of it. A death thus foretold, thus suffered, and for so noble an end, is it an act of feebleness? Ought it to be to the Jews an offence and to the Gentiles foolishness? Ought it not rather to be to both an object of admiration, of love, of gratitude, and the principle of a solid hope, and of the most entire confidence?

2. Of the necessity of this death. Jesus sets it forth *So must the Son of man be lifted up.* It must needs be that the malice, the disbelief of His own people should lift Him up on high on the Cross, and that He should die there. There is a *must* on the side of God, on the side of men, on the side of Jesus Christ Himself. On the side of God: He could without doubt have saved mankind in several other ways, but He has chosen and fore-ordained this one, because no other manner of saving man would have so fully repaid the outrage which sin had done to Him: no other would have so clearly set forth His greatness, His justice, His lowliness, and the hatred which He bears to sin; none other would have manifested so clearly His goodness and His mercy; none other would have made His glory and His wisdom shine forth so much, since, in this death alone, He has been able to satisfy the claims of His justice, and to temper them with the favours of His infinite mercy. There is a *must* on the side of men. This death was the fittest means to make them know the greatness of God, the enormity of sin, and the terrible punishment which it deserves, in order to make them understand the necessity laid upon them to crucify themselves, and to animate

them to do so courageously after the example of their Saviour: in order to knit them closely to God and their Redeemer by the bonds of the most perfect confidence, of the most lively gratitude, and of the tenderest love. Finally, there is a *must* on the side of Jesus Christ. A death so ignominious and so painful could alone satisfy the infinite love which He bore to His Father, and the ardent desire which He had to redeem us in the most complete manner and in the way which would glorify God the most, and be of the greatest service to us. This death alone could procure for Him that glory with which His Father willed to crown Him, by establishing Him as the Mediator between Himself and mankind. Oh what glory for this Divine Saviour thus to have reconciled heaven and earth, and to have done so in so noble and generous a way! If the Spirit of Jesus Christ was in us, we should understand that it *must* be, that it is necessary, that it is great, useful, and glorious to us, that we also should be crucified with Him. This truth would keep us from many complaints, would stifle in us many regrets and murmurs, and would change them into joy and thanksgivings.

3. Of the fruits of this death: Jesus foretells them, *That whosoever believeth in Him should not perish, but have everlasting life.* The first fruit then of this death is to save us from perishing by delivering us from the eternal damnation which we have brought upon ourselves by the sin of our first parent, and by our own. The second is to have gained for us eternal life, with all the graces and help necessary to attain to it. O lovers of life! why do ye neglect a life which is eternal, in order to attach yourselves to a perishable and mortal life? Sinners bowed down under the enormous weight of numberless sins, why will ye persist in perishing? Lift your eyes, behold Jesus on the Cross; His death has made satisfaction for you, ye will not perish, ye will live eternally. Believe only in Him, apply to yourselves the merits of His Blood, by making use of the means of grace which He has appointed. Believe

in Him, listen to Him as your Master, obey Him as your Lord, imitate Him as your Example, trust yourselves in His Hands as in those of your Saviour. Believe in Him and fear nothing. Believe in Him, and look forward with assurance of hope to the life eternal which He promises you, and which He has gained for you by His death. Christian souls, why these useless anxieties, which, without making you any holier, only disturb you and drive you away from your Deliverer? Your fears dishonour Him, your mistrust of Him is an outrage to Him. After having done all that is in your power, if you give yourselves up to fears and alarms, it is not because you have sinned, it is because you are wanting in faith.

THIRD POINT.

Of the love of God towards men, the motive of our love towards Him.

For God, our Saviour continues, *so loved the world that He gave His only begotten Son that whosoever believeth in Him should not perish, but have everlasting life.*

1. Consider that God has given us, in the person of His only Son, the object of His tenderness and His affection. If God could have given us all His Angels, and the entire universe, what parallel between these gifts, and that which He has bestowed upon us in the Person of Jesus Christ? In giving us His only Son, He has given us all things. This Son is the only heir of His Father. The Father, in giving Him to us, knew well that this liberal and generous Heir would make us partakers in His inheritance, and it is with this purpose that He gave Him to us. God, in giving Him to us has given us heaven, and Divinity Itself, of which this well-beloved Son has made us partakers, by procuring for us the adoption of children of God. What sublime truths! what goodness, what love! O God! if I do not belong to Thee entirely by the blessing of my creation,

what can I render Thee for the blessing of my redemption, and of such a redemption!

2. Observe to whom God has given His Son. To the world, to the children of a prevaricating father, prevaricators themselves, and stained with a thousand crimes: to a world, rebellious against its Lord, an enemy to its Benefactor, given up to idolatry, and all the abominations which are the consequences of it. It is not thus that Thou hast dealt, O my God! with the rebel angels. Hardly had they completed their disobedience, than for one single act of rebellion, without regard to their numbers, to the excellency of their nature, to the great evils which their despair would cause, to the great good which their conversion might have effected, Thou didst cast them down out of the height of Heaven down to everlasting Hell. What hindered Thee to treat us with the same severity? And where should we be, if Thou hadst so done? But instead of a punishment so justly merited, Thou gavest us Thine only Son to save us, and Thou didst give Him up to die for us all without exception.

3. Examine how God has given us His Son. Entirely. The gift which God made to us is without reserve. Jesus has been given wholly to us, His graces, His merits, His life, His labours, His Blood, His death, His glory, even His divinity. Jesus is our King, in order to govern us, our Master, in order to teach us, our Guide, in order to lead us, our Chief, in order to encourage us. Jesus is our Strength, our Light, our Consolation, our Joy, our Life. Jesus in the cradle has made Himself our Example, on the Cross, our Ransom, on the Altar, our Victim, at the Holy Table, our Food, and in Heaven our Reward. O divine, infinite, incomprehensible love!

4. Meditate to what end God has given us His Son. In order to save us, and to make us enjoy in Heaven an eternal happiness, and an eternal life. *For God*, says Jesus, *sent not His Son into the world to condemn the world; but that the world through Him might be saved. He that believeth on Him is not condemned; but he that believeth not is condemned already, be-*

cause he believeth not in the only Son of God. God has not sent His Son into the world to judge, to condemn and to punish it, as it deserved, but to save it. He that believes in Him is delivered from condemnation and has nothing to fear; but he that refuses to believe has no need of being condemned; he is so already and he lives in his condemnation, because he will not acknowedge the Only Son of God Who alone could deliver him from it. This new iniquity is the greatest of all and fills up the measure of the others.

Prayer. O my God, let me not be of the number of these ungrateful ones. Ah! grant me rather by the readiness, zeal and warmth of my heart to repair their outrages against Thy divine love. Grant, that by works animated by charity, fulfilled in Thee and for Thee, I may attain at last to possess Thee. I own myself a sinner, and the chiefest of all sinners; but, however guilty I be, I cast myself with confidence into Thy arms. The price of Thy death is boundless and far above my offences. I hope in Thee, O Jesus! increase my hope; I believe in Thee, O my adorable Saviour! increase my faith; I love Thee, O my Divine Redeemer! increase my love, that I may see Thee and love Thee eternally in heaven. Amen.

Meditation XXXIX.

THIRD AND LAST WITNESS OF JESUS CHRIST GIVEN TO HIS DISCIPLES.

Third and last witness of Jesus Christ given to his disciples.
S. John iii. 22—36.

After these things came Jesus and His disciples into the land of Judæa; and there He tarried with them, and baptized. And John also was baptizing in Ænon near to Salim, because there was much water there:

and they came, and were baptized. For John was not yet cast into prison. Then there arose a question between some of John's disciples and the Jews about purifying. Jesus Christ, after having won as a disciple the Jewish nobleman and scholar Nicodemus, withdrew from Jerusalem, shortly after the feast of the passover. Nevertheless He did not quit Judea, but remained some time baptizing there: although as we read He Himself baptized not, but His disciples. S. John the Baptist was no longer at Bethany, in the neighbourhood of the Jordan: the opposition of the scribes and the pharisees had apparently forced him to take refuge in Galilee, and here he was living at this time, and baptizing in a town which was under the jurisdiction of Herod the tetrarch, from whom he had hitherto received no ill treatment.

After a while disputes arose between some of the Jews and some disciples of S. John the Baptist concerning the administration of Baptism by Jesus Christ. These Jews defended the Baptism of Jesus Christ: they had now been witnesses of it for some time, and it may be, had been participators of it themselves: the disciples of John on the other hand were warm in the defence of their master's baptism, fearing that they were about to see the decline of his ministry through the disaffection which seemed likely to spring from this new administration of the rite. Burning with feelings of jealousy they hurried to the Baptist that they might pour out their grievances. Let us consider 1. these complaints which were carried by the disciples of John the Baptist to him, 2. the answer which he made to them.

FIRST POINT.

Complaints made by the disciples of S. John the Baptist to him.

These complaints were on three points: the person of Jesus Christ: His Baptism: and His disciples.

1. The person of Jesus Christ. These jealous disci-

ples approach S. John the Baptist with eager words: *Rabbi He that was with thee beyond Jordan to whom thou barest witness,* even a glorious witness, *behold the Same baptizeth;* every one is hurrying towards Him: *and all men come to Him.* We see here what are the features and the direful results of jealousy. 1. It bursts out into bitter words of complaint. Those who defended the Baptism of Jesus had made no complaints concerning John: beyond defending the cause they considered their own, they were quite quiet, and did not speak of it to the Saviour. Those who are constantly bringing accusations against others who do not retaliate, prove that they are actuated by passion and not by a sense of right. Let us beware of listening to, much less of believing any such complainers: let us try and reprove them, or at least let us hush them, by our own silence. 2. Jealousy shews itself in scorn and sarcasm. One can only speak with contempt of those whose honour is a reproach to ourselves. A jealous heart is only irritated with a brilliant and universal and well-earned reputation. And so it takes refuge in feelings of contempt which it strives to justify in itself and even to call forth in others. *Rabbi,* said the disciples of John, *He that was with thee beyond Jordan,* Who lived there as one of thy disciples, Who went about with thy disciples, *behold* He is now appearing as thine equal; nay, He is usurping thy position as Baptist, *the Same baptizeth.* These accusers do not condescend to mention Jesus by name; they appear to have entirely forgotten that He is the same Person Who so recently had healed their sick and worked divers miracles in their midst. 3. Jealousy breathes itself forth in the most malicious interpretations of the actions of others: it even turns against its opponent the very things which are really most to its advantage, or in its favour. Sometimes this is done in pure malice; sometimes, as in the case of John's disciples, it is, at best, a gross misrepresentation. *He to Whom thou barest witness.* They seemed to think that the witness which John the Baptist had borne to the Person and character of Jesus Christ only increased what they considered the wrongness and ingratitude of His conduct. Verily, a jealous spirit will see everything in a wrong light. Let the object of its envy be respected and defended by the whole world, by great and simple, by kings and peoples, by priests and nobles, even this universal testimony will only be regarded as a crime by a jealous soul. It will say, 'only ambition and cunning, intrigue and unheard of bribery can have brought about this general favour.' How truly blind is jealousy! and it is a fault by which, alas! even good people sometimes are overtaken! Let us examine our hearts in earnest upon this point, and not flatter ourselves that it does not concern us. If we find that we ourselves are the object of others' jealousy, we must not be disheartened: when we remember that even Jesus Christ allowed Himself to be the Victim of a wicked envy, how can we murmur?

2. Another subject for complaint which the disciples of John found to bring before him, was the Baptism of Jesus Christ. "*Behold*," they say, "*the Same baptizeth*." In what spirit and with what object is this report of the actions of Jesus made? It is in order to prejudice the holy Forerunner against the Messiah, in the hope that he may pronounce judgement against this new Baptism, which they consider as an unlawful usurpation of the ministry of their master. It is thus, O Jesus, that the first ordinance of the religion which Thou hast established, the first Sacrament which Thou hast instituted, has experienced the opposition of a false zeal, a zeal only born of ignorance and of envy, and in the same way Thy followers in undertaking work for Thy glory must expect to suffer opposition on all sides. Let us ever avoid criticising works of piety which we see undertaken, lest that same criticism should be brought to bear upon our own labours. Beyond all, let us, if called upon to suffer, strive to suffer patiently, without retorts, without feelings of hatred, without abusing those who are judging us unfairly. How must the heart of John

the Baptist have been filled with joy when he heard these words of his disciples "*Behold the Same baptizeth.*" With what feelings of satisfaction must he have heard these tidings, he who for so long had prophesied of this Divine Baptism; and we too should hear them with deepest feelings of emotion! They tell of good news for all mankind! At length Jesus Christ baptizeth, and in this Holy Baptism He imparts to all a new birth, He washes away all sin, He delivers us from the penalty of original sin, and He makes us children of God and inheritors of heaven.

3. The disciples of John make complaint to him concerning the number of those who followed Jesus. *All men come to Him.* They seem to consider it in the light of a schism, and they endeavour to persuade S. John that he will do well to turn to account the influence that he possesses over the minds of the people, by disabusing their minds and thus putting a stop to the evil. And now having seen the sad effects of jealousy, let us look for a moment, at the arts and devices which it employs in its cause; and first there is the weapon of exaggeration; a jealous spirit generally exaggerates to a great extent all that concerns those whom it envies, whether in the matter of position, or honour, of industry or of means, in order to establish its cause of complaint against them. A jealous soul in magnifying the advantages of his neighbour, lays the foundation for his own miserable envy, and also by this exaggeration gains a plea for finding fault with his neighbour's good fortune. Another weapon is that of deceit. The envious spirit takes the greatest care to hide the true motive of its complaint. The words it uses are *all men come to Him*, but what it means by those words is this, No one is following us. The jealous man would not venture to lay bare what it is that really troubles him: the exposure would not be to his credit: but all the while in complaining of an advantage which another has, the real complaint of his heart is that he does not possess it himself. And the third weapon is that of insinuation. The jealous soul

strives to kindle in the hearts of others the same spirit of envy which actuates itself. The truth was that these disciples of S. John the Baptist feared losing their own position and influence, but to S. John they dwell upon the fear they have that he is about to be forsaken. It is in this same way that feelings of envy are often spread, and its venom is communicated to those who by their high position should be most exempt from it. Let us strive to guard our hearts from this despicable fault of jealousy. Let us keep watch over our words, and see whether we are quite free from jealousy. Finally let us be on the watch against the evil insinuations of others.

SECOND POINT.

Reply of S. John Baptist to his disciples.

If these jealous men had been the disciples of the Pharisees, they would probably have been all their lives enemies and persecutors of Christ: but fortunately for them, their master was S. John Baptist, who knew how to instruct them without embittering them. His reply turns upon three principal points.

1. On that which regards himself, and one may gather from this first part of his reply, four maxims how to keep oneself free from jealousy. First maxim; every thing that is good comes from heaven. S. John answers them, *A man can receive nothing, except it be given him from heaven.* As if he had said: He of Whom you speak has a power which men cannot give, but which He has received from Heaven. Riches, honours, authority, influence, talents, success, every thing comes from God, Who orders all things as He will, without any one having the power to give himself any thing, against His supreme will, and independently of His Providence. What we have, God has given it us; what others have, God has given it them. Is not God the master of His own gifts? and who are we that we oppose ourselves to it, or find anything to find fault with it?

Second maxim; each one ought to be content within the limits of his calling, of his vocation, and to glory in it. *Ye yourselves bear me witness that I said, I am not the Christ, but that I am sent before Him,* as His forerunner in order to prepare His ways. That is to say, you say that I have borne to Jesus a glorious witness, and by that you acknowledge yourselves that He is more than I; for the witness I bare Him said two things: 1. that I was not the Messiah; 2. that I was His forerunner: that is in truth what He is, and that is what I am. Third maxim; one should only have God's glory, the interests of Jesus, and the good of souls at heart. *He that hath the bride,* says S. John, *is the bridegroom: but the friend of the bridegroom which standeth and heareth him, rejoiceth greatly because of the bridegroom's voice: this my joy therefore is fulfilled.* That is to say, Jesus is *the bridegroom* to whom the Church has been given as *bride.* Now that you tell me that the voice of the bridegroom has made itself heard, that He speaks Himself to His bride, that He teaches her, that He sanctifies her, *my joy is fulfilled:* Such will be the feelings of any one who will be *the friend of the bridegroom;* like S. John, he will rejoice in all that happens to the advantage of the Church, the edification of believers, and the salvation of souls, by whom ever that good may be effected. Fourth maxim. We should rejoice at the glory of Christ, even if it is promoted at the expense of our own. *He must increase, but I must decrease.* Such were the generous feelings of S. John Baptist. Jesus must increase by the celebrity of His name, the success of His labours, the splendour of His miracles, the sublimity of His doctrine, and the concourse of His disciples: but as for me, I must be forgotten, effaced, set on one side, thrown into the shade. With such feelings, one is inaccessible to jealousy, and one is in a condition to be able to cure others of it.

2. S. John explains himself respecting all which concerned Jesus. *He that cometh from above is above*

all; he that is of the earth is earthly, and speaketh of the earth: He that cometh from Heaven is above all. As if he had said, You make between me and the Saviour a comparison which dishonours Him, and humiliates me. The Messiah is a Man *come from Heaven*, and I am only a man who *is of the earth.* This God Man, *who cometh from Heaven*, is above Abraham and the patriarchs, above Moses and the prophets; in one word, He is *above all*, by the four advantages which distinguish him. First advantage, the divinity of His origin. Men, however great they may be, are only children of the earth; but Jesus, Who dwells in the bosom of Divinity, Who is both God and man, the only Son of God, Who is, in one word, the Incarnate Word, *cometh from above, cometh from Heaven*, where He was from all eternity before appearing on the earth, and cannot in any way be compared with any man. Second advantage, the force of His witness. Man is ignorant of the mysteries hidden in the bosom of God, and only speaks of them according to the limits of his mind, which although aided by the light of faith, is always infinitely bounded; but *He that cometh from above* has all the fulness of the divine lights which He has drawn forth from the bosom of God, and He enjoys a perfect and intimate acquaintance with all the mysteries of Heaven. Now *what* Jesus *hath seen*, continues S. John, *and heard, that He testifieth*: that is to say, He testifieth of that He knows of a certain and divine knowledge, and He supports His testimony by miraculous works, which can only come from God. Yet *no man*, he adds, *receiveth the testimony.* The perversity of mankind is so great, that there are few to be found whom His witness convinces so far as to bring them to make a profession of belief in Him. How different the language of love is from that of envy! The disciples of S. John complain that all men follow Jesus: but whoever loves Jesus, as S. John, can he restrain himself from exclaiming with the sainted forerunner, that no one follows Jesus: so small is the number of those who are truly devoted to Him? *He* nevertheless, continues S. John, with submission and respect, *that hath received His testimony hath set to his seal that God is true.* Shall we hesitate ourselves to certify this truth? The martyrs have sealed it with their blood: let us set our seal to it by the works of a lively faith, of a tender devotion, of an ardent charity, of a perfect love. Third advantage, the sublimity of His doctrine. *For He Whom God hath sent speaketh the words of God.* His doctrine is as far above that of men, as His origin is above theirs, and Heaven is above earth. He announces to us the secrets and the attributes of Divinity, as being the only possessor of them; He unveils to us the depths of the Godhead, impenetrable and inaccessible until now, and one cannot but feel that it is a God Who speaks. Fourth advantage; the excellence of the gifts which He has received. For God does not communicate His gifts to Him *by measure* and with reserve: *the Father loveth the Son* so greatly, that with the power of sanctifying mankind, of saving them and of ruling over them, He has also given Him that of teaching them all the mysteries of the kingdom of God. The Father loves the Son with an infinite, eternal, essential, necessary love. He communicates to the Son, in that He is God, all the essence of His Divinity, and makes Him equal to Himself; and to this Son, in that He is man, subsisting in the Word, and making with Him but one Person, He has communicated the Holy Spirit to Him without measure, and has given Him all the fulness of It. *God giveth not the Spirit by measure unto Him. The Father loveth the Son, and hath given all things into His hand,* and He has granted to Him a power without limits in the order of grace, and of that of nature, a sovereign power over all hearts and over all minds, over all substances corporeal and spiritual, for time and for eternity. What happiness to know Jesus, and to be of the number of His! what happiness to be united to Him, and to remain faithfully attached to Him! How worthy He is of our admiration, of our service, our reverence, our obedience, our love!

3. S. John explains himself with regard to those who believe in Jesus, and to those who do not believe in Him. *He that believeth on the Son;* Who hath been sent to teach and to save mankind, has already in him the germ of *everlasting life:* but *he that believeth not the Son* sent by the Father deprives himself of the happiness promised to believers: *he shall not see life,* and he will draw down upon himself the wrath of God. Thus, between him who believes, and him who believes not, we may remark four differences. First difference as regards his deserts. He who believes glorifies God, by acknowledging His sovereign Truth, by which He is incapable of deceiving us. He on the contrary, who refuses to believe, outrages God, as if God had not spoken distinctly enough, or as if He could deceive us, whether in the things which He reveals, or in the proofs which He gives us of revelation. Second difference, as regards his present state. He who believes has eternal life, the life of grace, which renders him a friend of God, worthy of Heaven, and which is in him, the pledge, the germ and the principle of life, of glory. He who does not believe is in death, in sin, which makes him the enemy of God, and the object of His anger. Third difference, as regards his future condition. In the world to come, he who believes will enjoy life in Heaven with Him, in Whom he has believed, and this life will be joy eternal, and the completion of all our happiness. He who does not believe, will have no part in this life: he will be shut out of Heaven, and this same man who was not able to forego here below a moment of terrestrial pleasure will be for ever deprived of the sweetness of heavenly pleasures, and plunged in a death eternal, which will be torments without end. Fourth difference, as regards eternity. Do we think indeed, Who it is that speaks to us, Who sends His Son to us, and Who exacts our faith, our obedience, and our love? Do we think indeed, that it is an eternal God, Who promises us eternity alone, Who threatens only for eternity, and Who has no design but for eternity? An eternity of happiness to him that

believes; but for him that believes not, an eternity of misery, in which he will be the object of an eternal wrath, which will continue for ever, and will weigh him down. This wrath is on him from this moment, but he does not feel it; but if through his unbelief, he dies in it, it will make itself felt by him in fearful and eternal torments.

Prayer. What hast Thou not done, what art Thou not doing still, O my God, in order to save me, to deliver me from this eternal death! Promises, threats, goodness, love, tenderness, Thou hast employed all these means, and dost still make use of them, in order to win me to Thee. Can it be possible that all this makes no impression on my heart? Ah! let Thy Spirit, which I have received at my baptism, but which I have profaned, breathe anew upon me; that He may deliver me from corruption, may give me a new heart, a new life. Oh holy baptism established by Christ, and perpetuated to our days notwithstanding the distance of places, and the long interval of so many centuries! how do I thank God that I have received its grace? If I have had the misery of violating the engagements which I entered upon in receiving it, I renew them to-day with all the fervour of which I am capable. I renounce the devil and all his works, the pomps and vanities of this wicked world, and all the sinful lusts of the flesh; I desire only to believe in Thee, and to be firmly bound to Thee only, for ever, O Jesus, my God and my Saviour. Amen.

Meditation XL.

CONVERSATION OF JESUS WITH THE WOMAN OF SAMARIA.

The sacred historian tells us in the first place what was the care which Providence employs in order to bring about this conversation; he then divides this same conversation in two parts, where, in the first part, the woman of Samaria acknowledges Jesus as a prophet, and in the second, Jesus discovers to the woman that He is the Messiah. S. John iv. 1—28.

FIRST POINT.

Of the care which Providence employs in order to bring about this conversation.

1. *Jesus is obliged to leave Judea.* *When therefore the Lord knew how the Pharisees had heard that Jesus made and baptized more disciples than John, (though Jesus Himself baptized not but His disciples,) He left Judea, and departed again into Galilee.* Jesus learnt from the conversation of men, that which He knew by the knowledge which He had of the secrets of all hearts, that the Pharisees had heard of that which He was doing. Persuaded and certain that after having insulted and banished the disciple, (S. John Baptist) they would not fail to employ a still more open violence against the master; seeing the storm gathering, and willing to complete the work His Father gave Him to do, before He suffered, He adopted the course of leaving Judea, and returning into Galilee, accompanied only by His four disciples, S. Peter, S. Andrew, S. James, and S. John. Oh Providence of my God, even Thy very enemies contribute, against their will, to the accomplishment of Thy designs! The learned men of the capital force their Saviour to leave Judea, and a sinner is about to persuade a city of Samaria to open its gates to Him, to beg Him to enter there, and to receive Him there.

2. *Jesus is obliged to pass through Samaria.* *And*

He must needs go through Samaria. Jesus had purposely placed Himself in Judea, so that in order to go from thence into Galilee, He must needs pass through the country of the Samaritans, unless He went by a long circuitous route, which the circumstances of an approaching persecution would not permit Him to take. Thus Jesus appeared only to be escaping from the persecution of His enemies, whilst He was hastening to the conversion of a woman that was a sinner, and of an entire people with her.

3. Jesus is obliged to sit down by the well of Jacob. *Then cometh He to a city of Samaria, which is called Sychar, near to the parcel of ground that Jacob gave to his son Joseph. Now Jacob's well was there. Jesus therefore, being wearied with His journey, sat thus on the well; and it was about the sixth hour.* Jesus, having journeyed all the morning, and in a very hot season, arrived towards noon with His four disciples in the neighbourhood of a city of Samaria called Sichar, anciently called Sichem. He found Himself so wearied with the journey, that He was obliged to sit down by a well, which was not far distant from the city, and which was called the well of Jacob. Thou dost weary Thyself, O good Shepherd, in seeking after the sheep that has gone astray, and Thou dost employ the time of Thy rest in winning her back, and teaching her. O fatigue of Jesus, how powerful Thou art! O rest of Jesus, how active Thou art!

4. The disciples of Jesus are obliged to go into the city in order to buy food, and leave Him alone. *For His disciples were gone away into the city to buy meat.* The disciples, seeing Jesus so wearied, went together to buy some provisions in the city in order to come and take their repast with Him. This solitude in which they left Him was not the effect of hazard; Jesus had brought it about, and it entered of necessity into the designs of His wisdom. It is in solitude that we have the fruition of God. There is no one so occupied, who

cannot find, if he will, many moments in which to converse with Jesus.

5. The woman of Samaria is obliged to come and draw water. *There cometh a woman of Samaria to draw water.* Come, happy woman, your Saviour awaits you! you will not see at first anything but chance in this casual meeting, where every thing has been brought about by His Providence, and His mercy; but in how few moments, He will bring about a change in you! How differently you will feel when you go back into the city to what you do at this moment that you are coming out of it. May my heart prove as docile as yours is about to be, to the lessons of our common Master!

SECOND POINT.

First part of the conversation. The woman of Samaria recognises Jesus as a prophet.

1. Jesus asks for water of her, and she replies to Him at first only with an expression of raillery. *Jesus saith unto her, give Me to drink. Then saith the woman of Samaria unto Him, How is it that thou, being a Jew, askest drink of me, which am a woman of Samaria? for the Jews have no dealings with the Samaritans.* The thirst which Jesus experienced was far less that which was caused by fatigue and heat, than the thirst for the conversion of the woman. Alas! we are, if not ministers, at least disciples of Jesus Christ. Where are our labours, our watchings, our wearinesses for the salvation of our brethren? What is our patience, our gentleness? Who feels a thirst like that of the Son of Man? When the Samaritan woman had drawn some water, Jesus was willing to abase Himself so far as to ask her for some, in order to have an opportunity of conversing with her, of instructing her and converting her. She did not refuse Him; but recognising by His dress, and His language that He was a Jew, she said to Him, as if turning the matter into jest; What! being a Jew as you are, and knowing that I am a woman of

Samaria, do you ask me for water to drink, for the Jews have no intercourse with the Samaritans*? She was ignorant that she was speaking to Him, Who was soon to reunite Samaritans with Jews, Jews and Samaritans with Gentiles, and to form out of all the nations of the earth one single faithful people: she was ignorant that, in a moment, she was about herself to become one of the members of that chosen people.

2. Jesus promises her a living water, and she asks Him whence He will draw it. Jesus gives no reply to the raillery which this woman throws into her words, He brings her back to more serious thoughts, by, in His turn, exciting her curiosity. *Jesus answered and said unto her: If thou knewest the gift of God, and Who it is that saith to thee, Give me to drink: thou wouldest have asked of Him and He would have given thee living water.* Ah! if we knew Him well ourselves, we should not refuse Him the little which He asks of us, and by yielding to Him in that slight constraint, that feeble subjection to our duties, those few acts of obedience which He requires from us at first, we should put ourselves in a condition to receive the fulness of the Heavenly gifts which He prepares for us. The words of Jesus led the woman of Samaria to suppose that He was something more than she had at first imagined, and she gives Him henceforth the title of Sir. Nevertheless, as she desired to know who He was, and as she suspected that some mystery lay concealed in His words, she answers Him in a manner to engage Him to explain Himself to her on the one or the other subject. *Sir*, she says to

---

* The Samaritans only accepted the five books of Moses out of the Holy Scripture; they refused to go to worship God in the temple at Jerusalem, and they mingled many superstitions with the divine worship which they offered to the true God. The Jews regarded them as heathen, with whom they were not allowed to have any connection, alliance or friendship; they were equally forbidden to receive any thing from them, to make use of the same articles of clothing, of the same table, or the same cooking utensils. The law, however, did not extend as far as to forbid traffic or dealings with them.

Him with respect, *Thou hast nothing to draw with and the well is deep: from whence then hast thou that living water? Art thou greater than our father Jacob, which gave us the well and drank thereof and his children, and his cattle?* What a picture the reasons and the difficulties which the Samaritan woman brings forward here is, of the frivolous protests which sinners allege, and the obstacles which they make to themselves, or which they oppose to the motions of grace and the salutary remorse of their conscience!

3. Jesus explains to her the qualities of the water of which He speaks to her, and she prays Him to give her some of it. Jesus takes no notice of the comparison which this woman made of Him with Jacob, not being willing to embitter a person whom He was seeking to gain over, or rather, He replied indirectly to it, by explaining to her the difference which there was between the water from Jacob's well and that which He promised her. *Jesus answered and said unto her, Whosoever drinketh of this water shall thirst again: but whosoever drinketh of the water that I shall give him shall never thirst: but the water that I shall give him shall be in him a well of water springing up into everlasting life.* How much difficulty a carnal mind has in understanding the things of God. It cannot imagine that there should be any thing else good save that which captivates the senses. If the woman of Samaria does not comprehend the entire meaning of the words of Christ, she begins to discern in them a mystery, the explanation of which she earnestly desires. It was enough to make her ardently long to have some of this water, and to make her resolve to ask for some. *The woman saith unto Him, Sir, give me this water, that I thirst not, neither come hither to draw.* The Samaritan woman asks indeed the Saviour for this living water, but she does not yet know its true virtue, and she is only actuated by the most material motives. As for us, who know more fully what that divine water is, which is none other than the grace of the Holy Spirit, let us de-

sire it, let us ask for it, not in order to be exempt from the necessities of life, but in order to be purified from our sins, to subdue the heat of our passions, to deliver ourselves from thirst after the pleasures and the good things of this world, in order to hinder ourselves from frequenting places which we know to be fatal to our innocence, and objects which defile us, which distract us, which absorb our time and our thoughts, and consume our strength, and do but excite our thirst instead of quenching it.

4. Jesus tells her to go and call her husband, and she answers that she has none. The woman of Samaria was awaiting with impatience the fulfilment of the glorious promises which Jesus had made to her, when He said to her, *Go, call thy husband and come hither.* In one sense, she had a husband, but in another, she had none, since he whom she had, was not her lawful husband. *The woman,* in order to satisfy the longing which she had for that living water which the Saviour had promised to her, *answered and said* with eagerness, *I have no husband.* She told the truth without meaning to tell it, and she thought as yet neither of acknowledging her fault, nor of confessing her evil conduct. It is thus, that in seeking to conceal the truth, the truth makes us speak: and when we are only thinking of suppressing it and hiding it, often our actions and our words betray it.

5. Jesus speaks to her of her sins, and she recognizes in Him a prophet. *Jesus said unto her, Thou hast well said, I have no husband: For thou hast had five husbands, and he whom thou now hast is not thy husband: in that saidst thou truly.* Such a declaration, which this Samaritan woman had no reason to expect, threw her into a state of extreme surprise; but the living water which she had asked for without knowing what it was, this grace of the Holy Spirit, beginning to spread abroad in her heart, made her feel that she was a sinner, and that He Who was speaking to her, was a prophet. She ceased to dispute the matter any further,

and only answered in a few words, which were the humble acknowledgement of her sins: *Sir, I perceive that thou art a prophet.* What a prophet! How penetrating is His discernment, and yet how sweet is His gentleness! In truth, whether the five husbands she had had, had been lawful ones, or whether they had not been so any more than the sixth, she was leading a sinful life; but Jesus does not reproach her with it, nor represent to her with harshness the enormity of her crimes; on the contrary, He takes the opportunity to praise her for having spoken the truth. He commends her sincerity, and does so at two different intervals. Oh infinite goodness! it is thus that Thou dost treat the sinner, when he humbles himself before Thee, and confesses his sin. Thou dost appear at once to forget his wickedness, in order only to see and hear the sincerity of his confession.

THIRD POINT.

Last part of the conversation. Jesus discovers to the woman of Samaria that He is the Messiah.

1. Question of the Samaritan woman respecting the religion of the Jews and Samaritans. The sinner of Sychar understood by the change which she experienced in her heart, that the water she had asked for had been given to her: thus she does not enter again upon that question, but proposes another to our Saviour. When a soul is sincerely turned to God, in all that regards its moral character, it does not rest easy in the path of error. This woman, who at the commencement of the conversation, had mocked at the scruples of the Jews, began to have some herself as regarded the religion of the Samaritans. And to Whom could she better propose her doubts than to Him Who had with such just right merited her confidence, and Who had wrought in her so great a change? *The woman saith unto Him, Sir, I perceive that Thou art a prophet,* but since Thou hast such certain knowledge of these things, condescend then to enlighten me on the subject of religion, on the questions

which divide us from the Jews, and which keep up a scandalous aversion between the servants of the same Master: instruct me, for I have resolved to embrace the right side, and to ensure my salvation. *Our fathers*, since their return from captivity, *worshipped* and offered their sacrifices in the temple, built *in this mountain: and ye say, that in Jerusalem is the place where men ought to worship*. On what ground do you maintain that the temple built on Mount Sion is the only place which God has chosen, and that it is there alone that He accepts the victims which are offered to Him in sacrifice? As for us, we maintain that it is on the mountain of Gerizim, which is before you, and in the temple which is built thereon, that men ought to offer up their worship: and as a proof we have the example of the patriarchs, who are our fathers. Thus did the Samaritans persist in their schism out of habit and from prejudice: and thus do those who have separated themselves from the Church rest even now-a-days upon the example of their fathers, who have built and frequented these places of worship: but if they would but go further back, they would find their fathers again in the same Church as ourselves, taking part in the same worship as ourselves. The schism of the fathers is no excuse for the children, and the children make themselves partakers in the schism of their fathers by continuing in it. Their plain duty is to return to the Church, from which their fathers have separated themselves. The woman of Samaria was not exactly under the same obligation, because as the Messiah was come, His reign was to take away the occasion of the schism by the destruction of the temple, and the abolition of the law of the Jews, so that it was only needful, for the future to believe in Him, and enter into His Church.

2. Answer of Jesus. *Jesus saith unto her, Woman, believe Me, the hour cometh when ye shall neither in this mountain, nor yet at Jerusalem, worship the Father.* It is no longer the time to occupy yourselves with these disputes, and soon the subject of this division between Jews and Samaritans will cease entirely: soon

it will no longer be a question either of your temple, or of that of Jerusalem, in order to worship God, and there will not be any place, fixed and determined on the earth, in which to render Him the worship due to Him. It is true, since you desire to know it, that the Jews have the advantage over you, that they do offer their public rites of worship and the ceremonies of religion in the place which the Lord hath chosen, and in this point they act conformably to divine revelation : for *ye worship ye know not what : we know what we worship : for salvation is of the Jews.* You worship God in your temple without being authorised to do so by any manifest sign of the will of God, and you do not know wherefore you do so : we, on the contrary, we know the will of God, and we only act conformably to His divine oracles. You do not know either the Father, or the Son, since you do not receive the books of the prophets, which would have made known to you both the One and the Other, and would have taught you that it is from the Jewish nation that the Son of God, the Saviour of the world was to be born. It is true that the Jewish worship is only in itself a material and figurative worship, setting forth in types the Saviour : *but the hour cometh, and now is, when the true worshippers shall worship the Father in spirit and in truth : for the Father seeketh such to worship Him.* The time is coming, and you are drawing close to it, when there will be no longer any immolation of legal victims, and when true worshippers will no longer be bound in the choice of times and places : when the blood of bulls and goats will no longer be poured forth. The carnal sacrifices which God has commanded should be offered to Him, were only the shadow of a more perfect worship which He now requires, of a true and sincere worship, interior and spiritual, which will only be shewn forth by the sacrifice of the mind and the heart : for *God is a Spirit, and they that worship Him must worship Him in spirit and in truth.* We see with our own eyes the fulfilment of this prophecy. The Church of Christ has existed for eighteen centuries. The temples of Samaria and Jerusalem have been destroyed, although the malice of an impious Emperor, Julian the Apostate, sought in vain to rebuild the latter. We live in that happy time, when a perfect worship has succeeded to Judaic rites and ceremonies, and a divine Sacrifice has taken the place of the carnal sacrifices of the law, but are we indeed of the number of the true worshippers, such as our Heavenly Father requires? Do we worship God in spirit and in truth? Let us unite ourselves to that Precious Victim that we may offer up to Him the sincere sacrifice of our minds, our hearts, our life, and all that we are.

3. The woman of Samaria declares that she is in expectation of the Messiah. She knew that it was the time when His arrival was to be looked for: she was not ignorant of the report that He had come, and that He was announcing His arrival already in Judea and in Galilee by the most striking miracles. In this disposition of mind, could she listen to this last discourse of Jesus, and reflect upon all that He had previously said to her, without having at least strong suspicions that He, Who was speaking to her, was Himself the Messiah? Now what a happiness, what an honour would it not have been for her to have quenched her thirst, to have confessed her faults to Him, and to have experienced the charms of His gentleness! But, on the other hand, she dared not flatter herself to that degree. Would the Messiah have been willing to converse with a sinner like herself, and would He have treated her with so much tenderness and consideration? Divided thus between hope and fear, respect for others not permitting her to discover her embarassment, she sought in a round-about way to enlighten herself on a matter which had become of such vital importance to her. *The woman saith unto Him, I know that Messias cometh, which is called Christ: when He is come, He will tell us all things.*

4. Jesus discovers to the woman of Samaria that He is the Messiah. Happy woman, your Saviour is not

ignorant of that which is passing in your mind. He knows the innocent artifice which you are employing: but because He sees that it is humility and love which have suggested it to you, He is about to satisfy your desires, and to fulfil all your longings. Be attentive then and listen well to these words, which make the joy of Heaven, and the hope of earth, those words which have never yet been uttered by His sacred Mouth, and which He is now about to speak. *Jesus saith unto her, I, that speak unto thee, am He.* O words worthy of all admiration: Jesus does not cease to speak the same words to us: are we attentive to them? Alas! Jesus speaks to us again and again, and we will not hearken to His voice. It is He Who speaks to us by the remorse which we feel, by that distaste of the world which we experience, by that sermon, by that discourse, by that word which touches us, by that poor man who asks our help, by that sickness, that affliction, that disgrace which humiliates us; if we were docile to that divine Voice, with what consolations would It not fill our hearts!

5. The disciples of Jesus arrive, and the woman of Samaria withdraws. When the woman had heard these words; *I am He*, who can say what feelings of joy, admiration, respect and love rose in her heart? But she has not time to express them. The disciples arrive at the moment: and she withdrew, or rather she sped to the city, in order there to breathe forth the sacred fire with which her heart was consumed.

Prayer. O Lord, Thy victory is complete, and Thy conquest assured. Of a woman that was a sinner, and of an unbeliever, Thou hast made an apostle; make also of my sinful soul, a soul that is penitent, Christian, and fervent. O Jesus! I am guilty in Thine eyes of sins, which in one sense are more heinous than those of the woman of Samaria, because I have had more light and more help given me whereby to avoid them; but if I have had the misery to offend Thee, I will seek at least, by the sincerity of my confession, to merit from Thee that pardon which she gained from Thee by speaking the truth to Thee. Give to me, as Thou didst to her, Oh divine Saviour, of that living water which so purifies our hearts from all earthly affections, that all my thoughts may be raised towards Heaven, and that the life eternal which Thou dost promise us there, may be the sole aim of all my desires. Amen.

Meditation XLI.

AS REGARDS THAT WHICH PRECEDED THE CONVERSION OF THE SAMARITANS OF SYCHAR.

Four objects ought to fix our attention here; 1. the astonishment of the apostles; 2. the zeal of the woman of Samaria; 3. the charity of Jesus; 4. the instruction which Jesus gave to His disciples. S. John iv. 27-38.

FIRST POINT.

The astonishment of the apostles.

1. This astonishment was honourable to Jesus. *And upon this came His disciples, and marvelled that He talked with the woman.* This surprise of the disciples points out to us how circumspect Jesus had always willed to appear in His conduct. It teaches us that those who have the spiritual charge of souls are much exposed to the censure and judgement of men, that their conduct forms the ordinary topic of public animadversion, and that they cannot too carefully avoid conversations, which might give rise to scandal, and which besides being useless, might prove dangerous to themselves. The conduct of Jesus Christ teaches us, that, on the other side, a wise and enlightened zeal ought to guide them in the difficulties of their sacred calling, so that they should give no cause of suspicion or of offence.

2. Their respectful astonishment shewn towards Jesus. *Yet no man said What seekest thou? or why talkest*

thou with her? The disciples did not venture to put any question to Him respecting that, which formed the subject of their astonishment. The flock ought not to judge the conduct of their pastor, nor even to be guided by appearances. That which might appear to furnish them with a subject of criticism, ought rather to lead them to be silent, because one is easily deceived. Let us learn to shake off this spirit of curiosity, which is naturally opposed to piety, and is as contrary to the simplicity of faith, as to the innocence of charity; of that habit of speaking evil which is to be found amongst those who make a profession of piety, as also amongst worldly persons; of that malignity, which is so common, and which is always ready to judge evil of everyone, and to interpret everything in bad part.

SECOND POINT.

The zeal of the woman of Samaria.

The woman then left her waterpot, and went her way into the city, and saith unto the men: Come see a man, which told me all things that ever I did: is not this the Christ? What ardour, what humility, what prudence, and efficacy in the zeal of the woman of Samaria!

1. Ardent zeal which makes her forget to take her repast, in order to go and publish throughout the city the blessed meeting which she had had. The zeal of faith and the love of truth, her desire and her joy, her surprise and her gratitude alike animate her, urge her on, and transport her. She hastens, and she listens only to the motions of the grace and ardour of that pure charity which Jesus Christ has enkindled in her heart. There is no torpor or want of animation in those souls who have the bliss of drawing nigh to God, and of listening with humility to those inward words which His Holy Spirit causes them to hear in their hearts.

2. Humble zeal. The woman of Samaria does not assume the tone of a teacher. Her words have nothing concealed, nothing which could prejudice others, or im-

pose on them. She does not lay a stress on the sublime knowledge which has been communicated to her, nor on the profound secrets which have been revealed to her: she only speaks of the revelation which has been made to her of her own actions and her own faults. Modesty and shamefacedness, feelings which have so much empire and strength over her sex; pride, fear, esteem of men which beset worldly persons: all these powerful motives are despised, all the strongest passions are sacrificed; every thing yields to the greatness of her faith, and of her zeal. Let her example condemn powerfully the worldly prudence and the base timidity of those who live in sin, and fear to blush at it, who have lost the fear of God, and yet cannot lose the fatal fear of the world!

3. Prudent zeal. She does not say that this man is the Messiah, and that she is herself assured of it: she contents herself with recalling the most striking circumstance of the conversation which she had had with Him, in order to animate those to whom she speaks, to go and find Him, to see and judge for themselves if this is not the Messiah. As ridiculous and unseemly as it is for a woman, however skilled she may be supposed to be, to mix herself up with dogmatism on the subject of religion, so much the more honour does she gain for herself, and so much more the good perhaps may she be able to do, when, in order to support the faith of others, or to inspire religious sentiments into them, she employs the charms of a gentle and skilful insinuation.

4. Efficacious zeal. *Then they went out of the city, and came unto Him.* At these words of the woman at Samaria, *Come see a man, which told me all things that ever I did,* all the city was moved, and a great number of the inhabitants prepared to go out to meet Him. If but all unbelievers would thus yield to this sweet invitation! Let us yield ourselves to it; let us go and see, that is to say, let us meditate on Christ, His actions, His words, and let us see how worthy He is of our love, our respect, and our confidence.

THIRD POINT.

The charity of Jesus.

1. Charity prevents Him from taking any food. *In the meanwhile, His disciples prayed Him, saying Master, eat.* Whilst the woman of Samaria was following the ardour of her zeal, and was calling the inhabitants of Sychar, the disciples of Christ put before Him what they had brought out of the city; and as they saw that He did not eat, they pressed Him to eat. Such was the occupation of the disciples; now let us see what was that of Jesus. Notwithstanding the fatigue of the journey, the heat of the day, the advanced hour, and the exhaustion of this divine Saviour, His thoughts are alone on the work of God which He has begun, and which the woman of Samaria is carrying on and which He wills to complete. O Jesus! Thy ardent charity, and the care of our salvation make Thee forget Thine own necessities, whilst we, we forget our own salvation and that of our brethren in following after imaginary wants, and frivolous amusements. Blessed are the pastors and those apostolic men, who, after Thy example, forget the care of their body, in order to labour for the salvation of souls! happy those faithful souls, who after the example of Thy disciples, render to their pastors those cares and that assistance of which they stand in need!

2. Charity supports Jesus with an unknown food. The disciples continuing to press Him to take some food, He says unto them, *I have meat to eat that ye know not of.* The Saviour turned everything into an occasion to edify and to instruct those who were with Him. The water which He had asked of the woman of Samaria, led Him to speak of the water of grace, which springs up into everlasting life, and the food which His disciples offered to Him, served Him as the subject of instruction on the duties of the ministry. The food, the nourishment of Jesus, is our sanctification; thus we offer Him a Heavenly food, when we shew ourselves docile to the impulses of grace: and we refuse it Him every time

that, indocile to His grace, we follow our own passions. Let us bear in mind those words of Christ; *I have meat to eat that ye know not of*, when friends, with too human a charity, urge us to relax somewhat of our practices of devotion, of mortification, or of zeal. Let us especially bear them in mind, when the devil, the flesh, and the world offer us those poisoned viands which bring about the death of the soul, by tempting the senses and our passions. Let us answer with Christ: I have meat to eat that ye know not of, and which has for me delights which render distasteful those which you offer to me.

3. Charity induces Christ to give an instruction to His disciples. *Therefore said His disciples one to another, Hath any man brought Him ought to eat?* The woman of Samaria understood nothing at first of that which the Son of God spake to her of the mystery of the heavenly water. The disciples are not more enlightened as to the nature, and the qualities of the divine food, of which Christ spoke to them. They had never felt any but bodily hunger, they did not know the hunger after truth, and the ardent thirst for righteousness: thus, not conceiving why Jesus should defer His repast, they imagined, that during their absence, some one had brought Him something to eat. Man is always the slave of his senses, unless the Spirit of God raises him above them, and puts into his mind worthy thoughts; and it was this, which led our divine Saviour to instruct His disciples on the duties of the apostolic office; oh boundless and indefatigable charity! Thus, oh Jesus! in preferring the necessities of others to Thine own, in shewing Thyself more occupied with the salvation of the Samaritans than with the hunger and thirst which Thou wert suffering, Thou didst teach not only the ministers of Thy Church, but all believers, never to omit works of charity, piety, and mercy which Providence may place in their way, never to prefer the necessities of life, or the care of their bodies, to the succour which the life of souls or the condition of sinners may demand of them,

as we have always time to take care of our bodies, but we have not always occasions favourable to the salvation of our neighbour.

FOURTH POINT.

The instruction which Jesus gives to His disciples on the duties of the ministry.

1. Jesus explains to them what is the food, of which He had spoken to them. *Jesus saith unto them, My meat is to do the will of Him that sent Me, and to finish His work.* As if He had said to them, Do not be surprised if I pay no attention to the needs of My body; the grace which My Father has bestowed upon this woman of Samaria, the blessed state in which I see her, enraptures Me and supports Me. Is it not in the natural order of things that the body shall yield to the mind? Is not the salvation of a soul to be preferred to material bread? If this preference is due to one soul alone, with much greater reason is it not due to the salvation of an entire city, and nation? That is the work God has appointed Me to do; I shall carry out His Will by completing the work of charity which I have begun, and such is My food. When we labour for the salvation of our neighbour, when we are fulfilling the duties of the ministry, when in fulfilling them, we are called upon to suffer, let us remember that it is the will of God which we are doing. Let us then labour at it with zeal, and joy, and let us taste the peace and consolation which are found in doing on earth what God wills us to do. Let us remember that it is God's work, and let us apply ourselves to carry it out as perfectly as possible: let us begin it and end it with an entire purity of intention, so that no human motive, no self-reflection, may rob Him of the least portion of it. Thus we shall find in the accomplishment of the will of God, a delicious food which will strengthen our souls, and make them grow in virtue, and lead them on to perfection.

2. Jesus explains to His disciples a proverb which the ministers of God may *not* apply to themselves. *Say not ye, There are yet four months, and then cometh harvest? behold, I say unto you, Lift up your eyes, and look on the fields: for they are white already to harvest.* The proverb ran thus; There are four months between the labours of sowing, and that of the harvest. The meaning of which was that it was not necessary always to work, but that there was a time for rest, and a time for work. The apostles might have thought that it was now the time of sowing the seed, and that afterwards they should have time to take rest: but our Saviour tells them that they are now to be engaged in the labours of harvest, that they must begin them without delay, and continue them without relaxation, and He encourages them by two motives First motive: the necessities of the people, and their disposition of mind. *Lift up your eyes*, He says to them, whilst pointing out the inhabitants of Sychar hastening up in crowds, behold the fields rejoicing, and only waiting for the sickle of the reaper. The cities, towns, and villages are prepared to receive you. It is time that you should bring to them the light of the gospel. Let us lift up our eyes, and see far off from us whole nations, who only ask, in order to receive the faith, to be instructed. Happy those whom God sends to them! Let us pray for them, let us entreat the Lord to increase their numbers. Let us see around us how many ignorant persons there are, who only ask to be taught, how many sinners, who sometimes need but a word, in order to bring them back to themselves, and to be converted. Let us do what we can on their behalf, let us speak, and let us pray. Second motive: the reward of our labours. *And he that reapeth receiveth wages, and gathereth fruit unto life eternal: that both he that soweth and he that reapeth may rejoice together.* These wages are nothing less than eternal life, and the sweet satisfaction of beholding there, those to whose salvation here below we have been instrumental. What joy, what love reigns amongst the blessed souls of

God's elect, between those who have been saved by the ministry of others, and those who shall have, in some way, contributed to the salvation of their neighbour, and those, who at different times, and in diverse labours have co-operated in forming this Church triumphant, this immortal assembly of the blessed! Can we, after that, spare ourselves, and not profit with ardour, by all the occasions which we meet with, for the salvation of souls? But what will be, on the contrary, the hatred, the rage, the fury, which will fill the damned against those who have neglected to instruct them and to reprove them, against those, who, by their examples, their discourses, and their writings, have contributed to their damnation! This thought ought to make the pen fall from the hands of those impious and sacrilegious authors, who only employ their talents in order to undermine the faith, and to corrupt the morals of others.

3. Jesus explains to His disciples another proverb, which may be applied to the ministry. *And herein is that saying true, one soweth and another reapeth.* 1. This saying is true in its proper and natural meaning, and it warns us of two things; the first, that we must not reckon upon life. It often happens that the one profits by the labour of others. Often we begin a work, and, death taking us away from it, it is another who finishes it; we sow, we labour, and death not permitting us to enjoy the fruits of it, another reaps what we have sown. The second, is that we must not work for ourselves alone. Those who have preceded us have laboured for us: we ought to thank God for their labours, and remember them in our prayers; and it is but just also that we should work for those who will succeed us. 2. This saying is also true when it is applied to the Apostles. *I sent you to reap that wherein ye bestowed no labour: other men laboured, and ye are entered into their labours.* The patriarchs, the prophets, the doctors of the law had sown, that is to say, had prepared beforehand the minds of men to receive the Messiah. When the Apostles announced Him, and con-

ferred on men His Baptism, they were reaping the field which others had sown. 3. This saying is also true when it is applied to the duties of the ministry in our days. The Apostles in their turn, and after them their successors, have ploughed up the ground, and sown the seed in the nations; their labours have been watered by their blood, and that of martyrs, and the faith has been thus handed down even unto us. With regard to each individual, it is true again that one sows and another reaps; the one teaches or gives rise to a good thought, the other succeeds in turning it to profit; the one directs in the paths of a holy life, the other gathers up the last breath of a saintly death. Thus the preaching of the Gospel forms as it were two chains, which have their commencement in Jesus Christ, the one of which goes back to the beginning of the world, and the other, which has come down to us, will continue on to the consummation of all time, and to the last harvest, which will be the time of the last judgment.

Prayer. Oh God! how worthy of admiration are Thy works! Happy they who have walked in the ways of Thy mercy, and laboured to carry out Thy purposes! O Jesus! if Thou dost will to forget the nourishment of Thy body in order to support Thyself, by doing the will of Thy Father, which is my sanctification, how earnestly ought I not to labour thereunto: I do resolve to do so, O divine Saviour! be with me to sanctify me, and to bless my efforts. Amen.

Meditation XLII.

CONVERSION OF THE SAMARITANS OF SYCHAR.

Consider with the sacred historian; 1. the docility; 2. the perfection; 3. the eminence of their faith. S. John iv. 39-45.

FIRST POINT.

The docility of their faith.

Admire three principal qualities in the faith of the Samaritans from the commencement of their conversion.

1. A prompt faith. *And many of the Samaritans of that city believed on Him for the saying of the woman which testified, He told me all that ever I did.* The Samaritans of Sychar were persuaded that the period marked out for the coming of the Messiah was at hand; there was nothing needed, to induce them to believe in Him, save the witness of the Samaritan woman. They could not suspect her witness; she could not be deceived as to the detail of that which had been hidden in her past life, and which had now been revealed to her; she could not wish to deceive her fellow-citizens, she had no interest in doing so, and she was known to be of a character, not to desire to do so. Those who seek the truth in good earnest are easily persuaded and convinced, when they have no self-interested motives in refusing to acknowledge it.

2. An active faith. *So when the Samaritans were come unto Him, they besought Him that He would tarry with them; and He abode there two days.* Many went out of the city, and came with the woman of Samaria to seek for Jesus, in order to pray Him to enter their city, and to make His abode with them, or at least to rest Himself there, and to remain there some time. Jesus consented to their wishes; He followed them, and abode with them two days. How merciful Jesus is! He goes willingly, He dwells and converses gladly with

those who pray Him to do so in a spirit of faith and love. What was the joy of these new proselytes! with what eagerness did the inhabitants of the city receive Him! And you, Oh zealous woman of Samaria, with what feelings did you behold this happy success of your exertions! with what satisfaction did you behold your divine Master received as it were in triumph by your fellow-citizens! with what ardour did you not follow Him wherever He went!

3. An attentive faith. *And many believed because of His own word.* They hastened to hear Jesus, and with what gladness did He not give instruction to hearts so well disposed! Thus the number of those who believed in Him increased greatly. The Apostles understood doubtless then of what food and of what harvest it was that Jesus had spoken to them. Alas! does not the number of those who believe in Jesus diminish rather than increase amongst us? Faith grows feeble, because we do not listen to Christ's voice, because instead of reading and meditating on His Gospel, we only read and lend our ears to that which may flatter our senses, or excite a vain and dangerous curiosity.

SECOND POINT.

Perfection of the faith of the Samaritans.

1. Their faith is perfect in its motive; they believe on the word of Jesus. The inhabitants of Sychar felt the value of the true faith, and they rejoiced to have received it. As the woman of Samaria took a special interest in all that took place, she was always to be found amongst His most zealous followers. They say unto her, *Now we believe, not because of thy saying; for we have heard Him ourselves.* Thus the teaching of the Messiah, despised at Jerusalem, was valued in Samaria. Jesus was listened to there with teachable hearts, and two days of preaching gained Him all hearts. The Samaritans are touched by the divine light from the first moment that it shines in their eyes; they believe in Christ, from

the moment they hear His words, and the Jew does not believe in Him, even when he sees Him work miracles! Thus we often see a Christian, doubtful in his faith in the midst of the greatest light, whilst the heathen, teachable and docile to the voice of God's ministers, believes, and lives conformably to his faith. The woman of Samaria gives no answer to the speech of her country people; far from being offended at what they say to her she rejoices that they should forget her in order to think alone of Jesus. Such is the character of true zeal, which is always full of love and disinterested motives. However great the humility of this woman was, it is nevertheless true, that if she had not believed herself in the first place, if she had not made Jesus known to her country people, they would have run a risk of not having been enlightened by the light of the Gospel. Wonderful links in the chain of grace! On the conversion of one, will depend often, the salvation and perfection of many. A first grace received with faithfulness, or rejected with obstinacy, is often the germ either of a perfected holiness, or of fearful damnation.

2. The faith of the inhabitants of Sychar is perfect in its object. *We have heard Him ourselves*, they say, *and know that this is indeed the Christ, the Saviour of the world.* How many truths are embodied in this single sentence! Happy citizens of Sychar, you are the first who have pronounced on earth this divine name of Saviour, since an angel announced it to the shepherds at Bethlehem. You bear witness that He is truly a Saviour, and not only the Saviour of the Jews, but also your own Saviour, the Saviour of all men and of the entire world.

3. The faith of the Samaritans is perfect in its duration. *Now after two days He departed thence, and went into Galilee.* After having remained two days at Sychar, Jesus went thence; but the fruits of His preaching did not fade away after His departure. Jesus, on leaving the inhabitants of Sychar, left them His grace, His spirit, and His love. With what regrets, with what

thanksgiving, with what protestations of faithfulness must not these fervent proselytes have accompanied their last farewell to Him! Could they ever forget the teaching He had given them, the honour He had done them by His Presence, and the graces He had so bountifully bestowed upon them?

THIRD POINT.

Eminence of the faith of the Samaritans.

1. An eminent faith, which condemned the infidelity of Nazareth, and the hardness of heart of Jerusalem. The first of these cities had heard Jesus, the second had seen His miracles. The first passed as the country of Jesus, because He had been brought up there: the second was so in reality, because it was the capital of Judæa, where He had been born. But the little fruit produced by His labours amongst them both, made Him do here as He had done after His Baptism; He advanced towards Galilee, where the inhabitants were more disposed than ever to receive Him and to listen to Him, He went to a distance from Jesusalem, and did not visit Nazareth: *For Jesus Himself testified, that a prophet hath no honour in his own country.*

2. The faith of the inhabitants of Sychar, eminent, and far superior to the faith even of the Galileans. *Then when He was come into Galilee, the Galileans received Him, having seen all the things that He did at Jerusalem at the feast: for they also went to the feast.* The faith with which the Galileans received Jesus was not exempt from all human motives. They regarded Him as their country-man, and they thought that the glory of His miracles would be reflected on themselves, and raise them above the Jews, who were wont to despise them. The inhabitants of Sychar, on the contrary, although strangers to Jesus, had believed in Him with a perfect faith, simply from having heard Him, and without having witnessed any miraculous display of His divine power, or at least any external exhibition of it.

3. The faith of the inhabitants of Sychar, eminent, and condemns the weakness and imperfection of our own. Alas! we have the words of Christ, we know His miracles, we see the fulfilment of His sayings, and yet it is more often from motives of self glory alone, and in order not to dishonour ourselves that we stand up in His cause, and call ourselves Christians.

Prayer. Oh blessed inhabitants of Sychar! your faith shall be the model of mine! O Jesus! these faithful Samaritans acknowledge Thee for their Saviour and that of the whole world; I acknowledge Thee for my Saviour also, and I desire no other happiness, no other knowledge, no other consolation than to serve Thee and adore Thee in time, so as to be able to glorify Thee in eternity. Amen.

Meditation XLIII.

JESUS, BEING AT CANA, HEALS THE SON OF A NOBLEMAN, WHO WAS SICK AT CAPERNAUM.

Admire here 1. the anxiety of this father; 2. his faith; 3. the benefits which he receives from Christ. S. John iv. 45—54.

FIRST POINT.

The anxiety of this father.

1. Observe the care with which he ascertains where Jesus is, and by which way He was journeying. *So Jesus came again into Cana of Galilee, where He made the water wine. And there was a certain nobleman whose son was sick at Capernaum. When he heard that Jesus was come out of Judæa into Galilee, he went unto Him.* This nobleman had a son, the object of his tender love, who had fallen sick at Capernaum: the sickness was so severe, that no hope of his recovery remained, unless it were by a miracle. Jesus had worked

many miracles in this city; but He was absent; a sad situation for an afflicted father, who was on the point of losing that which was dearest to him in the world. He enquires, he asks where Jesus is, he listens attentively to all that is told him about Him, and at length he learns that He has left Judæa, and that He is going into Galilee by way of Samaria. If we had the same earnestness as regards the salvation of our souls, as this father had in seeking the recovery of his son, we should enquire as he did, and find out all that might contribute to our healing, to our sanctification, to our perfection: nothing would appear indifferent to us which would help us to find Jesus, and in Him, a remedy for our own sicknesses.

2. Consider the journey which this afflicted father undertakes. Fearing that Jesus might arrive too late at Capernaum, he adopts the measure of going to meet Him, in order to entreat Him to hasten His arrival. He does not entrust this duty to any one else, he leaves his son in order to go and seek for succour for him: he sets off without being retarded either by the length or the fatigue of the journey. It is not thus with us, when it is a matter of working out our salvation; every thing alarms us, and we allow ourselves to be hindered by the smallest difficulties.

3. See the humility of the prayer. *And besought Him that He would come down, and heal his son;* for he was dying. He finds Jesus at Cana; he hastens to relate to Him the subject of his distress, and solicits Him with confidence and humility. If this prayer was faulty in some respects, at least it was fervent and reverent. Let us see that our prayers partake of both these qualities.

4. Admire the perseverance of this stranger. His imperfect faith needed to be taught, and Jesus imparts this instruction to him, and, ready to grant his demand, He yet conceals His willingness at first, as it were, under the cloak of a reproach, by saying to him, *Except ye see signs and wonders, ye will not believe.* We ought to observe how, on all occasions, our Saviour directed

his cares to the inner man before working on that which was external. It was as if He had said to this nobleman, Ye great men of this world, honoured for your birth or for your dignities, unless your personal needs force you to have recourse to Me, or if I do not reward your curiosity by working miracles, nothing else will persuade you that I am the Messiah: you require extraordinary signs, which should exalt you above other men, or miracles granted to your necessities: on these conditions, you feel disposed to believe, otherwise you do not even consider it a duty to seek instruction from Me. Alas! is it not thus that we act ourselves? When do we think of having recourse to God, unless when temporal afflictions befall us? Our sins, the danger in which we are of losing our salvation, all these things do not touch us in comparison with any disgrace, or any temporal misfortune. Jesus, by this reproof, humbled the pride of this nobleman, but He inflamed his desires, reanimated his hope, and exercised his faith; He exercised it so much the more, that in speaking these words, He did not appear prepared to depart, and this desolate father was counting every moment, and fearing always lest the remedy might be too late. Far from being rebuffed by this reproof, he humbles himself, and again repeats his entreaties. *Sir*, he says, *come down ere my child die; my child is in the last extremity*: deign to make haste. Happy father, your perseverance is about to be rewarded and that far above your hopes. *Jesus saith unto him, Go thy way, thy son liveth.* And in truth, at the same moment Jesus was healing him in Capernaum. Let us learn to know the Master Whom we serve; if He reproves us, if He appears to repel us, if He defers to grant our prayers, it is always His love which makes Him act thus, and it is only for our good that He deals thus with us. Let us ask of Him with resignation for temporal blessings, the success of our enterprises, or for bodily health; and if for our good, He refuses them to us, let us submit to His holy will. But let us ask for spiritual gifts with fervour, with perseverance, and He will always grant us more than we ask of Him.

SECOND POINT.

The faith of this father.

1. *The beginnings and the imperfection of his faith.* This nobleman, who to all appearance was a Gentile, and a descendant of those ancient Syrians established in Galilee, had formed but a very imperfect idea of Christ, from what had been told him at Capernaum. He believed indeed that He could cure his son: but he thought it was necessary He should see him, should touch him, and should speak to him. He was ignorant that Jesus could work His miracles as well at a distance, as at hand; that His presence was not necessary there, and that one single act of His will sufficed. He was far removed from believing that Jesus was the Son of God, God Himself, the Creator and Master of the universe. Have we the same idea of Christ? do we look upon Him as Such as faith presents Him to us, and requires of us to believe Him to be?

2. *The progress of his faith.* The reproof of the Saviour had made an impression on his heart, and when he heard Him say in a tone of authority, *Go thy way: thy son liveth*, he believed in the words of Jesus and went his way. He believed in the miracle, although he did not see it. He was not of the number of those of whom our Saviour had already spoken, who will not believe unless they see. Are we ourselves not of that number? Do we not sometimes hear persons amongst ourselves say, I would see a miracle? words of disbelief, which may provoke the Lord to anger; sign of a very languishing faith, well nigh, if not entirely, extinct. Let us learn from this nobleman to believe without having seen: in that consists the merit of faith: let us find our happiness and our consolation in so doing.

3. *The perfection of his faith.* Consoled by the firm persuasion that he had, that his son was healed, he sets off at once. The next day, he continues his journey, occupied doubtless with the words which Jesus had

spoken to him. He had not reached the city: for *as he was now going down, his servants* who had been the witnesses of the sudden recovery of their young master, *met him, and told him, saying, thy son liveth.* At these tidings, he does not give way to mere idle joy. He forgets himself in order to think only of his Benefactor, and to examine more closely into an event, which might have consequences more important still than the healing of his son. *Then inquired he of them the hour when he began to amend. And they said unto him, yesterday at the seventh hour* (that is to say an hour after noon) *the fever left him. So the father knew that it was at the same hour, in the which Jesus said unto him, thy son liveth: and himself believed.* He understood that Jesus had not only foretold to him the healing of his son, but that He had brought it about: and struck, as he ought to be, with a power so divine, he believed not only in the words of Jesus, but he believed in Jesus Himself; he believed that He was the Son of God, and the Messiah Who was expected, and to Whom mankind must cleave.

4. The zeal of his faith. *Himself believed, and his whole house.* True faith is not without zeal. A lively faith is neither dumb nor idle. The father makes known to his son and to his whole family and household the mercies which Jesus had bestowed upon them, and he speaks with a manner so penetrated with gratitude, that he leads all his family also to believe on Him. His conduct sets an example to all those in places of position, to all parents and masters. But in addition to these, each private person has in his outward and inward senses, and in all the powers of his soul, a sort of house and family which he governs, and which he ought to restrain by the regulations of a lively faith. Let then, wherever we may be, in the company of others or alone, in whatever occupation we may be busied, let our eyes, our ears, our tongue, our gestures, our behaviour, our imaginations, our memory, our mind, our spirit, our heart, our thoughts, our desires, our inten-

tions, our undertakings, our labours, our repose, let all be carried on in the spirit of faith, let all shew forth in us one who believes, and in whom every one believes. *This is again the second miracle that Jesus did, when He was come out of Judæa into Galilee.* This is the second miracle that Jesus worked at Cana in Galilee. If we look back upon many of the events of our lives, we shall find there much upon which to feed our faith and our love for God, we shall see there sensible and touching tokens of the goodness of God, of His Providence, of His infinite power; but we too often think only of enjoying the blessings God bestows upon us, without thinking of Him from Whom we receive them.

THIRD POINT.

The blessings which this father received.

1. The healing of his son. How often has God healed from sickness, ourselves, and those near to us! Have we thanked Him for this benefit? Alas! we have but too often no sooner received it than we have forgotten it.

2. The gift of faith, a thousand times more precious than life itself. We have received this inestimable gift: do not let us fail to render thanks to God for it.

3. The severity with which Jesus treated him. He reproved him publicly for his want of faith: but by that means, He made him humble, and made him commune with himself. He refused to grant his prayer by following him to Capernaum; but He worked in his behalf, a miracle far greater and more beneficial to him, than that which he asked for.

4. Even the illness of his son. Who would not have pitied this afflicted father, on seeing him on the point of losing a son, his only son? But that which made him so worthy of compassion in the eyes of men, was that which was to draw him nearer to Jesus, him and his house. How blind we are to our true interests, when we are discontented at God's dealings with us,

or murmur against the decrees of His Providence. Let us rather adore their depth and wisdom. Let us follow the example of this father and profit by sicknesses and afflictions, in order to have recourse to God, in order to unite ourselves to Him, and detach ourselves from the world. If God seems to make use of some severity towards us, if He refuses to grant us our requests, do not let us be discouraged: let us look upon His refusals and the severity with which He treats us, as favours from His hands, and let us be well persuaded that all which comes to us from Him is for our greater good.

Prayer. Give me, O Lord, the grace to know this truth, and to profit by it. Grant that I may know how to make use of all that Thy wisdom and goodness may will to bring about for my greater good. Let not my inclinations nor my weakness stand in the way; but rather do Thou deal with my feebleness by opposing Thyself to my wishes. Increase my faith, and render it constant, active, and perfect, like that of the nobleman in the Gospel. Grant to me the same zeal that he had, to make Thee known and loved. Deign to say to me in the depths of my heart these comforting words: Thy soul is healed, and it lives by the life of grace. It is not enough, O Jesus, to have delivered me from spiritual infirmities, but condescend also to give me grace to persevere in gratitude, faithfulness, and love, to the last moment in which the strife must be fought here below. Amen.

Meditation XLIV.

HEALING OF ONE THAT WAS POSSESSED OF A DEVIL.

Consider, 1. the Person of Christ, 2. the artifices of the devil whom Christ drove out, 3. the conduct of the people who were witnesses of this miracle. S. Mark i. 21-28. S. Luke iv. 31-37.

FIRST POINT.

Of Christ.

1. His zeal in teaching. *And they went into Capernaum: and straightway on the sabbath day, He entered into the synagogue and taught.* Capernaum was, as we have said, the centre of the mission of Jesus. This divine Saviour, accompanied by His four disciples, repaired thither from Cana. He did not take time to rest Himself: as soon as He had arrived, He began to teach. Besides the instructions which He gave every day in private, He taught publicly every Sabbath day in the synagogue, where the people were wont to assemble for prayer, and the reading of the Holy Scripture. The holy day of Sunday is to Christians what the Sabbath was to the Jews. On this day, the ministers of the Church offer up the divine Sacrifice, and preach the Word. To withdraw ourselves from the assemblies of believers, is to deprive ourselves of the grace and help provided for us by Christ, Who has set us an example, and also given us His commands so to do.

2. The authority of Christ in His teaching. *And they were astonished at His doctrine: for He taught them as one that had authority, and not as the scribes.* The scribes taught after the manner of men, who often do but convey with ostentation the various teachings and ideas of others, but it was not thus with Jesus: whether He was revealing to others mysteries, or explaining prophecies, or giving rules as to their conduct, He did it

without display or ostentation, but with definiteness and certainty, in the tone of a Master and Lawgiver, with a dignity and Majesty which were superhuman. It is thus that it befitted the Son of God to speak to men: it is thus it behoves men still to announce His doctrines.

3. The authority of Christ over the devils. *And there was in their synagogue a man with an unclean spirit: and he cried out, saying, Let us alone: what have we to do with Thee, Thou Jesus of Nazareth: art Thou come to destroy us? I know Thee who Thou art, the Holy one of God.* (ª) And Jesus rebuked him, saying, Hold thy peace, and come out of him. And when the unclean spirit had torn him in the midst, he came out of him and hurt him not. How much it costs an unclean spirit to come out of the soul of a sinner. This devil did not leave this unhappy man whom he had possessed until he had caused him violent tortures, fearful convulsions, and whilst uttering great cries, he threw him into the midst of the assembly, with such force, that there was room to fear lest he might have torn him in pieces: but his rage was powerless, the man who had been possessed found himself unhurt, whole in body, and free in mind. O Jesus! I adore Thy divine power, deign to exercise it on me; cause to be silent, and drive from my heart that spirit of murmuring, of criticism, and of slander which possesses it; cause to be silent and drive from the midst of us, the evil spirits of impurity and of heresy, who do not cease to lead astray souls which Thou hast formed to know and love Thee.

4. The reputation which Christ gained for Himself throughout the country. *And the fame of Him went out into every place of the country round about.* How well founded was this fame! How could it be possible

(ª) The devil seeks here as he had done in the wilderness, only to discover, by means of the words of Christ, if He were truly the Messiah, as he suspected Him to be: but Jesus, without giving any explanation, or permitting him to penetrate into this mystery, simply commands him to hold his peace, neither willing to tell him Who He was, nor to admit him to be a witness of His divinity.

not to acknowledge in these acts of goodness and power, the Deliverer Whom God had promised to the world? I rejoice, O my Saviour, that Thy Name begins to make Itself known: soon Thine apostles will carry It to the ends of the earth. Let all the people adore It! What can I do in order to contribute to Its spread, and the increase of Thy glory! Let me at least glorify Thee in myself, let me be occupied with Thy greatness! Let me have no other pleasure, no other thought, no other hope save in Thee, no other love save for Thee!

SECOND POINT.

Of the devil.

1. His complaints. *Let us alone, Thou Jesus of Nazareth*, that is to say, do not trouble us in our possession. What have we to do with Thee? Wherefore dost Thou seek our ruin, and declare war to us? Such are still the complaints of the devil, and especially those of the evil spirits of impurity and of heresy, against the zeal which pursues them, and which they look upon as a bitter, restless, and excessive zeal. They represent those who fight against them as restless and dangerous men, who only seek to satisfy their hatred, their ambition, and their jealousy under pretext of zeal, and in order to ruin persons under pretext of destroying their vices. Why do not they leave the world quiet, they say, and let each one have his own freedom to act and to believe as seemeth good unto him? Are we doing wrong to any one? Are we less good fellow-citizens, less faithful subjects, or less useful members of society? Hold your peace, deceitful spirits! Is not the loss of the souls whom you cast down into hell, sufficient to inflame the zeal of those who love Jesus, and to render it deaf to your clamours?

2. The artifices of the devil. After these complaints, the devil begins to confess Christ, and to exalt His holiness. *I know Thee Who Thou art, the Holy One of*

God. Complaints and praises, threats and flatteries, the devil employs them all in order to deceive and to seduce. Who praises more the goodness of God and His mercies than the evil spirit of impurity! Who speaks a language more devout, who affects more to employ the expressions of the scriptures and of holy men, who asserts himself as more versed in the knowledge of religion than the evil spirit of heresy? Hold your peace, impostors: these holy expressions become on your lips so many blasphemies by the meanings which you give to them, the false conclusions which you draw from them, and the perverse ends for which you employ them.

3. *The fury of the devil.* Forced to hold his peace, and to abandon his fury, he does not obey without manifesting his rage and his cruelty. A natural image of that which he makes a sinner suffer who seeks to drive him from his heart, and to become converted. What does it cost him to acknowledge his shameful falls! to own that he has been deceived, and that he has been in error! What struggles in order to renounce his evil habits, to break off his connections, to sacrifice that pretended happiness, that illusion which dazzles him. Courage, Christian soul! they are the last efforts of a cruel enemy from whom you are about to escape. Whatever it may cost you, persevere till you have broken your chains, and you will find true happiness in your freedom.

4. *The powerlessness of the devil.* In vain does he torment himself, in vain does he resist, he must obey; in vain, on leaving him whom he had possessed, did he throw him with violence into the midst of the assembly, he could not succeed in doing him any harm; his efforts and his fury do but show forth his weakness and his despair. Ah! how happy we are to have so powerful a Saviour! Let us cleave firmly to Him, and however cruel, however formidable the devil may be, let us fear nought.

THIRD POINT.

Of the people.

1. Their surprise with regard to the doctrine of Christ. *And they were astonished at His doctrine: for His word was with power.* Jesus Christ taught only the purest maxims, and the holiness of His life answered to the holiness of His discourses. This was what threw the Galileans into such a state of astonishment. They were not accustomed to see their doctors of the law and their teachers act in this manner in order to convert and to convince men. They knew how to preach and to give instruction, and did so with ostentation and with parade: but Jesus Christ, without affectation and without any display, announced, and convinced men of the sublimest truths. We should be in the same surprise as the Galileans, if we would but lend to Jesus an attentive ear to that which He speaks to us in the depths of our hearts; it is there that He teaches us in a divine and ineffable manner, and not after the manner of men: it is there that without revealing to us any other truths than those which faith teaches us, He makes us feel the value, the beauty, the richness and the importance of them; He makes us perceive, taste, and love them.

2. The admiration of the people with regard to the power of Jesus. *And they were all amazed.* They had seen Jesus exercise in Capernaum, although Himself absent, a sovereign power over all kinds of illnesses; but they had not seen Him command the evil spirits. This manner of teaching appeared to them so much the more strange and new, in that no one had ever heard that any prophet had exercised such power before. The manner in which He had just worked this wonder was not less admirable than the miracle itself. Three words had sufficed to Him in order to impose silence on the unclean spirit, and to force him to abandon his fury, notwithstanding his cries, his complaints, and his flatteries.

3. *The discourse of the people with regard to that which had just taken place.* *And spake among themselves, saying, What a word is this! for with authority and power He commandeth the unclean spirits, and they come out,* that is to say, this man preaches very differently to what our scribes and Pharisees do. He is as powerful in works as in words; miracles accompany His discourses, and it does not cost Him more to be obeyed by hell, than to shew the way to Heaven. Thus the people were occupied with nought else save the greatness and the power of Christ, and it was by this means that *the fame of Him went out into every place of the country round about.* Alas, with what do we occupy ourselves, what is the subject of our conversation save others, or ourselves? Why does not the greatness, the goodness, and the power of Jesus form the subject of all our discourses, and the matter of all our reflections?

Prayer. Grant, O my Saviour, that all the earth may know Thee, that all the world may speak of Thee, and that my heart may be penetrated with love of Thee. Be, O Jesus, the only Object of my admiration and of my love. What blessedness for me to have Thee as my Master! Teach me more and more, grant me the grace to be more faithful in practising Thy divine lessons. Renew in me, O powerful Deliverer, the operations of Thy mercy, deliver me from the tyranny of the evil spirit, grant me to triumph over it, never permit that I should be his victim in hell; but rather grant that I should be Thy conquest in Heaven. Amen.

Meditation XLV.

JESUS HEALS THE MOTHER-IN-LAW OF S. PETER.

Her illness, her healing, and the use which she makes of her health, three considerations which the sacred text proposes to us here. S. Mark i. 29—31. S. Luke iv. 28—39. S. Matt. viii. 14—15.

FIRST POINT.

Her illness.

Immediately after the deliverance of the man who had been possessed by a devil, *forthwith when they were come out of the synagogue they entered into the house of Simon, and Andrew, with James and John. But Simon's wife's mother lay sick of a fever.* Passions are the sicknesses of the soul; ambition, love of pleasure, self-interest, anger, slander, envy, avarice, pride, love of the world, hatred, are so many fevers, which by destroying the health of souls, take away from it the life of grace. Let us examine with what fever our soul is attacked, and let us see if it has more than one kind of these fevers. Let us mourn over our misery; and in order to encourage ourselves to desire our healing,

1. Let us consider the evils which these passions bring upon us. Like violent fevers, they torment us by continual agitations; sometimes they chill us with fear, fill us with suspicions, and despair, sometimes they inflame us with anger, spite, worldly love, hatred, with impure fires, with barren desires, with chimerical hopes. Sometimes they fight against one another, and tear us without mercy; they keep us in violent tortures, in perpetual perplexity, and troubling our reason, they throw us into a species of delirium. Every one perceives our folly: we alone do not perceive it, and soon we call that good, which is evil; honour, which is shame; liberty, which is slavery; pleasure, which is torment; we regard as a

sovereign happiness, that which is a sovereign misfortune.

2. Consider the condition to which we are reduced by our passions. Like fevers, they throw us into a state of weakness, of langour, of sleeplessness, and of disrelish for everything. We have no more strength to fight against the enemies of our salvation; we let ourselves be carried away by all the caprices of passion without making any resistance. If we still practise any acts of virtue, they are done out of habit, out of human respect, or even from hypocrisy. We have a positive distaste for all which regards truth, and perfection, and this distaste soon makes us abandon our readings, our meditations, our self-examination, communions and all our other devotional practices; and lastly, we come to know no longer that sweet repose which a fervent soul enjoys in prayer, in inward recollectedness, in the exercise of the presence of God, in submission to His divine will, in trust in the care of His divine Providence: how sinful is such a state!

3. Consider the change which passions cause in us. The longest fevers change a person less than does violent passion, whatever care we may take to conceal it. In that young person, formerly, one admired an amiable gentleness, a prompt obedience, a modest gaiety, a taste for piety and devotion which edified others: alas! it is now no longer the same: one finds no longer in her aught save a soured tone, scornful manners, an air of thoughtlessness, and an uneven temper. Sometimes one finds her plunged in gloomy melancholy, and sometimes abandoned to foolish joy, to excessive dissipation. Oh you, whose soul, formerly so pure and so beautiful, is now so shamefully disfigured, learn at least the source of your disease, and seek promptly for its remedy.

4. Consider the obstinacy and perseverance with which our passions cling to us. There is no fever so obstinate nor so difficult of cure, as a passion to which one has given a hold in one's heart. It would have been easy to resist the first attacks of vice, it would have been

possible to extirpate it whilst yet in the bud; we felt we could, and we flattered ourselves we should be able to do so always, and we said to ourselves that one day we should do so without difficulty; but soon we are forced to change our language; already we exclaim as to the uselessness of our efforts, we sigh, then we despair, and all our attempts are useless. Do not let us despair, nevertheless, we have a charitable and all-powerful Physician: let us have recourse to Him with confidence, let us redouble our efforts, and our recovery will be certain.

SECOND POINT.

The healing of the mother-in-law of S. Peter.

1. Observe the intercession of the Apostles. Jesus was not ignorant of the state of this woman; but it was befitting that His disciples, the witnesses of His miracles, and possessing a knowledge of His power, should at least make the advance, and should bear witness to their faith by asking of Him a miracle. They do so, as we see, with confidence in His willingness and His power. Let us recommend ourselves to the prayers of holy men on earth, and let us pray ourselves for others. Let us ask of Jesus, first of all, the healing of the soul, and then, as far as He shall see fitting, and in accordance with His glory and our salvation, the healing of the body; and if He does not grant it us, let us ask of Him patience, and the grace to make a good use of our sickness.

2. Observe the goodness of Jesus. *And He came, and took her by the hand, and lifted her up . . . And He stood over her, and rebuked the fever: and it left her.* I adore in every thing the divine power of Jesus, but that which touches me the most closely here, is His infinite goodness. Alas! O my God, how often hast Thou beheld me in the paroxysms of my senseless passion; Thou hast drawn near to me by Thy grace, and I have left Thee by my resistance: Thou hast touched my heart by poignant remorse, and I have stilled it by dis-

sipation and by new sins; Thou hast held out Thy Hand to me in order to draw me out of the abyss, and instead of laying hold on this Hand stretched out to succour me, I have withdrawn mine, in order to plunge anew in fresh disorders.

3. Observe the feelings of this sick woman. What was her consolation, although overwhelmed with suffering, when she saw standing by her, the Saviour of Israel! what was her hope, when she felt the impress of that All-Powerful Hand which touched her! what was her joy, when she heard the word spoken for healing, and found herself entirely cured! Jesus must first draw near to the sinner that He may take him by the hand, by touching him with His grace, in order to draw him out of the state into which he has fallen; but happy he who, touched in this manner, knows how to correspond to the grace of Jesus, by the practice of good works!

THIRD POINT.

The use which the mother-in-law of S. Peter makes of her recovery to health.

1. Her occupation. *And immediately she arose and ministered unto them.* Finding herself thus as perfectly as she was suddenly cured, she arises immediately. She causes food to be brought, and she has the happiness of ministering to Jesus and His disciples. What a lesson does this woman give us in the use which she makes of her health as soon as she has received it! She employs in ministering to Jesus, that very health which He has just restored to her. Let us also never make use of the gifts of God save in His service, and for His glory. If God has restored to us bodily health, or has granted the recovery of health to our souls by the forgiveness of our sins, let us strive to serve Him with renewed fervour. We serve Him by succouring our neighbour, comforting the afflicted, supporting the weak, assisting the poor, working for the Church and fulfilling faithfully the duties of our station.

2. *The diligence of this woman.* *And immediately she arose, and ministered unto them.* She arose without delay as soon as she felt herself healed. If we are in the enjoyment of bodily health, why do we waste the strength which God has given us in shameful repose, instead of employing it in useful work? If our soul has been healed by a sincere conversion, whence comes this idleness in our performance of our religious duties, whence this tardiness in the practice of good works? She arose without delay, because it concerned the service of Jesus. Ah! if it is a matter of serving the world or of our own interest, or pleasure, what diligence, what zeal! we have strength, we have health sufficient. But when it concerns the service of Jesus, is it not then that only idleness, cowardliness, or faint-heartedness are to be found in us?

3. *The attention of this woman.* It is easy to conceive that in ministering to Christ, she brought all her care to bear, that she made a study of doing well all that she did, that she was attentive to every thing, that nothing might be wanting, that, whatever pleasure she might have taken in listening to the words of the Saviour, she did not wait to listen to them, when her ministry was required elsewhere, and that, in the same way, when, without prejudice to that which she had to do, she could listen to them, she did not lose one of them; that finally, her heart was occupied with them, whilst her hands were busily engaged in waiting on Him. It is with the same earnestness and zeal, the same attention, and the same ardour that a converted sinner ought to arise, to act, and to labour. He ought to shew his gratitude for graces received by the practice of good works. If he has been truly raised from the death of sin, if he lives to God, he must shew it in his actions, sustained and animated by charity, humility, prayer, and in all the acts of holiness which a Christian life requires of him.

4. *The affection of this woman.* With what love must she not have ministered to Jesus and His disciples! She must have felt it an honour, when she thought

of the greatness of Him to Whom she ministered: she must have felt it a duty, when she thought of the benefits she had received from Him: she must have found a sensible satisfaction in it, in considering the goodness with which He accompanied His favours. We serve the same Master, and we have the same motives for serving Him; but do we do so with the same affection? When our service is done out of motives of love, it is a sweeter, and more careful service. Unless this affection is the mainspring of our acts of service, they are done with weariness, and with distaste, with impatience, and murmurings, and such services merit often rather to be punished than recompensed. Let us set before ourselves then, Jesus and His love, as the object of our actions: let us re-kindle our faith by these thoughts, and it will not then be difficult to re-kindle our fervour.

Prayer. I am resolved, O my God! to regulate my conduct for the time to come, only in accordance with that love which a humble and loving faith inspires, to resist no longer Thy tender entreaties, and to follow henceforth with faithfulness all the impressions of Thy grace. But command Thyself, O Jesus! command the passions which govern me: stretch forth Thy hand to me, take me by the hand, and lead me. Raise me, help me, lift me above temptations, above earthly and carnal desires, above the judgements of men, above myself. Raise me up to Thee, that I may remain united to Thee for ever. And may one day my feelings be like those of the mother-in-law of S. Peter, when in my last illness, Thou shalt deign, O Jesus, to come and comfort me in my sufferings, and visit me in the Sacrament of Thy Body and Blood, and not content with giving me Thine adorable Hand, Thou dost give Thyself wholly to me, and with Thyself, the assurance and pledge of eternal life. Speak then, command, O my divine Saviour, and at Thy word, my soul, delivered from the weight of the body, delivered from its sins, delivered from its sufferings, from death, will see Thee face to face, and will live eternally with Thee. O happy day, when wilt thou come? What can comfort me for the time that I must yet wait for thee, but the power that still remains to me to go myself and seek Christ, and receive Him with the same feelings which I desire to have at the last day of my life. Amen.

Meditation XLVI.

SEVERAL CURES WROUGHT BY CHRIST ON THE EVENING OF THE SAME DAY.

Jesus heals the sick, delivers those possessed by evil spirits, and by these miracles, accomplishes the prophecy of Isaiah. S. Mark i. 32-34. S. Luke iv. 40-41. S. Matt. viii. 16-17.

FIRST POINT.

Jesus heals the sick.

And at even, when the sun did set, they brought unto Him all that were possessed with devils. And all the city was gathered together at the door. And He healed many that were sick of divers diseases, and cast out many devils: and He laid His Hands on every one of them, and healed them.

1. The time of day is no hindrance to Jesus. Almost immediately after the healing of the mother-in-law of S. Peter, the sun set, and with its light the obligation of rest which was prescribed for the whole of the Sabbath day ceased also, as, according to the constant practice of the Hebrews, the Sabbath lasted from one evening to the next. The people awaited with impatience this moment, on which all those who were afflicted had set their hopes. As soon as it had arrived, they hastened to lead to Jesus, or to lay at His feet, every kind of diseased and sick person. This divine Saviour, yielding to the motives of His charity, laid His hands on each of them and healed them. We need not regard the time,

in order to ask for favours or graces from Christ: He is to be found at all hours, by night as by day: at all times shall we find Him willing to receive us, to listen to us, and to grant our prayers: His charity knows no inopportune moment. Is it so likewise with ourselves? Are we ready at all times to help our neighbour who has recourse to us?

2. The crowd does not keep back Christ. Almost all the city were gathered together around the house of S. Peter, and were besieging the door. From all quarters of Capernaum, they had led or brought the sick in order to present them to Jesus. The multitude neither overwhelms Him, nor drives Him back. The power and the will which He has to bless men and to gladden their hearts cannot be damped by the importunity and the crowd of suppliants: rather on the contrary, the more opportunity He has for spreading His benefits, the greater is the satisfaction to His goodness. It is a glad sight to His divine Heart to behold this crowd of people who come to Him with faith, in order to receive the alleviation of their sufferings. This sight is renewed often before our eyes: we see still believers hasten into our Churches there to worship Christ, and to seek for blessings from Him; let us join this multitude, let us seek to animate others by our example, or at least let us edify them by our recollectedness and earnestness.

3. The diversity of diseases does not exceed the power of Christ. All those who were brought to Him were healed, however great, however inveterate, however incurable their evils might be. *He laid His Hands*, says S. Luke, *on every one of them*. A pattern of the charity which Christians owe to one another, a pattern of the zeal which the ministers of Christ ought to have, always ready to visit the sick, to assist the poor, to comfort the afflicted.

4. The number of the sick does not exhaust the goodness of Christ. He did not heal all the sick who were brought to Him, by one single act of His will, by

a single absolute command, as He might have done: He willed to lay His Hands on each one of them, and listen to them each. He willed to give them all the consolation of seeing Him, of being seen by Him, of being touched by Him, however repugnant, however fatiguing, this office might be in itself. It is with the same goodness, that, in the Sacrament of His Sacred Body and Blood, He gives Himself to each one of us wholly, in order to serve us as Food, to heal us, to sanctify us, to unite us to Him. What goodness!

SECOND POINT.

Jesus delivers those who were possessed.

1. The devils are driven out by Jesus with a word. The Saviour Who healed sicknesses by touching those who suffered them, drove out all the devils by His Word, that He might make all these proud spirits feel the absolute power which He had over them. How powerful the word of Jesus is! Let us cherish it in our hearts, that we may be always ready to oppose it to the suggestions of the evil one. This enemy, all formidable as he is, cannot resist that powerful weapon.

2. The devils are forward to confess Christ. *And devils also came out of many, crying out, and saying, Thou art Christ the Son of God.* What does this acknowledgement of the devils imply, joined to the fearful cries which they are heard to utter? Their sin was, it is believed, that they refused to acknowledge the mystery of the Incarnation of the Word, and refused to submit to the Son of God, Who in the fulness of time, was about to become man; they seem to acknowledge Him now, but too late; they experience the effects of His power, they publish it, and yet they hate it. Alas! how sad it will be, because it will be too late; how sad for unbelievers, heretics, sinners, ungodly men, not to have known and not to have confessed Christ, until He shall drive them out of His kingdom and out of His Presence!

3. The devils are compelled to hold their peace. *And He rebuking them suffered them not to speak: for they knew that He was Christ.* Jesus assumes with the devils the menacing tone of an angry Master, and imposes silence upon them, because the devil never has any but evil designs in all that he does. If he praises, it is in order to inspire feelings of vain-glory, and to withdraw us from God, by making us the accomplices of his pride; if he leads us to good, it is only in order to disturb the work of God, whilst on the other hand, the guidance of the Holy Spirit is wisdom and gentleness. Jesus knew at what time and to whom He should manifest His divinity, and He was insensibly preparing men's minds to receive this great truth; but the devil would have wished to have brought this about in a precipitate manner, so as to disturb the order and the fabric of the wise Economy of God and to hinder the building of the Church from being raised on this solid foundation. It is, by the same artifice, that, when he cannot withdraw a soul from the service of God, he urges him to indiscretions, he presents to him the idea of a holiness and of virtues which are not suitable to him, he inspires him with the feeling of duty in undertaking acts of penitence beyond his strength, in order to disgust him and to overthrow thus the erection of his perfection. Let us avoid this illusion, let us conform ourselves to, and follow with simplicity, the drawings of grace, let us give ourselves up to the guidance of God, and let us content ourselves with following on step by step, according to the degree of light which is granted to us. Let us apply ourselves, before all things, to the duties of our state, and to the solid virtues of humility, obedience, charity, self-denial, and let us be on our guard against every hasty and ardent wish, which neither awaits reflection nor advice.

4. The devils are confounded in their knowledge. *And suffered not the devils to speak, because they knew Him.* Although the devils knew that Jesus was the Christ, they had not nevertheless a certain and exact

knowledge of this mystery; their knowledge was only a matter of conjecture. They had strong conjectures respecting the Divinity of Christ, because they were not ignorant of the promises, the prophecies, and the time of their accomplishment; but their uncertainty was such that they regarded this Divine Saviour as accessible to passions, to vain-glory, to ambition, to fear, to mistrust, to despondency. In vain nevertheless, did they put His virtue to the test during the whole of His life, they have always been confounded, all their efforts have only served to manifest His Divinity. Here, as every where else, they contribute, in spite of themselves, to His glory; whether by the words their fury extorts from them, whether by the silence which they are forced to maintain. How happy we are to have such a Saviour! What misery for us, if the devils having no power over Him, should succeed in separating us from Him, and hurrying us away with them! but as that cannot happen, save by our own fault, let us keep a watch over ourselves, let us keep ourselves closely united to Jesus, and their efforts will be powerless.

THIRD POINT.

Jesus accomplishes the prophecy of Isaiah.

That it might be fulfilled which was spoken by Esaias the prophet, saying, Himself took our infirmities, and bare our sicknesses. The manner in which the prophet foretells our redemption, and the manner in which Jesus Christ here accomplished the prophecy, are equally worthy of admiration. It is from sin, and from our spiritual infirmities, it is from the anger of God, and the slavery of the evil one, that Jesus comes to deliver us. This deliverance, though infinitely precious to us, was invisible to our eyes, and for that reason likely to make less impression on our hearts; but it becomes sensible to us, when it is applied to bodily infirmities, and to temporal evils, which are the just penalty of sin. It is then by these sensible evils, that the prophet announces our redemption, and it is by these that Jesus begins it. Soon we shall see Him Himself take our infirmities upon Him, here we see Him take them away from us. We see Him exercise an absolute empire over all kinds of infirmities, heal the sick, deliver the possessed, and by that means give a sensible proof that He is our Redeemer and our Saviour. It is for us now to shew our gratitude for the blessings we owe Him, and to strive to realize how it is that He has delivered us from these evils which we suffer besides, and at which perhaps we murmur.

1. Jesus has delivered us from evil by changing the nature of it through His merits. Our sufferings without Jesus, were sufferings which brought on us punishment for our sins, without expiating them; which tormented the sinner without purifying him; but this divine Saviour, by taking them upon Himself, has elevated them, ennobled, and sanctified them. They are, by His merits, a preservative against the sin we should be led to commit, and an atonement for the sins which we have committed; they are the purest homage which we can offer to God; O sacred sufferings! who would not desire thee, who would not value thee! Let us not suffer then any longer as children of Adam, but as members of Christ. Being delivered by Him from our sufferings, wherefore should we take them again upon ourselves? Being made by Him children of God, why should we return to the hard condition of slaves? Being enabled to suffer with so much glory, wherefore should we suffer still without the helps of religion, and without hope?

2. Jesus has delivered us from evil, in that He has taken away the opprobrium from it by His example. Having suffered for us, there is now only glory in suffering like Him, and for Him. What sufferings of body and mind can we have, which Jesus hath not suffered the like, and far greater besides? After the example of this God made a victim for us, can we complain of suffering too much, and not rather that we do not suffer enough? If the world still attaches an idea of oppro-

brium and contempt, to poverty, to humiliation, to sufferings; it is the opprobrium which Jesus has borne, and in which a Christian ought to glory since these sufferings gain for him the most perfect resemblance which he could have with the Son of God. Happy he who can rightly conceive this mystery. Let us ask for knowledge from Him, Who is the Divine Author of it.

3. Jesus has delivered us from evil in that He has softened the rigour of it by His grace. Our sufferings without Jesus, were an over-powering weight, under which our strength, and our courage were sinking; Jesus, by taking them upon Himself, has gained for us the grace which fortifies us, and which puts us in a condition to support them with patience, with resignation, and even with joy. What strength does not grace communicate to the weakest! what sweetness does it not make us find in the cup which is the bitterest to nature! The world cannot believe it; but the friends of Jesus know it by experience, and the world itself is sometimes forced to acknowledge this truth, in the facts to which it is the witness, in the examples which it admires.

4. Jesus has delivered us from evil in that He has shortened the duration of it by His power. Our sufferings, without Jesus, would have been eternal: but by having taken them upon Himself, He has changed them into temporal sufferings. He shortens them sometimes even in this life, when, in answer to our prayers, He restores health to us; He shortens them, lastly, by the end of life, with which end all sufferings for those who have known how to profit by them here, and who have by God's grace, let them work out the purpose for which they were sent. "For our light affliction which is but for a moment, worketh for us a far more exceeding and eternal weight of glory."

Prayer. O Jesus! since it is thus, I will not ask of Thee any miracles in order to free myself from my afflictions; I will only ask of Thee for grace to make a good use of them. Yea, Lord, let me suffer here below whatsoever it may please Thee, if only I may, by

Thy divine help, make so holy a use of my sufferings, that I may avoid the sufferings of hell which I have deserved, and enjoy that eternal happiness which Thou hast purchased with Thy blood, and promised to the faithful Christian, who is patient in tribulations. Amen.

Meditation XLVII.
JESUS GOES THROUGH GALILEE.

1. Jesus prepares Himself for His mission by prayer. 2. He sends away the Capernaites who opposed His mission. 3. He devotes Himself to His mission. S. Mark i. 35—39. S Luke iv. 40—44. S. Matt. iv. 23—25.

FIRST POINT.

Jesus prepares Himself for His mission by prayer.

And in the morning rising up a great while before day, He went out, and departed into a solitary place, and there prayed.

1. Jesus rises early in order to pray. The morning is the fittest time for prayer. He who loses the hours of the morning in sleep, does not gather up the heavenly manna. Interruptions present themselves, occupations press upon us, time fails, and one experiences no longer anything but distaste for prayer. The labourer and the artizan, the man of business, and the studious man rise early, at the call of duty, or of necessity, of interest, or of pleasure: the man of prayer ought to be animated by all these motives, and still more by the example of Christ. Our rising is the first action of the day; the manner in which we do it decides ordinarily the fervour or the faint heartedness of all the actions of the day: it is the first homage which we render to our Creator, Who, in raising us from sleep, raises us so to say, from nothing, gives us back our life, gives us back to ourselves, and seems to create a new universe for us. Let us hasten to enjoy His benefits, and to testify our gratitude to Him for them.

2. *Jesus withdraws into the desert in order to pray.* He rises before the sun, and leaving the house of Peter by the glimmer of the twilight, He retires to a desert place, where, far from the tumult of the city, He gives Himself up entirely to the fervour of His prayer. There is one kind of prayer which we can offer to God in all places, and in the midst even of our ordinary occupations, by inward recollectedness, by dwelling in the Presence of God, by uprightness of intention, and by fervent aspirations; but there is another kind to which we must give each day, a more connected time, and it is for that, that we must seek the desert. We find this desert in our Churches, open for prayer: we can find it in our own homes, and there pour ourselves out in prayer, before we give ourselves up to any other occupation: but where specially we must seek it, is in our own hearts. We shall never pray as we ought, till we have brought our hearts into the desert, into solitude, that is to say, until we have set it free from all cares, from all thoughts which distract it, from all objects which are foreign to the worship of God, in order to occupy ourselves solely with God, the needs of our souls, and the subject of our prayer, presenting ourselves before God, as if there were none other but Him and ourselves in the universe. For the want of this precaution or of this preparation, we kneel down to say our prayers, and repeat fervent prayers, even sometimes from a sense of obligation, but nevertheless we do not pray.

3. *Jesus prays in the desert.* As soon as Jesus was in a place apart, He began to pray. Happy those, who separated from the world, live in the desert of religion, if they know how there to pray! We leave our houses, we enter the Church, and what are we doing there, if we are not praying there? We find ourselves sometimes in solitude and without occupation, why do we not profit by this fortunate leisure in order to pray! How senseless we are! we prefer even to weary ourselves, to make others partakers in our weariness, to seek for distractions and frivolous amusements, sooner than to

enjoy in solitude the delights of prayer. O divine Saviour! for whom didst Thou devote Thyself thus to prayer in the desert? It is for me and for my salvation; it is in order to gain for me the graces of which I have need, and in order to give me the example of them: that, at Thy example, I may be punctual, recollected, constant, and fervent in my prayers.

SECOND POINT.

Jesus sends away the Capernaites who sought to keep Him back from proceeding further in His mission.

And Simon, and they that were with him, followed after Him. And when they had found Him, they said unto Him, all men seek for Thee. And He said unto them, Let us go into the next towns, that I may preach there also; for thereforth came I forth... And the people sought Him, and came unto Him, and stayed Him that He should not depart from them, and He said unto them, I must preach the kingdom of God to other cities also; for therefore am I sent.

1. The Capernaites seek Jesus. They seek Him with eagerness. From the morning they assemble, as they had done the evening before, around the house of S. Peter, where they supposed Jesus to be still, and they ask to see Him with all the eagerness which great needs, or deep gratitude inspire. They seek Him with love. It is no longer for their temporal interests or for the healing of their sick that they seek Him; but eager to learn His doctrines, they do so in order to hear Him and to profit by His lessons. They seek Him with constancy. Jesus was no longer in the house, S. Peter seeks for Him there, and not finding Him there, he follows Him with his brother Andrew and the other disciples into the solitude, where he thinks to find Him, in order to give an account to the Saviour of all that had taken place at Capernaum: but the multitude follows them, and leaving the city in crowds, they resolve to seek Jesus without sparing either pains, or fatigue, and they deter-

mine not to return without having found their benefactor. Is it thus that we seek Jesus? When we seek Him after this manner, we cannot fail to find Him.

2. The Capernaites find Jesus. They find Him by following S. Peter and the other disciples. It is thus by following the ministers whom God has set over us, and appointed as our guides, that we find Jesus. If we choose ways of our own seeking, we wander without guides in the desert, and we open out for ourselves, at the will of our own caprices, a thousand different ways, but none of which lead us to Jesus.

3. The Capernaites endeavour to detain Jesus. They see Him disposed to leave Him, and they will not consent to it: they beg Him not to forsake them, and even employ a kind of constraint towards Him. How agreeable to the heart of Jesus must these entreaties have been, and if He did not yield to them, how well He must have known to compensate to them for it! If we had but the same love to this divine Saviour, the same earnestness in detaining Him with us, and in remaining with Him, what would be our happiness! In vain did this grateful people entreat Jesus not to leave them; Do not detain Me, He says: the towns, the villages, and neighbouring cities await Me: I must preach to them the word of God, as well as unto you; they have a share in My mission. Let us go, He says to His disciples, come with Me, let us go through the towns and villages, in order that I may preach the Gospel there: for that purpose am I come into the world, for that end have I been sent. Such ought to be our rules with ourselves: for what purpose are we sent? to what end have we come into the world? Ah! it is not by the esteem, the love, the approbation of men that we ought to regulate our conduct, but by the will of God, the purpose of our calling, the duties of our station, without regard to our convenience, our rest, our self-interest, our own glory. When Jesus had thus spoken, the people insisted no longer, but returned to the city in the hope of soon seeing their Benefactor return

thither, and the four disciples remained with Jesus in order to accompany Him on His mission.

THIRD POINT.

Jesus gives Himself up to His mission.

1. His labours. *And Jesus went about all Galilee, teaching in their synagogues, and preaching the gospel of the kingdom, and healing all manner of disease among the people, and He cast out devils.* From the time that Jesus began His ministry, His whole life was only work and prayer: and it is thus that each of the days of His mortal life will be employed. The truly apostolic man ought to sustain his mission by continued efforts of charity and zeal, to fulfil with the same gladness of heart every office, whether it be obscure, or one that brings him into public notice, to labour with the same zeal for the salvation of poor or rich, and making war upon the devil, to drive him out of all the hearts of which he has possession. There is no place, and no person which ought to escape his zeal.

2. The miracles of Jesus Christ. *And His fame went throughout all Syria; and they brought unto Him all sick people that were taken with divers diseases and torments, and those which were possessed with devils, and those which were lunatic, and those that had the palsy: and He healed them.* The tidings of our Blessed Saviour's miracles passed from Galilee into Syria, and spread through that whole province. Even from that country, the inhabitants of which were for the greater part heathen, divers sick were brought unto Him, all of whom He healed. Shall we alone not have recourse to Jesus, to be delivered from our infirmities? We who have been taught by faith, and who knows with how many kinds of evils we are inwardly afflicted, shall we not do on behalf of our souls, what these people did for the healing of their bodies?

3. The success of His miracles. *And there followed*

Him great multitudes of people from Galilee, and from Decapolis, and from Jerusalem, and from Judea, and from beyond Jordan. What a sight to see these people collected together around Jesus, following Him in crowds in order to hear His divine instructions! let us go thither ourselves; let us join ourselves to these multitudes of believers, let us follow Jesus, and let us swell the glory of His triumph.

Prayer. I come to Thee, O Jesus! resolved to follow Thee, and not to leave Thee more. Give me an attentive mind that I may listen to Thy lessons, and a docile heart to practise them. I thank Thee, O divine Saviour! for the sufferings and fatigues to which Thou didst subject Thyself in order to preach to us Thy Gospel. Happy those to whom Thou hast entrusted the work of carrying on Thy labours, and who, whether in the towns or in the country, are occupied with instructing Thy people! give them the grace to imitate Thee, and to me that of labouring, according to my station, for Thy glory, by practising the commandments of Thy Holy Gospel. I join myself, O Jesus, to that crowd of such people whom Thou didst heal: there is none amongst them as miserable as I am. My soul is overwhelmed with all kinds of sicknesses, and there is none but Thee Who canst heal it. I adore Thy power, Oh adorable Redeemer, and I implore Thy charity: shall I be the only one whom Thou dost not heal? Heal me, Lord: my healing shall manifest Thy power, and contribute to Thy glory. Amen.

Meditation XLVIII.

PREACHING OF JESUS, AND THE MIRACULOUS DRAUGHT OF FISHES IN THE SHIP OF SIMON PETER.

1. Jesus preaches from the ship of Simon Peter. 2. Jesus causes S. Peter to make a miraculous draught of fishes. 3. Jesus points out the mystery hidden under this event. S. Luke v. 1-11.

FIRST POINT.

Jesus preaches from the ship of Simon Peter.

And it came to pass, that as the people pressed upon Him to hear the Word of God, He stood by the lake of Gennesaret, and saw two ships standing by the lake: but the fishermen were gone out of them, and were washing their nets; and He entered into one of the ships, which was Simon's, and prayed him that he would thrust out a little from the land. And He sat down, and taught the people out of the ship.

1. Consider the earnestness of the people. Jesus, being in the coasts of the lake of Gennesaret, found Himself surrounded by a crowd of people, who, famished to learn His doctrine, had assembled from different parts, and were pressing upon Him on all sides. How edifying this concourse was, and how agreeable to Jesus! Have we the same ardour in listening to, in reading, and in meditating on the Word of God? Do we not love better to read and to hear things which are useless, frivolous, dangerous, or evil? Let us examine here our hearts, and let us reform ourselves.

2. Admire the goodness of Jesus. The tumult was so great, that He could not have been heard except by a very small number of those who pressed around Him.

He wished to remedy this disorder, without disappointing these fervent auditors, whom He attracted around His person, and who responded with so much courage to the secret movements of His grace. He perceived two ships standing by the side of the lake; the fishermen had gone on land, and were occupied in washing their nets; one of the boats was that of Simon Peter into which Jesus entered. It is most probable that Jesus had arrived the evening before at Bethsaida, a city situated near the lake, and the native country of S. Peter: though He may even have been there some days, which may have been the reason which prompted S. Peter, and the two brothers James and John to go fishing. It also appears that Andrew was with his brother Simon, although he is not mentioned here. Jesus, having then gone on board the ship of Simon Peter, *He prayed him that he would thrust out a little from the land;* the people were drawn up on the shores; the Saviour seated Himself in the ship, and thence as from the pulpit of truth, He taught the multitude, who returned thence afterwards, praising and blessing God. What goodness, what condescension in Jesus thus to contribute to the instruction and the gratification of this people! He does not do any less for us: He provides that, in His Church, the teachings of the Faith should be multiplied to us. But do we take part in them, and do we seek only for instruction, for that which may edify us and encourage us in that which is good, and correct our faults? Or are we not too much occupied in judging the style, or the language of the preacher, or in seeking for any thing which may either please our intellect, or gratify our imagination?

3. Meditate on the happiness of S. Peter. Of the two ships which were on the shores of the lake, Jesus chooses his. By this ship, He sets before us, in a hidden figure, the ship of His Church, which should be governed by the successors of S. Peter and the Apostles, and should be to the end of time, "the pillar and ground of the truth." Do we then receive our teaching from

the Church? Do we acknowledge the authority of the ministry thus handed down to us by apostolical succession? Any teaching which we may receive out of this fold, however sublime the sentiments which it may appear to inculcate, however enlightened the maxims which it sets forth, is not the teaching of Jesus; it is the master of error and lying who is misleading us.

SECOND POINT.

Jesus causes S. Peter to make a miraculous draught of fish.

1. Observe the obedience of S. Peter. *Now when He had left speaking, He said unto Simon, Launch out into the deep, and let down your nets for a draught, And Simon, answering said unto Him, Master, we have toiled all night and have taken nothing: nevertheless at Thy word, I will let down the net.* A blind obedience by which Simon yields up his own understanding and experience. He knew better than any one else that broad day light was not a time as favourable for fishing as night time would be; he knew, by more recent experience that there were no fish in this place: but reasoning has no place when it is a matter of obedience. Obedience is not perfect, if we do not sacrifice to it our own understanding. An obedience full of confidence. If S. Peter set before our Saviour his thoughts and his reflections, it was not in order to induce Him to revoke His commands, but only to shew Him how great the confidence he had in Him, was. Notwithstanding all that, he said to Him, *at Thy word, I will* without deliberation, *let down the net*, which does not mean only, I am going to do it in order to obey Thee, because Thou commandest it, which would only have been obedience in judgement and in will; but I am about to do it at Thy word, persuaded that by acting in Thy Name, and at Thy commands, my labours will not be in vain, useless, and without success. Lastly, a prompt obedience. Hardly had Peter finished these words, than

he and his companions threw down the nets without awaiting from the Saviour either answer, or explanation, or fresh orders, or renewed assurance. Is it thus that we obey those who are " over us in the Lord," and who hold to us on earth the place of Christ ?

2. Observe the success of S. Peter's obedience. *And when they had this done, they inclosed a great multitude of fishes: and their net brake. And they beckoned unto their partners, which were in the other ship, that they should come and help them. And they came, and filled both the ships, so that they began to sink.* Hardly had they cast the net into the sea, than they felt a number of fish collecting there. They feared to see the net break under their hands, and despaired of drawing it out without help. They made a sign to the fishermen in the other ship to come and help them. They drew near, and the draught of fishes was so abundant, that the two ships which were filled were on the point of sinking. Can we, after such a miracle, doubt the power of our Lord, and fear to obey Him?

3. Observe the feelings which the miracle brought forth. *When Simon Peter saw it, he fell down at Jesus' knees, saying, Depart from me, for I am a sinful man, O Lord. For he was astonished, and all that were with him, at the draught of fishes which they had taken: and so was also James and John, the sons of Zebedee, which were partners with Simon. And Jesus said unto Simon, Fear not.* The disciples had seen their Master work many miracles: but this one filled them with dread. Fishermen by profession, they were better able to understand the miracle. They had seen, without being afraid, their Master command on land the devils, and had seen them obedient to His Word; and had seen Him speak the word and the sick were healed: but when they saw that His power extended even to the depths of the sea, that He could call together the fishes from thence, and assemble them at His will, they were so terrified at it, that fear rendered them, and those that were with them, dumb, and as it were motionless. They

dared not raise their eyes to their Benefactor. Peter, whose feelings were always rather quicker than those of the rest, overcoming his fear, and summoning up all his strength, threw himself at the feet of Jesus, and said to Him, Lord, I am not worthy that Thou shouldest remain in my ship; withdraw from a sinner, such as I am; I am not worthy to possess Thee. O Holiness so much to be feared! how is it that we dare to appear before Thee, or rather how is it that we do appear before Thee with such little respect and fear? *Jesus said unto Simon, Fear not.* Thou willest, O my God, that we should learn by these words, that Thy will is equal to Thy power: both are infinite. No, it is not those who fear Thee, and who love Thee, who ought to keep away from Thee: sinners though they be, if they do but humble themselves in all sincerity before Thee, Thou dost disperse their fears, and dost re-assure them: Thou dost bestow favours on them. To believe ourselves to be unworthy of Jesus through reverence for His Greatness, and to preserve at the same time a tender love for His Person, such are the sure means by which never to be separated from Him.

THIRD POINT.

Jesus points out the mystery hidden under this event.

Jesus said unto Simon, Fear not: from henceforth thou shalt catch men. That is to say, be not afraid, far from going away from Me, understand on the contrary, that it is important for you to leave all and follow Me. What you have just seen done in a figure, I am about to bring about through your ministry: from fishers of fish you are about to become fishers of men. These words determined the first disciples of Jesus, who from that time forward became closely attached to Him, and were never more separated from Him. *And when they had brought their ships to land, they forsook all and followed Him.* By these words, Jesus makes known to us, that this draught of fishes was not only a miracle, but was further a figure, and a prophecy of a still greater miracle, namely, the propagation of the Gospel by the Apostles and their successors. A prediction which is of great comfort to us, who see the literal accomplishment of it.

1. In the abundance of this spiritual draught of fishes. Every part of the world, every kingdom of the earth, every clime, every tongue has received Christianity. The ship of the Church has crossed every sea: its mysterious nets have been stretched from one end of the world to the other, from the east to the west, from the north to the south. The inhabitants of the old and new world have gathered together in crowds, and these fishers of fish have become teachers of all nations. Could we believe such a prodigy if we were not eye-witnesses of it?

2. Accomplishment of the prediction of Jesus Christ in the manner in which this draught of fishes has been accomplished. It has been accomplished in the manner, which would have appeared the least fitted for its success. It has been carried on in the open day, and the Christian religion has been offered to the world, such as it is, without circumvention, without dissimulation, without artifice. To the wisdom of this world, it has profferred the sublimity of its dogmas without reasonings; to the corruption of the world, it has imposed the severity of its morals without palliation; to the superstition of the world, it has offered the unity of its worship without reserve; to the persecution of the world, it has offered the truth of its faith without disguise; and notwithstanding this publicity, with this simplicity and this candour, it has overcome the world, it has attracted it, gained it over, and triumphed over it.

3. Accomplishment of the prediction of Jesus Christ in these by whom this draught of fishes has been accomplished: that is to say, by the Apostles, and their successors. It is thus that the prediction hidden under the figure of this miraculous draught of fishes has been

verified in mankind: it is thus that the Saviour taught His disciples, by setting before their eyes, in a sensible manner, the history of His Church, the detail of their labours, the rule of their duties, and the image of their success. This manner of teaching belongs only to a God. No other sect which has separated off from the Church, has any share in this miracle. Heretics may have perverted Christians indeed, but they have never made any. Their zeal, always in accordance with their own self interest and their own passions, has never led them to leave all for the preaching of the Gospel. There is no Christian Church, which does not acknowledge as its first apostle, one of those called and sent by Christ to preach the Gospel.

Prayer. I thank Thee, O my God, that Thou hast caused me to be born into Thy Holy Church: grant that nothing may separate me from it; multiply labourers in it, who shall preach Thy Gospel, gather together all nations into it, and bring back into Thy fold all those who have had the misery to forsake it. Amen.

Meditation XLIX.

SERMON ON THE MOUNT.

OF THE TWO FIRST BEATITUDES.

Observe first of all, what was the preparation for this discourse, and meditate then on the two first beatitudes. S. Matt. v. 1—14.

FIRST POINT.

Preparation for this discourse.

And seeing the multitude, He went up into a mountain: and when He was set, His disciples came unto Him: and He opened His mouth, and taught them, saying. After the miraculous draught of fishes, Jesus, accompanied by His four disciples, continued His journey, and His mission. People assembled in crowds from all sides, in order to see Him and to hear Him. Finding Himself one day overwhelmed by the crowds, He went up into a mountain, and when He had seated Himself, He began to teach.

1. Consider Who it is that teaches. It is Jesus, the Word of God made man, uncreated Wisdom, God Himself: let us listen then to Him with reverence and in a teachable spirit.

2. Consider the place where He teaches. It is a mountain, visible and accessible to everyone. The ancient law had been given on a mountain: and it is on a mountain that Jesus begins to give the new law: but this latter was not like that of Sinai, surrounded by thunders and lightnings, and fire and smoke: but all is calm and peaceful here, all invites confidence, everything breathes here love and peace. O Blessed Jesus! Oh Law-giver worthy of love!

3. Consider those whom He teaches. They are all those who follow Him and are desirous to hear Him. When Jesus was seated, His disciples drew near to Him, that is to say, not only S. Peter, S. Andrew, S. James, and S. John, but several others besides who already made a profession of being His disciples, and of following Him every where. The rest of the people followed, and all listened in silence. Nothing hinders us from drawing near to Jesus; we should therefore be more disposed to listen to Him, and more resolved to practise His lessons.

4. Consider the manner in which He teaches: it is by Himself. He had spoken to mankind at first by the mouth of angels; He spoke to the Jews in the wilderness by Moses, and to Moses by an angel. He had opened, in the Old Testament, the mouths of prophets; and He will soon speak by the mouth of His apostles; but here it is by Himself that He speaks to us: it is His sacred mouth which has uttered the oracles on which we are about to meditate. What goodness on His part! what

gratitude, what teachableness has He not the right to exact on our's?

5. Consider the doctrine which He teaches: it is the way of true happiness and of perfection. It is not those vain speculations which only excite the curiosity of men without satisfying it, and which can neither render us happier nor better; it is the knowledge of true happiness which Jesus gives us, it is the means by which we may attain to it which He teaches us. What could more closely concern us? Let us receive then with eagerness and earnestness those divine instructions which He is about to give us. Human wisdom has never invented any thing like them; they are the strongest proof and the best apology that our holy religion can offer to her enemies. A law-giver who frames such laws, who gives such lessons, and who makes Himself followed, can be none other than the messenger and the Son of God.

SECOND POINT.

First beatitude.

Blessed, says Jesus Christ to them, *are the poor in spirit, for theirs is the kingdom of Heaven.* There are those who are poor in spirit, whether in regard to the riches which are without a man, or with regard to those which are within him: let us examine both, and let us then meditate on the happiness which those different kinds of riches procure for him.

1. There are those who are poor in spirit with regard to the riches which are without them. With respect to these riches, there are poor of three kinds; those who are poor by choice, poor from necessity, and poor in will. The poor by choice, who are so voluntarily, are those, who by a free renunciation, have despoiled themselves of their wealth, have taken upon themselves a vow never to possess any thing of their own in this world, and to be entirely dependent on others for all they use. Those are poor in spirit, if they maintain the spirit of

detachment, humility, and self-mortification, with which they ought to have entered on this renunciation. The poor by necessity are those, who by their condition, their birth, or some accident appointed for them by Providence, find themselves without earthly possessions, or with but few, who live on straitened means, and experience the hardships of indigence. These are poor in spirit, if, content with their lot, they bear it with resignation and humility, if they do not desire to change it, and are not envious of the rich. Lastly, the poor in will, are those who by a kind of necessity, find themselves placed in a position of wealth. They are poor in spirit, if they possess riches without fixing their hearts on them, without pride, and without anxiety to increase them : if they are ready to lose them without murmuring: if they only make use of them with sobriety and moderation, if they make use of them for the relief of their neighbours, the spread of the faith, the service of God, and not for display, luxury, and the enjoyments of this life. Are we amongst the number of these different kinds of poor in spirit ?

2. There are those who are poor in spirit with regard to the riches which are within them. There are, or there may be, in man, three sorts of riches from which poverty of spirit ought to detach them : the first are the riches of the body, such as strength, beauty, health : the second are the natural riches of the soul, such as knowledge, powers of mind, talents, and that which these advantages procure for us from others, such as love and esteem : the third are the supernatural riches of the soul, which are not necessary to our perfection, such as spiritual consolations, a sensible pleasure and delight in our devotions. We ought to receive all these sorts of riches with gratitude from the hand of God, as a poor man receives alms; we ought to possess them with humility as belonging to God, and not to ourselves: we ought to make use of them with fear, and only to employ them to the glory of God : we must suffer their loss with resignation, and believe that, created not for ourselves, but for

God, it is not to His gifts, but to Himself alone that we must cling. The more we advance in this poverty of spirit, in this entire despoiling of ourselves, the further shall we advance in perfection and in the ways of God.

3. Of the blessings which belong to the poor in spirit. The poor in spirit are blessed, because the kingdom of heaven is their's. The kingdom of heaven may signify; First, in heaven, the possession of God in all His glory; the poor in spirit have an assured right to it, by the promise of God Himself. What happiness! what an exchange! A few earthly possessions, which we own but for a moment, for an eternal kingdom! Secondly, in our hearts, sanctifying grace, habitual righteousness, the state of grace in which God, His love and His justice reign in our hearts. It is the poor in spirit who possess this heavenly kingdom, who strive to strengthen themselves in the possession of it, to perfect themselves, to enrich themselves by works of piety and virtue, and by the use of Sacraments, and other means of grace, while the rich of this world, entirely occupied with the riches of this world, live in forgetfulness of God, and often with a conscience laden with crimes and acts of injustice. Thirdly, in the Church, the Gospel of Jesus Christ. It is to the poor in spirit that the kingdom of God has been announced; for they alone have received it and keep the commandments with simple obedience. The love of riches, the fear of the loss of fortune have hindered a multitude of heathen from embracing Christianity, many heretics from returning to the Church, and still prevents many who glory in calling themselves Christians from keeping the faith in its integrity, from taking an interest in that which concerns the faith, and of taking up its defence on occasions when they are most specially called upon to do so. O miserable riches! who would not fear thee and distrust thee! O sacred poverty! who should not love thee, seek for thee, and desire thee? Blessed and holy detachment from all which is not God, thou art the first lesson which Jesus gives us, and the first beatitude which He sets before

us; when we possess thee, how easy it is to acquire the rest.

THIRD POINT.

Second beatitude.

Blessed are the meek, for they shall possess the earth. The second distinguishing mark of the true believer is meekness. Let us learn to know it in all its extent.

1. Consider in what consists the practice of meekness, and first of all in what way we should exercise it. It should be Christian, having as its principle, charity and humility, and not caprice, or temperament, policy, self-interest, the desire to please or to win over others: it must be sincere, and not feigned or apparent; it must shew itself in our whole self, in the expression of our faces, in our gestures, in our words, in the tones of our voices, and above all, it must dwell in our hearts. 1. Is it thus that we practise this virtue? 2. On what occasions ought we to practise it? These occasions are frequent and daily. It is in small as well as in great events, that we must exercise meekness; we must bear all that is vexatious, without irritation, and without bitterness. 3. Towards whom must we exercise this meekness? Towards our superiors, our inferiors, and our equals, towards great and small, towards every one in general, and towards each one in particular. They have all a right to be borne with by us, in that which may perhaps displease or annoy us on their part, as we desire ourselves that they should bear with us.

2. Examine what are the excuses we make to ourselves in order to palliate this want of meekness. 1. It is the object which is offensive to us. We find it so troublesome, so irksome, that we persuade ourselves that it is impossible, or at least very difficult to bear with it: but it is the characteristic of virtue to overcome difficulties, for without them there would be no virtue, and consequently no merit. 2. It is our own natural disposition: that is to say, we are naturally quick tempered. But do we pretend only to practise the lessons

of Christ, when they are conformable to our own natural characters? What He requires of us, is it not to overcome these very natural inclinations, to put a curb upon our passions, to check its outbursts, to destroy our evil habits, and to cultivate in their stead those which are good? He who only makes feeble efforts to that end, flatters himself in vain that he is His disciple and will have any part in the rewards He has promised to His faithful followers. 3. It is our zeal for good order. But true zeal is full of gentleness: if it assumes occasionally a tone of severity, it is without any passion and without harshness. Let us beware of neglecting a virtue which our Lord places here in the second rank, which He has several times recommended, and of which He has given us so perfect and so constant an example. We flatter ourselves easily that the sins we commit under this head are only trivial sins; but we do not perceive the scandal which quick temper causes, we do not see the mortal wound which a hard or cutting word makes in the heart of our neighbour.

3. Meditate on the blessing promised to meekness. Those who are gentle are happy, because *they shall possess the earth.* Doubtless this signifies the land of the living, the promised land, heaven, where they shall enjoy in eternal peace the delights of perfect love; but besides this they shall possess the earth, that is, the empire of their own hearts. Our heart is, in each one of us, a country, a kingdom, where a thousand seditious motions arise unceasingly; meekness stifles them from their birth, and then we possess our souls in peace, and in our souls the God of peace. There can be no inner life, where this peace does not reign, which is produced by the victory gained over our passions; therefore it is not without reason that our Lord makes use of the expression; *They shall possess the earth.* Yea, even on this earth which we inhabit, meekness gives us successes which we might seek in vain to procure for ourselves by other means. How many startling conversions have there been, how many pious institutions

which meekness has been the means of effecting, and which would have fallen to the ground without it. Is it not through meekness that Christianity possesses now-a-days the earth, which heathenism possessed for so long a time?

Prayer. O Jesus! be Thou henceforth my example, teach me to be as Thou art, meek and humble of heart, to possess my soul in peace, to banish trouble from my spirit, bitterness from my words; give me that gentleness of spirit, that affability, so opposed to disputes and quarrels, that gentleness which wins every one, that store of patience which is never exhausted. Grant me that self-abnegation, that evangelical poverty to which Thou dost reserve the treasures of Thy mercy. Amen.

Meditation L.

FIRST CONTINUATION OF THE SERMON ON THE MOUNT.

Of the three following beatitudes. S. Matt. v. 5—7.

FIRST POINT.

Third beatitude.

Blessed are they that mourn, for they shall be comforted. Tears, which in the opinion of men, only befit the unhappy, are, in the judgement of the Son of God, tokens of happiness; but it is from the source whence flow these tears, that spring the claims we have to this beatitude. Now, we may distinguish three different, and consequently three kinds of tears; tears of nature, tears of religion, tears of prayer.

1. Tears of nature. 1. Examine who are these, who, by nature are condemned to tears. Alas! it is every one; no one is exempt from them. The world is full of miserable persons who weep; tears flow on all sides,

and for how many different causes! The loss of wealth, of honour, of health, the death of friends and of neighbours, the jealousy of our rivals, the persecution of enemies, and a thousand other causes of misery, cause, in all conditions of life, bitter tears to flow, which religion alone can soften. 2. Consider on what conditions those can be happy who weep from the necessity laid upon them by nature. Those who weep thus are happy, if they make use of their afflictions in order to detach themselves from creatures, and to attach themselves to God : if, looking upon their troubles as coming to them from the hand of God, they suffer them with patience and resignation, in a spirit of penitence for their sins : if they come at length to suffer them gladly and thankfully as sent by a God Who is chastising and purifying them, and thereby making them like unto His Son. 3. In what are these that thus weep, happy? They are happy, because they will be comforted. They will be so in Heaven, whence every cause of sorrow will be removed, and where they will possess in God a perfect happiness : they will be so on earth, by inward consolations, by particular graces which will make them understand that their afflictions are weighed and measured, that each moment of them is counted by God, and that none of them will be without its reward : they will be so besides on the earth by external consolations, because God does not send us trouble on all sides : if He sends us on the one hand affliction, He multiplies His benefits on the other. But ungrateful as we are, we murmur at the blessings of which He deprives us, and far from thanking Him for the mercies He showers down upon us, we abuse them and thereby offend Him, and lose our own souls!

2. Tears of religion. And in the first place, who are those who by religion, are dedicated to tears? First of all, all Christians, who by their baptismal vows have renounced the pomps and vanities of the world: and then, those who, amongst Christians, make a profession of a more holy and more perfect life, whether they are living in the world, or whether they are separated from

it by their state of life. In the second place, on what conditions are these latter happy? They are happy, if entering truly into and maintaining the spirit of their vocation, they despise the happiness of the world, they abhor the vain show and pride of the world, and lead on the contrary a serious, retired, laborious and penitent life. In the third place, in what does their happiness consist? They are happy, because they will be comforted. They will be so in Heaven, where they will enjoy a pure bliss, proportioned to their repentance, to their fervour and their tears: they will be so on earth through the inward consolations, which a good conscience brings to those who fulfil the duties of their Christian calling: they will be so besides on earth by the outward consolations which they will receive from good men, whose esteem, confidence, and love, without being either the motive, or the reward of their virtue, will aid them in supporting the weight of their trials.

3. The tears of prayer. What are those tears? Prayer opens the sources of innumerable tears. Tears of zeal, at the sight of the scandals which are committed, of the outrages which sinners offer to the Divine Majesty, at the sight of the infinite number of souls who give themselves up to a life of sin, and who perish for ever: tears of repentance, at the sight of our sins, and our daily unfaithfulness: tears of sadness, in considering the length, the misery and the perils of our exile: tears of compassion, in meditating on the sufferings of Jesus Christ: tears of devotion, in adoring Him in the Holy Eucharist: tears of tenderness, in uniting ourselves to Him in the Communion; tears of desire, in longing to see Him in His glory: tears of hope, in thinking of the eternal blessings which are prepared for us; tears of love, in contemplating the sovereign goodness of God, and universality of His benefits, the immensity and eternity of His love. Who could name all the sources of the tears which the Holy Spirit causes to spring up in a heart which is faithful and docile to His operations? They who thus weep are blessed, because they shall be

comforted. They shall be so in Heaven, where all tears will be wiped away, and where they will enjoy fully and for ever the God of all consolation; they will be so in death, because it will only have sweetness for them, which shall be the foretaste of the eternal blessings for which they have sighed; they shall be blessed even in their tears. Ah! who can say what is the sweetness of those tender tears which divine love causes to flow? If we did but know their value and their delights, we should have no difficulty in banishing from our hearts frivolous joys in order to give ourselves up entirely to tears, we should consecrate to them all the moments which we could steal from our occupations, we should feed upon them by day, we should drink of them by night, we should make them the sole delight of our life.

SECOND POINT.

Fourth beatitude.

Blessed are they that do hunger and thirst after righteousness: for they shall be filled.

1. What is this blessing of righteousness, and wherein is it desirable? By righteousness is meant here the habitual practice of every virtue, and the accomplishment of all our duties. It is what we call besides, holiness, perfection, sanctifying grace, love of God, union with God: and as we can always grow in righteousness thus understood, we ought to desire both to acquire it, and also to make fresh progress in it every day. Righteousness taken in this sense is our only good, the only one which belongs to us, which belongs quite entirely, intrinsically and inherently to our soul, of which it forms the greatness, the beauty, and the nobleness. All other possessions are without us, and we can be despoiled of them in spite of ourselves. Even knowledge and talents are of this number. The soul has only a passing use of them: as for the capital, it is as it were in deposit in the organs of the body, of which one single fibre dis-

arranged, suffices to make it lose all, and to make the whole vanish away. Righteousness is a pure and unmixed possession: all others carry with them their poison. Knowledge puffs up, pleasures enervate us, honours dazzle us, riches harden us; but righteousness includes every virtue, and is opposed to every vice. Lastly, righteousness is an eternal and incorruptible possession. Alas! we lose it but too often; but it is always through our own fault. Death will despoil us of all our other possessions, without our being able to retain any of them: but death will not take from us our virtues, on the contrary, it will bring them to perfection, and will consummate them. What folly then to give ourselves so much trouble to acquire, and to desire with so much earnestness and constancy, these frivolous possessions, and not to seek after the one only true good, that is our sanctification and our growth in grace.

2. What is the desire after righteousness, and what ought it to be? This desire ought to be lively and ardent like hunger and thirst: it ought constantly to occupy our minds, to follow us everywhere, to glow in our hearts day and night; it ought to stifle every desire which is contrary to it, and rule all that is not in accordance with it. This desire ought to be active and efficacious like hunger and thirst: it ought to make us attentive to all the opportunities which may present themselves of becoming more holy, and make us zealous in seeking for them, and prompt in making use of them: it should pervade all our actions, all our words, all our sufferings, all our undertakings, all our prayers. What do we not do, to what do we not make up our minds in order to satisfy our hunger and thirst? Again, these desires should be regulated and kept within the bounds of reason, as hunger and thirst are in a man in health. We must not lend ourselves to chimerical ideas of a holiness which is not suitable to our station in life; but by practising every day the same duties, we may grow each day in holiness, and love, and advance towards perfection. We ought not to desire keenly sublime and

extraordinary gifts, such as are sensible delights, or revelations, but to content ourselves with that most precious of all gifts, namely that of doing the will of God, and let us strive to do it each day in a more generous spirit, more inwardly, more purely. Lastly, we must not hope to attain to perfection, even in the exercise of the virtues which belong to our station. Let us desire, and strive to avoid all sins, and all imperfections: and if we fall into some sin, as will always happen to us, do not let us be cast down, let us not despair; let us humble ourselves, condemn ourselves, let us repent, and keep ourselves more on our guard; and continue to desire righteousness with more earnestness.

3. How is this hunger and thirst after righteousness to be satisfied, and where shall we find it? This hunger and thirst is satisfied even in the desire after righteousness. Profane longings torment and tear the heart, which gives itself up to them, because their object is distant, difficult, and sometimes impossible to obtain, always incapable of satisfying, even when it is possessed. The desire after righteousness, on the contrary, fills the soul with consolation, because it contains its object, and bestows it on it. In desiring to love God and to be united to Him, already we love Him and become united to Him. Blessed longing, which is the possession of the God we long for! Let us desire unceasingly to grow in righteousness, and to go on to perfection, and we shall progress unceasingly. We find this desire after righteousness is satisfied in all the events and in all the actions of our life. If we seek above all to become sanctified, we shall become more holy. Nothing in the world can hinder us: on the contrary, everything can contribute to it, everything may be a help to us. We find this desire after righteousness to be satisfied in the doctrines of the Gospel. In them, an upright soul who truly seeks righteousness finds wherewithal it can be fully satisfied. It finds there the true idea of righteousness: it finds the rules, the motives, and the perfect Example of it. Out of that, nothing that satisfies, no-

thing that can fill a soul, either in this life, or in that which is to come. We find again this desire after righteousness is satisfied in the use of the Sacraments and of the means of grace, which are the source of all graces and righteousness: but especially in that sacred Banquet of the Eucharist, where we receive Him, Who is Righteousness Itself, and Who wills indeed to be our Righteousness. Happy is the soul that is hungering and athirst for this Food! it shall be satisfied, its thirst shall be quenched, and it shall be filled in proportion to the hunger and thirst which it brings with it there: open thy mouth wide, and I will fill it. Let us then enlarge our desires; the greater they are, the more will they be satisfied. The treasures which are offered to us are infinite; we shall never be able to exhaust them, but we shall partake of them in proportion as we desire them. O blessed desire! oh hunger! oh delicious thirst! consume then my soul, that it may be filled, and quench its thirst with large draughts from that infinite source of blessings and delights. Lastly, this desire after righteousness will be satisfied in Heaven, where, for ever freed from sin, and for ever separated from sinners and admitted into the assembly of the just, we shall live with them in the kingdom of righteousness, and possess, without fear of losing Him, God, the Author of all righteousness.

THIRD POINT.

Fifth beatitude.

Blessed are the merciful; for they shall obtain mercy. We may succour our neighbour, either in his bodily needs, or in his spiritual needs, or even in his faults.

1. Of mercy in succouring our neighbour in his bodily wants. To feed the hungry, and to give drink to the thirsty, to clothe the naked, to minister unto prisoners, to visit the sick, to harbour the strangers, to redeem those in captivity, and to bury the dead; such are the corporal works of mercy. How do we exercise them?

Do we profit by the occasions which present themselves to us in order to exercise them? Do we do them as we would that others should do unto us, if we were in the same necessities? Do we fulfil them as we desire that God should do towards us? Now, how does God exercise these acts of mercy with regard to us? He has provided us with benefits, He has given us wherewithal to nourish ourselves, to clothe and lodge ourselves, perhaps even with luxury; we enjoy health and freedom. Let us thank God for so many blessings with which He loads us, and let us remember that it is not for ourselves alone that He bestows them upon us; that the greatest happiness which we can find in them, and the greatest profit we can draw down from them, is to share them with those in need, and by that means, to respond to His designs, to imitate His goodness, and to draw down upon ourselves the abundance of His graces.

2. Of mercy in succouring our neighbour in his spiritual needs. The works of spiritual mercy are especially to correct with prudence and charity those who are in fault, to comfort the afflicted, to instruct the ignorant, to counsel those who have need of it, and to pray for others. How do we exercise these works? Do we not omit to reprove out of want of courage, or from human respect, or do we do so in temper, or in a spirit of criticism, and with bitterness? Are we watchful over the instruction given to those dependant on us? Do we instruct them ourselves or see that they are taught their duty towards God, and what they should believe respecting the sacred mysteries of religion? Or are we content that they should be instructed in worldly knowledge, in the literature and sciences of this world? Do we give them, when occasion offers, lessons of piety and virtue? Or are not the lessons we give rather lessons of worldliness, impiety, and irreligion? Do we lend our ear to those in distress, and do we visit them? Do we not rather avoid them, repel them, and add to their sorrow rather than diminish it? Are the counsels we give, worldly counsels, or such as the Gospel teaches? Do they tend to

the salvation or the ruin of souls? Lastly do we acquit ourselves of our duties towards others, by giving them the help of our prayers? Alas! in all our conduct, what cruelty, what inhumanity do we shew, instead of that mercy which the Gospel recommends to us so expressly! But how does God exercise these works of mercy with regard to ourselves? He reproves us by salutary remorse, in which His goodness makes itself felt. How often have we not sought to stifle it in ourselves and perhaps in others also? He has caused us to be born in His Holy Church, He has surrounded us with teachings and opportunities of grace; have we not neglected them in the search after frivolous and useless knowledge, or perhaps by following the ways of the world, of error, or of impiety? In our sorrows, God is ever ready to listen to us, to comfort us; has He no reason to complain that we do not hasten to Him in our griefs, and that we seek for our comfort only in the creature rather than the Creator? A thousand good thoughts fill our minds every day, and lead us to good; what faithfulness do we manifest in following them? Let us thank God, that, notwithstanding our ingratitude, He has not entirely withdrawn His mercy from us, and in order to draw it down more and more upon ourselves let us shew it forth ourselves with more care towards others.

3. Of mercy in bearing with our neighbour in his failings. There are many things which we must bear with in our neighbour, and from our neighbour. There are injuries, and heavy wrongs, which we must pardon generously: there are more often lighter offences which we must shew ourselves easy to forget, there are always failings, humours, annoying and offensive modes of action which we must bear with indulgence. How do we exercise these works of mercy? Do we forgive injuries with sincerity and without any desire of revenge? Do we forget offences without allowing the remembrance of them to foment in our minds, without exaggerating them in our imaginations, without embittering and resenting

them in our hearts, without recalling them in our conversations, and making them known to those whom we think by that means, to be able to influence against those who have offended us? Do we bear with the failings of our neighbour, without drawing attention to them in a sort of ill will, or amusing ourselves at his expense? Do we think that we never offend others, and that we have no failings which others have to bear with? Ah! what need have we not that God should shew forth His mercy towards us?

Prayer. O God, where should I be without Thine infinite goodness! Numberless and heinous crimes, offences multiplied daily, gross faults, continual imperfections, actions opposed to Thy Holiness, such is the whole of my life, and the recollection of it would drive me into the horrors of despair, if I did not know that Thy mercy is boundless. Thou dost only require, in order to pour upon me the divine rays of Thy mercy, that I should shew mercy myself towards others; if I forgive all, Thou dost pardon me all; it is Thyself Who hast assured me of it; and who am I that I should compare myself to Thee! Oh sweet law, Oh condition of mercy! O Jesus, I will shew forth mercy to others in its fullest extent, that I may be partaker of Thy eternal mercy. Amen.

Meditation LI.

SECOND CONTINUATION OF THE SERMON ON THE MOUNT.

Of the three last beatitudes. S. Matt. v. 8—12.

FIRST POINT.

Sixth beatitude.

Blessed are the pure in heart, for they shall see God. What is purity of heart? What are the prejudices which people adopt against this virtue? What will be its rewards? Let us enter into these details.

1. What is purity of heart, and in what does it consist? We may distinguish three degrees in purity of heart. The first is the state of grace which belongs to the purgative life. In this first degree, is a heart, which is pure and washed from the stain of mortal sin, and set free from all hankering after venial sin, so that the love of God reigns there, and sanctifying grace dwells there: that is what is called being righteous. The second degree is a state of virtue which belongs to the illuminative life. In this second degree, a heart is pure from which evil habits have been rooted out in order to fill their places with holy ones, so that passions are mortified in it, and subjected to the exercise of virtue: that is what is called being virtuous. The third degree is a state of holiness which belongs to the intuitive life. In this third degree, a pure heart is a heart which is detached from every creature, and lives only in God. Nothing created touches it; it is only touched by God; it has no pleasure and comfort, no sorrow and grief, no desires and no fears, no affections nor love except according to God, for God, for His glory, and His interest and the accomplishment of His Holy Will; that is what is called being holy. To rest contented with the first degree, real or pretended, without applying ourselves in earnest to attain to the two others, is what is called being in a state of lukewarmness; a state very dangerous in the matter of salvation. Our heart is as it were a centre to which every thing converges. Our external senses delight in spreading themselves over, and in filling themselves with a thousand impure objects, which penetrate thence into the heart: we must gain the mastery over our senses, and bring them into captivity in order not to permit them to have any hold over us beyond what is absolutely necessary. Our mind, our imagination, our memory are turbulent faculties which raise up unceasingly a thousand mists, the evil influence of which attacks our heart; we must bring them into subjection, and banish by force every thought, every image, every memory, not only dangerous or licentious, but even use-

less. Lastly the heart itself is an ungrateful soil, which oftenest produces only thorns and poisons, illregulated affections, unlawful desires, criminal intentions: we must root out without compassion those impure productions to the very last fibres, and that as often as they spring up.

2. What are the prejudices which people adopt against this purity of heart? First prejudice; that to live such a life, must be to lead a sad and unhappy life. What then? does our happiness spring only from sin, from our passions, from created objects? Is it not from these, on the contrary, that all our sorrows, all our griefs, all our misfortunes arise? is it not from this cruel empire that we experience the hardest and most fatal slavery? How many delights does a soul enjoy who has broken these chains, and has set itself at liberty, and clings only to its God! Second prejudice; that this constant attention is something impossible. But grace renders every thing possible. There have been saints, pure souls who have lived a life of purity in all conditions of life, in that in which we are placed. In truth, there are difficulties, to be met with, and it will cost us pains and exertion on our part in order to acquire this purity of heart; but nothing that is good can be acquired without trouble. Arts and sciences have their difficulties, which do not hinder men from learning them. These difficulties become smoothed away in proportion as we advance, and the happiness we find in having surmounted them makes amends to us for the trouble which they may have cost us. That which appears impossible at the beginning becomes easy to us by habit; these difficulties are moreover a means to us of testifying our love to God; and what love commands us, however difficult it may be, becomes sweet and easy. Third prejudice; this perfect purity of heart is not a precept. What an error! it is on the contrary, an indispensable precept, a precept which essentially springs from the greatness and holiness of God; and in truth does not the least impurity suffice to close Heaven to us, into which nothing defiled can

enter? and in order to purify our souls from which nothing but the deepest repentance will avail? Ah! let us then understand what folly it is to shrink from that which by purifying us, might have gained for us an eternal bliss.

3. What are the rewards of purity of heart? *They shall see God*, they shall see Him in His works, in the government and foundation of His Church, in the sacred writings which contain His will, in all the events which are the ordering of His Providence; they shall see Him in His inward graces. Yes, the consolations, the inspirations, the supernatural delights with which God is pleased from time to time to inundate a pure heart, are something so divine, so ineffable, that all carnal delights and all worldly delights are but as torments in comparison. Lastly, they shall see Him in Himself in Heaven. When the pains of the last agony, the prayers of the Church and the last Communion shall have purified that soul, and a holy death shall have set the seal of final perseverance to its faithfulness, it shall be admitted to see God face to face, to possess Him, and to love Him with a beatific and eternal love. O recompense worthy of the goodness and greatness of a God! can I do too much in order to attain to it, and not to fail in it! O purity of heart, how precious thou art, and how worthy of all my care!

SECOND POINT.

Seventh beatitude.

Blessed are the peacemakers; for they shall be called the children of God. Let us examine what are the duties of the peacemaker, with regard to public peace, with regard to private and domestic peace, and in what his blessedness consists.

1. What are the duties of the peacemaker with regard to public peace? 1. The love of public peace requires care, that we may not be of those who disturb the peace. In order not to trouble the tranquillity of the state, or that of a city, or commonalty, let us obey the laws, and

those in authority without murmuring, without criticism, without complaint. In order not to trouble the peace of the Church, let us submit ourselves to her laws, and the decisions of her pastors without equivocation, and without evasion. In order not to trouble the public peace, let us never bring forward our private quarrels, by writings, satires, or any way by which we may form parties, or cause any divisions in men's minds. 2. The love of public peace requires zeal in order to restore it when it has been disturbed. We shall contribute to it by taking no side amongst private persons, by declaring ourselves always on the side of the obedience and submission which are due to lawful authority, by striving, on all occasions, to soothe, according to the degree of our influence, men's minds, to bring them back to their duty, and to the ways of peace. 3. The love of public peace requires patience and prayer. When we can effect nothing in order to restore it, let us be content to mourn and to pray; our complaints and our lamentations are useless, let us keep silence, let us sacrifice ourselves; if peace were banished from the whole earth, nothing hinders us from possessing it in our hearts, in being at peace with ourselves and with God.

2. What are the duties of the peacemaker with regard to private and domestic life? 1. He ought to take care not to be of those who disturb the peace; to watch over his tempers in order to control them, over his words in order to measure them, over his actions in order to regulate them, so that he should not be wanting in any of the duties of respect, courtesy, or charity which are due to his neighbour. 2. He must have zeal in order to contribute to the restoration of peace amongst those who have lost it; a zeal full of gentleness and love, in order to soften men's minds, and to conciliate them; full of prudence in order not to enter into quarrels, in which nothing can be done for the preservation of peace. 3. He must make sacrifices in order to preserve peace with those who trouble it, a sacrifice of his own interests, of his rights, of his reputation, and even of his honour: a sacrifice

of everything, excepting the interests of God, of religion, and of his conscience. He who will sacrifice nothing for the blessing of peace, does not love peace: thus, to words, he must offer no reply; to reports, no credence; to offences which are offered, no heed; to want of courtesy, no resentment; to pretensions, no resistance. The world may look upon us perhaps as spiritless and stupid, as cowardly and without feeling; let us leave the world to say what it will, and let us think only of what Jesus Christ says to us.

3. What is the blessing of the peacemakers? 1. They are blessed in that they are the children of God, Whose will they fulfil, Whose example they follow, and Whose Name they cause to be blessed. Those who disturb peace are, on the contrary, the children of the evil one, whose inclinations they follow, whose words they imitate, and whose designs they promote. 2. They are blessed, because they will be acknowledged as children of God, not only on earth by good men, whose good opinion is always a great help and comfort, but even by the wicked themselves at the day of the last judgement. Behold, they will say, those whom we have despised, ill-treated, and whom we looked upon as fools; what glory surrounds them! How are they placed among the ranks of the children of God. Ah! it is we who have been deceived, it is we who have been the fools. 3. They are blessed, because they will be dealt with as children of God, admitted to the inheritance of their heavenly Father, where they will enjoy a perfect, delicious and eternal peace, whilst the dwelling-place of those who shall have disturbed the peace of others will be a place of punishment, where an eternal strife will reign.

THIRD POINT.

Eighth and last beatitude.

Blessed are they which are persecuted for righteousness sake, for theirs is the kingdom of Heaven. Let us examine in what consists this persecution of the world, whether it be against the virtue of the righteous, or against the zeal of the apostles, and let us meditate on the advantages of this persecution to God's ministers.

1. Persecution of the world against the virtue of the righteous; there are several sorts of persecution. Open persecution, in which menaces, force, bad treatment are employed in order to lead others into sin, to corrupt their faith, to turn them away from a pious life. Malignant persecution, by which virtue and those who make profession of it are turned into ridicule, scoffed at, and exposed to contempt. Hypocritical persecution, by which, under pretext of remedying abuses and faults, people inveigh against devotion and devout persons, and then against God's ministers. Ah! if they were really touched with the failings which are sometimes to be found in good men, as they desire to make believe, they would mourn over them in secret, sooner than speak of them; and if they speak at all of them, it would be in other terms, in other places, in another tone, and in a less injurious manner. Observe how great is the crime of persecutors. They outrage the friends of God, whose prayers they ought rather to ask: but do they believe that God will not avenge them? They cause the ruin of souls, of whom many do not dare to enter, and others dare not persevere in, the path of virtue, acting thereby the part of the devil, and contributing to the success of his hatred, and of his jealousy against mankind. They close to themselves the path of return to God, and place themselves in a state of hardness of heart from which perhaps nothing will recover them. Let us beware lest we be of that number. If we have not courage to be in earnest ourselves, at least let us not be so sinful as to hate those who are so. Let us on the contrary love them, esteem them, encourage them, and take their part when opportunity offers. 2. What is the blessedness of those who are persecuted! O ye who are the object of the persecution of this world, do not be discouraged, but rather rejoice, because this perse-

cution from the world establishes in you the kingdom of God and of His grace: because it assures to you the possessions of the Gospel, whose laws you follow; because it gives you a claim to the kingdom of Heaven, to which no one can attain but through suffering, and that already that kingdom belongs to you.

2. Persecution of the world against the zeal of the apostles. *Blessed are ye,* continues Jesus Christ, *when men shall revile you, and persecute you, and shall say all manner of evil against you falsely for My sake.* Our Saviour has set before us the other beatitudes in one sentence; but He enlarges upon this beatitude, and develops it, because it was of the greatest importance for His Church, and equally needful for the apostles in order to sustain them in their ministry, and for true believers, in order that they might not fail to recognise them as apostles. Unhappy Jerusalem, which persecuted and put to death the prophets, thy hardness of heart is complete and without remedy! Let us beware of participating in her crimes, let us honour those who suffer for God, for religion, for the interests of virtue: when opportunity serves, let us defend their cause; blessed for us, if by that means, we merit to have some share in their opprobrium!

3. The advantages of persecution to God's ministers. *Rejoice,* continues Jesus Christ, *and be exceeding glad: for great is your reward in heaven: for so persecuted they the prophets which were before you.* The first advantages which persecution procures to them, is, that it guards their virtue from the shoals of vanity and self-love, from dissipation and the love of the world, from security and remissness. The second advantage is that it increases their reward. Oh! how great it will be in Heaven: rejoice then, let a thrill of joy enter your minds at the thought of so great a happiness, ye blessed persecuted ones: it is Jesus Christ Himself, Who invites you to it. How worthy of envy is your lot! The third advantage is that it sets the seal to their glory. Persecution has rendered apostles like unto the prophets, and

it renders God's ministers not only like to prophets and apostles, but like unto Christ Himself. Do not then relax in persecutions, ye ministers of the true God: look upon them as the glorious appanage of your mission: and if they are wanting to you, fear lest this fatal calm should be the effect of your own indolence, your indifference, your compliance with the world, its vices, and its errors: fear lest it should soon become to you a cause of growing lukewarm and of becoming corrupted: fear lest the world, which does not persecute you, because you do not in any way contradict it, may soon come to despise you; and that, at length, the Lord, wrath at your faint-heartedness, should put into your place more faithful labourers, who should draw down upon them the persecutions you have avoided, and should take away from you the crown which you have not had the courage to win.

Prayer. In order to live in Thy fear, and in holiness, O my God, I must then expect to pass my life, despised by the world. What glory for me, if I have no enemies but Thine, O Jesus! happy if I may suffer something for Thee, Who hast suffered so much for me: grant that the evils which I may endure, may never, Lord, be brought upon me from any other cause than my faithfulness in Thy service, and my love for righteousness, and not be brought down on myself by the requirements of Thy divine justice. Give me the spirit of peace with the enemies even of peace, a spirit of goodness, of affection, of care, and of tenderness towards all men, a spirit of union which prompts me unceasingly to strive to reunite all hearts and minds, to banish discord, to smooth away differences, to stifle dissension; lastly give me not only in regard to others, but also in regard to myself, that peace which passeth understanding, and which the world cannot give. Purify my heart by Thy Holy Spirit, O my God! kindle there the fire of Thy love: grant that always enlightened by His Light, and burning with the fire of His divine unction, I may lead a pure and spotless life, that I may shew forth in my life and conduct that innocence, and purity of soul which alone is worthy of Thy love here below, and which can alone for ever possess Thee in Heaven. Amen.

Meditation LII.

THIRD CONTINUATION OF THE SERMON ON THE MOUNT.

OF THE FULFILMENT OF THE COMMANDMENTS.

Jesus Christ teaches us here what are the ways, the obligations, and the motives for fulfilling the commandments. S. Matt. v. 13-20.

FIRST POINT.

Ways of fulfilling the commandments.

These ways are drawn from the ministry of the apostles and the pastors of the Church. The commands which Christ has laid upon His ministers and the privileges with which He has honoured them are all on our behalf, and the means which they should employ in order to fulfil these commands which they have received, concern ourselves.

1. Jesus Christ has endued His apostles with His authority in order that they should correct and reprove. *Ye are the salt of the earth; but if the salt have lost his savour, wherewith shall it be salted? It is thenceforth good for nothing, but to be cast out, and to be trodden under foot of men.* The apostles and ministers of Christ are the salt of the earth, in order to preserve men from the corruption of sin by the wisdom of their counsels, of their exhortations, of their corrections, their preachings, and the administration of the Sacraments. Their employment is an exalted one, but it is not without its dangers for them; for if the minister fall, who shall raise him up again? If he fail, who shall correct

him? If he wander from the right way, who shall bring him back again to it? If he loses the taste for his calling and its duties, who shall restore it to him? Will he not be rejected of God, and despised of men, as a useless and cumbersome thing, which one throws out in the streets, where the passers by tread it under foot? How difficult it is for a priest who has forsaken his God to find the way of repentance! Blindness and hardness of heart follow but too closely on these first falls! But it is for them to meditate on the threatenings of Jesus Christ, that they may be steadfast in fear and humility, and it is for us to examine with what docility, with what earnestness, and gratitude we receive this salt, which is not denied to us, and to examine what fruit we draw from it.

2. Jesus Christ has entrusted to His apostles and ministers His doctrines to teach. *Ye are the light of the world. A city that is set on a hill cannot be hid. Neither do men light a candle, and put it under a bushel, but on a candlestick, and it giveth light unto all that are in the house.* The apostles and Christ's ministers are the light of the world: a sure light which leads men to their true End, to God, to truth, to eternal happiness. Every light drawn from any other source is but error, darkness, and can only lead to ruin. An universal light which lightens the whole world, and which all men ought to follow: a pure light which admits neither of being divided, nor of being mixed; a sublime light, raised above ourselves, above all prejudices, above our reason; a bright light, visible to all who desire to see it and who do not obstinately turn aside in order not to behold it. The body of the first apostles, Catholic and Apostolic doctrines, in one word, the Church, in its teaching, is here compared by Christ to a city that is built on a high mountain, which no one can hide. The whirlwinds of dust which men endeavour to raise around her cannot reach to her, and hide her from our sight; they will serve rather to blind those who stir them up. He who has an upright heart cannot

be mistaken there; he beholds clearly the Church which Christ has founded, he follows without ambiguity what that Church teaches. Each particular Church, compared here to a house, is subject to its own pastor, whose teaching is the light which ought to be set on a candlestick in order to give light to those who are in the house. If the pastor through fear keeps the light hidden under a bushel, or lets it go out for want of drawing fresh supplies from Him, Who is the Light of the world, he brings down a curse upon himself: but the Light of the world continues to shine for ever, and to that only, in such a case, we must look for enlightenment. Is it in the brightness of that Light that we are walking; is it this doctrine which we are following?

3. Jesus Christ has communicated to His apostles and pastors, His holiness for the edification of their flocks. *Let your light so shine before men, that they may see your good works, and glorify your Father Which is in Heaven.* The preaching of the apostles, although accompanied by miracles, would have had no success, if it had not been also accompanied by holiness of life. What success then can a pastor, a minister of the Church have, to whom the power of miracles is not now granted, if he be also without holiness? The greatest means of persuading others, is by setting an example ourselves: but this precept of edifying others by a holy life, is not meant only for God's ministers: it is obligatory also on parents, masters and mistresses, on all those who are in places of authority, and even on all true believers in particular. How do we imitate the apostles and holy men? How do we profit by the good examples which are set before us? What good examples do we ourselves set? and when we do anything that is good, is it of the glory that will accrue to our Heavenly Father that we think, or of that which will fall on ourselves?

SECOND POINT.

Obligation laid on us to fulfil the commandments.

This obligation is founded on the nature itself of the commandments, which are a divine, Christian, and unchangeable law.

1. A divine law. *Think not, says Jesus Christ, that I am come to destroy the Law or the prophets: I am not come to destroy, but to fulfil.* These commandments have their source in God Himself, and can have no other origin, since it is God alone Who knows perfectly what man owes to God, what man owes to himself, what he owes to those with whom the Creator appoints that he should live. This law, God has revealed to the patriarchs, and has engraven it in the hearts of all mankind; but the children of men forget the revelation which has been made, and efface in themselves the impress of it, in order that they may transgress it with more hardiness and with more ease. God wrote them with His Hand on the tables which He gave to Moses; but the Israelites neglected often the study and the practice of them. The prophets sent by God, often recalled them to mind, set forth the necessity of fulfilling them, and left behind them in their writings, these witnesses of their zeal. These are the unchangeable precepts of the moral law, contained in the commandments, and explained in the prophets, and which Jesus Christ often calls the law and the prophets; it is that divine law, taken in this sense, which our Lord has not come to destroy, and of which He inculcates here the entire and perfect fulfilment.

2. A Christian law, that is to say, renewed by Jesus Christ in His Gospel, explained and established by Christ in all its purity and holiness, perfected even by Christ, in order to adapt it to the more perfect worship which He has founded amongst men. It is thus that He is not come to destroy the law of God, but to set it before us in all its fulness, its extent, and its perfection.

3. An unchangeable and indispensable law. *For verily I say unto you, Till heaven and earth pass, one jot or one tittle shall in no wise pass from the law until all be fulfilled.* Whilst heaven and earth shall last, whilst there shall be under the heaven or on the earth

men capable of knowing God, the divine law of Jesus Christ shall last, and shall be obligatory upon them; it shall have to the end of time, faithful disciples, and none of the precepts which it contains, however slight we may imagine them to be, shall be transgressed with impunity. Jesus Christ distinctly sets before us that no single point of His law shall be set aside or forgotten; but nevertheless how often is it not broken, how many prevarications in its observance! Jesus Christ is the Truth: He is the absolute and unchangeable Author of His laws, and what He says is infallible. If Heaven and earth shall perish sooner than one jot or tittle shall pass from His law, or that His word and His will shall be set aside, let us tremble; and if we will avoid an inevitable loss, let us adhere inviolably to that which He requires of us.

THIRD POINT.

Motives for the fulfilment of the commandments.

These motives are taken; 1. from the misery which those experience who have broken God's commandments, and taught others to break them. 2. from the bliss of those who shall have kept God's commandments, and taught others to observe them; 3. from the insufficiency of worldly virtues.

1. The misery of those who have broken God's commandments, and taught others to break them. *Whosoever therefore*, continues Jesus Christ, *shall break one of these least commandments, and shall teach men so, shall be called least in the kingdom of Heaven.* By the kingdom of Heaven, all commentators understand here the last judgement. Now, if it should be but the least of the commandments, or rather one of those which the world regards as little, which any one should have broken, or taught others to break, he will be at the day of judgement, rejected to the lowest place, below that of simple transgressors. What will then be the lot of those who shall have broken or taught others to break the greatest commandments, those which even heathens have

believed themselves bound to observe! When these corruptors shall see the thousands whom their discourses, their books, their pictures shall have corrupted and brought to eternal damnation, what will be their shame, and what punishment must they not look for, and not only they themselves, but also 1. they who shall have been partakers in their crimes, by selling or promulgating, lending or making known these criminal publications; and 2. those who having the power in their hands, have not had either sufficient watchfulness, or sufficient determination to put a stop to them.

2. The blessedness of those who shall have observed God's commandments, and taught others to do so. *But whosoever shall do and teach them, the same shall be called great in the kingdom of Heaven.* Those who shall have observed God's commandments, and taught others to do so, whether by example, or by their discourses, shall be called great at that last day. O greatness worthy of envy, can it be then that those to whom God has given talents should be insensible of this solid and immortal glory! Let us strive then, according to our station, not only to practise these commandments, but also to teach them, and to contribute, with all our power, to establish in all around, the love of the divine law, and we shall have a share, according to the measure of our labours, and of our zeal, in the glory and the reward of the Apostles.

3. Insufficiency of worldly virtues. *For I say unto you, That except your righteousness shall exceed the righteousness of the scribes and Pharisees, ye shall in no case enter into the kingdom of Heaven.* The righteousness, that is to say, the virtue of the Scribes and Pharisees had three defects, as we shall see by the reproaches which our Lord uttered against them hereafter. It was entirely external, without any care being given to that which was within; they made clean the outside of the cup and of the platter, but within they were full of extortion and excess. It was punctilious, laying great stress on minor observances, and neglecting what was

essential. They paid tithe of mint, and anise, and cummin, and omitted the weightier matters of the law, judgement, mercy, and faith; having neither love towards God, nor charity towards their neighbour. Lastly it was hypocritical, seeking only the esteem of men, without caring for that of God. They prayed in order to be seen, they required others to salute them with respect, to receive them with marks of honour, and to be placed in seats of distinction. With such righteousness men cannot hope to enter the kingdom of heaven. Is our's more perfect, more inward, more true, more humble? We have no longer Scribes and Pharisees to corrupt the commandments, but we have worldly Christians who bring them down to an apparent and superficial propriety of conduct, and who substitute for the maxims of the Gospel the maxims of the world, more corrupt still than those of the Pharisees. The virtue of the world, the virtue of parade, and ostentation: virtues insufficient to give an entrance into the kingdom of heaven: feigned virtues, which conceal real vices, which merit eternal condemnation.

Prayer. I will apply myself, oh my God, with Thy Divine help, to practise the true virtues which Thou dost require of me, by observing Thy commandments in their full extent, according to the letter, and according to the spirit, with purity of intention, and fulness of obedience. Oh divine and holy commandments; how blessed am I to know them, how miserable am I to have so often broken them. Pardon me, O Lord, my past transgressions, give me the love of Thy holy commandments, that I may make them for the time to come my study, and the only rule of my conduct. Amen.

Meditation LIII.

FOURTH CONTINUATION OF THE SERMON ON THE MOUNT.

Explanation of three precepts of the law concerning murder, adultery, and false swearing. S. Matt. v. 21—37.

FIRST POINT.

Of murder.

1. Of the sins forbidden under the head of murder. *Ye have heard that it was said by them of old time, Thou shalt not kill; and whosoever shall kill, shall be in danger of the judgment: But I say unto you, That whosoever is angry with his brother without a cause, shall be in danger of the judgment; and whosoever shall say to his brother, Raca, (i. e. vain fellow) shall be in danger of the council: but whosoever shall say, Thou fool, shall be in danger of hell fire.* By this precept, are forbidden all sins in deed, such as to kill, to strike a person without cause, or without authority, out of anger, hatred, revenge, or caprice; sins in word, such as words of slander, of calumny, contempt, insult, cursing, uttered from hatred, malice, or anger; sins purely inward, such as motions of anger, hatred, by which we are inwardly carried away against our neighbour, and we either rejoice at his misfortune, trying to do him some evil, or wishing that some evil may befall him. All these sins are very enormous at the tribunal of God. Let us observe the tradition of which our Lord makes use here. The scribes and Pharisees, in explaining this precept of the law, spoke only of murder; which crime is regarded by the whole world as a capital crime worthy of punishment; now our Lord places the simple act of anger in the heart, without any outward manifestation

of it by word or deed, on the same footing as the Pharisees placed that of murder, and as worthy of judgment, that is, as deserving to be carried before the tribunal of these superior judges who had the power of condemning a criminal to death. Our Lord places also an abusive word, although containing but a slight offence, if said in anger, on the same level as the greatest crimes which were judged by the council or the great Sanhedrim, which only took cognizance of crimes against the State or against religion. Lastly, He places a word containing a grievous insult, as a crime beyond all human justice and all the punishments it can award. Thus does Jesus, the sovereign Judge of the universe, pronounce and decide respecting this matter. Let us then watch with the greatest care not only over our actions, but even our words, that we may not give offence to any: let us regulate even the most hidden motions of our hearts.

2. Of the obligation we are under to make entire reparation for the evil which we have caused to our neighbour. *Therefore, if thou bring thy gift to the altar, and there rememberest, that thy brother hath aught against thee, leave there thy gift before the altar, and go thy way; first, be reconciled to thy brother, and then go and offer thy gift.* If you have done wrong to your neighbour, as regards his possessions, if you are keeping back what is his, if you have caused him any loss or damage, you must restore it and indemnify him entirely. If you have injured his reputation, his honour, or his credit, you must employ every means, in order to reinstate him, in the same degree of honour and consideration in which he formerly stood. If you have offended, wronged, or vexed him, you must seek to pacify him and to give him satisfaction. Lastly if you believe that your neighbour hath ought against you, even if it should be nothing really wrongful, and even if you should have given no occasion for it, you should omit nothing in order to clear away his prejudices, to remove his suspicions, to dissipate the umbrage he has taken, to re-

establish charity in his heart: and to revive betwixt you and him unity and a good understanding. Until you have taken these steps, and you have reconciled yourself with him in good faith as far as lies in your power, you must not hope that God will receive your prayers, or your offerings: do not, above all, presume to present yourself at the holy Communion, to receive there the Lord of peace and love, Who has Himself laid these obligations upon us.

3. Of the obligation laid upon us to repair quickly the evil done to our neighbour. *Agree with thine adversary quickly whiles thou art in the way with him; lest at any time the adversary deliver thee to the judge, and the judge deliver thee to the officer, and thou be cast into prison.* Repair the wrong done to your neighbour at once, if it be possible. The longer you delay, the greater your sin will be, and the more difficult to expiate, the greater will be the harm done and the more difficult to repair, the deeper will be the wound, and the more difficult to heal. Do not defer till your death, which may perhaps take you by surprise, and which, in all probability, will fill you with other cares, and will leave neither leisure nor freedom to fulfil the obligation you are under to your neighbour, or at best will only permit you to acquit yourself of it but imperfectly. You and the person whom you have offended, are like two suitors who are about to appear before their common Judge. Before you arrive there, whilst you are still on the way, agree with your opponent; you will make better conditions with him, than if justice should take your matter in hand, because then it would judge you with the utmost rigour. At least, when death comes, if you have had the misfortune and the folly to defer it until then, do not be foolhardy enough to cross that terrible pass, without setting in order such an essential matter. Bethink yourself, that it is of the greatest importance for you, that time presses, and that the wrongs of your neighbour whom you have injured, will accuse you before the tribunal of God, your Judge, Who will condemn you with all the rigour of His justice.

4. Of the punishment of those who die without having repaired the evil done to their neighbour. *Verily I say unto you,* our Saviour continues, *Thou shalt by no means come out thence, till thou hast paid the uttermost farthing.* The bare idea of prison makes you tremble; but what are the most fearful dungeons in comparison of those prisons of fire to which Divine justice will condemn the guilty? If your fault is venial, you will not come out of your prison till you have satisfied the rigour of Divine justice; but if it is mortal, never, never will you leave your prison and the fire with which it is filled, because you never will be able to pay your debt, and you will never succeed in doing so.

SECOND POINT.

Of adultery.

I. How shameful the sins of impurity are in the eyes even of men! *Ye have heard that it was said by them of old time, Thou shalt not commit adultery.* Those who are guilty of sins of impurity, would rather suffer every thing, than that their intrigues should be discovered, and their sins revealed. If the secrecy with which they seek to cover their shame is sometimes laid bare, what scandal does it not cause to the world, what confusion and what disgrace to themselves. What will not a person do in order to preserve himself from such dishonour! What other sin has made people make more sacrilegious confessions and Communions than this? How often, tormented by their conscience, and not being able to support the disgraceful secret with which they feel themselves oppressed, they have been to the feet of the priest without daring to discover the depth of their sores? How often, in laying bare even their crimes, they have suppressed through shame, essential circumstances regarding them, and have rendered useless the imperfect avowal which they had begun! How often, struggling between shame and the fear of God, they have yielded to the former, and have kept away from means of grace, sooner than bring themselves to make the necessary acknowledgement of their sins! Their companions in sin, are ashamed of their mutual crimes, and blush at the remembrance of them, and when the frenzy of their passions leaves them some interval of reason, they cannot prevent themselves from mutually despising one another. Even those who glory in their shame, would nevertheless be covered with confusion if the detail of the horrors to which they abandon themselves were made known. The atheist and the deist, although insensible to other opprobrium which they bring on themselves, are sensible of this, and would persuade us that this shameful vice has no part in their irreligion. Now, if this sin is so infamous in the eyes of men, what must it be in the eyes of God? What can a soul, stained with sins which inspire even sinners with horror, be in the eyes of God?

2. How little is needed to make us guilty of impurity in the eyes of God. *But I say unto you, That whosoever looketh on a woman to lust after her, hath committed adultery with her already in his heart.* A thought which is entertained with complacency, a desire consented to, a look which accompanies this desire, suffice to bring adultery into the heart. But if he who casts this look, commits this sin, is she who attires herself in a manner to attract it, innocent? Alas! how many hidden sins there are which we seek to dissimulate to ourselves! We keep our reputation clear perhaps through pride; the fear of the consequences prevents us perhaps from yielding to actual sin; but if the fear of God does not penetrate us, and restrain all our senses, the heart soon becomes guilty, and as soon as our heart is soiled, we have lost our innocence and our honour in the eyes of Him Who sees our heart.

3. What sacrifices we must make in order to keep ourselves from this sin. *If thy right eye offend thee, pluck it out, and cast it from thee; for it is profitable for thee that one of thy members should perish, and not thy whole body should be cast into hell. And if*

thy right hand offend thee, cut it off, and cast it from thee; for it is profitable for thee that one of thy members should perish, and not that thy whole body should be cast into hell. That is to say, that cost you what it may, you must, by a generous sacrifice, renounce all that is dearest and most necessary to you in the world, if it is to you an occasion of falling, and a stumbling-block, were it, so to say, your right eye and your right hand. If this proposal frightens you, you have then forgotten that it is a matter with you of avoiding hell; in such a case, is any thing dear, is any thing unnecessary? But it is here a matter of gaining eternal life; can you, at that price, find anything too difficult, and ought not all to appear easy to you? But your sacrifice ought not only to be generous, but it must be entire; it ought to have no delay, no compromise. Pull out your eye, cut off your hand, that is to say, tear out of your heart that inclination, the object which causes it, and lose even the very remembrance of it; break off those attachments and those connections, retrench those pleasures, those amusements, flee from those companions which are the shoals on which your innocence may be wrecked; lastly let your sacrifice be irrevocable, so that it may no longer be open to you to withdraw from it. After having pulled out your eye, and cut off your hand, you must besides cast them away from you. It is not enough to hide from your neighbour's eyes those books, those verses, those songs, you must throw them into the fire. If the whole world *offend thee*, put an insurmountable barrier between the world and yourself. Ah! would it not be better for you, to live eternally in heaven, after having been ignored, despised and humbled in the world, than to burn eternally in hell fire, after having enjoyed your freedom, and your pleasures in the world, or rather after having been the slave in the world of your pretended freedom, the victim of your imagined pleasures?

4. How severely God punishes impurity. We will not speak here of the heavy punishment the sinner brings down upon himself in this world; such as the oppro-

brium and disgrace, which are sometimes reflected on an entire family; or the dissipation of property and the total ruin of a household; the diseases and fearful sufferings, which after having for a long time tormented the body, bring it to the tomb; but of that which awaits the sinner, who appears before the tribunal of God with his heart defiled with impurity, and which is nothing less than to be cast into hell fire, there to burn eternally. At this sentence, the impure man trembles, is troubled, cries out, and asks what proportion the pleasure of a moment bears to eternal punishment. For that very reason of the proportion which pleasure bears to suffering, it would be needful then to deny also the existence of the temporal sufferings, which impurity so often causes, and which far exceed the pleasure which has been tasted; but nevertheless these sufferings do exist and destroy this spurious reasoning. But it is not by the feeble lights of reason that God's sentences are regulated. God alone knows what is the crime, and what ought to be the punishment of a creature who disobeys his Creator, who despises equally His authority and His love, His rewards and His threats. God alone knows what barriers it is necessary to oppose to our depravity, and with what threats it pleases Him to terrify sinners. How many saints have owed to the terror with which the thought of hell inspired them, the sovereign happiness to which they have attained, whether through a complete innoceney of life, or by a true and sincere repentance? Why do we not imitate them? Why do we not deprive ourselves of those pleasures of which we know the nothingness, and the short duration, in order to preserve ourselves from those punishments which, according to us, are so disproportioned? Why do we not apply ourselves to deserve the eternal rewards which have been promised us, and which are still less proportioned to the sacrifices which are required of us, however great they may appear to us?

THIRD POINT.

Of swearing.

1. Of swearing by the Holy Name of God. *Again, ye have heard that it hath been said by them of old time, Thou shalt not forswear thyself, but shalt perform unto the Lord thine oaths; but I say unto you, Swear not at all.* Let us see in the first place what the ancient law forbade on this subject. As regarded an oath, with respect to the past or the present, and by which we affirm that a thing is or has been, it forbad in express terms that God's name should be taken in vain: that is to say, to perjure oneself or to swear falsely by the name of God. As to the oath which had regard to the future, and by which any one promised or engaged that a thing should be, it forbad that any one should fail in performing the vows they had made unto the Lord, or the promises they had made to their neighbour with an oath, when these engagements had nothing unjust or unreasonable. In reality, in these two cases, the perjury or the false oath is one of the greatest crimes which any one can commit, since it is to render God a witness, a guarantee, and so to say, an accomplice in the falsehood; it is a crime which God, even in this life, punishes often with severest penalties. Let us see now how this law of Jesus Christ bears upon this subject. It gives to the ancient law its full extent and strength; it commands in the first place, that we should not swear at all, that is to say, not only that there should be no false swearing, but that there should not even be any useless oaths taken, although they were truthful, because it was to fail in the respect due to the majesty of God, to employ the authority of His Name without necessity, either in vain utterances, or yet more in wicked or unlawful matters. It commands that no false or useless oath should be taken in the holy name of God, but also that no oath even should be taken in that of His creatures, because that to swear by the works of

God, is in some way to swear by Himself, as our Lord goes on shortly afterwards to explain. It forbids all swearing; which does not mean that it is never and on no occasion permissable to take an oath. This sense has only been adopted by some schismatics, anabaptists and others, who paying no attention to the passages which precede, and to those which follow after, have interpreted it according to their own fancy. We have the example of S. Paul, who sometimes takes God to witness of the truth of that which he sets forth: and the practice in courts of justice, to require an oath from the witnesses who are being examined, has been approved of by the Christian Church, and an oath of obedience and faith is required of those whom she admits to any office in her ministry. Of such oaths it cannot be said that they are contrary to the mind of God, and the teaching of Christ.

2. Of swearing by any created thing. *But I say unto you, Swear not at all; neither by heaven; for it is God's throne; nor by the earth; for it is His footstool; neither by Jerusalem; for it is the city of the great King: neither shalt thou swear by thy head, because thou canst not make one hair white or black.* Created things represent to us God and His divine perfections; it is in this respect that they are made use of in an oath; for the things themselves could not testify to the truth which we are setting forth; it is then to swear by the name and truth of God Himself, if we swear by that which He has created. Therefore the one is not more allowable than the other, and we must observe in both cases the same rules. The oath which we take by ourselves, being of a different nature, is also forbidden for a different reason. The oath taken by the name of God or that of His creatures is a simple assertion of the truth of that for which we take God to witness. The oath taken by ourselves adds to the assertion, an imprecation by which we bring down upon ourselves punishment or death, if what we say is false: and this is forbidden to us, because we are not our own, but we belong to God,

and to do so is to dispose of ourselves, which we cannot do in any case save such where the law requires it of us.

3. Of the idea of created things with regard to contemplation. The idea under which our Lord represents to us the relation of created things with God is so noble and great, that it may serve not only to set before us the nature of an oath, but also to raise our minds to God by sublime contemplation. 1. The Heaven *is God's throne;* it is there that Jesus Christ is seated at the right Hand of the Almighty Father; it is there that the Holy Trinity, the only and Eternal God, manifests all His glory, and communicates all His happiness to His creatures. Let us reverence that blessed abode. 2. The earth *is His footstool;* as long as we live on the earth, we are unceasingly at the foot of the Throne of God. It is there that the Lamb without spot has been offered up, that His Blood has flowed, and that It is daily offered up for us as a perpetual Sacrifice: it is from thence that we can send up our prayers, appease the justice of the Most High, and draw down upon us His mercy: it is there that pardon is granted, and that graces are poured down upon us. How then can we profane it by swearing, by our sins? 3. Jerusalem *is the city of the great King.* Jerusalem was the seat of the kings of Judah, and as such it belonged to Jesus Christ. It possessed the only temple in the universe which was set apart for the lawful worship of the true God; and as such, it was the holy city, and the centre of religion. Let everything then that belongs to God inspire us then with a holy and religious respect. We cannot even, in the dependence on God in which we are, and not having even the power to make one hair of our heads black or white, we cannot swear by our heads without uttering a vain, and useless oath, and one which is injurious to the divine sovereignty.

4. Of the simplicity of our conversation. *But let your communication be Yea, yea, Nay, nay, for whatsoever is more than these, cometh of evil;* We ought

then to avoid not only an actual oath, but still more all which approaches to it, such as many words which offend pious ears, and which are commonly regarded as an oath, and all expressions which savour of exaggeration. We ought to avoid this superabundance of words, because evil, danger, and scandal are always to be found mixed up with them; because they come from the evil spirit, our enemy, who seeks all occasions to make us fall; because they spring from an evil principle which is in us, namely pride, love of display, presumption, anger, infatuation, self-love, avarice or self-interest. Let us then examine our words, and regulate them scrupulously by the heavenly doctrine of our Blessed Saviour at Whose tribunal we shall have to render an exact account of them, without any one of them escaping from His knowledge and His justice.

Prayer. Inspire me, O God, with a holy reverence for Thy Divine Name, and all that belongs to Thee. Oh that I might be able to repair, by my homage and my love, all the blasphemies, and all the false oaths, which dishonour Thee, either in Thy holy Name, or in Thy creatures! Grant that knowing Thee both in Thyself, and in all which sets Thee before us, I may be watchful over all my words, and that there may not be one which may not glorify Thee. Grant me to serve Thee with a chaste body, and to avoid all occasions of sin, in order that I may be well-pleasing in Thy sight by the purity of my heart. Give me the grace to stifle in myself even the least motions of anger and hatred. Engrave on my soul a law of unchanging gentleness. Pardon me all that I have done, said, or thought, that has been against charity. Give me the courage to humble myself in order to make amends for my faults, and watchfulness that I may not commit new faults for the time to come. Amen.

Meditation LIV.

FIFTH CONTINUATION OF THE SERMON ON THE MOUNT.

Of the duties of the Christian towards his neighbours on three sorts of occasions. S. Matt. v. 38—48.

What are the duties of the Christian towards an unjust and passionate neighbour, towards an inconsiderate and importunate neighbour, and towards a neighbour who is an enemy and a persecutor? Let us learn them from Christ Himself.

FIRST POINT.

The duty of a Christian towards an unjust and passionate neighbour.

Ye have heard that it hath been said, An eye for an eye, and a tooth for a tooth; but I say unto you, That ye resist not evil. The law of the gospel forbids all persons to make use of the law of retaliation, and substitutes for it, rules of perfection, which in certain cases, become duties of obligation. What is called the law of retaliation, by which a guilty person is made to suffer the same evil that he has done to another, was the law which Moses gave for the regulation of the judgements of magistrates; but the authority which gave this law to the tribunals of justice was usurped by private persons, and each one arrogated to himself the right to render to his neighbour, when he could, all the evil which he had received from him. Our Lord opposes to this abuse, the precept to make no resistance to injustice and violence. This new law of Jesus Christ does not forbid without distinction, in all cases, and to all Christians, that recourse should be had to public authority in order to demand justice; this law specially had respect to the Apostles and persecuted Christians, who were often obliged to obey this injunction to the letter; even now-a-days, Christian ministers, and Christian men may find themselves under the same necessity; but the general obligation laid upon us all, is to take this precept in its spirit, and to take special care not to allow ourselves in the opposite extremes. Let us examine ourselves then on this point. Do we not still fall into the offences which our Saviour here seeks to warn us against? Are we not in the constant habit of rendering evil for evil? Do we not treasure up the remembrance of offences we have received, until we have found an opportunity of rendering the like? Are we even content to render, according to the terms of the ancient law, an eye for an eye, and a tooth for a tooth? but do we not rather follow the blind impulses of passion and hatred, which always break through the bounds of moderation? Let us here sound our hearts, and reform ourselves by the law of the gospel; for it is by this law that we shall be judged. Our Lord, after having thus set forth this duty in a general manner, applies it to three different cases, and explains it by three examples.

1. When any one insults us so far as to ill-treat us by blows. *Whosoever will smite thee on the right cheek, turn to him the other also.* Let us compare our patience with this maxim. If the insults, the ill-treatment, we complain of are of this nature, let us see with what generosity we ought to bear them; but if it is only a word, a gesture, a person's manner, a mere nothing at which we take offence, let us blush to find ourselves so far removed from the perfection of the Gospel, and cherishing feelings so opposed to those of Jesus Christ.

2. When any one despoils us of our goods, so far as to ruin us. *And if any man will sue thee at the law, and take away thy coat, let him have thy cloke also.* Let us compare our conduct with this maxim. If the wrong that is done to us is carried to excess, see with what disinterestedness we ought to regard it; but if we are carried away by passion, if we give way to anger at the least loss, at the least diminution of a profit in our income which leaves us still in easy circumstances: if

we betake ourselves to law-suits for a possession of little value, for a claim which is of no consequence, for a point of honour which only wounds our vanity, let us acknowledge how far removed we are from following the example of Jesus Christ.

3. When any one molests us, so far as to treat us as slaves. *And whosoever shall compel thee to go a mile, go with him twain.* Let us compare our feelings with this maxim. If the vexations which we suffer are as unjust as this, see with what gentleness we ought to bear them; but if what is required of us is laid upon us by lawful authority, if it is conformable to our station and our employments, if it is honourable to us, if it has for its object, public usefulness, the glory of God, and the relief of our neighbour, we shall do well to see that in complaining as we do, we have as yet learnt nothing in the school of Jesus Christ.

SECOND POINT.

The duty of a Christian towards an inconsiderate and importunate neighbour.

1. In his demands. Here is the law of Jesus Christ. *Give to him that asketh thee.* If ever your neighbour should ask of you something which would be useful to you, but which he should judge suitable to him, give it him. Your charity, your obedience to the law of Jesus Christ, will be a thousand times of more value to you than that which you have given to him; but if that which is asked of you is only a service, a favour, a help, counsel, or a moment's attention, how can you refuse it him? Let us examine now, how far we make refusals daily which are against the spirit of this law of disinterestedness and patience which Jesus Christ lays down for us here: and let us also bethink ourselves, that, besides that, our refusals are against the law of charity, if that which is asked of us is a needful relief of indigence, of need, or of distress into which our neighbour finds himself thrown; let us remember that our refusals are still more against the law of justice, if that which is asked of us is a duty

of our station, or an obligation laid upon us by our office or position, or that which devolves upon us through engagements we have entered upon; if it is a creditor who demands that which is due to him, a servant who claims his salary, a workman, or a tradesman who demands his payment.

2. In loans. Here is the law of Jesus Christ. *From him that would borrow of thee, turn not thou away.* How many subterfuges, how many false excuses, how many evasions, in order to rid ourselves of those who ask us for a loan! and in all these excuses, what lies, what ill-will! The usurious loan is to the avaricious man a source of unjust wealth; the loan made in the spirit of Christianity may become to a true believer, the source of blessings, so much the more abundant, in that opportunity of lending is more frequent, and therefore more assured, and that this good deed is less flattering to our self-love and vanity.

3. On many occasions, we find besides an obligation to bear with the want of consideration and importunity of our neighbour. Do not let us weary of being yielding, and compliant, because in that we follow the law of Jesus Christ; do not let us fear to be the dupes of our kindliness; if it costs us something, He Who has made the law, will know well how to compensate us for it. When it is an impossibility for us to grant to our neighbour that which he asks of us, let us at least shew him our good-will to oblige him, and the sorrow we feel at being unable to do so. Do not let us begin by repelling him; let us take care not to make him feel his want of consideration, or to reproach him with it; let us also take care not to speak or complain of it to others: in one word, let us enter thoroughly into the spirit of this law, which is a law of love. Let us deal with regard to our neighbour on all occasions as if he were a tenderly loved brother; that is the spirit of Jesus Christ; let us clothe ourselves with it, if we would be His disciples, and have a share in His most intimate favours.

THIRD POINT.

The duties of a Christian towards a neighbour, who is an enemy and a persecutor.

Ye have heard that it hath been said, Thou shalt love thy neighbour, and hate thine enemy. But I say unto you, love your enemies. The Jews abused the law which commanded them to destroy the nations which were their enemies and idolaters, by applying these commands to their private enmities; the law did not even lead them to hate the people whom they were fighting against. The law of Jesus Christ does not forbid Christian people to take up arms in just and neccessary wars; but it forbids us to hate any one; it commands us to love all men, even our enemies.

1. A Christian ought never to be the enemy of any one. We may be an enemy in our hearts, in our actions, or in our words. In our hearts; we hate, we have antipathies, aversions, dislikes; we rejoice in the evil, in the chagrin, in the humiliation which befalls a person; we are sorry at any good fortune which happens to him, his success, or his rejoicing: if we find that such feelings rise in our heart against any one, let us fight against them earnestly, and never let us rest contented till we have entirely extirpated them from our hearts. In our actions; we persecute, we vex, we thwart, as much as we can, a person whom we do not like. Is there no one who is not thus the object of our persecutions? In our words; we contradict, we speak sharply, we criticize, blame, censure, or interpret as evil all which a person whom we hate, either does, says, or undertakes; we point out their faults, we speak of them, or publish them, we exaggerate them, we slander the person. When we speak of any one, do we ask ourselves: Is it thus I should speak if it were a friend I loved? In this way we should be enemies to none. If any one believes us to be his enemy, let us use all our efforts to undeceive him, and in the same way do not let us persuade ourselves easily that any one, be he who he may, has a dislike to us.

2. A Christian must not treat any one as an enemy. *Bless them that curse you, do good to them that hate you, and pray for them which despitefully use you, and persecute you.* That is to say, if you have an enemy whom you cannot gain, who manifests the hatred he bears you, who persecutes you, and calumniates you, his injustice ought not to have any effect on your charity towards him. These are your duties; you must love him in your heart, be sorry for his misfortunes, rejoice at his prosperity, and desire that still greater success may await him: in your actions, you must do him good when the opportunity presents itself, assist him, succour him, defend him, anticipate his wishes, and show him nothing but good will; in your words, you should never speak of him but in good part, and never complain of his wrong doings towards yourself: if you speak to him, it must always be with gentleness and in terms of kindness; lastly, you must pray for him, not only for his conversion, in doing which you might perhaps deceive yourself, but also for his health, his prosperity, and the success of all that may be useful to him. How many enmities would cease, if only one of two parties would observe these rules!

3. What is the pattern of the Christian in order to attain to this perfection? 1. It is a divine Pattern which we must imitate. *That ye may be the children of your Father Which is in Heaven; for He maketh His sun to rise on the evil and on the good, and sendeth rain on the just and on the unjust.* Ah, if we complain of the difficulty we find in fulfilling the law which Jesus Christ has given us to love our enemies, let us remember that we are Christians, children of God, adopted in Jesus Christ! Is it then too much to require of us that we should imitate our Heavenly Father and our Saviour? Now, let us see with what goodness this tender Father causes the light to shine, and sends down the dew alike for the benefit of those who serve Him, and of those who sin against Him. Did not our Saviour die for His enemies? Did He not pray for His murderers? Shall we

take into account only our own weakness, and shall we account as nought the succours of His grace?

2. It is a human pattern which the Christian ought to surpass. *For if ye love them which love you, what reward have ye? do not even the publicans the same? And if ye salute your brethren only, what do ye more than others? do not even the publicans so?* What! are even publicans held up to us as an example? But let us confront ourselves with them, and perhaps we shall find that we are no better than they? We love those who love us, we are kind and courteous to those who are so to us, we willingly do good to those who do so to us, or from whom we hope for good; now, doing thus everything for ourselves, everything for the world, and nothing for God, what reward do we expect from God? Perhaps we do not expect any at all! But we will hope that we have not yet come to that point; but nevertheless is it not true at least that if we were looking for anything from our fellow men, if our fortune depended on our love for that enemy, we should love him and nothing would seem hard to us? And yet an eternal reward which may be won at the same price, makes no impression on us? But let us remember, that if we are insensible to the eternal rewards which Jesus Christ promises us, we shall not be able to escape the eternal punishments with which He threatens us.

3. It is a universal pattern which the Christian ought to set before himself in all things. *Be ye therefore perfect, even as your Father which is in Heaven is perfect.* It is not only in this matter, but in the exercise of all the virtues that we ought unceasingly to have before our eyes the infinite perfections of our Heavenly Father, that we may act, judge, and will as He does, and by the conformity of actions, of judgement, of will, render ourselves in all things like unto Him. How beautiful is this law, how sweet, how divine, and truly worthy of the Son of God, Who lays it upon us.

Prayer. Everything is possible with Thy grace, O God! grant it to me, and I shall be faithful to it. With the help of Thy succour, Thy perfection shall be the rule of mine. Not only will I suffer without resistance, without ill will, all the evil that may be done to me; I will be always ready to despise myself, to lend, to give, I will love those who do me evil, I will love them even at the time when they make their hatred to me most keenly felt, I will love them with a sincere and tender affection, in doing them good, and praying God to bless them. Who could appear odious to me at the moment when Thou dost command me to love them? O my God! Can I do too much in order to deserve to belong to Thee, as to my Father, by the true spirit of Thy children, which is charity? Amen.

Meditation LV.

SIXTH CONTINUATION OF THE SERMON ON THE MOUNT.

OF THREE SORTS OF GOOD WORKS.

1. With regard to our neighbour, the sacrifice of our possessions by almsgiving. 2. With regard to God, the sacrifice of our mind by prayer. 3. With regard to ourselves, the sacrifice of our body by fasting. S. Matt. vi. 1—18.

FIRST POINT.

With regard to our neighbour, the sacrifice of our possessions by alms.

Take heed that ye do not your alms before men, to be seen of them; otherwise ye have no reward of your Father which is in Heaven. That is to say, take great care to steer clear of the shoals of vanity. The good works which you do, such as almsgiving, prayer, and fasting, let them not be done in the presence of men, with the intention of having them seen, and of drawing attention to yourself; otherwise they will only be valueless deeds, which will gain you no reward from your Father

Which is in Heaven. This precept is not opposed to that which Christ gave us above, to edify our neighbour by our good works, because, in a man, who lives a holy life, there are also many good works which cannot be hidden, and which edify our neighbour, and there are also others which must be hidden, and have God Alone as their witness. Besides, even in the good works themselves which we are necessitated to do openly, either in order to avoid giving offence, or to edify others, we must not seek our own glory in doing them, but only the glory of God, and the edification of our neighbour. Now, the most efficacious means, to assure ourselves on these occasions, of the uprightness of our intentions, is to do many good works in secret, between God and ourselves, and out of the sight of men. *Therefore,* says Christ, *when thou doest thine alms, do not sound a trumpet before thee, as the hypocrites do in the synagogues, and in the streets, that they may have glory of men, verily I say unto you, they have their reward. But when thou doest alms, let not thy left hand know what thy right hand doeth, that thine alms may be in secret: and thy Father, which seeth in secret, Himself shall reward thee openly.* Amen.

1. We must practise almsgiving. It is a precept which Jesus Christ assumes that we know already and practise: but let us consider here with attention how we fulfil it. Do we give alms as liberally as we might? Let us consider first, that 1. It is God our Father and the common Father of all men, Who has given us all that we have. Whether He have given us little or given us much, He wills that we should share what we have with our brethren who have less than ourselves, or who are in need. If He has loaded us with wealth, it is not that we should squander it in luxury, in pleasures, and in superfluities, whilst our brethren are in indigence. What useless expenditure might we not retrench, if we really desired to relieve the poor! We ought never to spend anything on ourselves, without at the same time giving to the poor their share. 2. God rewards alms-

giving. He sees what we give, He sees of what we deprive ourselves, He sees the manner, and the generous spirit in which we give. The reward which He destines for us is infinite and eternal. The money we lay out on ourselves is valueless; it brings no reward with it, and all our wealth will perish; we shall only keep that which we have given to God and for God. Let us then practise so excellent a work, let us urge all who are entrusted to our care to do the same, let us set before them the blessings of almsgiving. Christian fathers ought to accustom their children, from their earliest years, to almsgiving. Their tender hands can as yet only perform this good work, and their heart is more susceptible than it ever will be of feelings of compassion for the miseries of a neighbour. To lay the foundation of charity in their hearts, so that it should grow with their growth, this is indeed to leave them an inheritance more precious than wealth, it is to teach them the most glorious and most useful way in which to employ it.

2. We must give alms, without seeking in doing so, to gain the esteem and applause of men. To purchase the esteem of men at the price of almsgiving is to purchase it very dearly, since it is to purchase it at the price of Heaven Itself, which would have been the reward of our almsgiving. Alas! how many good works do we not lose through the poison of vanity which creeps into them, and makes us lose all their merit! Let us examine how many things we do in order to be approved and praised of men, and let us remember that all that is lost for us, and that we shall receive no reward for them from God. Ah! what a loss! And what folly to give ourselves all this trouble, and yet afterwards to lose all the merit of our acts of virtue.

3. We must give alms, without indulging in vanity in our own hearts. Let us conceal from our own eyes our good works, by never reflecting on them, by forgetting them, or if we think of them at all, only doing so in order to reproach ourselves with the little we do for God, the faint-heartedness with which we do it, and the

want of love which animates our actions. Do not let us seek as witness of our actions any but Him, Who should be the judge of them. Let Him, that Heavenly Father, from Whose eyes nothing escapes, see them hidden now, that He may one day make them known to the assembled universe, when He comes to reward them, which He will do for us with so much the more glory in Heaven, as we shall have sought for less on earth.

SECOND POINT.

With regard to God, the sacrifice of our mind by prayer.

There are three faults to be avoided in prayer.

1. Hypocrisy. *And when thou prayest, thou shalt not be as the hypocrites are; for they love to pray standing in the synagogues, and in the corners of the streets, that they may be seen of men. Verily I say unto you, they have their reward.* Hypocrisy includes singularity, dissimulation, and human respect. In order to avoid singularity, let us not offer up prayers in public save in the places set apart for that purpose. Let us not pray but with a modest demeanour and appearance, such as that of really religious persons, without affectation, and without any of those postures which may draw attention to us and make us remarkable. In order to avoid dissimulation, let us take care really to pray when we are engaged in prayers, and in the posture of a person who is praying; otherwise we are deceivers. In order to avoid human respect, let us pray because we are in the presence of God, and not because we are seen of men; otherwise we shall lose all the fruit of our prayers. Alas! how many lost prayers, how many hypocritical prayers, prayers of the presence of our bodies, prayers of our presence in God's House, prayers of our tongues in which our hearts take no part, phantom prayers, pure delusion, lost time, lost reward. Let us strive to repair the past by sincere and true prayers.

2. Distraction. *But thou, when thou prayest, enter*

into thy closet, and when thou hast shut thy door, pray to thy Father Which is in secret, and thy Father, Which seeth in secret, shall reward thee openly. We must avoid distraction, whether in our private prayers, or in the public worship of God. When we are engaged in private prayers, let us choose a free time, let us enter into our own rooms, and shut to our doors, and there alone with God, and putting aside every thing else, after having placed ourselves in His Holy Presence, let us address our prayers to Him as if there was no one but Him and us in the world; let every other object disappear from our sight. Let us hold with Him the most secret and most intimate converse. Perhaps we have never yet tried to pray in this manner. How many hours we have in which we do not know what to do, or which we employ uselessly, which we might give up to such a holy purpose! The time would not be lost: God would see us in this solitude, He would prepare for us a reward in Heaven, and He would give us the foretaste of it on earth by the inward consolations with which He would inundate our souls. When we pray in the public places of prayer, let us enter into the secret chamber of our own hearts, let us close all the doors of our senses; let our ears be only open to the divine service, let our eyes only behold the ceremonies of divine worship, let our tongue only utter the words of sacred praise which are offered up to God there. Our Heavenly Father will see us there, He will mark us out there, and there He will reward us. Nothing is so common as the complaints which are made with regard to the distractions which occur during prayer; but what do we do in order to prevent them? If we enter into prayer without any preparation, and without precautions, without even thinking what we are about to do, only intent upon setting ourselves free as soon as possible from an obligation which is burdensome to us; if we carry with us to our prayers, a heart, full of distractions, occupied with a thousand worldly objects which we do not give ourselves either the time or the trouble to lay aside; if instead of giving our thoughts to prayer, we allow ourselves to see every thing and to remark every thing that is going on; if we do not even fear to speak and to converse with others there, do not let us complain any longer of our distractions, but let us complain of ourselves. Our Father knows well our weakness, and He forgives the distractions which we are not entirely able to drive away; but for those which only spring from our own fault, our want of reverence, and our want of love to God, there is no excuse.

3. The multitude of our words. *When ye pray, use not vain repetitions as the heathen do: for they think they shall be heard for their much speaking.* Our Lord here condemns the abundance of words in our private prayers, as being contrary to the very spirit of prayer. A humble and contrite heart speaks little. The more a person speaks the less he prays: and we do not pray at all, when the words we utter do not come from the heart. A discourse and prayer are two very different things. The former is the work of the imagination and the mind: the latter is the work of the heart, and of the heart which feels its needs. Feelings rather than words ought to compose prayer. Besides which, our petitions are only part of the exercise which is called prayer. Prayer contains, besides that, praise, oblation, adoration, thanksgiving, which is carried on by the singing of Psalms and hymns, by reading the Scriptures and holy books, and by all the liturgy and services of our Church. It is not to prayer, taken in that sense, that we must apply this prohibition of our Lord, but to prayer which each offers to God, in order to ask of Him that of which he is in need, or some particular grace: that is to say our Lord forbids us to multiply words with ideas like unto those of the heathen. The heathen had not the same ideas of their false gods which we ought to have of the true God: they believed that their gods might be absent or far removed from them: they looked upon them as being ignorant of their wants: and as not being always willing to relieve them: they thought then that

by dint of words, they should make themselves heard by them, that they should move them, and thus obtain the fulfilment of their requests. It is not thus with our God, with our Father; He is always present, He hears us everywhere, He sees our desires, and He desires to relieve them. *Be ye not therefore like unto them;* adds our Saviour: *for your Father knoweth what things ye have need of, before ye ask Him.* What a motive for us of love and confidence! Lastly, although God knows our wants, and wills to deliver us from them, He wills nevertheless that we should pray to Him, in order to keep us in a salutary dependence on Him, in order to preserve humility in us, by the knowledge we must have of our needs before we can make them known, in order to establish between Himself and us an intercourse full of faith, love, confidence and thanksgiving. Let us then pray with fervour and perseverance.

THIRD POINT.

With regard to ourselves, the sacrifice of our body by fasting.

When ye fast, be not, as the hypocrites, of a sad countenance; for they disfigure their faces, that they may appear unto men to fast. Verily I say unto you, They have their reward. But thou, when thou fastest, anoint thine head, and wash thy face; that thou appear not unto men to fast, but unto thy Father, which is in secret: and thy Father, which seeth in secret, shall reward thee openly. There are three kinds of sadness to be avoided here.

1. The sadness of vanity, in order to be praised for our acts of fasting. We wish to let men know that we do fast: and if the fast is an appointed and public one, we wish to let others see how much it costs us, how mortified and strict we are, and how great our fervour is in observing these religious exercises; and thus we yield our body up as a sacrifice to the devil by this very act of self-mortification which is prompted by vanity.

In this sadness of countenance put on to satisfy our pride, and to draw upon ourselves the esteem of men, what does the divine Creator see? He does not see His image there any longer, but the proud image of the evil one, a double-minded spirit, an unfaithful heart, a hypocritical soul.

2. There is a sadness of dissimulation. We put on an appearance of feebleness and langour that we may make others believe that we are not in a condition to fulfil our Lord's commands of fasting. We have strength enough to give ourselves up to tumultuous pleasures, far more capable of deranging our health than the most austere fasts: but when it is a question of fasting, then we are infirm, and out of health: an hypocrisy of a new kind far more common in our days than the former.

3. There is a sadness of sensuality that we may not be made uncomfortable by our fasts. We complain of the number of fast days and days of abstinence enjoined by our Church: we complain of all which in our fasting is mortifying to us: we even turn our fasting and our abstinence into an occasion of gratifying our tastes. But this is to fast before men and not before God. The fast which God looks upon and rewards, is that which is a true mortification, and which is accompanied by the spirit of repentance, and of a humble and contrite heart; it is that which is undertaken to satisfy the justice of God, to punish ourselves for our faults, and to bring into subjection a rebellious flesh, which has been the cause of them; it is that by which we deprive ourselves of the pleasures of the senses, in order to render ourselves more capable to enjoy those of the spirit, by which we detach ourselves from all the delights of the world, in order to long with greater ardour after those of Heaven. Alas! of how many fasts and abstinences have we not lost the fruits, because instead of doing them to God and in the spirit of repentance, we have only done them out of human respect, out of display, or to gain the praise of men.

Prayer. Ah Lord, since Thou art so gracious as to

reward these mortifications which are done to Thee in secret, I will not lose the fruit of my self denials; the little that I do shall be done at least with the single and upright desire to please Thee, and to sanctify myself. I will apply myself to pray, and to pray well, that is, to pray with faith, with attention, and with love. I will help my brethren in need: but I will seek to have Thee, my God, alone, as the witness of my almsgiving, my prayer, and my fasting, that so, by Thy Mercy, I may not lose the reward which Thou hast promised me in Heaven. Amen.

Meditation LVI.

SEVENTH CONTINUATION OF THE SERMON ON THE MOUNT.

OF THE LORD'S PRAYER.

Before examining the three petitions, which have reference to God, and the four other petitions, which concern ourselves, let us consider the sentiments with which we ought to repeat this prayer. S. Matt. vi. 9—15.

FIRST POINT.

Of the feelings with which we ought to say the Lord's Prayer.

1. In relation to Him Who has taught us this prayer, gratitude and fidelity. *After this manner therefore pray ye.* Is it not an infinite condescension on the part of our Lord, to have taught us in what way He wills that we should pray to Him: to have, so to say, framed the petition which He wills that we should present to Him? Could He, after that, refuse to receive it, or not grant us our requests? This prayer, having God for its Author, cannot but be perfect. It is, in reality, the abridgment of the whole Gospel; it contains all that God has done for us, and all that we ought to do for Him; it contains

all our duties and all our needs; it ought to regulate our thoughts, our feelings, our life, all our movements, so that our heart should long unceasingly for those things which we ask for in this prayer, desire them continually, and have no other desires.

2. In relation to Him to Whom we address this prayer, love and confidence. It is to God that we address it; but by what Name are we commanded to call Him to our help? It is not by that of Lord, of Creator, Judge, Almighty, but by that of Father. *After this manner therefore pray ye; Our Father.* O Name full of sweetness and delight! we call God our Father; it is Jesus Christ Who commands us so to do, and it is He Who gives us the right to do so. When He speaks of God in relation to us, He says always, Your Father seeth you, your Father will reward you, your Father knoweth your needs. What glory, what happiness, what a ground of trust!

3. In relation to ourselves, who use this prayer, brotherly charity. We are all children of God by creation; but, besides this blessing which is common to all mankind, we are, besides, children of God by a still closer title, which is that of our adoption in Christ. By this title, and in virtue of our being Christians, we are all brethren in Christ. We make up but one family with Him, Who is the first-born amongst men, the interests of which are common, and the petitions of which ought also to be common. Can there be between us a stronger and more sacred bond of the sincerest and tenderest charity?

4. In relation to the place whence and whither we address this prayer; reverence, detachment from this earth, and longing for Heaven. *Our Father which art in Heaven.* It is to that Throne of Thy glory that we raise our thoughts and our wishes, O tender Father! Who hast formed us in Thine image, Who hast given us the life of grace, Who hast always provided for our needs. As Thy children, what respect, what obedience, what fear, and what love do we not owe Thee! O Al-

mighty Father, Who reignest in the Heavens, what is the earth in Thy sight? What power have all creatures against Thee, and against those whom Thou dost protect? Our Father which art in Heaven! have pity on Thy children who are on the earth, and at such a distance from Thee? What pleasure can I take here below, separated from Thee, O my Father Who art in Heaven, whilst I am still here below on the earth? When wilt Thou recall me from my exile, O loving and compassionate Father, that I may come to my true country? when wilt Thou re-unite me to my brethren, who are with Thee, that I may never more be separated from them, to my brethren who reign in Heaven with Thee, that I may reign for ever with them?

SECOND POINT.

Of the three first petitions, which have reference to God.

1. First petition, *Hallowed be Thy Name.* May It be sanctified, known, adored and glorified, by the public and universal worship of all nations: may all, renouncing their superstitions, acknowledge and adore no other God but Thee. May He be hallowed by every tongue; may all praise Him and bless Him in adversity as in prosperity; may none blaspheme or dishonour Him, may there be no one who does not know Him, and love Him with all their hearts, who does not serve Him as He deserves to be served. Grant, that in particular, I, who am more favoured with Thy graces, may serve Thee with so much fear, earnestness and watchfulness, that it may appear by my works done to the glory of Thy holy Name, that I worship in Thee, the true God, the holy and all-powerful God. The glory of the Lord, which is the object of this petition, ought then to form the first object of our desires: but what zeal do we shew forth for the glory of God? What do we do in order to promote it? Do we strive as much as we can to make known the Lord, to make Him obeyed and loved, and to know Him, serve Him, and love Him ourselves?

2. Second petition. *Thy kingdom come.* That is to say, the reign of Thy Gospel, of Thy Church, in all the kingdoms of the world. 1. May all nations acknowledge Him Whom Thou hast given them as Messiah, as King, Saviour, and Judge. 2. May the reign of Thy grace soon come in our hearts. Reign there as Sovereign, may all be subjected to Thee, and may nothing resist Thee. 3. May the reign of Thy glory come after this life; grant that our sins may not deprive us of it, that repentance may restore us to the path which leads to it, and that Thy mercy, by granting us the gift of perseverance unto the end, may put us in possession of that peaceable and happy reign, where plunged in the joys of an eternal life, we shall enjoy abundance of all sorts of delights; that is to say delights worthy of Thee, O God, worthy of our divine Birth and of the holiness of our condition! Such are our desires, doubtless; but let us labour with all our power to establish in others, and especially in ourselves the kingdom of God, and to destroy there the reign of the world, of sin, of self-love, and of evil passions.

3. Third petition. *Thy will be done on earth as it is in Heaven.* May all men, without distinction, Jews and Gentiles submit to Thy will; may Thy will be done on earth by all Thy creatures who know Thee, as the angels and the blessed fulfil it in the abode of bliss. Let there be no longer, on earth as in Heaven, any hearts but those which are submissive to Thy laws. I submit my own to Thee; I embrace, adore, and accept with all my heart the accomplishment of Thy supreme will, which, without in any way depriving men of their free will, governs every thing on earth as in Heaven, makes every thing subservient to the designs of His glory and the designs of His Providence. In all the events of my life, even those which seem to be the most unfavourable, I will recognise, O my God, Thy adorable will which is thus fulfilled, and which is not less holy and adorable in that which it permits on earth, than in that which it appoints in Heaven. Thus this continual

thought of the will of God, which was the ruling principle of our Saviour, ought also to be the main spring of our desires and of our actions; but do we enter into these feelings? We utter these words: but do we not rather do the contrary of that which we ask? In Heaven, every thing obeys God with promptness, exactness, punctuality, joy, and love; is it thus that we obey Him, whether in His commands, or in the person of those who stand to us in His place? Is not our will, with regard to His, what our flesh is with regard to our minds, in a manifest opposition, in a fatal and continual contradiction? Oh self-will, without which there would be no hell! wilt thou never submit thyself to that sovereignly lovely and perfectly loved Will, which makes the joy of believers on earth and the bliss of the blessed in Heaven? We may perceive in these first petitions the mystery of the Holy Trinity, and address each of them to each of the three Divine Persons. The first to the Father, as to the source of all holiness; the second to the Son, Who has established the reign of God on earth; the third to the Holy Spirit, Who is the Will and the Love of the Father and the Son. We can moreover bring to bear upon these three petitions the acts of the three Theological Virtues, regarding the first, as specially relating to faith, the second, to hope, and the third, to charity.

THIRD POINT.

Of four other petitions, which relate to ourselves.

1. Fourth petition. *Give us this day our daily bread.* That is to say, 1. The material and earthly bread for the temporal life of our body. Give us, not riches, not the conveniences of life, but that which is necessary for our subsistence, as much as necessity requires, without luxury, and without abundance: moreover we only ask it of Thee for to-day, for why should we disquiet ourselves respecting a morrow which we are not certain may ever come? 2. Give us the spiritual bread of the Word, in instruction, in reading, in meditation, and in

prayer, for the spiritual food of our souls: give us, lastly, the Heavenly Bread of the Holy Eucharist for the support of our souls, the resurrection of our body, and the eternal life of body and soul. Let us examine here what is our ardour, and what our relish for these sorts of bread: and if we have been commissioned by God's Providence, with the office of distributing them to others, let us see with what pains we acquit ourselves of our duties.

2. Fifth petition. *And forgive us our trespasses, as we forgive them that trespass against us.* My most pressing need, O my God, is to be delivered from the immense debts which I have contracted towards Thee by sin. I venture then to conjure Thee to forgive me them, as I forgive sincerely all those which my brethren have contracted towards me. I know that there is no proportion between my sins and the wrongs which others may have done to me; and what is the indulgence I am capable of shewing to others, compared with Thy infinite Goodness? We pronounce by these words the sentence of our own absolution, or of our condemnation. God wills to forgive us all our offences, however great they may be, and to pardon us entirely, forget, wash out, and do away all our sins; He wills to pardon us every day, because every day we sin against Him: He wills to pardon us as soon as we ask Him to do so; He anticipates us even by His grace, and by His ministers, He is the first to entreat us to return to Him. We ought then on our side to forgive also, and that is what we promise to do; that is what we pledge ourselves to do when we repeat this prayer. Therefore let us forgive every thing without making any exception: let us forgive entirely, let us forget, bury in silence, and efface from our hearts the offences which we forgive, without treasuring up either resentment or remembrance of them, without allowing ourselves even to speak of them and to complain of them: let us forgive, day by day, without letting any thing exhaust our patience, or put bounds to our charity; let us forgive as soon as a fault is acknowledged; let us even

smooth the way for its acknowledgment, and make the first advances ourselves. Is it thus that we forgive? How easily do we not persuade ourselves that God forgives us, that He forgets our sins and unfaithfulness! How difficult it is to us to forget the wrong which has been done to us! What an insurmountable opposition do we not offer to the desire others shew to gain our forgiveness! What injustice is it not on our part, and how little do we know our real interests!

3. Sixth petition. *And lead us not into temptation.* Put afar from us all those occasions of sin which the devil puts in our way, and of which he so often takes advantage in order to ruin us. There are some which are so dangerous, there are situations so critical, that the strongest and the most courageous can with difficulty bear up against them. Thou alone, O my God, Thou alone, by Thy Providence, canst put far from us these kinds of temptations: suffer not that we should be exposed to them. There are some temptations which are inevitable, and which Thy Providence permits that we should meet with; of whatever kind they are, forsake us not, and suffer not that they should enter into our soul by our yielding to them, or hearkening to them. Grant, Lord, that we may draw back from them as soon as we perceive them, may resist them, strive against them, guard ourselves against them, and repulse them: grant moreover, that temptation, thus surmounted by Thy grace, may turn to our advantage; but whilst we ask this of Thee, O powerful God, we promise Thee ourselves to avoid temptation, to look closely into everything that may be an occasion of falling to us, to observe the places, or the persons who may be a cause of temptation to us, or who perhaps have already been such, and have caused our fall, and to avoid them absolutely with all our power: we promise Thee that we will not ourselves lead others into temptation, so as to be to them a cause of sin, an occasion of scandal, and to do nothing, and say nothing, write nothing, and neither give nor lend anything, which may be prejudicial to their salvation or to their Christian perfection.

4. Seventh petition. *But deliver us from evil.* From temporal evil; send us no affliction nor calamity which may become to us an occasion of falling, which may produce in our minds either forgetfulness or neglect of our duties. Bring us not down to an extremity of poverty which may lead us to murmur, and thrust us into despair, or lessen our faith. Deliver us from the temporal calamities which we deserve but too well through the abuse of Thy blessings: deliver us above all from the spiritual calamities which surround us, from the evil of sin, from the evil of hell: deliver us from the evil spirit, from Satan, or from the man, who does the work of the devil, by leading others into sin. Deliver us from the tyranny of our own passions, and make us worthy to enter that blessed state of peace and liberty which Thou dost reserve for Thy children: a happy state, where there will be no more sin, no falls, no cause of offence; where virtue will be pure, and piety will prevail, holiness will be perfected, and our happiness assured. There remains sometimes a difficulty with regard to the fifth petition of the Lord's Prayer. I have sinned, says one, but has God forgiven me? Listen to the words of our divine Saviour, and admire His goodness: He takes pains to calm our anxieties, and to reassure us. *For if ye forgive men their trespasses, your Heavenly Father will also forgive you:* and in order to cement more firmly amongst us the most sincere charity, He adds; *But if ye forgive not men their trespasses neither will your Heavenly Father forgive your trespasses.* How then could we not forgive, and in forgiving, hope for all?

Prayer. Ah! far be it from me, Lord, to draw near to Thee in prayer with a heart filled with bitterness! In order that Thou mayest hearken to Thine infinite goodness, I will myself hearken to my duty. Charitable and compassionate towards my brethren, I shall experience that Thou art a Father full of goodness and mercy. Thou dost make me in some way, the arbiter of my own lot, and Thou willest to receive from me the measure of Thy long-suffering; could I then not shew myself willing to look with mercy on the faults of my brethren towards myself, faults so light in comparison to those which I have committed against Thee? It is with these feelings, O Heavenly Father, that I will often utter that divine prayer which Thy Well Beloved Son has taught me. Each day, and without ceasing, I will ask with faith, love and attention, the sanctification of Thy Name, the coming of Thy Kingdom, the perfect fulfilment of Thy holy Will, all things that are needful both for body and soul, the forgiveness of my sins, and grace not to commit them any more, deliverance even from my evil inclinations which lead me into sin, and from all my misery, by a holy death, and a glorious resurrection. Amen.

Meditation LVII.

EIGHTH CONTINUATION OF THE SERMON ON THE MOUNT.

Of detachment from the things of this world, and of taking pains to enrich ourselves with those of Heaven.

Consider, 1. the difference there is between earthly and Heavenly possessions; 2. what is a common delusion on this point; 3. the pretext which people employ in order to make excuses for this delusion. S. Matt. vi. 19—34.

FIRST POINT.

Of the difference which there is between earthly and heavenly possessions.

The difference of these possessions is found in their nature, in their acquisition, in their preservation, in their possession, and in the enjoyment of them.

1. In their nature. *Lay not up for yourselves treasures upon the earth, where moth and rust doth corrupt, and where thieves break through and steal; but*

lay up for yourselves treasures in Heaven where neither moth nor rust doth corrupt, and where thieves do not break through and steal: The treasures of earth consist in gold and silver, in precious stones, rich apparel, magnificent ornaments, superb furniture: add to these estates, houses, costly dwellings, vast possessions. Now, what is all that, but mire and mud? What are the other riches of the world, glory, reputation, honours, pleasures? Wind and smoke, nothingness and the source of corruption. Heavenly treasures consist in acts of virtue, of mortification, temperance, patience, charity, submission to God's commands, resignation to His will, in works of mercy, in almsgiving, in prayers: such are the true riches worthy of men, worthy to be placed in heaven. About which of these two kinds are we occupied?

2. These possessions are different in their acquisition and in their increase. Earthly riches are difficult to obtain. We need talents, opportunities, a fair start, and very often all these things are wanting to us. Again they cannot be acquired without depriving some one else of them, and often this other gains them, and deprives us of them. Heavenly riches are at our disposal; in order to acquire them, it suffices but to desire them. Grace is obtained by prayer. Opportunities for the practice of virtue present themselves to us of themselves, and at every moment of our lives. The endeavour to enrich ourselves with those heavenly possessions injures no one else, and no one can injure us in this undertaking. The riches of heaven and earth are different in their increase. The heart is equally insatiable, whether it abandons itself to the love of heavenly treasures or to the love of earthly treasures; it desires unceasingly to increase those possessions in which it makes its happiness and its treasure consist: but he who desires only heavenly riches has alone the consolation of being able to increase them every day and every moment of the day. A sigh, a desire, a simple thought increases his treasure. Well or ill, asleep or awake, nothing can hinder him

from enriching himself more and more. Whatever he does or suffers, if he does and suffers it for God, all is counted to him. Senseless that we are to give our thoughts to any other treasures than those in heaven.

3. These possessions differ in their preservation. To what accidents, to what mischances are not the possessions of this world exposed? The rust eats into them, the worms gnaw them, old age destroys them, thieves carry them away, the fire burns them, shipwrecks swallow them up, law suits exhaust them, a thousand accidents dissipate every day the most brilliant fortunes; other possessions are not more durable. Glory is withered by calumny, envy, or intrigues; pleasures are troubled by censure, jealousy, and clouded by sickness or disappointment: greatness falls of itself; the weight alone of its own vanity suffices to bring it down, and if that did not suffice, that which men's passions have raised up, the passions of others will overturn. What anxieties does not at the least the fear of all these dangers bring with it, and the precautions we take to guard ourselves from them? He who has his treasure in heaven is sheltered from all anxiety and from all accidents; he has nothing to fear but himself.

4. These riches differ in their possession. The possession of earthy riches debases the heart and blinds the mind. The heart participates in the nature of the things to which it clings. *For where your treasure is, there will your heart be also.* Thus what is a heart that sets its happiness on earthly treasures? Base-minded, grovelling, material, low, earthly, vile and despicable, delighting only in idle fancies, and frivolous pleasures. Is it for that that it has been created? On the contrary a heart which works only for God, and which has its treasure in Heaven, is a noble and generous heart, elevated, sublime, heavenly and divine. Do we desire then to know where our treasure is, let us examine where our heart is: let us examine towards what object it tends of itself, and as it were, naturally, with what object it occupies itself willingly, and for the longest time, if it is

of earth or Heaven. Possession blinds both the mind and reason. *The light of the body is the eye: if therefore thine eye be single, thy whole body shall be full of darkness. If therefore the light that is in thee be darkness, how great is that darkness!* That is to say, your mind, your judgement, your reason are to your soul what your soul is to your body. If your eyes are good, clear, and not vitiated by any extraneous matter, your whole body is in light; you know how you are and where you are, where you put your foot, or where you lay your hand, what you must do, or what you should avoid; in a word, you are and you act in the light, and that is for you a point of security. Such is the lot of him who labours for heaven; he feels that he is, and that he is walking, in the light, that he has taken the good part, and that he will not go astray; he sees things as they are, and esteems them at their right value. But if your eye is vitiated, if it is not single, if it is, so to say, made double by a thick film, how can you discern objects? Alas! what is the blindness of him who loves only the things of this world? How does he look upon things, and to which does he give the preference? He has no taste, he has no affection but for the things of the earth, he doubts if there are any other, if there is another life, a Paradise or a hell; sometimes even he persuades himself that there is none. Now, if his reason, which was given him in order to guide him and to regulate his movements, is obscured by such thick darkness, what will it be with all the other powers of his soul, which have no light of themselves, and which can only be governed by the light of reason? In what abyss of crimes do not covetousness, his inclination to evil, all the unregulated passions and affections of his heart precipitate him? In vain would he make a display of a pretended integrity; reason blinded by passion acknowledges no other integrity than the art of concealing one's crimes. How necessary is it then to purify unceasingly this eye of our soul, to strengthen it with the light and religion of faith, and not to let it be obscured by the maxims of the world, the suggestions of the devil, and the delusion of passion!

5. These possessions differ in their enjoyment. We only enjoy the riches of the world during our life time, besides which it is needful that we should enjoy them all our lives, and enjoy them fully, quietly, and in a manner to be able to be truly happy. Our enjoyment of them is at least but an imperfect enjoyment, unquiet and of short duration; death will terminate all, and will take us away from every thing; on the contrary, the enjoyment of heavenly possessions will be perfect, eternal, and secure in its eternity of duration. What folly then to attach oneself to the earth and to a passing possession, whilst we might gain heaven and eternal happiness.

SECOND POINT.

Of a common delusion on this subject.

This delusion consists in that people seek to lay up for themselves at the same time a treasure on earth and a treasure in heaven, to serve God and the world, to be happy in this world and in the next, to enjoy during this life the good things of this world, and in the future life the blessings of the next world, in a word to serve two opposite masters, which cannot in any way take place. *No man can serve two masters; for either he will hate the one, and love the other; or else he will hold to the one, and despise the other; ye cannot serve God and Mammon.* The reason of this impossibility is, that each of these masters require of us that which we cannot share between them.

1. Our love. We have only one heart, and that heart cannot belong to two objects at the same time, and especially to two objects as different as are the Creator and the creature, Heaven and earth, the present life and the future life, virtue and vice, charity and covetousness. One cannot love the one without hating the other; we must, of necessity, in attaching ourselves to the one, forsake the other: our own experience makes us feel it sufficiently.

2. Our esteem. It is none the less true we cannot share our esteem and give it at the same time to two masters. He who esteems those happy who live in abundance, luxury, honour, pleasures, what value can he set upon voluntary poverty, a humble, hidden, and mortified life? He looks upon it only with a sovereign contempt, and it appears in his eyes as pure folly.

3. Our obedience and our services. The impossibility of sharing our services and our obedience between these two masters makes itself yet more felt, since the laws which they impose upon us, and the commands they give us are entirely opposed. The avaricious man overlooks the laws of justice; how should he then obey those of charity and of almsgiving? The ambitious man disowns those of modesty; how should he obey those of humility? The voluptuous man disowns the law of moderation and of decorum; how should he obey these of self-denial and repentance?

4. Our inclinations and our likings. We cannot relish the things of heaven, and at the same time, those of earth, delight ourselves in God, and find our pleasure in the world. We complain perhaps that we do not experience any relish in our religious exercises, that we find no sweetness in the practice of devotion; but we ought not to be surprised at it, it is because we seek to serve two masters, to divide our services between them, and to follow their laws by turns. Let us undeceive ourselves, let us renounce the world, our passions, and ourselves, in order to attach ourselves wholly to God, and then we shall relish all that has relation to Him, and belongs to His service.

5. Our cares and our thoughts. This multiplicity of thoughts which beset us, and which importune us in prayer, come from the same source. We complain of our distractions; oh! let us rather complain of our delusion. We wish to serve two masters, and that is impossible. If we served but one, if God alone was the Master we sought to please, and in Him alone, our love, our esteem, our services, our inclinations, our likings,

our cares, and our thoughts were centred; in Him alone we should find our happiness both in time and in eternity.

THIRD POINT.

Of a pretext which people make use of in this matter.

The pretext which people make use of in order to make excuse for the excessive care they take to procure for themselves the good things of this world, is the fear of being in want of them; but this pretext comes from the depravity of our hearts.

1. Of an ungrateful heart, which, forgetting the benefits already received, does not see that they are a pledge of those which we may expect. *Therefore I say unto you*, our Saviour adds, *Take no thought for your life, what ye shall eat, or what ye shall drink, nor yet for your body what ye shall put on. Is not the life more than meat, and the body than raiment?* God has given us body and soul, He has joined our soul to our body, and that is what makes our present life; how could we fear after that, that He should let us want those things which are necessary to sustain our life, and clothing to cover our body?

2. This pretext comes from a heart which is distracted, and does not reflect on the miracles of Providence which the world offers to our eyes. *Behold the fowls of the air; for they sow not, neither do they reap, nor gather into barns, yet your Heavenly Father feedeth them. Are ye not much better than they? Which of you by taking thought can add one cubit to his stature? And why take ye thought for raiment? Consider the lilies of the field, how they grow; they toil not, neither do they spin. And yet I say unto you, That even Solomon in all his glory was not arrayed like one of these. Wherefore, if God so clothe the grass of the field, which to-day is, and to-morrow is cast into the oven, shall He not much more clothe you, O ye of little faith? Therefore take not thought, saying, What shall we eat? Or what shall we drink? Or, Wherewithal shall*

we be clothed? See the birds which fly in the air, with what care God feeds them; see the flowers which cover the earth, and are only to last a day, with what magnificence, what splendour, and what variety God has clothed them; nevertheless He has given neither to the former the power to sow and reap, nor to the latter the industry to weave and spin: and you think that God will forget you, He Who is not only your Creator, but likewise your Father; you for whom He has made all that is in heaven, and on earth; you whom He has endowed with reason, industry and talents, you whom He has destined for an immortal life of happiness: oh! where is your faith?

3. This pretext comes from a heart, which has no trust in God, and which does not hope for any thing from Him. *(For after all these things do the Gentiles seek;) for your Heavenly Father knoweth that ye have need of all these things.* Do you think then that the God Whom we adore is, like those heathen gods, a God, Who is blind, powerless, without feeling? Ah! He is a Father, and more a Father than any other. Shall we never shew Him the feelings of trust which are suitable to children? That endearing name of Father which we give Him every day, is it only an empty title?

4. This pretext comes from a proud heart, which places its trust in itself, and which only torments itself needlessly. *Which of you by taking thought can add one cubit unto his stature?* In truth, what do all our anxieties avail? Have we any power over nature? To what purpose do all these reflections serve, all these conversations about the weather, the winds and the rain? Superfluous words which only serve to shew how much our thoughts cling to the things of this world. Let us acknowledge our powerlessness, and the sovereign might of Him Who has created and Who governs the world, and let us place our trust in Him. The time which we lose in fanciful reflections, would be much better employed in prayer, and in working out our own salvation.

5. This pretext comes from an irrational heart, which seeks that which does not depend on its researches, and does not seek that which does depend on it. *Seek ye first the kingdom of God and His righteousness: and all these things shall be added unto you. Take therefore no thought for the morrow, for the morrow shall take thought for the things of itself. Sufficient unto the day is the evil thereof.* Let us think only of our own sanctification, let us strive to gain the kingdom of God which has been promised to us, let us exercise ourselves in works of righteousness, let us enrich ourselves with heavenly goods, and those of earth will not be wanting to us. The care of working out our salvation, and of doing all the good works that we can, has never ruined any one; that which brings ruin with it, is too often the very desire to gain more, luxury, gambling, revelling, and idleness. Let us do each day what we have to do, and what is required of us, without any anxiety for the future. To each day its own troubles, cares and labour are sufficient. It is not nevertheless that a wise and moderate foresight is forbidden, but a useless anxiety, which turns away our thoughts from our present duties, and which makes us unsettled and disturbed in mind, and which we do not restrain within due bounds; for He Who forbids us to be thus over-careful, commands us also to work.

Prayer. Ah Lord! can I then still have so much eagerness in the pursuit of the necessaries of life, and the false and frivolous things of this world! No, all my thoughts, all my desires shall be turned henceforth towards Heaven, towards those true riches whose possession is eternal, and ought to fill for ever all my desires. In heaven shall be my treasure, and consequently my heart: and it is by good works, pure and holy in their motives, that I will enrich myself for my true and eternal home. Two masters, whose service is opposed to each other, shall not any longer have rule in my heart: I will not hesitate any longer, O my God! There is no rule more just, more sweet, and more reasonable than that of Thy love; and no rule more unjust, more cruel, and more blinding, than that of the love of riches, of the world, and of myself. Far from me then this love of life, and that which it exacts! I will even be without anxiety as to the necessaries of life. Can Thy Providence forsake me, if I do but commit myself to it? After working and taking reasonable cares, I will rest from my wants on Thy Fatherly Heart, and feel that Thou wilt do what is best for Thy child whom Thou hast formed in Thine own image and destined to eternal happiness. Yes, Thou art my Father, and Thou knowest all my needs, I shall never then be in want of anything, unless I render myself unworthy of Thy care by my mistrust. I will then only employ myself above every thing, with the care of gaining Heaven and acquiring the virtues which may assure me the possession of it. Amen.

Meditation LVIII.

NINTH CONTINUATION OF THE SERMON ON THE MOUNT.
OF THE THREE DUTIES ESSENTIAL TO SALVATION.

These duties are, 1. with regard to our neighbour, the duty of charity; 2. with regard to God, the duty of prayer; 3. with regard to ourselves, the duty of self-denial. S. Matt. vii. 1—14.

FIRST POINT.

With regard to our neighbour, the duty of charity.

1. Let us avoid doing any injury to our neighbour, and hurting him by our thoughts, in judging evil of him. *Judge not, that ye be not judged. For with what judgment ye judge, ye shall be judged, and with what*

measure ye mete, it shall be measured to you again. And why beholdest thou the mote that is in thy brother's eye, but considerest not the beam that is in thine own eye? Let us not judge nor condemn the actions and the words of our brethren, if we do not wish to be judged and condemned ourselves. Let us take in good part that which will bear a good interpretation, let us not blame that for which we can make an excuse, or rather let us not even examine into the conduct of our neighbour of which the charge is not entrusted to us; let us not penetrate into his intentions, but take it for granted always that they are good; let us excuse his failings, and only occupy ourselves with our own. The reason of this duty is; that our judgement is, on our part, incompetent, because we are not constituted the judges of others; it is, that as regards our neighbour, our judgement is always unjust, because his cause is absolutely unknown to us, and that we cannot know what passes in his heart: it is, that in relation to God, our judgement is injurious, because in judging, we usurp His rights: a judgement which has even something repugnant in it, in that, sinners as we are, we set ourselves up as judges, and that we undertake to judge those who stand before the same tribunal that we do, and who are often much less guilty than we are. The reward or the punishment of the fulfilment or the transgression of this duty, is that if we do not judge nor condemn our neighbour, if we make excuse for him in all ways, we shall not be either judged or condemned, we shall be forgiven and treated with leniency: on the contrary, if we condemn our neighbour with rigour and severity, we shall be treated in the same manner. It is for us to choose how we will that God should act towards us, for He will measure His conduct by our own. If we are lenient judges towards others, we shall find Him full of indulgence towards us; if we are pitiless, and severe critics, and censors, we must expect judgement without mercy. This duty has regard only to our conduct amongst ourselves, it does not take away from those who are called to the office of judge, any of their duty in so doing. The Church and magistrates have this duty laid upon them in a different manner, and our duty is to yield to the judgement of those who have authority given them to exercise it.

2. Let us avoid injuring our neighbour by our words, in reproving him for his faults. *Or how wilt thou say to thy brother, Let me pull out the mote out of thine eye, and behold, a beam is in thine own eye? Thou hypocrite, first cast out the beam out of thine own eye, and then shalt thou see clearly to cast out the mote out of thy brother's eye.* Do not let us meddle with others by reproving them without authority; much less by blaming them, or censuring them, or criticising them in their absence: zeal, which is the ordinary pretext for such censure, is only an hypocritical zeal, because it hides the malignity of an evil heart which only rejoices in the evil of another, and loves to make it known; because it hides a secret pride which takes pleasure in another's humiliation, which rises in proportion as it abases a neighbour, and which desires to make others believe that one is so much the more exempt from failings as one is zealous in reproving others; because it conceals a deplorable blindness, by which, at a time that we are looking at the mote in our neighbour's eye, we do not perceive the beam which is in our own. Hypocrites that we are! if we have zeal, let us begin by taking away the beam which blinds us, and we shall see how to take out from our brother's eye, the mote which disturbs us. Let us also follow this rule, when our position or charity require that we should reprove others; before reproving them, let us look into our own hearts, and it will not then be difficult to us to reprove with gentleness and charity.

3. Let us avoid injuring our neighbour by our actions, by doing things which give him occasion to sin against God. Let us never do any thing which can lead others to do wrong, or make them more sinful than they are. *Give not that which is holy unto the dogs, neither cast*

ye your pearls before swine, lest they trample them under their feet, and turn again and rend you. It belongs to prudence regulated by the light of God, to distinguish mischievous and rash judgements from the thoughts and feelings, the zeal and the duty which the Lord requires: to discern those whom it befits to keep away from the sacred mysteries, and to know the occasions when it is needful to hold one's peace, in order not to aggravate the wrong doers, from those when one must speak, even at the peril of one's life. As for ourselves, do not let us imitate those furious swine, but let us bear with humility the wholesome denials we receive, let us listen in a teachable spirit to the good advice which is given to us, and let us profit carefully by the precious instructions which we meet with.

SECOND POINT.

With regard to God, the duty of prayer.

Examine the object, the motive, and the conditions of this duty.

1. The object of prayer. *Ask, and it shall be given you; seek, and ye shall find; knock, and it shall be opened unto you.* The duty of prayer consists in asking of God, His grace. We must ask it with ardour, because we have a pressing need of it; with humility, because we are unworthy of it, and that God bestows it out of no obligation, but of His own free will; with perseverance, because it is a precious treasure, and merits to be constantly solicited, because we have often abused it, and have rejected it when it was offered to us. This duty of prayer consists in seeking the kingdom of God, that is to say, that in asking God for His grace, we must on our part, with the grace which He gives us, do what depends upon us, seek the means whereby we may please Him, fulfil His commandments, conquer our evil passions, sanctify ourselves, and work out our salvation. Let us seek this reign of God in meditation on eternal truths, in reading religious books, in the practice of good

works, in frequenting the Blessed Sacrament, let us seek it in Church, in retreat, and in the society of religious persons. But alas! where do we seek, and what do we seek? We seek to distract ourselves, to content ourselves, but not to sanctify ourselves. Man is in a continual agitation, and it is evident that he is seeking for something; but what is he seeking for? What cares, what exertions to gain fortune, pleasure, and glory! Why does he not strive thus for his salvation? People complain of their passions and their bad habits, which they say they cannot conquer; but do they seek the means of conquering them? Do not they seek, on the contrary, all that may inflame them and feed them? Lastly, the duty of prayer consists in knocking, that is, in solliciting constantly in order to enter into communication with God, in order to converse with Him in a more intimate manner, and with a greater degree of familiarity. This God of goodness calls us to this high degree of honour, and He offers Himself to admit us to His confidence, if we esteem it sufficiently to desire it. Let us stand then like assiduous supplicants at this mysterious door of which Jesus Christ speaks; let us remain there especially in prayer and in Communion by a deep recollectedness, awaiting the blissful moment when it will be opened to us. Let us knock with reverence by our ardent desires, and groanings full of love. Let us persevere with courage, let us beware of letting any distraction, let it be ever so small, take possession of us, or remove us from our place, lest we should lose the favourable moment. Lastly, let us enter with confidence as soon as the door is opened to us, let us enjoy the favours our God deigns to bestow on us, let us taste with gratitude the sweetness of His converse, and let us not come forth but with a renewed desire to return thither as soon as possible, and to knock anew at that door. Whatever enlightenment God communicates to us, and to whatever degree of confidence He admits us, we have always more to gain, and further to advance, and consequently we have always to knock, until the door even of heaven should be opened to us. Ah! if we knew the ineffable blessings which a soul partakes of in these divine communications, how willingly should we renounce the world and ourselves in order to be able to partake of them!

2. The motive which ought to lead us to fulfil the duty of prayer, is the assurance that we shall succeed in obtaining that for which we ask, and in finding that for which we seek, and entering where we knock; *for every one that asketh, receiveth; and he that seeketh, findeth: and to him that knocketh it shall be opened.* This assurance is founded on the promise of Christ, and His word standeth fast. It is founded also on the goodness of God; God being the Sovereign good, and Sovereign goodness, He only asks to communicate Himself to others. It is founded on His title of Father, which God takes upon Himself with regard to us. *What man is there of you*, our Saviour asks, *whom if his son ask bread, will he give him a stone? or if he ask a fish, will he give him a serpent? If ye then, being evil, know how to give good gifts to your children, how much more shall your Father which is in heaven, give good things to them that ask Him?* God is a Father more tender, more filled with love for His children, than any earthly father; when shall we then bear towards Him those feelings of confidence which are suitable to children? Why should we look upon Him always as an absolute Master, as an inexorable Judge, and a severe Avenger, and never as a tender and beneficent Father? Ah! it is because we feel that we are rebellious, ungrateful, and indocile children; but let us become obedient and submissive, and then let us hasten to Him with confidence, let us ask, seek, knock, and we shall find it will be granted to us, the door will be opened. But no, we ask, and no one gives to us; we seek, and we find nothing; we knock, and the doors remain closed. O what folly! we run after things which elude our pursuit, and we flee from those which are offered to us; and thus losing both, we prefer to live in misery, in irksomeness, surfeited with things of this

world, rather than to have recourse to Him Who only can enrich us, glorify us, render us happy?

3. What are the conditions of the duty of prayer, or rather of its success? *Therefore all things whatsoever ye would that men should do to you, do ye even so to them; for this is the law and the prophets.* God engages to grant our prayers, but on condition that besides this duty of prayer towards God, we should also fulfil that of love to our brethren; on condition that our neighbour should obtain from us that which he asks of us, that he should find at our hands the help he seeks for, and that we should open to him when he knocks, and that we should act towards him, as we desire that men and God should act towards us. These two duties are essentially bound up together. All that we will that men should do to us, let us do the same to them. This maxim is short, it is the abridgment of all our duties to our neighbour, it comprehends all that the law has prescribed, and all that the prophets have set forth on this subject. Let us examine how we practise it, or in how many ways we go astray from this command. God wills that this maxim, which is the bond which unites men together, should be also the bond which unites men to Him. It is the condition which He sets to all the promises which He makes us; let us not lose it out of sight; it is in right of His relationship to us as the Father of all mankind, that He requires it, and He will never set us free from this obligation.

THIRD POINT.

With regard to ourselves, the duty of restraint and self-mortification.

Enter ye in at the strait gate; for wide is the gate, and broad is the way that leadeth to destruction, and many there be that go in thereat; because strait is the gate, and narrow is the way, which leadeth unto life; and few there be that find it. Men have before them, and open to their choice, two opposite ways, the one, narrow, and the other, spacious.

1. What is this broad or spacious way, what is the gate of which the entrance is wide? This way, this gate, are those which we enter without inconveniencing ourselves, and almost without perceiving it. We enter them by following all our corrupt inclinations, all our propensities, our ideas, our passions. We walk along in this way as we entered it, without troubling ourselves, without looking where we are going, without thinking what we are doing; we think, speak, and act in it just as it pleases us; and as this way is much frequented, the numbers of those who walk in it embolden one another by the example of the rest, reassure them mutually as to the dangers which sometimes present themselves to their minds, so that they become animated, and encourage one another, and lead one another on, to advance with rapid strides in so pleasant a path, where all is smiling and strewn with flowers; but in the end this path leads to perdition. Senseless that ye are! will this truth never strike your hearts, will it never be the subject of your most serious reflections? Whither are you going, whither are you hastening? Where will these pleasures, these fortunes, these greatnesses lead? In what will a life full of sins and crimes end? In perdition, in hell, in eternal punishment. What will it then avail you to have lived according to your perverse inclinations, to have been happy, if you will, during a few days which have disappeared like a dream, and to have precipitated yourself in unending misery?

2. What is the narrow way, what is the gate of which the entrance is small? They are those, in order to enter into which, we must humble ourselves, and deny ourselves, humble our minds beneath the yoke of faith, and restrain our inclinations within the bounds of the law. We cannot expect to walk at our ease in this path, we must pay attention to all our steps that we may not stray from the right way. The restraint of our passions demands a continual effort on our part, and it needs constant watchfulness and care in order to check them; the mind has its consolations in the struggle; but nature suffers

through it. This way is but little frequented; there are some who do not even know it, who do not concern themselves about it, and do not even know where it is and in what it consists. There are few who enter it, and still fewer who persevere in it. Some begin well, but soon they weary of the restraint, and allow themselves more liberty; and insensibly they return to the broad way, and perish there. Lastly, this path conducts to life; but to what life? To the only true life, to the life which is above all, to the life in comparison of which the present life is only a continual death. It is the sight of this blissful and eternal life which makes men fervent in serving God, which supports them in this narrow way, and which makes them walk in it and persevere with joy; it is the forgetfulness of this eternal life which makes men faint-hearted, inconstant, and untrue to their Christian calling. Ah! how sweet it is, in the moment of death, to have walked in the straight way. Trials and sufferings will then have passed away, and the reward will never be ended.

3. Reflect on what our Saviour says to us of these two ways. i. The words of our Lord respecting these two ways, that is to say, as to the great number of those who are treading the path of perdition, and the small number of those who attain to life, have nothing in them which ought to surprise us. It is a truth, alas! too palpable and too visible, that the greater number amongst men only seek to please themselves in the short space of this present life, in defiance of God, His Commandments, and His gospel; and that but very few live habitually in a state of grace.

ii. The words of our Saviour have nothing which ought to offend us. The sinner says, Then will every body be damned? No, there are some, whom we see, and there are some whom we do not see, who find the way of salvation, and in whose salvation the wisdom of God will be justified, and the folly of the sinner condemned. He says moreover, Has God then created so many men in order to condemn them? No, since He ceases not to enlighten them, to warn them, to urge and entreat them to follow that which is good; but God condemns to hell whoever having wilfully committed mortal sin, remains in that state, and dies under the anger of God. The number of sinners makes no difference; on the contrary, the great numbers of them can but increase His displeasure, whilst the small number of the good renders them still more precious in His sight. Ah! were it not for this small number, for whose sake He withholds His thunder-bolts, He would exterminate the sinners from off the earth.

iii. The words of our Saviour have nothing in them which ought to discourage us. However small may be the number of those who are saved, were it yet smaller, we might be of the number. God calls us to it, and nothing is required of us but to follow His voice, and to correspond to His grace. On the contrary, the smaller the number is, the greater will be the glory to be of that number; even the very difficulty ought to encourage us. Men love so much distinction on earth; can there be a better opportunity than this in which to distinguish ourselves for eternity! Let us be ashamed to mix ourselves up with the great multitude of lost souls, who forget God in order that they may defile themselves with sins. Let us place ourselves on the side of that small number who have the courage to devote themselves to a life of holiness, to declare themselves for God, in the midst of the perversity of the times, which has become almost general.

iv. The words of our Saviour ought only to instruct us and to forewarn us. Let us learn from them not to regulate our conduct by the multitude, to distinguish between the two ways, and to make a good choice. I am offended, and the desire of revenge rises in my heart; to follow it, is the broad way; to repress it, to pardon and forget the offence, is the narrow way; and thus it is with other occasions of avoiding evil, and practising virtue. Let us learn besides to keep ourselves humble, and to mistrust ourselves. Since there are so many who are lost, I may be lost also. I am sure of nothing; all depends on my faithfulness, my constancy, my perseverance: why am I then always weak, fickle, inconstant?

Prayer. Thou art alone my strength, O my Saviour! I will cling to Thee, I will not leave Thee any more; do not Thou forsake me a single moment, that I may never lose Thee out of sight. With Thy help, I trust I may be of the small number who will choose Thee in life, and will praise Thee in eternity. Amen.

Meditation LIX.

TENTH CONTINUATION OF THE SERMON ON THE MOUNT.

OF THREE SORTS OF DELUSIONS, IN THE MATTER OF SALVATION.

Delusions in doctrine, delusions in words, delusions in knowledge. S. Matt. vii. 15—27.

FIRST POINT.
Delusions in doctrine.

1. Jesus Christ lays upon us the obligation to take heed of false prophets. *Beware of false prophets, which come to you in sheep's clothing, but inwardly they are ravening wolves.* The artifice and the malice of the false prophets oblige us to be thus ware of them. They are unwilling to shew themselves such as they really are, to lay bare their designs, to expose freely their thoughts and their feelings: they hide themselves, they disguise themselves, and cover themselves with the garb of sheep. They give themselves out for followers of the Church, submissive and obedient children: but they are never wanting in falsehood, evasions, and subterfuges. They appear to employ themselves in working for God, and call themselves His messengers, and promise to guide

men into the way of salvation; they rest their promises on the austerity of their lives; and gain authority by their regularity in religious observances, their zeal, and their modesty. Their outward demeanour is edifying and composed: but under an exterior so simple, so apparently mortified, they conceal a spirit of anger, and carry with them every where division and devastation; these are ravening wolves in the midst of a flock. The sheep ought to flee from them, and the shepherds ought to drive them away. To say, in excuse, that one does not care to meddle in religious controversy, is to set little value on one's salvation and one's religion, or to make no distinction between two very different matters. It is not required of every one to sift to the bottom the controverted points between members of the Church and heretics; but all are obliged to take care not to give their confidence to false teachers, not to accept a false doctrine, a doctrine which is contrary to the true faith; that is a precept laid upon us by Jesus Christ Himself. If for want of this precaution, we are led astray, we are without excuse. To say besides that we do not wish to judge any one, is to take the words of our Lord, in a wrong meaning, and not to reflect that in the same chapter where He has forbidden us to judge others He has also commanded us to beware of those who may lead us astray.

2. Jesus Christ teaches us the way by which we may discern false prophets. *Ye shall know them by their fruits. Do men gather grapes of thorns, or figs of thistles? Even so every good tree bringeth forth good fruit; but a corrupt tree bringeth forth evil fruit. A good tree cannot bring forth evil fruit; neither can a corrupt tree bring forth good fruit.* Every one has it not in their power to discern the artifices which prevail in the discourses and in the writings of false teachers: and besides which, it is not possible to specify all the books which contain false teaching, nor all who impart false doctrine. But how shall we then distinguish the false doctrine or the false teachers, which are hidden and

disguised? There remains one way, which is not difficult to those who have an upright heart; the tree is known by its fruit. We have only to consider the fruit which their doctrine bears, and the end to which their discourses tend. If their words and their affectation of piety only end in self-interest and avarice, in sensuality and depravity; if a spirit of reform, the language of pure charity, an austere and rigorous zeal only lead to independence and contempt of lawful authority; or if on the contrary, easy-going rules, lax maxims cause them to walk in ways but little conformed to the Gospel, by a broad and spacious road, where it costs but little or no self-denial, the mask has fallen, the veil is raised from that moment, and the artifice is made known; and no one is deceived, but those who are so wilfully. Such fruits can only come from a bad tree. On the contrary, an extreme attention to purity, a continual watchfulness over one's self, an assiduous endeavour to do violence to one's self and to mortify one's self, humility of heart, and submission to all lawful authority, real charity, a zeal which has nothing excessive or bitter in it, an unchanging gentleness, silence under wrongs, and patience under affronts, these are fruits which cannot be suspected, and which can only come from a good tree.

3. Jesus Christ sets forth to us the punishment of the false prophets, and of those who follow them. They will have the fate of a bad tree. *Every tree which bringeth not forth good fruit shall be hewn down, and cast into the fire.* False prophets have their followers who praise them and extol them; but Jesus Christ condemns them; they are the idols of their disciples, but they are judged by Jesus Christ, and they will be the prey of hell. What will it then avail them to have unsettled others, and triumphed over the credulity of an ignorant and misguided people, whilst they who have been the leaders of this rebellion, with all those who have followed them and are dead in their crimes, will burn in eternal fire? Ah if we did but think earnestly on this terrible fire, which will be the portion of those who

die in sin, we should not forsake so easily the only secure and safe path, to follow those who lead us in paths of error. Once more, let us beware, let us think of the consequences, let us be on our guard against false prophets. Our Lord has taught us how to know them; and He repeats to us yet again, *By their fruits ye shall know them.*

SECOND POINT.

Delusions in works.

We must do good works. Not every one that saith unto Me, Lord, Lord, shall enter into the kingdom of heaven; but he that doeth the will of My Father which is in heaven. It is not sufficient to raise sighs towards heaven, to acknowledge Jesus Christ as our Lord and Master, to call upon His Name sometimes, to ask for grace from Him; we must, with that divine grace, put our own hands to the work, and fulfil the will of His Father, such as He has revealed it to us. Sighs, idle regrets, and a barren invocation do not open to us the kingdom of heaven, we must add to them works. But do not let us deceive ourselves as to the nature of these works; there are many which appear good in our eyes, and in the eyes of men, which are quite otherwise in the sight of God. In order to be really good, they must be done according to the will of God, for God, and in His love.

1. Our works must be done according to the will of God, that is to say, in the station of life which God has appointed to each one of us, and according to the rules of obedience which we owe to our lawful superiors. Thus works which are the holiest in themselves, and the most striking, if they are done to the prejudice of the duties of our station, in disobedience to those whom God has set over us, without our being called upon to do them, and according to our own inclinations, and not according to the will of God, are so many useless, and even sinful works, for which we can hope for no

reward; on the contrary, he who confines himself entirely to follow God's will, if he only performs the commonest duties, and works without any show or display, both in the eyes of men, and of our self love, he it is who will enter the kingdom of heaven, and there receive a full reward. How consoling and instructive is this truth!

2. Our works must be done for God. *Many will say to Me in that day, Lord, Lord, have we not prophesied in Thy Name? and in Thy Name have cast out devils? and in Thy Name done many wonderful works? And then will I profess unto them, I never knew you.* To preach, to write, to reprove, to convert sinners, to perform acts of charity, even miracles, if all these are done out of vanity, self interest, ambition, or self love, all will be lost to those who have had no other motive for their actions, and Jesus Christ will answer them that He does not know them, that they have never been in His service, that they have never done any thing for Him, that He has never known them. On the contrary, He will acknowledge those as His, who in the little that they have done, have had no other aim than to please Him, to fulfil their duties, and to make Him known and loved, and to glorify Him.

3. Our works must be done in the love of God, and in a state of grace. A passion which we cherish in our hearts, any secret impurity, or unlawful affection, a criminal attachment, a feeling of hatred, aversion, or jealousy against our neighbour, any grievous slander, calumny, or great wrong which we have not repaired; in a word, a single mortal sin which has not been atoned for, and washed away, suffices to annihilate and corrupt all the good which we might otherwise do, and no good work can counterbalance it. Our Saviour, when He comes to judgement, will count all the rest as nothing. He will single out in us this sin, amidst all those good works which dazzle our eyes; He will behold, so to say, only this sin, which will place us in the condition of a sinner and a castaway. If after this, we count

upon works done in such a state, and present ourselves with them before God, this is the answer which He assures us Himself, that He will make us, *Depart from Me, all ye that work iniquity.* Alas! how many deceive themselves and blind themselves now, who will be undeceived at the great day! But then it will be too late. Let us therefore undeceive ourselves now, while we have yet time to correct our error.

THIRD POINT.
Delusions in knowledge.

1. How great is the necessity to know and make ourselves acquainted with the law of Jesus Christ. *Whosoever heareth these sayings of Mine.* All human knowledge is of no avail, if we do not employ it for our salvation and the glory of God. Each one according to his station, ought to cultivate the study of the arts and sciences, but if we stop short there, if we place all our happiness, all our glory in them, and neglect the knowledge of salvation which Jesus Christ came to teach us, into what a deplorable delusion do we not fall? How many wear themselves out in study and vigils who would not give a moment to the meditation of the law of God, to the study of the Scriptures, or of some religious book. Blind that ye are, ye glory in your enlightenment, and ye are in darkness! Death will rob you of all those frivolous and transitory acquirements, and will shew you that the knowledge which you have neglected, was the only one which merited your attention. You will understand then that the use you ought to have made of the talents which God has given you, was to study His commandments, to meditate on them, to search them out, and make them your delight.

2. What is the wisdom of him who knows and practises the commandments of Jesus Christ. *Whosoever heareth these sayings of Mine, and doeth them, I will liken him unto a wise man, which built his house upon a rock, and the rain descended, and the floods came, and the*

winds blew, and beat upon that house; and it fell not; for it was founded upon a rock. It is not sufficient to know the commandments of God, we must practise them. It is not a question here of one of those sciences of speculation or of display, but of a science of practice. He who hears the words which I have just uttered, our Saviour continues, in conclusion of the Sermon on the Mount, he who regulates his life by the doctrine which I preach to you, is like unto him who has built his house upon the rock. The rains fall, the torrents overflow their banks, the winds blow, every thing joins together in order to overthrow the building; but because it is founded on a rock, it withstands all attacks, it resists all the storms, and remains immoveable. Such is the blessedness of him who puts in practice the words of Jesus Christ; adversity, and misfortunes may fall upon him; passions, and persecutions may arise and roar around him; the devils may be unchained and employ their rage against him; but his faith, his religion, his virtue, are this edifice built on the rock, that is, on the constant practice of the precepts of Jesus Christ, and nothing can shake it. Death even will not overthrow it, it will only strengthen it, consecrate it, and place it beyond the reach of all harm.

3. What is the folly of him who knows and does not practise the faith of Jesus Christ. *And every one that heareth these sayings of Mine, and doeth them not, shall be likened unto a foolish man, which built his house upon the sand: and the rain descended, and the floods came, and the winds blew, and beat upon that house; and it fell: and great was the fall of it.* To listen to the words of Jesus Christ without profiting by them, to hear His precepts without practising them, is to make one's self like to a foolish man who built his house upon the sand. The rain came, the floods overflowed, the winds blew, the building which was without a foundation crumbles to the ground, and presents no longer ought save vast ruins, and sad remains. What a loss for this unhappy man! But also what folly. Ah! far greater still

is the folly of him who hears the word of God, who knows His laws, and does not practise them. Without support against adversity, its weight overwhelms him; without strength to resist his passions, their impetuosity carries him away; without principle to withstand the devil, his artifices deceive him. How many falls, how many crimes! Soon he loses faith, hope, and thinks only of stifling the little remorse that remains, which would be his salvation if he would but listen to it, but which becomes his punishment and foretells his entire ruin, because he struggles against it. Alas! are we not ourselves like that foolish man! Every day the words of Jesus Christ are repeated to us, every day God's commandments, His will, His punishments and His rewards are set before us in His Holy Word; we take part in His public worship, we listen to them, and we come away as cold as if all that had been said did not concern us. Occupied with a thousand frivolous objects, we work, we exert ourselves, but we build on the sand; senseless that we are! death will destroy all these useless buildings which we have erected with so much trouble, and there will remain to us only the shame of being deceived, the grief of being no longer able to repair our mistake.

Prayer. Oh deplorable misfortune! When shall I then begin to be wise and to build upon the solid stone? Alas! how miserable I am. I know Thy commandments, O my God! I admire them, I resolve to follow them, I promise Thee to practise them; but alas! when the moment of temptation comes, when I ought to follow them, I hearken to my passions, I satisfy my own inclination, I forget my resolutions, I violate my promises. What wilt Thou say to me, O Jesus, when I appear before Thy judgment seat? Shall I not appear like a barren tree, which produces no fruit, or rather which has only borne bad fruit? Wilt Thou not be justified in rejecting me as having only been a worker of iniquity? Alas! my life is filled with iniquity, and as it were imbued with sin. What would become of me, O Saviour, if Thou didst not have pity on me? Enlighten my mind, captivate my heart, so that, truly contrite, I may make amends for my sins; so that, undeceived as to my false virtues, I may begin to practise those only which are true, and which may be acknowledged as such by Thee in eternity. Amen.

Meditation LX.

CONCLUSION OF THE SERMON ON THE MOUNT.

ASTONISHMENT OF THE PEOPLE.

This astonishment has as its object, 1. the doctrine which Jesus taught; 2. the authority with which He taught it; 3. the manner in which He taught it. S. Matt. vii. 28, 29.

FIRST POINT.

Admiration of the doctrine which Jesus Christ taught.

And it came to pass, when Jesus had ended these sayings, the people were astonished at His doctrine. The first object of their astonishment was the doctrine of Jesus Christ. Let us wonder also and admire it ourselves so that we may cling more and more closely to it.

1. Perfect doctrine, because it regulates and perfects the entire man. And first of all, with regard to himself, it teaches him to despise and reject all that would debase and corrupt him. It makes of him a true man, real, constant, generous, chaste, disinterested; and then with regard to his neighbour, it renders him gentle, modest, humble, submissive, compassionate, benevolent, affable, and sincere: lastly, with regard to God, it unites him to Him by a filial love, by the tenderest confidence, by the continual desire to please Him, and to do His holy will.

2. Perfect doctrine, because it enlightens the entire man. It teaches him not only all his duties, but it teaches him besides the nobility of his origin, which is God Himself, his Creator; the misery of his fall, and his consequent corruption, his natural weakness, and his bondage under the empire of the devil; the blessings of his redemption, and his consequent elevation, his adoption, his end, and his glorious destiny.

3. Perfect doctrine, because it strengthens the entire man, by fixing the levity of his mind, by the immutable rules of faith, by animating his heart by motives proportioned to his condition and his needs. Motives of fear, but of a fear capable of arresting the most headstrong passions, and of quenching their fire by the thought of so terrible an end, which no one could think of without a shudder. Motives of hope, but of a hope capable of making us undertake every thing and suffer every thing, in the thought of an infinite and eternal happiness, the possession of which is promised to us, if we are faithful. Motives of love, but of an ardent and generous love, capable of sustaining us under any trial whatever it might be, since the object of that love is none other than a God-Creator, Infinite in every perfection: a saving God, become like to us in order to put Himself at our head, and to give us the example of it: a sanctifying God, Who pours His love into our hearts, supports us and animates us by the inward strength of His grace. O Heavenly doctrine! can any not admire thee? can any not love thee? What are in comparison, the doctrines of men, of philosophers, of unbelievers? They are monstrous doctrines, which leave man in his weakness, abandon him to himself, without any help: which leave man in darkness, without teaching him either whence he comes, or whither he is going, or for what purpose he has been sent into the world; which leave man in all his corruption, and precipitate him still deeper into it, harden him in all kinds of crimes and infamy, render him vile and degraded below the conditions of brute beasts. Abominable doctrines, which

can only find followers amongst men of perverse minds, depraved, without shame, or those who are hypocrites in practice.

SECOND POINT.

Their astonishment at the authority with which Jesus taught.

For He taught them as one having authority. The second object of the astonishment of the people was the authority with which Jesus taught.

1. The authority of Jesus Christ incontestable. It was founded on divine rights. The authority of a law-giver. *I say unto you. It was said by them of old time, but I say unto you.* The authority of a Mediator between God and the world, to which all men must look. *Blessed are ye, when men shall revile you, and persecute you, and shall say all manner of evil against you falsely, for My sake. Ask, and ye shall receive, seek and ye shall find; knock, and it shall be opened unto you.* Authority of the Son of God. *Not every one that saith unto Me, Lord, Lord, shall enter into the kingdom of heaven: but he that doeth the will of My Father which is in heaven.* Authority of the sovereign Judge of all men. *Many will say to Me in that day, Lord, Lord, have we not prophesied in Thy Name, and in Thy Name have cast out devils? and in Thy Name done many wonderful works? And then I will profess unto you, I never knew you: depart from Me, ye workers of iniquity.*

2. The authority of Jesus Christ such as cannot be assumed by others. Never has man on earth ever spoken with that authority, neither those whom God has sent to instruct men, such as Moses, nor those who have appeared in order to deceive mankind, such as many false teachers who have formed different sects. None of these, however desirous they may have been to gain credit, have ever carried their audacity so far as to usurp such glorious titles, which they have not been in a position to support, and which by that means would

have rather contributed to destroy than to affirm their authority. If in the course of centuries, we have seen some fanatic dare to imitate some expressions of this divine language, we have seen his pretensions vanish with himself, and sometimes before himself. It is only Thou, O Jesus, Who couldest assume these divine titles, and support the greatness of them. Thy holy religion, founded on these titles, has stood the proof of the researches of philosophers, and the persecution of tyrants. Under these titles, I render Thee homage, I hold fast to Thee, I listen to Thy words, and I desire in all things to conform myself to Thy divine law.

3. The authority of Jesus Christ, matchless. And who then are those who in our days dare to raise themselves up against Thee, O Jesus, and gainsay Thy doctrine? Whence come they? what are their titles? what is their authority? They do not even appear, they dare not show themselves, nothing is to be seen of them but some furtive writings to which they do not even venture to sign their names: and are these the teachers to whom I should listen, whom I should trust! Is it possible, O divine Light, that any one can forsake Thee in order to follow leaders so contemptible and so obscure, without name, or authority?

THIRD POINT.

Astonishment at the manner in which Jesus taught.

And He taught them, as one having authority, and not as the scribes. His manner of teaching was,

1. Simple and suited to His audience. Without ornamentation, or affected eloquence, without display and without pride. He made plain and intelligible all that He said, and He put it within the reach of every one.

2. It was noble and touching, full of Majesty, and of feeling.

3. It was clear and precise, without equivocal ambiguity, without disputation or controversy. It is on this model that the apostles formed themselves, and it is that

by which the preachers of the Gospel should still form themselves. It was not thus that the scribes and Pharisees taught. Not only could they not announce a doctrine so sublime, nor speak with the same authority, they did not explain themselves with that grandeur, that simplicity, that clearness, and that elevation of thought, and that divine unction which made men love in Jesus Christ, both the Preacher Who taught, and the virtues He inculcated. Feebleness in reasoning, uncertainty and changeableness in doctrine, affectation and vanity in language pervaded their discourses; and such is still the language of unbelievers and of impious men; sophisms and false reasonings, equivocal dissimulation, artificial insinuations, bitter satires, and unfitting railleries; and the fruit of these writings in those who read them is to bring disquiet into their souls, doubt into their minds, estrangement from God, distaste of virtue, aversion to what is good and the practical contempt of every kind of duty.

Prayer. Remove far from me, Lord, these dangerous men, these seductive books which only flatter the ear in order to corrupt the mind and heart. Let me never listen to these vain teachers, may I never suffer myself to read their corrupting books. Grant that I may have no relish but for Thy holy word, and for those who teach and explain it according to the authority which comes alone from Thee. I submit myself to this divine, simple, sure, unchangeable teaching, with all my mind and my heart; and I resolve, by the help of Thy grace, to conform to it in all my conduct. Amen.

Meditation LXI.

JESUS HEALS A LEPER.

The state of this leper, the steps he takes, his healing, and that which follows his healing: four circumstances which merit our attention. S. Matt. viii. 1—14. S. Mark i. 40—45. S. Luke v. 12—16.

FIRST POINT.

The state of the leper.

When He was come down from the mountain, great multitudes followed Him. And behold there came a leper and worshipped Him. Nothing represents better the condition of sin than the state of the leper. Let us then picture to ourselves the diseased state of our soul from that which the body of this unhappy man suffered.

1. Leprosy was an evil which was horrible in itself. The unfortunate man of whom we are speaking was quite covered by it: he was an object of horror to every one, he was an object of horror to himself, and could not bear himself. Each sin being a stain of the soul, ought I not to confess that I am quite covered with sins, since my whole life is only one continuation of crimes? What should I be in my own eyes, if I could see the stains which disfigure my soul? What should I be in the eyes of men if they could know me? But what am I in the eyes of God, Who sees them, and knows all the ugliness and the deformity of them? Shall I then remain always in this state without having recourse to the Physician Who can heal me?

2. Leprosy was a disease contagious to others. Sin is so still more; it can be communicated by our eyes, by our words, by our actions, by our example. Without speaking here of those enormous crimes, dishonourable even to reason and yet so common in the world, let us think whether our dissipation, our want of modesty, and of self-restraint, our irregularities, our acts of impatience, our murmurings, our dislikes, our aversions,

our slander, raillery, and criticisms, have nothing contagious to others?

3. Leprosy was an evil less fatal in its contagion, than sin, 1. in that the leprous man, in communicating his evil, did not increase his own, whilst all the stains of sin which we occasion in others become so many fresh stains on our souls; 2. that while the leprous man did not increase his malady by holding communication with other lepers, in the case of sin, however defiled we may be already ourselves, we become still more so every day, by partaking in the defilements of others. Alas! without the sins which spring up from our own evil nature, without the sins which we communicate to others, how many sins do not others communicate to us! Let us acknowledge with confusion before the Lord, that we should not be able to count their number, and that our souls are in the most dangerous state, if that heavenly physician does not have compassion on them.

4. Leprosy is a disease humiliating to him who was afflicted with it, since it excluded him from all intercourse with other men. It was not permitted to a leper either to inhabit or to enter a city, and every one was forbidden, be he who he might, to touch him; obliged to wander about in the country, avoided by every one, he hardly found sufficient means of subsistence, and people were obliged to throw to him whatever charity they wished to bestow on him. Ah! if justice was rendered to me, should I not be treated in the same manner! Should I not be banished from society, avoided as contagious, despised and hated by every one? Alas! have I not often by my conduct, forced good and virtuous persons to separate themselves from me! My sentiments on religion, my conversations which seem a breach of charity, my haughty, capricious, hasty tempers, my worldly and dissipated manners, and a thousand other evil habits which I have indulged in, do they not drive away from my companionship those who really love and serve God?

SECOND POINT.

The proceedings of the leper.

And it came to pass when He was in a certain city, behold a man full of leprosy; who seeing Jesus, fell on his face, and besought Him, saying, Lord, if Thou wilt, Thou canst make me clean. Let us omit none of these circumstances.

1. The leper sees Jesus. That was not exactly his merit, it was in reality the goodness of the Saviour, Who prevented the unhappy man by offering Himself to his gaze: his merit consisted in his looking upon Jesus as Him whom a number of acts of healing already announced as the Messiah and the Son of God: it was his believing, and hoping in Him, and feeling what a happiness it would be for him to be able to approach Him. We have the same happiness; do we feel it, do we profit by it? Jesus prevents us and offers Himself to us by looks, by flashes of light, by lively inspirations, by the holy desire to give Himself to us. Do not let us turn away our eyes in order to avoid His sight, He is our Physician, our Saviour; do not let us look for help to others, none but He can save us, cleanse us, and make us happy.

2. The leper goes to Jesus. As soon as he sees Him, he comes to Him. What pains do we take to go to Jesus, to visit Him, to repair to His Presence in His House of Prayer, to receive Him in His Sacrament, to call Him to our succour in temptation? But alas instead of going to Him, do we not go every where where we know well that we shall not meet Him?

3. The leper worships Jesus. In approaching to the Saviour, he falls on his face before Him, and prostrates himself with his face to the ground in order to adore Him. How do we behave ourselves in the presence of Jesus Christ in His House of Prayer, before His Altar, or when we address Him in our private prayers? Let us bethink ourselves that we are in the presence of our God, of Him from Whom Alone we can hope for salvation.

4. *The leper prays to Jesus.* He *besought Him saying, Lord, if Thou wilt, Thou canst make me clean.* A short but fervent prayer! How much is expressed in those few words! What faith in the power of the Saviour! what trust in His goodness! what humility, what submission to His will! He acknowledges himself unworthy of the favour which he asks: he only hopes for it as a free gift from Jesus Christ, he believes that He can grant it him, that He only needs to will it, and he hopes that He will grant it. Why do we not pray in this manner in order to obtain purity of soul, especially in the temptations which we experience? After those few words, the leper, always prostrate at the feet of Jesus, awaits the decision of his fate. In this state of expectation, what feelings do not arise in his heart? Feelings of a sweet joy, caused by the firm hope to be soon healed and cleansed; feelings of a tender love for Him from whom he hoped for His salvation, with a firm resolution to attach himself to Him and to serve Him; feelings of fear at the thought of his own unworthiness, such as a person always experiences when they await a great favour which they do not merit! But the goodness of Jesus does not keep him waiting. *And Jesus moved with compassion, put forth His hand, and touched him, and saith unto him, I will; be thou clean; and as soon as He had spoken, immediately the leprosy departed from him, and he was cleansed.* Observe here in Jesus, His feelings, His actions, His words, and the miracle He worked.

THIRD POINT.

Healing of the leper.

1. *The feelings of Jesus.* It was not either in Him a feeling of horror, of contempt, of disdain at the sight of the leper, but a feeling of the most tender compassion. Let us learn to know Jesus Christ. Confused sometimes, and troubled at our misery, we dare to go to Him, because we know that He is holy and just: but let us know also that He is tender and compassionate to those

who give proofs of true sorrow for their sins, and a real desire to be cleansed from them; let us turn then to our God with full confidence in His mercy.

2. *The action of Jesus.* He stretches out His Hand, and touches the leper. Oh Almighty Hand! Oh salutary touch! what impression didst Thou not make on that happy suppliant! His flesh and his heart trembled with joy. Was it not enough, Lord, to heal him? Must Thy sacred Hand needs touch flesh infected with leprosy, which no one could even see without experiencing a feeling of horror? How great is Thy goodness, O God! It is that which engages Thee to come to us, however wretched we may be, not only in order to touch us, but to unite us to Thyself, and to serve us as food.

3. *The words of Jesus.* In touching him, *Jesus saith unto him, I will; be thou clean.* Our salvation is assured as soon as we truly desire it and do on our part all that God requires of us; because on the part of Jesus Christ, we are sure of His will; and that will is all-powerful, and when we do not put any obstacles in the way, it is always followed by accomplishment. How infinitely guilty then are we, if, far from profiting by these dispositions of our divine Saviour in order to purify ourselves, to sanctify and save ourselves, we abuse them by our resistance and our delays.

4. *The miracle which Jesus works.* As soon as He had pronounced these words, *I will; be thou clean,* the leprosy disappeared; he who had prostrated himself at the feet of our Saviour a leper, rises pure and without stain, as whole as if he had never been a leper. It is thus that we shall be cleansed from our pride, from our undue attachment to the things of this world, and its pleasures, from our jealousies, our acts of impatience, in a word from the leprosy of sin, if we will but turn to Jesus with humility and trust, if we will ask Him to deign to look upon us, to have compassion on us, to touch us, and to speak to us.

FOURTH POINT.

Of that which took place after the healing of the leper.

And He straitly charged him, and forthwith sent him away; and saith unto him, See thou say nothing to any man; but go thy way, shew thyself to the priest, and offer for thy cleansing those things which Moses commanded, for a testimony unto them. But he went out, and began to publish it much, and to blaze abroad the matter, insomuch that Jesus could no more openly enter into the city, but was without in desert places; .... and great multitudes came together, to hear, and to be healed by Him of their infirmities. And He withdrew Himself into the wilderness and prayed. Jesus gave us here the most striking example of subordination and obedience to the law of modesty, and of avoiding praise, of retirement and prayer, of charity and zeal.

1. Subordination and obedience of Jesus Christ to the law. The leper desired to remain with his benefactor, and not to leave Him again. Jesus does not permit it. He even speaks to him in a severe and menacing tone and obliges him to withdraw, in order to go and present himself to the priest, to whom by the commands of the Highest of all Priests and in His stead, was entrusted the duty of examining into the cure of leprous persons, and readmitting them into their civil relationships. Jesus enjoined him to make the offering appointed by the law, to serve as a witness to the priests and all the people that the cure was a perfect one.

2. Modesty of Jesus Christ, and the pains He took to avoid praise. Jesus forbade him to mention to any one, either by whom, or how he had been healed; but this leper, obliged to obey the command to withdraw, did not think himself equally bound to obey that of silence. His gratitude shone forth, and he published every where the miracle. This event made so much noise, that Jesus was some time without shewing Himself in the city, in order to avoid the applause and acclamations of a crowd of admirers. The Saviour did not

fear ostentation; but He willed to give us an example of that humility, which cannot bear to witness the good it does, and which hides with care the good which God gives us the grace to do.

3. *The retirement of Jesus Christ, and His prayer.* The people were coming from all parts both in order to receive from Him instruction, and for the healing of their sick; but Jesus withdrew from their assiduity, and betook Himself into solitude in order there to give Himself to prayer. It is more often by prayer than by discourses that the ministers of Christ obtain the graces which are needful for the flock which is confided to them; and where can prayer be offered with more profit than in silence and retirement?

4. *Charity and zeal of Jesus Christ.* A congregation do not feel discouraged when their minister leaves them only to spend his time in prayer, they have more confidence in him, and more anxiety to have recourse to his advice. However profound might be the solitude to which the Saviour withdrew, the people came to find Him there, and Jesus, Who gave the night to prayer, gave the day to instructing the people and healing the sick. It is thus that Jesus employed His whole life for our sakes, that He provided for all our needs, instructing us alike by His discourses and by His example.

Prayer. O my God, a leprosy far more horrible than that of the leper in the Gospel disfigures my soul! *If Thou wilt, Thou canst make me clean,* stretch forth also over me Thy healing hand, touch my heart, that it may resist Thee no longer. Cause my soul to hear those consoling words, *I will; be Thou clean.* Amen.

Meditation LXII.

JESUS HEALS THE CENTURION'S SERVANT.

Meditate here, 1. on the words of the Centurion to Jesus; 2. on the words of Jesus to the by-standers; 3. on the words of Jesus to the Centurion. S. Matt. viii. 5—13.

FIRST POINT.

Words of the centurion to Jesus.

These words are full of charity, trust, humility, and faith.

1. Full of charity. *And when Jesus was entered into Capernaum, there came unto Him a centurion beseeching Him, and saying, Lord, my servant lieth at home sick of the palsy, grievously tormented.* Jesus having entered into Capernaum after His retirement in the wilderness, a centurion, that is to say a Roman officer who had the command of a company of a hundred men, came to implore His succour; he did it with the simplicity and frankness of a man who was both religious, and who possessed faith in Him of whom he came to ask for help, with that nobleness and open-heartedness which win men's hearts, and also win for them from God the success of their prayer. Charity animated his request; it was not for himself that he was making this request, it was for his servant, kept a prisoner to his bed by an attack of paralysis which made him suffer much. Do we shew the same charity towards our servants, our inferiors, our brethren? Let us feel it at least towards our own souls; have they not been for a long time as if they were paralysed and motionless, as regards heavenly things, and good works, whilst they are so eager, and so ardent in seeking after earthly things?

2. The words of the centurion full of trust in the goodness of Jesus Christ. He asks for nothing, he contents himself with laying before Him the condition of his sick servant, and that suffices to the heart of Jesus.

Let us lay before Him ourselves with a like trust, our soul with its infirmities, its wounds and its diseases, its sins and its lukewarmness, and He will heal *it*.

3. The words of the centurion full of humility. *And Jesus saith unto him, I will come and heal him.* Ah, Lord, answers the centurion confused, I dare not aspire to such an honour; Thou come to me! that is not what I ask of Thee. *I am not worthy that Thou shouldest come under my roof; but speak the word only, and my servant shall be healed.* Admirable words, which must express the feelings of every Christian at the moment of communion. Let us utter them then with the deepest feelings of reverence for the Admirable Person of Jesus, our Saviour and our God.

4. The words of the centurion full of faith in the power of Jesus. Without leaving the place where Thou art, Lord, he continues, deign only to speak the word; the most obstinate diseases will obey Thee; command, and my sick servant shall be healed: *For I am a man under authority, having soldiers under me; and I say unto this man, Go, and he goeth; and to another, Come, and he cometh; and to my servant, Do this, and he doeth it.* The centurion had formed a just idea of the power of Jesus. The manner in which he carried out his thoughts was noble and striking. What a profession of faith for a Gentile! He represents so to say to our Saviour, that having a sovereign, independent, and unlimited power, He could in an absolute and efficacious manner lay His commands as a master on every kind of disease, and on all nature, and that He has but to speak in order to be obeyed. Shall we then never form a like idea of the power of Jesus Christ? Wherefore, in addressing ourselves to Him, do we shew that timidity, that mistrust, that secret disquietude which close our hearts? Ah! it is because we neither know His power nor His goodness, it is that we have neither faith in the one, nor trust in the other. Let us learn then now to know our Saviour. Let us begin to believe in Him, that is to say, to put our whole trust in Him.

SECOND POINT.

Words of Jesus to the by-standers.

These words are full of commendation of the centurion, of comfort for the Gentiles, of terror for the Jews, and of threats for bad Christians.

1. Full of commendation of the centurion. *When Jesus heard it, He marvelled and said to them that followed, Verily I say unto you, I have not found so great faith, no, not in Israel.* When shall we give to Jesus Christ, this satisfaction to behold and praise in us a lively and perfect faith? A stranger has more faith than the Israelites. A man engaged in the world, and in the profession of arms sometimes shews more faith than those who are consecrated to the ministry of God, and the service of His Church. How glorious is this contrast for the one, and how humiliating for the others! If we are living in retirement from the world, let us profit by the blessings of our condition, and not let ourselves be out-done by those who have not the same advantages with ourselves. Let a holy emulation unite us all in charity, and animate us all to testify to our Saviour, our faith and love.

2. The words of Jesus full of comfort for the Gentiles. *And I say unto you, That many shall come from the east and the west, and shall sit down with Abraham, and Isaac, and Jacob, in the kingdom of heaven.* It is we who are the objects of the prophecy which our Lord utters here; we see the happy accomplishment of this prediction. We are associated in the faith of these holy patriarchs, when shall we be sharers in their bliss? Ah, what misery, if after so many blessings, we should come, through our own fault, to be cast out from it.

3. The words of Jesus full of terror for the Jews. *But the children of the kingdom shall be cast out into outer darkness; there shall be weeping and gnashing of teeth.* The children of the kingdom who shall be cast into this eternal darkness, where tears are their only food, and where there is nought but gnashing of

teeth, torments and despair, are the unbelieving Jews, who having had the blessing of being born in the midst of the true worship of God, and of having had their minds prepared for the Gospel by the law and the prophets, were the first called and destined to live under the empire of Christ, have yet rejected Him and refused to acknowledge Him. We see the thick and palpable darkness in which this unbelieving nation lives. The accomplishment of prophecy, and the sight of all nations united by Jesus Christ in the worship of the One true God, and His Son, Jesus Christ, cannot dispel their blindness; let us add more; a shameful exile, and the punishment which has fallen on them for nearly two thousand years cannot conquer their hardness of heart. But in hell, what will be the punishment of these unhappy people? What will be their torments to see themselves driven out of that kingdom of light, which was destined for them, and which will be possessed by heathen and idolaters who have been truly converted and substituted in their place!

4. The words of Jesus Christ full of threats to bad Christians. Let us apply to ourselves these threatenings of our Saviour. Having become the children of the kingdom in the place of the Jews, let us take care not to lose its faith, its works, and its rewards; let us beware, lest, by our unfaithfulness, we let our inheritance pass into other hands. What despair will fill the hearts of the damned, when they compare themselves with the blessed inhabitants of heaven, of Christians by birth with savages newly converted, of masters and the great of this world with their servants and their subjects, of rich and learned men with the poor and ignorant, of priests and those in religious orders with laymen and seculars? Ah! who cannot but shudder and tremble at this thought? Let this fear be for us the motive of new fervour, and of increased watchfulness.

THIRD POINT.

Words of Jesus Christ to the centurion.

These words are full of goodness, condescension, and instruction.

1. Words of Jesus Christ full of goodness. Hardly had the centurion laid before Him the state of his servant, than, without giving him the time to say more, without waiting that he should entreat Him, or solicit Him, He answers him, *I will come and heal him.* How plainly marked out here is the willingness of Jesus Christ to relieve our sufferings, why are we not as eager for the healing of our soul, as He is willing to do that which we sincerely ask of Him? How could anything be wanting to us? How could we languish in the dangerous state in which our soul is, having a Saviour, Who is so amiable, so condescending, so merciful, and so anxious to relieve us?

2. Words of Jesus full of power. *And Jesus said unto the centurion, Go thy way; and as thou hast believed, so be it done unto thee.* O power of Jesus! Thou art not less amiable than worthy of admiration, Thou art only occupied in loading us with benefits, and delivering us from all evils.

3. Words of Jesus full of condescension. If we seem to desire Him to come, He offers Himself to come; if we will that He remains with us, He consents to remain; He is always content, if He can testify His love to us; satisfied, if He can heal our wounds; glad, if He finds in us a great faith, and the opportunity of rewarding it.

4. Words of Jesus full of instruction. In saying to the centurion, *As thou hast believed, so be it done unto thee,* He teaches us that the effect of our prayers depends on our faith, that it is in proportion to our faith, that the profit we draw from the practice of good works, from frequenting the Blessed Sacrament, and from the exercises of religion, depends. If we only gain but little or no profit from all these things, if we only ex-

perience lukewarmness, langour, distaste, let us carry the remedy where the evil is, let us rekindle our faith, let us act according to our faith, and it will be done unto us according to its extent, its measure, and its ardour.

Prayer. I believe, O my Saviour, like the centurion, that Thou canst heal me with a word; say then to me as Thou didst unto him, *Go thy way: and as thou hast believed, so be it done unto thee.* At the moment when Thou dost utter these salutary words, I shall feel my strength return, and rousing myself from the inaction into which the palsy of my soul has reduced me, I shall run in the way of Thy commandments. Amen.

Meditation LXIII.

JESUS PASSES OVER TO THE OTHER SIDE OF THE LAKE.

Jesus departs in order to take ship and pass over to the other side of the lake. S. Matt. viii. 18—22.

Now when Jesus saw great multitudes about Him, He gave commandment to depart unto the other side. Our present life is a voyage: the world is a sea known for its shipwrecks. We will consider this lake of which the Gospel speaks to us here, as representing to us the narrow way, the holy, repentant, retired life, and punctual in our religious duties, which true Christians and faithful souls ought to lead. Now how must we undertake the passage across this figurative sea? It must be with confidence, with courage, and without delay, this is the plan of our meditation.

FIRST POINT.

With confidence.

1. That which ought to animate our confidence, is

the multitude whom we leave behind on the shore. This multitude is the world, that is to say, that world which our Saviour so often condemns, and against which He uttered most terrible anathemas, that world which walks in the broad way of pleasure and of indulgence of its passions, and which is hastening to perdition. Either this life which the multitude of worldly persons lead, has its delights for us, or else it only causes us weariness: if it pleases us, we are in evident danger of losing our salvation, and we cannot take too many precautions in order to withdraw ourselves from it: if, on the contrary, this tumultuous life only produces weariness and distaste in us, why do we not give it up altogether, and follow the path of piety, devotion, and holiness? Let us separate ourselves from the multitude from this present moment; at least let us separate ourselves from them in heart, if we do not wish God to separate us from them at the day of His last judgment.

2. That which ought to animate our confidence, is the chosen company which we follow. Jesus is at our head, what have we to fear under such a Chief? Is He not powerful enough to sustain us, and good enough to will to do so? Let us join ourselves to Him without fear; it is He Who invites us to it, it is He Who commands us. His disciples accompany Him and go with Him. O what a blessing for us to be of that number! how many holy souls follow Him with fervour! without doubt we know many such; shall we rest contented always with admiring them; cannot we do as they do, why should we not imitate them? Let their example then animate our confidence, and urge us on with a holy emulation, otherwise they will be one day a subject of condemnation for us.

3. That which ought to animate our confidence, is the passage we have to make; it is short, and it will open to us a future which will have no end. Life passes with a rapidity which we have already experienced. Besides which, for the greater number, it comes to a close just when we think it would last much longer, the

longest life is in itself only a day, an instant; in a word it has an end, and it is finished by an eternity which will have none. In whatever manner we pass our life, it will come to an end. The man who has spent his life in pleasures, and the penitent, will equally find the end, the one of his pleasures, the other of his sufferings; both will enter equally upon an eternity without end, for the one an eternity of punishment, for the other an eternity of bliss. Let us think of this happy or unhappy eternity, which we shall soon reach, and let us make a choice for which we may bless God eternally.

SECOND POINT.

With courage.

1. It requires courage to make a beginning. Jesus having given command to His disciples to make preparations to cross over the lake, *a certain scribe came, and said unto Him, Master, I will follow Thee whithersoever Thou goest.* There was in this scribe a good impulse, a holy desire, a right resolution; but all this was but the beginning. He was still walking on the land, for Jesus had not yet embarked. Let us offer ourselves to Jesus in the words of this scribe, let us form good resolutions, let us make good purposes, that is well; but let us remark that up to that point, nothing is yet done. Projects for the future cost us nothing: it is a question of making a beginning, and of putting our hand to the work; it is this beginning which costs us trouble, and it is of him who has made a good beginning that one can say that he has half done; but of him who makes promises, who plans and yet begins nothing, that one can say with truth that he has done nothing, and according to all appearance, he will never do anything. How many have died in this manner without having ever begun to serve God! let us fear to be of that number, if from to day we do not make a beginning.

2. It requires courage to continue and support such

trials. The scribe or doctor of the law promised himself much from this zeal. Jesus put it to the trial, and he soon belied himself. Do you know Me well, the Saviour seems to say to him, and have you meditated enough on the profession which you have made to Me? Learn what is the life I lead. *The foxes have holes, and the birds of the air have nests: but the Son of man hath not where to lay His head.* I, the First-born and chief among men, I have not a dwelling place, not a place which belongs to Me, or where I can rest Myself; to whatever place I withdraw Myself, there I am a stranger; such am I on earth, and such must be those who follow Me. See, consult now your own courage. The Christian life has its sufferings, we must not hide it from ourselves; but has not the world also its sufferings? But, between the two what a difference there is! In the sufferings, which try a penitent life, of whatever nature they may be, we have our Saviour at our head, Who goes before us. He will never put us to trials as severe as those through which He has willed to pass Himself out of love for us. Each of our trials in particular is present to His eyes, and He will render to us a faithful reckoning of them. We may forget them: but He will never forget them, and none of them shall pass without reward. Our sufferings will soon end with life, and the happiness which will follow them will never end. Ah! it is not thus with the sufferings of the world, which are the fruit of sins and of the indulgence of our passions!

3. It requires courage in order to persevere unto the end. Without this perseverance, all is useless: let us then ask it of God every day, and it will not be refused to us. On our side, let us keep up our watchfulness, and examine our progress; and if sometimes we find ourselves relaxing in our religious practices and in virtue, do not let us relax our efforts until we have recovered the ground we have lost. Let us pray, weep, sigh, let us fear the fatal consequence of the least decline in our fervour; for it is then that perseverance begins to van-

ish from us, and it will disappear entirely if we do not apply a prompt remedy.

THIRD POINT.

Without delay.

Three things, that is to say, grace, our will, and life take flight too rapidly for it to be safe for us to defer for a single moment our conversion.

1. Grace. *And another of His disciples said unto Him, Lord, suffer me first to go and bury my father. But Jesus said unto him, Follow Me: and let the dead bury their dead.* Jesus was advancing at this moment towards the lake in order to take ship. There was not a moment to be lost: either he must go with Him, or he must give up any hope of following Him. Could this disciple hope that, in order to wait for him, Jesus should stop short in His journey, and defer His embarcation? Grace urges us, entreats us, makes known to us its commands, and our obligations; but it does not wait for us, and does not make itself dependent on our caprices. We can deceive ourselves, and cover our faint-heartedness under the most specious pretexts; but we do not impose upon God, Who sees the depth of all hearts. Nevertheless, they were, in the sight of Jesus Christ, but false pretexts. The presence of this disciple was not necessary at the burial of his father. Let us leave the dead, that is, worldly people, those who are dead in sins and trespasses, dead to grace, to bury their dead, to set their affairs in order, to arrange their quarrels, and bring their law suits to an end; but let us seek to profit by the moment of grace, the accepted time, and give ourselves to God. If we have affairs which require our attention, instead of first concluding them, and then thinking of our own conversion, let us first give our thoughts to God and our own souls, and then we shall be more fit to conduct our business.

2. Will. This disciple was quite resolved to come and

join Jesus when he had buried his father; but who had assured him that he would continue in this resolution? After the burial of his father, would he not find himself engaged in the distribution of his father's possessions, in the arrangement of the various interests of members of the family? Become master of his patrimony, would he have continued in his desire to share the poverty of Jesus Christ, and would he have thought of joining him? This is what we do not know; but what we do know, and what experience teaches us every day, is that one thing involves us in another, that a first obstacle is followed by a second, that during these multiplied delays, the warmest resolutions are lost, and that a conversion which is deferred is almost always a conversion which never takes place.

3. *Life.* In deferring it, life passes, the devil beguiles us, and we do not perceive it. Might not this disciple, in going to his father's burial, die himself by some sudden accident? We mark a time for our conversion with as much assurance as if we were masters of our time; when the time we have marked out for ourselves has arrived, we justify our first act of imprudence, and commit another more dangerous still by putting off our conversion to a still more distant period; thus life passes in planning, and in putting off, till a despairing death comes to put an end to these senseless projects, and these foolhardy delays.

Prayer. O irreparable misfortune! O eternal despair! is it possible that I can have exposed myself to it till now? Ah, Lord, it is done; Thou dost make me hear anew in my heart this sweet invitation: *Follow Me.* I will not defer any longer, nothing shall turn me aside any longer from Thy service, nothing shall separate me any more from Thee; notwithstanding all the obstacles and all the trials which it shall please Thee to lay upon me, supported by Thy grace, O my adorable Saviour, I will belong to Thee without delay, unchangeably in time and in eternity. Amen.

Meditation LXIV.

CALMING OF THE TEMPEST.

Dangers of the present life. These dangers concern either our body, our soul, or the Church. S. Matt. viii. 23—27. S. Mark iv. 35—40. S. Luke viii. 22—25.

FIRST POINT.

Of the dangers which concern our body.

I. How ought we to behave ourselves before danger? Jesus was advancing insensibly to the shores of the lake, whilst imparting useful lessons to His disciples; the closer He drew to it, the more the people pressed around Him. *It was late; and without delaying any longer, Jesus entered into a ship and His disciples followed Him. And He saith unto them, Let us pass over unto the other side. And when they had sent away the multitude, they took Him even as He was in the ship: and there were also with Him other little ships.* Could one have believed that this voyage, undertaken at the express command of the only Son of God, the Saviour of the world, could have become dangerous? Nevertheless more than once those who were on the ship thought themselves lost. It is not only on the sea that life and property are endangered. All the elements, all nature, a thousand accidents menace us on all sides, and come to assail us at the most unexpected moment; we ought then to persevere constantly in the grace of God, and be always ready to appear before Him. We ought daily to commend our life, with all those in whose welfare we are interested, and all that belongs to us, to His divine protection, Who is the Master of all events. We ought to do nothing, to undertake nothing, without imploring the help of God, and the protection of His holy angels. What foolhardiness to live in the midst of so many dangers, with a conscience stained with sin, to enter upon journeys, to brave the perils of the sea, or of war, in a state of sin.

2. How ought we to behave in danger? *But as they sailed He fell asleep; and there came down a storm of wind on the lake; and the waves beat into the ship so that it was now full. And He was in the hinder part of the ship, asleep on a pillow; and they awake Him, and say unto Him, Master, carest Thou not that we perish. Lord save us: we perish. And He saith unto them, Why are ye fearful, O ye of little faith.* In danger, we must act with calmness, and do what depends on ourselves; we must pray and offer up to heaven, religious vows and sincere promises, we must hope in the goodness and power of Him Whom we invoke, we must submit ourselves to the commands of Providence, and the will of our sovereign Master. If then any illness should really threaten our life, any misfortune disturb our peace of mind and deprive us of our worldly possessions, let us act and pray, let us submit ourselves and hope.

3. How ought we to behave ourselves after the danger is past? *Then He arose, and rebuked the wind and the raging of the water; and they ceased and there was a calm. And He said unto them, Why are ye so fearful? How is it that ye have no faith? And they feared exceedingly, and said one to another, What manner of man is this, that even the wind and the sea obey Him!* After the danger is past, our gratitude ought to burst forth in praises and thanksgivings mingled with admiration, with fear and love for Him Who has delivered us; it ought to shew itself in a prompt and exact fidelity in acquitting ourselves of the vows and promises which we have made to Him, but especially in a sacred use of the life and the tranquillity which He has restored to us. Which of us has not found himself in some pressing danger, in occasions or in critical affairs, from which he has only escaped by a sort of miracle? Let us recall here the special benefits of God on our behalf. What gratitude have we manifested towards Him?

Was it then in order that we should offend Him, was it then in order that we should live as we are doing that He has preserved our life? Ungrateful, we have called upon Him in danger, we have promised Him to be faithful to His commandments, if He would deliver us; He has delivered us, and we have equally forgotten our promises and His benefits.

SECOND POINT.

Of the dangers which concern our soul.

1. How should we behave ourselves before the danger? 1. We must fear it, because every thing depends upon our conduct then, since we risk the loss of grace, innocence, faith, our souls, and eternity. The least danger which threatens our life makes us tremble; it is not necessary to exhort us to fear it, we fear it often to excess, whilst we do not fear Him who can take from us the life of grace, and precipitate us into eternal misery. 2. We must flee from danger, because few escape, and the greater number perish; let us burn those books, those pictures, those songs which suggest evil to us; let us renounce that society, those plays, those conversations which we find corrupting. As soon as we feel that there is any risk for our soul, let us tremble, let us shudder, let us flee from it. If of our own free will we expose ourselves to peril, if we love it, if we seek for it, we are already half conquered, we shall perish. 3. We must keep ourselves always on our guard, because danger is frequent and hidden. It is to be found everywhere, it is to be found where we had the least ground to suspect it. If we are not continually on our guard, we find ourselves besieged, deceived, led away almost before we are aware of it. 4. Lastly we must pray, because God only can keep danger away from us. Let us ask Him then every day for this grace for ourselves, and for those in whose welfare we take an interest; let us ask it of Him before we undertake anything, at the beginning, and in the course of all our actions.

2. How ought we to behave ourselves in danger? 1. We must either flee from the danger, or else fight bravely against it from the very first. If we find ourselves suddenly engaged in some occupation which is dangerous to our souls, let us beware not to advance further, nor to stand still on the brink of the precipice, let us draw back at once with fear as at the sight of an insidious serpent, let us break off that conversation, leave that place, drive away those thoughts, shut that book, turn away our eyes from that object, control all our senses; if we defer ever so little, the temptation will enter into our heart, or to speak more truly, we shall enter ourselves into the temptation, it will lay siege to our hearts, and we shall succomb. 2. We must pray. However little strength we may feel we have to do so, let us do it nevertheless, if we do nothing else than repeat the saving Name of Jesus, or cry out repeatedly, *Lord, save me, or I perish.* 3. We must have trust. The temptation will not last for ever, the calm will return: and what joy will it not be then to us to have resisted, and to have remained faithful to God. In the violence of the storm, it seems as though all were lost, and that nothing remains to us but to yield ourselves up to our misery. Let us be careful not to give credence to this suggestion of the tempter. Whilst we withhold our consent to it, there is nothing lost as yet, we have received no hurt as yet. If some weakness have betrayed us already, if we have yielded any thing to the enemy, let us beware not to yield to him any further, let us rekindle our courage; if our victory is not complete, let us act so that at any rate our defeat should not be a complete one.

3. How ought we to behave ourselves after the danger is past? 1. Let us humble ourselves. Let us ask pardon of God for the faults which we may have committed amidst the temptation, whether in exposing ourselves to it, or in making but a faint resistance to it. 2. Let us thank God that He has upheld us in the danger, and has not permitted that we should perish.

3. Lastly, let us form good resolutions and take wise precautions for the future, because what has happened to us under these circumstances may happen to us under many other circumstances. Let repentance, recollectedness, prayer, work, fear, the avoidance of all occasions which may lead us into temptation, the love of Jesus, union with God, the frequenting of the blessed Sacrament, serve to us as preservatives against dangers to come.

THIRD POINT.

Of the dangers which concern the Church.

The ship is the figure of the Church.

1. The Church, like this ship, is exposed to most fearful storms, and often appears to be on the point of being swallowed up. Who would not have thought that she would have been destroyed a hundred times by the sword, submerged by error, overthrown by crime, scattered by schisms, annihilated by politics? But she exists in the midst of the storms. The evils which she suffers afflict her children, but they do not discourage them. There is nothing surprising that false religion should enjoy tranquillity amongst mankind, whose inclinations they flatter, and whose delusions they encourage, any more than that in the midst of such men we should see the Church, which teaches the truth, attacked, persecuted, and fought against; but that this Church, assailed at all points, against which are united and set loose every error, and every evil passion, should exist and continue on her way, in spite of all contrary waves and winds, that is a wonder which we cannot too much admire.

2. The Church has Jesus always with her. In the Church, as in the ship, Jesus is present. He knows the assaults she has to endure, He regulates their duration and their strength. If He appears to be for a time powerless, motionless, and without action; if He seems to shut His eyes to the insults which are offered to His Spouse, it is only in order to purify her, to prove her

faith, and to manifest to her with greater brightness His tenderness and love. We awaken Jesus by prayer, but it must be a prayer full of charity, calmness, and confidence. The true Christian makes use of no other arms in defence of the Church; he sets forth in all their simplicity the truths which she teaches, and defends them without bitterness; he remains firmly attached to them without regard to human respect, suffers without murmuring, he dies in blessing him by whom he is condemned, and embracing him who strikes him. Such is the spirit of a true Christian martyr.

3. The Church is assured of calm when it will be helpful to her. In the Church, as in the ship, Jesus, when it pleases Him, and according to the ordering of His infinite wisdom, makes the most profound calm succeed to the most stormy tempests, and the serenest day to the most obscure night. Sometimes by brilliant prodigies, and sometimes by the secret unction of His grace, He changes the hearts of nations and of kings. The former become submissive to the Church, and the latter become its nursing fathers and protectors. It is thus that Constantine, Clovis, Charlemagne, S. Louis and many other pious monarchs have procured for the Church not only peace and freedom, but also dignity and splendour.

Prayer. It is in the bosom of Thy Church, O Divine Jesus, that I desire to live and die. Woe be to me, if, having had the happiness to be admitted into her, I should leave her, or if whilst believing myself to belong to her, I should be indifferent to the evils by which she is afflicted. Conduct her, O Jesus, this ship of the Church, this militant Church, to the haven of eternity, notwithstanding the storms and persecutions which agitate her unceasingly. But that which this Church, Thy Spouse experiences, I also experience. Multiplied temptations assault me from within and without; speak, and the tempest will be scattered; command especially those passions which rend my heart, that they may be calmed, so that I may no longer follow ought but the peaceable and gentle guidance of Thy love. Amen.

Meditation LXV.

THE TWO MEN WHO WERE POSSESSED OF DEVILS IN THE COUNTRY OF THE GERGESENES. A TYPE OF IMPURITY.

Meditate 1. on the possession; 2. on the deliverance of the two unhappy victims of the devil. S. Matt. viii. 28—32. S. Mark v. 1—18. S. Luke viii. 26—33.

FIRST POINT.

Their possession.

And when He was come to the other side into the country of the Gergesenes, there met Him two possessed with devils, coming out of the tombs, exceeding fierce, so that no man might pass by that way. There met Him out of the tombs a man with an unclean spirit—he wore no clothes, neither abode in any house but in the tombs. S. Mark and S. Luke only speak of one man who was possessed, doubtless because the possession of the one of the two of whom S. Matthew speaks, being more remarkable, they did not think it needful to speak of the other. Let us consider 1. what was the devil by whom these men were possessed; 2. what was the nature of this possession; 3. what was their condition during the time of their possession.

1. What was the devil by whom they were possessed? It was *an unclean spirit*. Although all the devils are unclean spirits, one cannot fail to recognize the devil of impurity by the characteristics which this one presents to us. First, his cruelty. Not content with tormenting him whom he possessed, he threw himself with fury also on the passers-by. The profligate seeks every where for sharers in his guilt, and accomplices in his crimes. Woe to him who passed by the dwelling place of these possessed men! but yet more is the profligate to be feared; woe to all who have any intercourse with him, who draw

near to him, or are on terms of intimacy with him! Parents, be on your guard, if you love your children. 2. He is known by his strength. *And no man could bind him, no, not with chains, because that he had been often bound with fetters and chains, and the chains had been plucked asunder by him, and the fetters broken in pieces; neither could any man tame him.* Who can curb the man who is abandoned to his evil passions; who can restrain him? Neither the loss of his reputation, nor the ruin of his health, nor the disgrace which he brings on his family, nor the bonds of friendship and of blood, nor the duties of religion, nor the sacred office of holy orders, nor sickness, nor the sight of recent death, can check the impetuosity of his unbridled passions. A miracle only of the grace of Jesus Christ can drive out of the heart an evil spirit so strong, so obstinate, and so formidable. 3. He is recognized by his name. *And Jesus asked him, What is thy name? And he answered saying, My name is Legion: for we are many.* Legion is the true name of the spirit of impurity; he never goes alone, he takes along with him every other vice, he takes possession of all the senses, and all the faculties of the soul, and takes entire possession of the man. Let us tremble at the thought of so hateful an evil spirit. If we have been his prey, let us open our eyes to the odiousness of his character; if we have been preserved or delivered from him, what gratitude ought we not to have for our Deliverer!

2. What was the nature of this possession? 1. A lengthened possession, for it was a *long time* that they had been possessed. When any one begins to give themselves up to impurity, they flatter themselves that it will only be for a time. Sometimes a person thinks to himself that it is but one act of sin that he is allowing himself to commit; but the first sin brings many others in its train. The time we have proposed to ourselves for our conversion, is deferred again and again, and most often is postponed till decrepit old age and till the grave. If we rise out of it for an instant, we fall back into it

for years, to rise finally no more. 2. A continual possession. *And always, night, and day, he was in the mountains and in the tombs.* It is the same with the profligate; day and night, in the country and in solitude, in the house and in the Church, every where and at all times, he carries his passions with him, he is occupied with them; he is tormented with them; what a continuation of crimes, what a multitude of sins! 3. A cruel possession. *Crying and cutting himself with stones.* The passions of the profligate are yet more cruel, and tear him more pitilessly by remorse, by shame, by jealousy, by unfaithfulness, by spite, dishonour, disease, and by the just fear of an eternity of punishment. Oh cruel passions! all the pleasures which you promise are nothing in comparison with the torments which you cause.

3. What was the state of these unhappy men during the time of their possession? They were naked like the brute beasts; *they wore no clothes,* they would not suffer on themselves any kind of garment; such was the shameful condition to which this evil spirit had reduced them. And is not this still a distinguishing mark of the evil spirit of impurity? Ah! is it not he who has introduced into engravings, into sculptures, into dress, that which is opposed to purity? Is it not he who has introduced so many indecent fashions, which are so contrary to Christian modesty? Are not these the livery of the devil, and do not those who wear them range themselves under his laws, and submit to his empire? Let us turn away our eyes with horror from every thing which is indecent or impure; let us detest, and drive far from us, and banish out of our houses every thing which offends against purity; let us observe a strict and exact modesty in private as well as in public, and as much with regard to ourselves as with regard to others. 2. These unhappy men lived far from the dwellings of men *in the tombs,* dark and infected places. And what are the profligate, and such like sinners, who have been long dead to grace, but whitened sepulchres? They have consci-

ences seared with sins and fearful stains; their bodies are wasted by dissipation, and are sometimes more tainted than the dead bodies which lie in the tombs. 3. These unhappy men wandered about sometimes *in the wilderness* and sometimes *in the mountains*, filling the air with fearful groans, a true picture of the restless, fierce appearance which is so often to be seen in a profligate man, of the wild passion which governs him, and makes him avoid the society of good men, and of the cries and groans which his passion draws from him in spite of himself. What a life, O my God, what a life for a Christian! Such are then the pleasures which the devil gives to those who follow him. Ah impostor! were these what he promised them?

SECOND POINT.

Their deliverance.

The evil spirit of impurity is also to be here recognized by his acts, his complaints, and his prayers.

I. The steps he is compelled to take. And one of them, *when he saw Jesus afar off, he ran and worshipped Him, and fell down before Him.* As soon as Jesus had landed, the evil spirit felt his conqueror, he could no longer remain in his gloomy subterranean habitations; an invisible power drew him forth from them in spite of himself, and summoned him, so to say, before the tribunal of his Judge. He hastened to meet Him, and as soon as he perceived Him, this fierce spirit, whom no human power had been able to tame, became yielding, and trembling, fell at His feet, acknowledged his Master, and adored Him. A forced adoration, which fear alone drew forth from him, and which could not be pleasing to Jesus. Thus it comes to pass that however abominable the profligate may be, nevertheless, urged on by remorse, he yet will prostrate himself before God, he will strike his breast, and acknowledge his sin; a blessed beginning, a praiseworthy action, but which the devil but too often finds the means to render of no avail.

2. Injurious complaints. *And cried with a loud voice, and said, What have I to do with Thee, Jesus, Thou Son of the Most High God? I adjure Thee by God, that thou torment me not. For He said unto him, Come out of the man, thou unclean spirit.* The devil makes a complaint that Jesus has declared Himself his enemy, that He had come to trouble and torment him before the time. On what are founded these complaints? On the command of this Saviour-God, that he should come out of the bodies of which he had taken possession. Jesus, in commanding him to do so, did not will to force him to do so at first, in order to give him time to manifest his malice and his shamelessness, and to give us an opportunity of knowing him and of detesting him. It is then to torment thee, impure and cruel spirit, to prevent thee from doing us hurt! Thou didst bethink thyself that thou wouldest be left in possession of thy power to the end of the world. Nay, nay: Jesus has come, and has delivered us from thy odious yoke, and henceforth thou wilt have no power but over those who give themselves up to thee of their own will. Immortal praise be rendered to Thee, O Divine Redeemer! and woe be those who will not profit by the precious fruits of Thy adorable blood! The devil puts the same complaints now-a-days into the mouth of the profligate. 1. He complains of God, that He sets Himself against his crimes. What harm am I doing? he exclaims, I do wrong to no one. As if the Spirit of God was not essentially opposed to the spirit of impurity; as if the essential precept of the love of God could be compatible with sinful affections and the flames of impurity. 2. He complains of those who have zeal in the salvation of souls. If the enormity of his crimes is set before the profligate, and salutary remorse is stirred up in him, he will seek to evade it by saying that he is being disquieted before the time. Unhappy time of youth! thus dost thou let thyself be deceived; but canst thou be certain that thou wilt ever reach this time which thou dost promise thyself; or if thou dost attain to it, then and even to thine

old age wilt thou not be the plaything and the prey of the devil whom thou dost cherish!

3. *Sinful prayers.* *And he besought Him much that He would not send them away out of the country,* and *that He would not command them to go out into the deep. Now there was there, nigh unto the mountains, a great herd of swine feeding. And all the devils besought Him, saying, Send us into the swine, that we may enter into them. And forthwith Jesus gave them leave. And the unclean spirits went out, and entered into the swine; and the herd ran violently down a steep place into the sea, (they were about two thousand) and were choked in the sea.* The devil first asks to be allowed to remain in the country; wherefore? in order to do harm there; he then asks not to be precipitated into the abyss, where he will dwell at the end of the world, but to remain always on this earthly region; wherefore? in order to exercise his fury, in order to tempt and ruin mankind. To take away this power from him, is what he calls, tormenting him. Lastly, he asks that at least he may be permitted to enter into the swine which were feeding in the neighbourhood; wherefore? in order to precipitate them into the sea, and thus to make the Saviour odious to all the inhabitants of that country. Jesus grants him this last request. We shall see what were His reasons for so doing in the next meditation; but let us here examine what are the secret desires and the dearest wishes of the profligate. What do they desire, what do they request? That they may not be condemned to hell. They desire to escape it without putting an end to their own crimes; they desire that there should be no justice in God, no punishment for sin; lastly, they desire to be like brute beasts; they envy their lot; they seek to persuade themselves that there is no difference between their condition and that of their own, and often God, by a just punishment, permits them so to persuade themselves, or at least, they live as if they were persuaded of it.

Prayer. Ah! Lord, I offer to Thee to day a prayer

very different to this; suffer me not to become like those brute beasts, but make me like unto Thyself. If in order to be delivered from the devil and from my evil passions, I must needs lose all that I possess: if I must leave the country where I am, leave the world, my family, and give up every thing, I am ready to sacrifice all, sooner than lose my soul, and live under Thy displeasure. Sustain me, O divine Jesus, in these resolutions; strengthen me against Thine enemies and mine. Amen.

Meditation LXVI.

OF THAT WHICH TOOK PLACE AFTER THE DELIVERANCE OF THE TWO WHO WERE POSSESSED, IN THE COUNTRY OF THE GADARENES.

Consider here, first, the conduct of the Gadarenes, then that of the two who were possessed, and lastly that of Jesus Christ. S. Matt. viii. 33—34. S. Mark v. 14—21. S. Luke viii. 34—40.

FIRST POINT.

Of the Gadarenes.

1. *The flight of those who kept the swine.* *And they that fed the swine fled and told it in the city, and in the country, and what was befallen to the possessed of the devils.* Those who were entrusted with the care of the swine, fled away each to his own master, some to Gadara, some to the neighbouring villages, where they spread the tidings of so surprising an event. Ah! who would not have been frightened at the sight of such a spectacle? If we could see the number of sins and of evil spirits from whom a sinner who is converted, is delivered, we should be seized with astonishment, and it was doubtless, in order to give us a true idea of what sin really is, that Jesus granted to the devil the petition which he had made.

2. *The groundless fear of the Gadarenes.* *And behold the whole city went out to meet Jesus, to see what it was that was done; and they came to Jesus, and see him that was possessed with the devil, and had the legion, sitting, and clothed, and in his right mind; and they were afraid. And they that saw it, told them how it befell to him that was possessed with the devil, and also concerning the swine.* The crowd of those who hastened to the spot, in order to learn what had taken place, was so great, than any one would have said that the whole city was assembled in order to learn the circumstances. Jesus and His disciples were to be seen, with the possessed of the devils at His feet, and specially the one who had been the most furious, clothed, calm, and in his right senses, and listening to the words of the Saviour. The sight struck the inhabitants of Gadara with fear rather than with reverence; they thought only of the loss of their herds; they feared for their swine, of which the law forbade them to make any use for food, but which they did not consider that it was forbidden to rear as an article of trade. The faith of these people was not proof against so base an interest. If they had sustained this trial which Jesus had laid upon them, their future happiness would have been secured. ' Is it not this very spirit of self interest, and of avarice, is it not this attachment to the things of this world which animates us and which ruins us ?

3. *The insensate prayer of the Gadarenes.* *Then the whole multitude of the country of the Gadarenes round about besought Him to depart from them; for they were taken with great fear; and He went up into the ship and returned back again.* Senseless fools that ye are! Of Whom do ye thus deprive yourselves? Of Him Who would have delivered all your possessed of devils, healed all your sick; of Him Who would have preached the truth to you, and would have loaded you with graces and blessings. Alas! How many say daily to Jesus, Withdraw from me, come not to me, not out of respect or from humility, but in order not to be obliged

to part with that in themselves which is displeasing to Jesus Christ! Thus the moments of salvation are allowed to slip by unused, when the grace which would draw us does not accord with our own interests; thus, in order to spare our cherished passions we reject the heavenly Visitor, and despise the advances which our Saviour graciously makes to us.

SECOND POINT.

Of the men who were possessed.

What was their conduct, 1. when they were delivered, 2. when Jesus was about to withdraw Himself, 3. when they returned to their own homes?

1. When they were delivered. Jesus having permitted the evil spirits to enter into the swine, the unclean spirits came out of the two who had been possessed by them, who found themselves at that same instant entirely free, and in their right minds. Coming back to themselves, they clothed themselves decently, and became perfectly calm and quiet, and remained seated at the feet of Jesus. Such is the image of a converted and penitent soul: everything becomes changed in it, its ideas, its affections, its person, its feelings, its habits, its garments, its surroundings, its expenditure. The evil temper is no longer to be perceived; no vestige of its former passions are to be seen; it places its whole happiness in remaining at the feet of Jesus, its Saviour, and its Deliverer: gratitude makes it cling close to Him, and love fills it with delights.

2. Conduct of the two men who had been possessed, when Jesus was about to withdraw Himself. What a separation for hearts penetrated with gratitude! The one who had been the most cruelly tormented by the evil spirit could not persuade himself to this separation; he offered himself to Jesus to follow Him, and entreated for a place amongst His disciples, protesting with sincerity to Him that he would never be separated from his benefactor; but Jesus, touched by his gratitude,

destined him for another employment, that of publishing abroad the mercies of God, an employment of which he acquitted himself with fidelity. *And when He was come into the ship, he that had been possessed with the devil prayed Him that he might be with Him. Howbeit, Jesus suffered him not, but saith unto him, Go home to thy friends, and tell them how great things the Lord hath done for thee, and hath had compassion on thee.*

3. Conduct of the possessed on their return home. Jesus had commanded them to return to their own homes, to rejoin their families, and to publish the blessings which they had received from God. With what zeal and what gratitude did they not do so, and especially the one who had been the most wretched! *And he went his way, and published throughout the whole city how great things Jesus had done unto him.* But not content with having manifested to his family and the whole city of Gadara, the power and glory of Jesus, *he departed, and began to publish in Decapolis how great things Jesus had done for him, and all men did marvel.* He went through all Decapolis, doing the work of an apostle, and, shewing himself especially as an evident proof of the power of the Saviour, he filled all the cities and villages with astonishment and admiration, and disposed them thus to receive the Gospel. Gratitude forms apostles in all conditions of life, and how many victories would this excellent virtue gain for God, if all those on whom He lavishes His graces would shew forth grateful hearts! Let then our hearts be penetrated with a like gratitude, with a similar love; and without being apostles, how many of the works of an apostle might we not do!

THIRD POINT.

Of Jesus.

And all men did marvel. Let us do so also, and marvel,

1. At the power of Jesus which summons the evil spirit before Him, asks him questions, and drives him

out. If this unclean spirit did harm to animals like the swine, he could only do so by the express permission of the Saviour. What have we then to fear if Jesus is with us? Let us be faithful to Him, and nothing can be against us.

2. Let us marvel at the wisdom of Jesus, Who makes known to us in this event, the character, the malice, the strength, and the weakness of the enemy of our salvation; and Who proves the inhabitants of Gadara, by the loss of a possession of moderate value.

3. Let us admire His goodness in delivering those two unhappy men, and procuring to their family the consolation of seeing them and possessing them once more; His goodness which leads Him to withdraw Himself from the country of the Gadarenes without complaint of their conduct, even leaving them a means of salvation by the command He gives to those who had been possessed to publish abroad His mercy; lastly, His goodness which yields to the entreaties of those who were awaiting Him anxiously on the other shore of the lake. *And when Jesus was passed over again by ship unto the other side, much people gathered unto Him: and He was nigh unto the sea; and the people gladly received Him; for they were all waiting for Him.* How good Jesus is! Happy is he who profits by His Presence! happy he who in His absence sighs after His return! happy he who receives Him with love!

Prayer. Inspire me, O Lord, with that holy ardour, that eagerness which this people had for Thy word. Speak to my heart, and it shall be healed. O divine Jesus, speak, command the devil, Thine enemy and mine, and all the powers of darkness which attack my soul, all the passions which reign in my heart will be dispersed and set to flight. Open my eyes, O charitable Saviour, and suffer not that I should hasten to my ruin, like those senseless and vile animals. Make me taste the happiness which those enjoy who possess Thee, and which those lose who lose Thee. Lastly, dwell in me, O my God, after having taken possession of me, and grant that I may be Thine in time and in eternity. Amen.

Meditation LXVII.

JESUS HEALS A PARALYTIC MAN IN THE PRESENCE OF THE PHARISEES.

1. That which precedes this miracle; 2. the manner in which the miracle is worked; 3. that which follows it. S. Matt. ix. 1—8. S. Mark ii. 1—12. S. Luke v. 17—26.

FIRST POINT.

That which precedes this miracle.

1. The teachableness of the people. *And again He entered into Capernaum after some days; and it was noised that He was in the house. And straightway many were gathered together, insomuch that there was no room to receive them, no, not so much as about the doors; and He preached the word unto them.* How the eagerness of the people is about to be rewarded! The Saviour is about to make them witnesses of a striking miracle which will fill them with the sweetest consolation. Jesus Christ is the Way and the Light; He alone can enlighten us, can heal us, and He is ready to pour down upon us the gifts of His mercy; gifts which He will shed down in proportion to our eagerness to receive them, and of our obedience towards Him. We have ourselves only to blame if we continue always blind or ill. We have the blessing of being in the House where He teaches, and where He works His wonders, that is to say, in His Church; let us not remain there in vain, whilst others come thither from all parts in order to receive there the graces which they need.

2. The jealousy of the Pharisees. *And it came to pass on a certain day, as He was teaching, that there were Pharisees and doctors of the law sitting by, which were come out of every town of Galilee, and Judæa, and Jerusalem; and the power of the Lord was present to heal them.* The people came to Jesus to be healed of their sicknesses; but the doctors came there

in order to contest these cures, in order to criticise the doctrine of Him Who performed them, and to cry Him down with the people. Never could they have a better opportunity for becoming acquainted with our Blessed Saviour, that Man whose fame was so widely spread, and Who caused them so much umbrage. This Divine Saviour was seated in the house, and they were seated around Him. They saw Him, they heard Him, they censured Him; but they only carried confusion away with them, and their obstinate resistance to the evidence of facts only increased their blindness, strengthened their hardness of heart, and animated against Jesus a hatred, which from that moment, remained implacable. The just punishment of those who hear or read the word of God, or who examine into His works with the same disposition of mind as the Pharisees.

3. The charity of those who brought in the paralytic man. *And behold, men brought in a bed a man which was taken with a palsy; and they sought means to bring him in and to lay him before them.* A laborious charity; this unhappy man was so crippled in all his limbs, that it needed four men to carry him stretched out on his bed, and there were those to be found who were charitable enough to do so. Charity does not shew itself in words, but in deeds. A persevering charity; the sick man and those who carried him were well persuaded that if they could but reach Jesus, the cure would be effected; but the difficulty was to reach Him. What ever effort they might make, after having sought for a long time to penetrate the crowd, they could not even get near the door. They were not disheartened. True charity is only stimulated by obstacles, and God only permits them in order that it may shine forth more abundantly. An industrious charity; *and when they could not find by what way they might bring him in because of the multitude, they went upon the house-top, and let him down through the tiling, with his couch, into the midst before Jesus.* Not being able to open for themselves a passage through the crowd which was

besieging the door, they went a roundabout way, and approaching the house on another side, they carried the sick man by an outside staircase on to the roof, which according to the custom in Palestine, was a platform. They made there a large opening, by which they let down the paralytic man lying in his bed, and placed him in the midst of the assembly, at the feet of the Saviour. Let us imagine to ourselves the surprise of the spectators, but above all what were their expectations. The trial was a strong one, a pretender would have failed in it. Those who were outside the house were not less eager to know what the result would be, than those who were within. Jesus increased the expectations of both, and left them time to exercise their faith, their conjectures, or their criticism, by deferring the cure, or rather by announcing it with wonders more secret yet, and of a higher order.

SECOND POINT.

Of the manner in which this miracle was worked.

Jesus in the place of one miracle, worked three, the first of which was the greatest; the second was the most striking, although secret: the last was the most evident, and the proof of the other two.

1. First miracle: the forgiveness of sins. *Jesus, seeing their faith, said unto the sick of the palsy, Son, be of good cheer; thy sins are forgiven thee.* 1. Consider here the teaching which Jesus gives us. He teaches us that all human infirmities have their source in sin; that the greatest of all evils, and that from which we ought first of all to ask for deliverance, is sin; that bodily afflictions ought to be borne in expiation of sin; lastly, that in the exercise of zeal and all our actions, we must act according to God's will, with a holy freedom, without regard to the pharasaical objections which evilly disposed and irreligious minds may raise against us. 2. Observe the consolation of the paralytic man. With what joy was not his heart penetrated when he heard those tender

words, *My son, be of good cheer.* The remission which he obtains for his sins, the precious and glorious name of son which Jesus gives him, what motives are those for joy, admiration, and love! 3. Reflect on the offence which the Pharisees take at these words. They were seeking for a ground of offence, and they find it. *But there were certain of the scribes sitting there, and reasoning in their hearts, Why doth this man thus speak blasphemies? Who can forgive sins but God only?* Ought those doctors to have been ignorant that, according to the prophets, an essential characteristic of the Messiah was that He was to be the Son of God, God with us, and that He must in consequence, according to their own Scriptures, have the power of forgiving sins. Jesus in doing so was only fulfilling his character as the true Messiah. It is true that an imposter might usurp this language; and that many have done so; but when their power has been put to the proof, they have been found at fault. It was therefore needful at least that they should suspend their judgement, and await the result; but this is what unbelievers never do; they blaspheme a religion of which they never give themselves the trouble to search out the depths; and they separate always its incomprehensible mysteries from the proofs which render them obvious, and place them within the reach of the simplest minds. Let them then come hither, those pretended geniuses, and if they are not entirely hardened let them await the event, and they will be convinced.

2. Second miracle: the knowledge of men's hearts. *And Jesus, knowing their thoughts, said, Wherefore think ye evil in your hearts?* Full of the idea that Jesus had been guilty of blasphemy, the scribes and Pharisees promised themselves to make use of the event, in order to disabuse the people of the high opinion which they had formed of the holiness of the new prophet. They dared not declare themselves publicly; but they found it needful to be cautious in the measures they adopted, for fear of exciting a revolt amongst the bystanders who were in expectation of a miracle. Jesus Christ read the depths

of their hearts. What thoughts are occupying your minds, what suspicions are you inwardly forming against Me? *Why reason ye these things in your hearts?* A very precious warning, which we shall do well never to forget. Of what avail is it to us to feign, and to conceal ourselves from the eyes of men? Jesus sees our hearts, and what He sees there will form the subject of His judgment; He sees there the thoughts we entertain there, thoughts of vanity, of ambition, of sensuality, and of impurity; He sees there those suspicions against our neighbour, those rash and precipitate judgments, those murmurs, those feelings of impatience. He sees there those motives which direct our actions, motives of vain glory, of human respect, of self-interest, of self-love, those motives which are but too natural, and so often tainted either in part or wholly. Let us examine here our heart, and apply ourselves henceforth to keep it pure in the presence of Him Who sees it.

3. Third miracle: the healing of the body. Be attentive, scribes and Pharisees, the decisive moment is at hand, in which it will be easy to know who it is who has blasphemed, whether it be Jesus or you. You will not be taken by surprise, you will be prepared for what is about to follow, for it is being announced to you now. Judge of the efficacy of the first words which Jesus spoke to this paralytic man for the healing of his soul, by the efficacy of those which He is about to say to him for the healing of his body; and if, by a single word, He heals his body, acknowledge that He has the power, which He claims for Himself of healing his soul, of forgiving his sins; acknowledge in consequence, that He is God, that He is the Saviour of men, the King of Israel, the expected Messiah. Jesus, continuing His discourse, says to them, *Whether is easier, to say, Thy sins be forgiven thee; or to say, Rise up and walk? but that ye may know that the Son of man hath power on earth to forgive sins, He said unto the sick of the palsy, I say unto thee, Arise, and take up thy couch, and go unto thine house. And immediately he rose up before them, and took up*

that whereon he lay, and departed to his own house, glorifying God. Let us thank Jesus Christ for this great miracle which He has worked, and for the way in which He has brought it about. How glorious is this day for Him and how blessed to us, in which He confounded His enemies, gave proof of His Divinity, relieved the suffering man, gave joy to Heaven and consolation to earth!

THIRD POINT.

That which follows the miracle.

1. The conduct of the paralytic man which we ought to imitate. At the command of the Saviour, he arises, and without help, in the sight of the assembled multitude, he carries away with him his bed, and takes the road to his house, publishing on his way the mercies which God had showed to him. When Jesus, by the means of His minister, grants to us forgiveness of our sins, does our conduct prove our healing and our gratitude? Do we arise? Do we come forth from our evil habits, our faintheartedness and lukewarmness, our indolence, our spiritual palsy? Are we firm in our resolutions? Do we fall back no more into the same infirmities, into the same love of repose, and of idleness, into the same attachments to created beings rather than to the Creator? Have we the strength and the courage to carry away, to take away, and cause to disappear all the tokens of our infirmities, all the objects which have drawn us aside, all the occasions of sin which have made us fall? Have we the generosity to triumph over them, and to raise up a trophy of them to our Deliverer? Do we withdraw to our own house, and there remain in silence and in retirement, in recollectedness and in prayer? Do all our life, and all our actions glorify the Lord? Do we consecrate them to His glory and our own salvation?

2. The acclamations of the people, to which we ought to join ourselves. *But when the multitude saw it, they marvelled, and glorified God, which had given*

such power unto men. And they were all amazed, and glorified God, and were filled with fear, saying, We have seen strange things to-day. We never saw it on this fashion. When those who were in the house saw the paralytic man rise up and take up his bed, when those who were without, saw him come out and pass forth in the midst of them, there was but one unanimous cry to the glory of God and of His Christ. The acclamations of the bystanders were mingled with the thanksgivings of the paralytic man. On all sides the people exclaimed, No, the Saviour has never worked amongst His people wonders more striking; it is of a truth on this day that God shews Himself forth to mankind by the marvels which we behold! Blessed be God that He has thus communicated to our feeble and mortal nature so divine a power! Let us bless Him ourselves, this God of mercy; for what would become of us, miserable sinners that we are, if He had not granted to us remission of our sins? This power which He has bestowed upon His Apostles, and through them, to their successors, remains in His Church, to be a means of peace and assurance to us in our disquietudes, our resource in our falls, and our support in times of difficulty. Unhappy they who forsake a Church which is so favoured, in order to follow sects which are destitute of this divinely given power!

3. The silence of the Pharisees, whose conduct we ought to abhor. How should they contrive to bring back the people from a pretended delusion, or to put a stop to their first acclamations? They do not attempt to do so; the fact was too evident, and spoke too plainly. Why should they not then join their voices to those of the people? This is the effect of wilful blindness, of jealousy and of hatred; of a determination taken up in passion, in which they obstinately persist, and from which they will not desist; and such is still the conduct of the unbelievers of our days. Let them disabuse us of our error, let them shew us by what way of deception the Gospel, such as it is, has come down to us; in what

century mankind has been imposed upon, in order to make them believe the Gospel history. It is assuredly not in our own; we only believe what was believed in the last century, and so on until the beginning of Christianity; and then, if the things had been false, would they ever have been believed, and would they ever have reached to us? But no, they will not undertake to disabuse us; they content themselves with saying that, for their part, they are not convinced. But if you are not, how inconsistent you are then. Are you then well convinced, are you well assured of the new and strange dogmas which you propound, that all comes to an end with our life, that our soul is only matter, and that it dies with the body? Are your proofs unanswerable? Produce them to us. Blind and senseless that ye are! ye believe without proofs the absurdities and the falsehoods which flatter your passions, and ye reject the truth which is founded on obvious proofs, which ye dare not even attack save by denying them, and in this inconsistency, ye hasten to the grave, and eternity will soon open upon you!

Prayer. O Jesus, I acknowledge Thee, and I adore Thee, as my Saviour and my God. Let the Pharisees murmur at the words, *Thy sins are forgiven thee;* as for me, I believe and I confess that Thou only couldest expiate my sins by Thy Blood, that Thou alone couldest, with a sovereign authority, pardon me them by Thy grace. Let Thy mercy, O divine Jesus, cause my soul to hear those consoling words, *Son, be of good cheer, thy sins are forgiven thee.* Amen.

Meditation LXVIII.

THE CALLING OF S. MATTHEW.

1. Jesus Christ calls S. Matthew. 2. He partakes of a repast in the house of S. Matthew. 3. the Pharisees murmur against Him. 4. He replies to the murmurs of the Pharisees. S. Matt. ix. 9—13. S. Mark ii. 13—17. S. Luke v. 27—32.

FIRST POINT.

Jesus calls S. Matthew.

And He went forth again by the sea side: and all the multitude resorted unto Him, and He taught them. And as He passed by, He saw Levi, the son of Alpheus,— a man named Matthew, sitting at the receipt of custom, and said unto him, Follow Me. And he arose and followed Him. Observe first who it is whom Jesus calls, then how He calls him, and lastly, how He is obeyed by him.

1. Who it is whom Jesus calls. A publican, a man employed in collecting for the Romans the public taxes and imposts; a profession which was odious to the Jews, who only endured with great unwillingness the Roman rule; a lucrative profession, but which, generally, by multiplying riches, only increased the desire for them, and attached the heart to things of this world, and led to the forgetfulness of God: a dangerous profession, by the facility which it offered to those who practised it, to commit injustice, by the impunity which they could promise themselves in committing it. It was a man of this profession whom Jesus called to the ministry, to the practice and to the preaching of poverty and renunciation. How deep and impenetrable are Thy designs, O my God! how powerful is Thy grace! how ineffable is Thy goodness. Let us never despair of any one, nor judge any one: those who appear to us the farthest from the kingdom of God, and whom perhaps we despise, may become saints, and rise up one day in condemnation against us.

2. *How did Jesus Christ call the publican?* He called him as He was passing by. Jesus loses not a moment, He leaves Capernaum, and goes to the sea shore: as He goes along, He teaches the people who follow Him in crowds, and as He passes by, He calls a publican and makes him an apostle. The greatest graces depend often on a passing moment. Woe be to him who lets this precious moment escape! Jesus calls Matthew as he was actually sitting at the receipt of custom. The moment of conversion is that of grace, and that of grace is independent. Often it is in the tumult of business, in the midst of the greatest dissipations, in the midst of pleasures, even in the midst of crimes that God touches the heart, and calls it back to Himself. To defer to yield one's self up, is not to await a more favourable time, but it is to lose the moment of grace, perhaps never to regain it more. Jesus calls Matthew by a word: *Follow Me.* O word of power! O adorable word to him who knows its value! How often have I not heard it! how often have I made as though I heard it not, *or* have I had the unhappiness openly to resist it?

3. *How is Jesus obeyed by him whom He calls?* He is obeyed promptly. At the words, *Follow Me*, S. Matthew rises, without any business, any consideration, any human respect being able to stop him for a moment. Jesus Christ is obeyed sincerely and effectually. This rich man leaves all, despoils himself of all, reserves for himself of all his goods only wherewithal to testify to his Master his gratitude on this one single occasion. He leaves great possessions and great hopes, but earthly possessions and earthly hopes, the enjoyment of which would soon have passed, for heavenly treasures which he still enjoys, and which he will enjoy for ever. Why do we not make the same choice? Jesus Christ is to be obeyed with all generosity. The new disciple follows his Master through the whole course of his life; he preaches Him after His death, he writes His history, becomes the first sacred writer of the New Testament, and confirms lastly what he has written and what he has

THE CALLING OF S. MATTHEW.   469

preached by shedding his blood for his Master's sake. O holy apostle! O holy evangelist! faithful imitator of thy Master! may we have grace to profit by thy preaching which we find in thy writings; and may we have the same spirit of detachment, fervour, and humility, of which thou hast given us an example.

SECOND POINT.

Jesus partakes of a repast in the house of S. Matthew.

And Levi made Him a great feast in his own house: and there was a great company of publicans and others that sat down with Him and His disciples, for there were many, and they followed Him.

1. Consider the preparations for the feast. The new disciple, who was to have the honour of receiving his Master in his house, was only occupied with the care of treating Him in such a manner as to testify to Him his attachment and his love. He looked upon this day as the happiest and most glorious of his life. He hastened to invite to share in his happiness, relations, friends, publicans employed with him or under him, men whom the Jews called sinners, and the greater number of whom did not affect any great regularity of life, but who were not far removed from the kingdom of God, and several of whom had already begun to follow Jesus Christ. He was careful that nothing should be wanting to celebrate this great day, and the repast was a splendid one. *He made Him a great feast.* Is it thus that we prepare ourselves to receive this same Jesus, no longer mortal Man on earth, but reigning in heaven, and present in the Eucharist: no longer in order to feed Him, but to be fed by Him ourselves: no longer in order to receive Him into our houses, but into our inmost hearts and souls? Do we feel how much happiness and glory one day of Communion may procure for us, and what cares and watchfulness is required that we may reap the fruits of it?

2. Observe what was the joy of the feast. 1. It was

pure, because temperance, modesty, peace, gentleness, and charity reigned there with true freedom. 2. It was holy, because of the presence of Jesus there. All eyes were fastened on Him, they listened to His words, and their minds were filled with holy thoughts. 3. It was perfect, because at the same time that the body was being nourished, the mind and heart were also receiving their food, a thousand times more delicious. It is thus that the first Christians celebrated their Agapes, or love feasts, and that Christians now should take their repasts.

3. Examine what were the fruits of this feast. These fruits were the abundant graces, which were stirred up in the hearts of those who were present, a new fervour in the service of God, a new desire to hear His word. a new courage to follow Jesus, and to declare themselves on His side. S. Matthew was the most favoured of them all. From that moment, he gave up all, became one of the followers of the Saviour, and never forsook Him more. If we desire to have any part in His favours, as we cannot minister to Christ in His own person, let us do so in that of His members, who are the poor.

THIRD POINT.

Murmurs of the Pharisees against Jesus.

But the Scribes and Pharisees, when they saw Him eat with publicans and sinners, murmured against His disciples, saying, Why do ye eat and drink with publicans and sinners? Why eateth your Master with publicans and sinners? The murmurs of the Pharisees arose from jealousy, of which the characteristics, which are easy to be recognized here, are curiosity, malignity, and cowardice.

1. Curiosity. How did the Pharisees know that Jesus was at a feast at the house of S. Matthew, and with whom He was eating? The jealous man spies out every thing, sees everything, enquires into everything. Unhappy curiosity, which disturbs the peace, destroys

charity, and finds fault sometimes even with religion and the conduct of God Himself. What does it matter to us what this or that person does, respecting whose conduct we have no concern? What does it matter to us where they go, to whom they speak, or with whom they associate? Let us think of ourselves, and leave others in peace.

2. Malignity. Wherefore, say the Pharisees, does your Master eat, and wherefore do ye yourselves eat with sinners? The jealous man finds mystery and design in every thing; he takes offence and finds fault with everything. Instead of giving others credit for good intentions, which they often are, instead of looking upon things at least as indifferent and matters of little consequence, as they mostly are, he turns everything into evil, he finds abuses, crimes, scandals everywhere.

3. Cowardice. The Pharisees do not carry their complaints to Jesus, but to His disciples. Jealousy never attacks in person him who is the object of it, and who would be able to reply to its charges; it is in secret and in the absence of the person against whom it is directed; it is to their friends, to those with whom they are intimate, to whom it inspires its mistrust, that it insinuates its suspicions, and that it seeks to communicate its venom. It is not either to men of established character that the unbeliever dares to propose his doubts and his blasphemies, but to those whom he knows well are not sufficiently well instructed to refute him. In the presence of the former, he keeps silence. But Jesus hears all, and does not forsake either His own cause nor that of His disciples. He still raises up men who are capable of confounding calumny, and of enlightening those who desire to be enlightened, and one day He will avenge with a high hand His own glory and that of His servants.

FOURTH POINT.

Answer of Jesus to the Pharisees.

This answer, Jesus draws, 1. from a comparison to

earthly things; 2. from a text of the Holy Scriptures; 3. from the purpose of His mission on earth.

1. *From a comparison to earthly things.* *When Jesus heard that, He said unto them, They that be whole need not a physician, but they that are sick.* O charitable Physician! Thou dost exercise here Thine office well with regard even to Thine enemies. Thou dost not reproach them with their sickness, although it is one which they have wilfully brought upon themselves; Thou dost not grow angry with them, guilty as they are; Thou dost not set before them even their injustice and their malignity: Thou dost instruct them with gentleness. Thou dost seek only to heal them and to gain them over. O powerful Physician! Why do we not consult Thee in our sicknesses! we should then enjoy perfect health, and assure ourselves of eternal life. What! So much pains spent on the health of body which physicians cannot guard from death, and so little care for the health of a soul which will never perish, and to whom the heavenly Physician can and will procure eternal life.

2. Jesus draws His answer from a text of Holy Scripture. *But go ye and learn what that meaneth, I will have mercy, and not sacrifice.* That is to say, mercy and sacrifice are equally commanded; but when the two duties clash in a manner that it becomes impossible for us to reconcile them, you ought to lay aside the sacrifice in order to exercise mercy. A work of charity towards our neighbour is more agreeable in My Eyes, than the holiest work of the law, such as the offering of victims. Let us meditate on these words, and let us understand well their meaning. Yes, God prefers works of mercy to sacrifices and to all works of piety. To make a pretext of devotion in order to dispense one's self from the duties of charity, is an abuse; to think that one is pleasing to God by the practices of piety, whilst our heart remains hard towards our neighbour through indifference, contempt, harshness, hatred, is a delusion: to leave God for our neighbour, in order to comfort him in his sorrows, to console him in his afflictions, to instruct

him in his ignorance, in order to convert him, to bring him back from his wanderings, that is leaving God for God, that is acting according to the heart of God, so much does He love us, and so dear to Him are our interests; that is what the Scripture teaches us, and what Jesus teaches us by these words and by His example.

3. Jesus draws His answer from the purpose of His mission on earth. *For I am not come to call the righteous, but sinners to repentance.* That is to say, in drawing around Me those whom you call sinners, and in gaining them over to My Father by My benefits, I am fulfilling Scripture, I am giving the preference to works of mercy; sinners have more need of it than the righteous; and as I am sent into the world in order to bring them to repent, and to practise the Gospel from which they are further removed than the righteous, therefore this is the reason why My Ministry is less needful to the righteous than to sinners.

Prayer. O infinite goodness of God! we were all sinners, and therefore Thou didst cast upon us the eyes of Thy mercy; yea, it is for us all, it is for me in particular that Thou didst come. Ah divine Jesus! Thou didst come to seek sinners; behold me, the greatest of all. It is for that very reason I lay claim to Thy mercy. Behold me before Thee, humble and contrite. Thou dost call me to repentance; I repent with my whole heart. Support my courage, break my chains, that I may follow Thee with the same promptness and love which S. Matthew shewed to Thee; root out and destroy all my sinful affections, which are continually springing up anew, that, persevering in Thy grace as did this holy apostle, I may hope that from the depths of repentance Thou wilt call me to Thy glory on high, there to dwell with Thee. Amen.

Meditation LXIX.

ANSWER OF JESUS TO THE COMPLAINTS OF THE PHARISEES, AND OF THE DISCIPLES OF S. JOHN BAPTIST.

1. The complaints of the Pharisees and of the disciples of John; 2. the reply of Jesus to those complaints. S. Matt. ix. 14—15. S. Mark ii. 18—20. S. Luke v. 33—35.

FIRST POINT.

Complaints of the Pharisees and the disciples of John.

And the disciples of John and of the Pharisees used to fast, and they come and say unto Him, Why do the disciples of John and of the Pharisees fast often and say prayers, but Thy disciples fast not?—but eat and drink?

1. Observe the inconsistency which is to be found in the reasonings of the Pharisees. Jesus had justified His conduct with regard to sinners, and He had concluded by saying that He came only to call sinners to repentance. To that the Pharisees answer, and this is to what their reasoning amounts: How can you say that you are come to call sinners to repentance, you whose disciples do not shew any outward tokens of it. The disciples of John are to be seen undergoing frequent fasts and long prayers; the disciples of the Pharisees follow the same rules: but your disciples eat and drink at will, without fear of displeasing you, and you impose upon them neither fast nor prayers. It is thus that they attacked our Saviour, and that they pretended to make Him contradict Himself, as if repentance did not consist essentially in change of heart, and the observance of His law, in hatred of sin, and the love of God, in detachment from earthly things, and in a teachable spirit. Austerities and fastings are but the externals of repentance, are not always suitable to every one, and but too often the ostentation with which they are practised, does away with their merit. It is thus that people still now-a-days

attack the teaching of our Blessed Lord; they pretend to shew contradictions in dogmas, in books, in decisions, in the history of religion, because they are mistaken regarding the terms in which they are expressed, and of which they will not give themselves the trouble to penetrate the meaning.

2. Consider the imprudence which manifests itself in the union of the disciples of John with those of the Pharisees. Then the disciples of John drew near to Jesus, and uttered the same complaint, or rather made to Him the same reproach as did the Pharisees. Wherefore, say they to Him, do we and the Pharisees, besides the fasts prescribed by the law, observe so many others of supererogation, whilst Thy disciples observe none whatever? But how did the disciples of the forerunner, the humblest and the least censorious of men, venture to join themselves here with the greatest enemies of the Saviour, in order to find fault with Him and His disciples? How did they come to borrow the language of a sect which had been condemned, and which was only upheld by its pride? Alas! do we not too often see Christians make themselves, on different points, the echoes of unbelievers, of irreligious men, and of heretics, and offer to the Church, her pastors, her ministers, and those who defend her, the same reproaches and the same insults? We see those who are orderly and regular in their own conduct, speak against devout persons, whether ecclesiastics or those devoted to a religious life, in the same tone as worldly persons or as unbelievers do.

3. Let us examine into the unseemliness which prevails in the complaints of the Pharisees and of the disciples of John.

i. An unseemliness through the pride which shews itself there. Both practised several fasts; nothing more edifying than that; but wherefore boast of them? Not content with having spoken of their fasts in the third person, they add in S. Matthew's account, *we fast*. As for me, I practise such and such things, I am so devout; as for me, I have not these faults. How much vanity and unseemliness there is in such language! how rarely necessity requires us to make use of it! The subterfuges and the pretexts which we employ in order to speak good of ourselves do not impose on any one: pride shines forth through them all, and every one perceives it.

ii. An unseemliness through the contempt of others which appears in them. *We fast*, and ye fast not; *we fast*, wherefore do ye not fast also? How many persons condemn the conduct of the Pharisees, and yet imitate it daily? We compare ourselves with others, an odious comparison; we prefer ourselves before others, a sinful preference: we lay claim to the subjection of others to our ways of thinking and acting, an unjust pretension. Let us think of ourselves, and not concern ourselves what others do. If others do not practise such and such acts of virtue, or such and such works, they practise others which we are ignorant of, and which place them, in God's sight, perhaps far above ourselves. Each one has his special grace and his inclination which he ought to follow; but inward humility is necessary to all, and is the foundation of all virtue.

iii. An unseemliness through the malignity which is concealed in them. The Pharisees only sought, by these discourses, to decry before the people a Man Who caused them umbrage. The disciples of John perhaps themselves also were not wholly exempt from all jealousy, and in that, they had but ill-conceived the spirit of their master, and they were far removed from sharing in his feelings towards Jesus. It is this malignant jealousy which is but too generally the source of all that we say to the disadvantage of our neighbour, and which we seek to cloke under various pretexts. Let us examine here our words and let us search out our hearts.

SECOND POINT.

Reply of Jesus.

Jesus answered them: *Can the children of the bride-*

chamber mourn, as long as the bridegroom is with them ? but the days will come, when the bridegroom shall be taken from them, and then shall they fast. In this answer, Jesus sets forth His title of Spouse of the Church, foretells His own death, and announces the future condition of His Church.

1. Jesus sets forth His title of Spouse. The Church is the bride which He has gained for Himself, at the price of His Blood, and with whom He will reign for eternity. The apostles and S. John are *the children of the bridechamber*, the friends of the bride. How great this mystery is! how comforting! The union of a husband and of a wife is only the figure of the union of Jesus with His Church, and with each holy soul which is in her. O my soul! dost thou indeed understand what thy happiness and thy glory are! thou art also the spouse of Jesus Christ. O Divine Spouse, full of love and of delights! why cannot I respond to all Thy tenderness! render me worthy of Thee, transform me into Thyself. Can I love, can I esteem any other object than Thee? Is there any thing which can appear difficult to me when it shall be a matter of pleasing Thee? What misery, if sin should separate me for a moment from Thee! what despair, if it should separate me from Thee for ever!

2. Jesus foretells His death. It was by His death that Jesus was to gain His spouse, and to merit all the graces which He willed to bestow upon her. He had always this death present to His mind; He desired it ardently, and spoke of it in all His discourses. Precious death, striking proof of the love of Jesus Christ, how can I ever forget thee? The Church commemorates it daily; how ought I to take part in this Commemoration? The days will come, yea, they will come, and they are not far distant, when those same Pharisees, who put to Thee today, O my Saviour, those insidious questions, will demand Thy death and will obtain it. Thou wilt die, O Divine Spouse, and Thou wilt be taken away from Thy Bride; but, by a prodigy of Thy wisdom, of Thy power, and of Thy love, whilst Thine enemies take away from her Thy

visible presence, Thou wilt give Thyself to her, Thou wilt remain with her by a real Presence, although invisible, of which the fury of the Jews, of tyrants, and of heretics can no longer deprive Thee, which will make her happiness on earth, until she shall be called to see Thee in the splendour of Thy glory, and to share with Thee in the delights of Thine eternal kingdom.

3. Jesus announces the future state of His Church. *Then shall they fast.* After the death of Jesus, His ascension into heaven, and the descent of the Holy Ghost, the life of Christians was only a life of fasting and of prayer, of suffering and of tears, of detachment from this world, and of sighs towards heaven. *Then shall they fast in those days.* Those days are to last to the end of the world. During all that time, the Church will sigh after her Spouse, she will perpetuate on earth the sufferings and the atonement of her Spouse, and by that means, she will render herself worthy of Him. We live in those days of fasting, of suffering, mortification, and trial. Where are our fastings, our self-denials, our sufferings, our prayers, our tears, and our sighs?

Prayer. O Divine Spouse of my soul, when shall I see Thee, when shall I possess Thee? can I enjoy any pleasure here below whilst separated from Thee? Ah! I can have none other save that of loving Thee, of serving Thee, of being united to Thee, of humbling myself, and of suffering for Thee. Thou dost demand this of me, O Divine Spouse; I promise Thee to do this, and to do all which may lead me to Thy glory in Heaven. Amen.

Meditation LXX.

JESUS CONFIRMS HIS PRECEDING REPLY BY THREE COMPARISONS.

Let us observe here, first of all, the mysteries which we may consider under the figure of these three comparisons; then the reply to the complaint of the Pharisees which we may discover in them; and lastly, the rules of conduct which we may draw from them. S. Matt. ix. 16, 17. S. Mark ii. 21, 22. S. Luke v. 35—39.

FIRST POINT.

Of the mysteries which may be considered as hidden under the figure of these three comparisons.

Our Lord set forth sometimes the deepest mysteries under the covering of the most familiar comparisons. It is for piety to enter into these sacred depths, in order to meditate on them, and not in order to raise disputes as to the meaning of the words of Jesus Christ. We hear them as much as is needful for us, as soon as we learn to draw from them only instruction and edification. Jesus was always filled with the thought of His great work, the establishment of His Church. He has just declared Himself to be her Spouse as we have seen; it appears that, in the three following comparisons, He continues to exalt the advantages which belong to it above those of the synagogue, and to foretell the divine privileges which belong to it.

I. First comparison, of a piece of cloth or of a new garment, out of which people do not cut a piece in order to mend with them an old and worn garment. *No man putteth a piece of new cloth into an old garment, for that which is put in to fill it up taketh from the garment, and the rent is made worse.* We can understand, under this comparison, the new law which it is not permitted to any one to disfigure, and, so to say, to dissect. Some of the Jews, from the beginning of Christianity, as S. Paul complains in his epistles, were desirous thus to blend them, retaining circumcision and the ceremonies of the ancient law with the truths of the Gospel. Mahomet mingled his doctrines in this way, and wishing to amalgamate some truths of the new law with the ancient law, he perverted both, and set up a monstrous religion. Heretics make this mixture, by following some dogmas of the new law, and paring off others in order to make them agree with the ancient prejudices of a blind reason, which loses itself in the systems which it constructs. Sinners do the same when receiving the Gospel, they cut off some of its precepts, or imagine that they can bend some of its rules to the will of their erring consciences. The dogmas and the precepts which the Church has received from Jesus Christ, and which she teaches every where, are, in some manner, this piece of cloth, this new garment with which we must clothe ourselves, and from which it is not permitted to diminish ought. If we do so, we do not in any way benefit the old garment which we wish to preserve, and we are guilty of spoiling the new garment which has been given to us; we offend Him Who has given it to us, and we draw down upon ourselves the whole weight of His anger.

2. Second comparison, of the new wine, which is not put into old vessels, but into new ones. *Neither do men put new wine into old bottles, else the bottles break, and the wine runneth out, and the bottles perish; but they put new wine into new bottles, and both are preserved.* We can understand, under this comparison, the spirit of the new law and the Sacraments. The Holy Spirit, with Whom the Apostles were filled on the day of Pentecost, was not given to them for themselves alone, but that they should also communicate Him to believers. But in order to receive this newly given Spirit, this Spirit of fire and of love, it was needful that they and true believers, should after having been initiated into the dogmas and precepts of the new law, be regenerated and made new creatures by baptism. It is needful also that the Christian, who has lost the grace of baptism should recover it by repentance, before he presumes to partake of the Sacrament of the Holy Communion, in which the grace of the

Holy Spirit is anew bestowed upon him; otherwise he profanes the Sacrament, dishonours the Holy Spirit, treads under foot the grace which is offered to him, and the fool-hardy man, who in this state of decay and of the old man, receives it, does so only to his condemnation and his loss, but on the contrary, if he receives this new gift into a new and purified heart, all is in order, all is preserved.

3. Third comparison, of the new wine which a man accustomed to the old wine does not relish at first. *No man also having drunk old wine straightway desireth new: for he saith, The old is better.* Nothing is so consoling nor so agreeable to any one as to lead a regular, orderly life. No, there is no sweetness which approaches the peace of a good conscience, and such is the happy condition to which a truly Christian life leads us. But a soul which begins to change its life does not feel all at once the sweetness of peace, and the happiness which there is in belonging to God. Religion has its hardships, and that the sinner experiences at first; accustomed as he is to the pleasures of a sensual and worldly life, a slave of his passions and of the old man, having always acted according to his own desires, and having judged of things only by the ill-regulated inclinations of his own heart, how can he change all his habits without difficulty and without repugnance? It needs prudence to restrain the first fervour of a soul which is deeply conscious of the wanderings of its past life; lest he should be tempted to undertake austerities which are too hard, and thereby fall into a snare of the devil, or a delusion of his self-love. No one can pass at once from the indulgence of his passions to the transports of a pure and perfect love, and of a charity which is complete.

SECOND POINT.

Of the reply of Jesus Christ to the complaints of the Pharisees.

The disciples of Jesus Christ were not less capable

than those of John of prayer and fasting: but they were at present in a different situation; which Jesus Christ had already explained under the emblem of the bridegroom: and they had a different lot before them in the future; which Jesus Christ signifies under these three comparisons. The answer which is there to be found is only a confirmation of that which He had already given, and we ought to find there the same meaning, covered with the same obscurity to the adversaries of Jesus Christ.

1. An old garment is not mended with a new piece of cloth, or with a new garment. That is to say, My disciples belong to a new law, they are destined to publish it and to establish it. This law of love and of union will have its fitting prayers and fasts, with new motives for praying and fasting. When My disciples shall have published this new law, they will recommend it by the virtues and the holiness of their lives. I cannot then withdraw them from that for which they are set apart, in order to subject them to the practices of the ancient law which are now abolished, nor require of them that they should keep them in their old age, by practices of self-denial and piety, which I reserve for them to the time of the new law.

2. New wine is not to be put into old vessels. That is to say, My disciples who are set apart to receive the spirit of the new law, a spirit of zeal and of self-denial, of love, and of union with God, have no need to be filled with the spirit of the ancient law, and to fulfil its works: they must wait for the new Spirit which they are about to receive, and when they have received It, and have communicated It to others, then they will fast and pray.

3. A man who is accustomed to old wine does not desire at first the new wine. That is to say, My disciples, who are destined to drink and to distribute to others the cup of the New Testament, a cup of blood and of suffering, of sacrifices and of martyrdom, do not need to accustom themselves to the cup and the self-denials of the Old Testament; it would be a hindrance to the de-

signs which I have for them, and they would only have more difficulty in becoming accustomed to the new wine, the cup which I destine for them. Such then was the destination of the Apostles, and is it not ours also? We have received the new law, its spirit and its cup; does our life correspond to the gifts which we have received, and to the engagements which we have entered upon, in receiving them?

THIRD POINT.

Of the rules for our conduct which we may draw from these three comparisons.

1. The first may be applied to sinners who need conversion, and whose consciences must be purified. How much patience does it require to search out and know the miserable condition in which they are, and all the stains which have soiled the robe of innocence with which they were clothed at their Baptism? How much gentleness and skill does it not need in order to turn to the best profit the few good feelings which remain to them, in order to animate their confidence without giving them false hopes, and to set before them their misery without discouraging them? How much wisdom is needed in the choice of means in order to proportion them to the weakness of the object, and not to destroy all the good that has been done by practices which are too hard, and so to say, too new to them.

2. The second comparison may be applied to the beginners, to new converts, who must be guided aright, or their fervour is often imprudent; they do not know their own weakness, and they desire to do more than they can; it is therefore necessary to moderate their zeal. Their fervour is ambitious; what they have read in the life of saints has enchanted them, and they are desirous to imitate them all at once; it is therefore necessary above all that they should learn to lay the foundations deep in humility, and not anticipate the moments of grace. Their fervour is passing and inconstant; one way of establishing it and of making it more solid, is to

keep it in check, and to defer the performance of that which they so ardently desire. Through the want of these precautions, the brightest beginnings have belied themselves, and the most fervent souls have returned to the excesses of the most licentious lives.

3. The third comparison may be applied to religious persons, who need progress. There are a great number who content themselves with the avoidance of mortal sin, with frequenting the Blessed Sacrament, with observing some practices of devotion, but who, with that, remain always in the same state, without making any progress in their spiritual life, and have always the same self-love, the same attachment to earthly objects, the same distractions, the same imperfections in their conquests over their passions: they do not seek to advance in the love of God and in union with Him, in the knowledge and imitation of Jesus Christ; they do not apply themselves to mortify their senses, to raise their thoughts, to purify their intentions, to detach their hearts, to increase their faith, to perfect their love, to animate their hope; they do not delight in God, nor do they feel the sweetness which He communicates to souls which are truly recollected; they cannot think of death without fear, and they serve God more from a spirit of fear than from love. Zeal is needed in order to rouse them out of this condition, that they may not continue to languish in it: but great prudence is also needed to draw them out only little by little, by accustoming them first to meditate, and to commune with themselves from time to time, and to overcome themselves in easy things. Insensibly they will find a relish in these new exercises: and in proportion as they make progress in them, they will acquire new graces, new ardour, and they will find in this new wine a strength which will make them despise the old wine which till now they believed they could not give up.

Prayer. Grant me this grace, O God! give me a new heart, fitted to receive the new wine of Thy Gospel, and which can relish its highest commands. Reform me, and renew me by an abundant outpouring of Thy Holy Spirit: Thou hast obtained for me this Divine Spirit, at the price of Thy Blood: I belong to Thy New Covenant, give me a perfect understanding of it, that, practising what Thou hast taught in all its fulness, and conforming myself to the spirit of Thy new law, I may have a greater love for sufferings, more inclination for hardships, and an intimate union with Thee both in time and in eternity. Amen.

Meditation LXXI.

THE PRAYER OF JAIRUS.

Examine, 1. how this prayer was offered; 2. how it was received; 3. how we offer up our prayers. S. Matt. ix 18—19. S. Mark v. 22—24. S. Luke viii. 41—42.

FIRST POINT.

How this prayer was offered.

1. With reverence. *While He spake these things unto them, behold, there came a man named Jairus, and he was a ruler of the synagogue: and he fell down at Jesus' feet, and worshipped Him, and besought Him that He would come into his house.* Is it in this posture and with these feelings that we present ourselves to offer up our prayers, and that we place ourselves in the presence of God?

2. With earnestness. *And besought Him that He would come into his house, for he had one only daughter, about twelve years of age, and she lay a-dying.* It was the life of a dearly-beloved child which depended upon His coming, a child who was the sole hope and comfort of this afflicted father. What more pressing interest could there be for a father? Ah! if we did but think that, in our prayers it is the salvation of our soul which is at stake, our only soul which is always in danger of death, and that, a death eternal, would it be needful to exhort us to pray with as much earnestness as reverence?

3. *With simplicity.* This tender father contents himself with laying before the Saviour the sad state to which his child is reduced. *My little daughter lieth at the point of death.* My child is actually without hope and without resources. All our care is in vain, the disease has gained the upper hand, we only await her last breath. I look upon her as dead, if Thou dost not succour her. In what state is our soul? Is it not dead? Is it not at least sick, languishing, and at the point of death? Ah! it is not without hope, since we have Christ with us. Let us profit by His Presence; let us lay before Him with simplicity our condition, and let us hope for every thing from His power and goodness, health, strength and life.

4. *With faith. I pray Thee, come and lay Thy Hands on her, that she may be healed: and she shall live.* The faith of Jairus was great, but it was not perfect, it did not equal that of the centurion; therefore the Saviour rewarded it, but without praising it. How good Jesus is! He compassionates our weakness, and He pardons us many faults by reason of our trust in Him.

SECOND POINT.

How was the prayer of Jairus received?

1. Jesus received it with an unequalled goodness, which shone forth in His promptness to follow this afflicted father. *And Jesus arose, and followed him, and so did His disciples.* Jesus was seated in the midst of a numerous assembly, to whom He was speaking and whom He was instructing, or rather whose reproaches He was confuting, by justifying the doctrine and the conduct of His disciples, when Jairus presented himself before Him. Nevertheless He rises at once, leaves everything, and s ts out to follow him who implores His succour. Is it not still thus that this God and Saviour is ready to answer our prayers as soon as we call upon Him?

2. Jesus received the prayer of Jairus with an unequalled goodness, which appeared in His silence. The

Saviour answered nothing to this ruler of the synagogue; but He rose immediately, and set out with him. This silence, joined to action, ought to have been very comforting to Jairus, on the one hand, it showed him how truly Jesus took part in his affliction, on the other hand, how assured he ought to be of the succour which he had come to request. Jesus walked in silence, which He only broke in order to confirm the faith of Jairus, and to give him new motives for comfort.

3. Jesus received the prayer of Jairus with an unequalled goodness, which showed itself in His patience in bearing the importunity of the people. *But as He went much people followed Him, and thronged Him.* Jesus was followed, not only by His disciples, but by an innumerable crowd of persons, who were eager to hear Him and curious to behold the miracles which He wrought. They did not know how to observe any moderation. Without regard for the sacred Person of Him for Whom they were filled with admiration, and only hearkening to their own eagerness and anxiety, they threw themselves upon Him, they pressed upon Him, and thronged Him; but Jesus utters no complaint.

4. Jesus received the prayer of Jairus with an unequalled goodness, which manifested itself in His condescension in perfecting the faith of this man. It was not by reproaches for his want of trust that the Saviour sought to increase the faith of Jairus; no, his afflicted state would have made them too bitter. It was not either by an instruction by word of mouth, which with regard to a ruler of the synagogue, would have added humiliation to his affliction; it was by working a miracle in his presence for which he had not asked, and a still greater miracle in his favour than that for which he had asked, as we are about to see. O divine Saviour! woe be to him who loves Thee not. O divine goodness! how ill do I imitate Thee! Have I the same promptness to succour my neighbour, the same care to comfort him, the same patience to bear with him, and condescension to instruct him?

THIRD POINT.

How do we offer up our prayers?

Prayer is the soul of the Christian life, and the manner in which we fulfil this duty can only shew us what progress we have made in our spiritual life. In order to guide ourselves in so important an examination, let us take a sentence out of S. Luke's Gospel which we could not enter upon fully in its place. It says that Jesus, our divine Example, passed the night which preceded the choice of the apostles in prayer to God, that is to say, in one long and fervent prayer. Let us then distinguish here four kinds of Christians who pray, and let us examine which we ourselves are.

1. There are those who never pray at all, or scarcely ever pray. Their prayers consist in a short formula, repeated in the morning in haste, and in the evening in a sort of drowsiness; such is all the homage they pay to their Creator and their Saviour; such is all the praise they yield to Him, all the gratitude they testify towards Him, all the requests they make to Him, and all the intercourse they have with Him! Is that a christian life? Is that prayer to God? Is it not rather a prayer of form, of routine, and of habit?

2. There are others who offer up long prayers. Whether those prayers are imposed by themselves as an obligation, or whether they consider them as incumbent on them, they will not miss them, they persevere in acquitting themselves of this duty; and in that they are praiseworthy. But if these prayers are repeated without any aim, without any effort to maintain themselves in the necessary state of recollectedness: if in repeating these prayers, they take no pain to restrain their senses: if they let their minds wander at will, and occupy themselves with every thing else, is that prayer to God? Is it not rather prayer of the lips, and if one may speak thus, a prayer of one's self, a prayer said in order to satisfy one's self, and after which one is satisfied with one's self? But is God contented with us?

3. There are those who spend a long time in the place of prayer. They pass much time in Church; they are assiduous in attending the services of the Church, and thus far is edifying; but if all the time is passed in idleness or in distraction; if God is present neither in their minds nor in their hearts, however reverent, as we may suppose, the presence of their body may be, it is not prayer to God; it is at the least prayer of the body, a prayer of men, a prayer of the world, and of the public. Such nevertheless are the greater part of our prayers; prayers of ceremony, prayers of our lips, prayers of our body, and in no other way whatever, prayers to God. Is it surprising after that, that our prayers should be without effect? Instead of being heard, do we not rather deserve to be punished for such prayers?

4. Lastly there are those, who whether they pray in words or mentally, in their house or at Church, pray with their minds and with their hearts, have always their hearts and minds filled with God, praise Him and thank Him for all, love Him above all, enjoy His Presence, and commune over His blessings, His mercies, the benefits He bestows upon us and those which He has promised to us. They pass their days thus in prayer to God; they obtain what they ask for, and like Jairus, beyond what they ask for. We envy their lot; but it only depends on ourselves to obtain for ourselves the same blessings. Let us begin by purifying our hearts from all useless and vain thoughts, let us take care to collect ourselves often: let us persuade ourselves earnestly that the spirit of prayer is essential to Christianity, to our perfection, to our salvation; let us ask, but like Jairus, with reverence, with earnestness, with simplicity, and with faith, and we shall obtain; in a word, let us reform our prayers, and we shall soon have reformed our whole life.

Prayer. Yea, Lord, I will seek to imitate the humility and the earnestness of the prayer of this ruler of the synagogue; or rather, knowing better than he did, the extent of Thy power, I will plead with Thy goodness by prayers more humble still, and more fervent, and Thou wilt cause me to feel the effects of Thy power and of Thy goodness both in time and in eternity. Amen.

Meditation LXXII.

HEALING OF THE WOMAN WITH THE BLOODY ISSUE.

The secret healing of this woman and the confirmation of her healing will form the two points of this meditation. S. Matt. ix. 20—22. S. Mark v. 25—34. S. Luke viii. 43—48.

FIRST POINT.

The secret healing of this woman.

1. Consider the sad condition of this woman. *And a certain woman, which had an issue of blood twelve years, and had suffered many things of many physicians, and had spent all that she had, and was nothing bettered, but rather grew worse, when she had heard of Jesus, came behind Him.* I. The state of this woman was one of the saddest that could be conceived from the nature of her disease. It was a distressing illness, the nature of her infirmity brought much confusion on her: it was an inveterate illness, for it had lasted for twelve years: it was a constant illness, which gave her no respite, and left her no interval of health; it was an afflicting illness, which rendered her incapable of doing anything, which excluded her from society, and was a constant cause of distress to her from day to day. Let us examine the state of our souls, and see whether they have not some sickness which is akin to the characteristics of this illness. 2. A condition which was sad from the remedies which she had employed. Remedies which were painful, because she had expended all that she had on them; remedies that were useless, because she had

not been able to gain a cure from any of them; remedies that were costly, because far from having received any relief from these physicians, she found herself in a worse state than before. The remedies she had made use of had served only to exhaust her strength, and to add poverty to her infirmity. When the health of the body is concerned, we sacrifice every thing for remedies which are often useless, and always uncertain. If the health of the soul is concerned, and there are infallible remedies which we may procure, we will take no trouble, we will not inconvenience ourselves in the slightest degree. We ought to pray, to read, to meditate, to fast, to mortify ourselves; no, we have not the strength for it; we ought to give alms, to procure good books, to ask others for their prayers: no, we have not time for it. Thus, every thing for our bodies, and nothing for our souls. Others imagine to be able to calm their passions by gratifying them, whereas they do but excite them the more. Reason and philosophy undertake in vain to cure us. It is only Jesus and religion which can work this miracle. 3. A condition which was sad from the despair of recovery. If Jesus had not worked a miracle in favour of this woman, she would have been without resources and in despair. Alas! where should we be without Jesus! But with Him what need we fear, and what may we not hope for?

2. Examine the happiness of this woman. *When she had heard of Jesus, she came in the press behind, and touched His garment.* It appears that she was not a native of Capernaum, but from some distant place. Thus 1. her happiness was that she had heard of Jesus. Happy those who are assiduous in attending the services of public worship, that they may hear of Jesus! happy those who frequent the company of those who speak to them of Jesus! happy that society, those companionships where Jesus is conversed of! happy those families in which it is a habit to join in spiritual readings in common in order to hear of Jesus! happy those who converse within themselves of Jesus, of His power, and His goodness! happy

those who spread abroad to distant regions the glory of His Name, and the sound of His wonders! 2. Her happiness was to have come where the Divine Saviour was. She left it to others to discourse over the wonders which were related of Him, to examine them or believe them, to admire or criticise them; she only bethought herself of profiting by them. Let us follow her example, let us think only of our salvation, and let us leave others to discourse or dispute. 3. Her happiness was to profit by the first opportunity which she had to see Jesus. If she had found Him in the house where He was wont to reside, if she had found Him in the country, occupied in teaching and healing the sick who were brought to Him, the occasion would have been favourable, it would then have been easy to accost Him, and to obtain from Him the grace which she had just besought of Him, but He was actually on His way, accompanied by the ruler of the synagogue, who was conducting Him in haste to his house, that He might heal his daughter, who was at the point of death; He was walking, surrounded by an innumerable crowd of people. Less than this would have been needed in order to discourage us; but all this did not dishearten her, she did not await a more convenient opportunity, she looked upon this circumstance on the contrary, as being so much the more favourable to her design. When we go in all sincerity to Christ, we profit by every thing, nothing keeps us back, and we make for ourselves means out of the very obstacles we meet with.

3. Observe the plan which this woman forms for her cure. 1. A plan founded on a lively faith, a deep humility, and a great simplicity. She was well aware, that, under the present circumstances, it was impossible for her to speak to Jesus, to lay before Him her affliction, or even to present herself before Him. If she could have done so, yet she judged herself unworthy to draw near to Him, and she shrunk from making known her condition, in the presence of all the people. She formed the plan of approaching to Jesus from behind, and of touch-

ing the border, which according to the custom of all the Jews, who observed the law, He wore at the edge of His garment. *For she said within herself, If I may touch but His garment I shall be whole.* This woman had never heard of any one having been healed in this way; in truth, no one ever had been. Her faith was then not only great, but without example; nevertheless, it was still very imperfect, if she imagined that she could touch the garment of Jesus without His knowing it. Ignorant people often mingle very defective ideas of religion with the fervour of their devotion, with the worship which they render to God. Our duty is to help and instruct them, and not to criticise or laugh at them. The ignorant, with all their simplicity, know how to obtain what they ask for, whilst sometimes the wise man with all his knowledge, does not even know how to ask for it. 2. A plan executed with courage. In spite of her illness, in spite of her weakness, she *came in the press behind*, she mingled with the crowd without fear of being overpowered; she made an effort, she made her way through them, and advanced little by little until at length she reached Jesus, from Whom she awaited her salvation. Alas! it is not thus with us. We form the most specious plans of conversion and of perfection; but when the moment for their execution comes, the least difficulty hinders us, we only see vexatious mischances, and insurmountable obstacles. 3. A plan crowned with the happiest success. From the moment that she found herself close behind the Saviour, her faith increased, her boldness grew; she bent low with reverence, she touched the hem of the Saviour's garment, and raised herself without being perceived. *And straightway the fountain of her blood was dried up; and she felt in her body that she was healed of that plague.* Alas! we touch, not only the garment of Jesus Christ, but Jesus Himself and His glorious Flesh; we receive Him, we become incorporated into Him, and yet we are not healed. What is wanting to us then? Is it teaching? No, but it is humility, faith, and even the desire to be healed. Oh! how this woman esteems herself happy at this moment! how she rejoices over the innocent deception which she believes herself to have practised upon Jesus! But she did not know yet the great favours which were in store for her, and of which she is about, after a moment of trial, to taste all the sweetness.

SECOND POINT.

Public confirmation of the healing of this woman.

1. Enquiries of Jesus. 1. An enquiry full of knowledge. *And Jesus, immediately knowing in Himself that virtue had gone out of Him, turned Him about in the press, and said, Who touched My clothes?* Jesus required an acknowledgement of what had taken place, and was not seeking for information. He was not ignorant who had touched Him, He knew all the actions of this poor woman, He knew all the thoughts of her heart. But Jesus acted therein as though He had no other knowledge than that of a purely external and human experience. Let us admire this infinite knowledge of Jesus, and remember that every where we are present to His eyes. 2. An enquiry full of majesty. At this movement of Jesus, and at the interrogation, the crowd drew back, every one excused themselves and denied that it was them. Such are we, always ready to excuse ourselves. Untruth itself costs us nothing when it is a matter of avoiding the least blame or the least reproach. What will become of me, Lord, when in the day of Thine anger, Thou wilt cast a terrible look upon sinners, and that Thou wilt ask then, not who it is that touched Thee, but who it is that has pierced, crucified, despised, and outraged Thee, who has profaned Thy Sacraments, abused Thy grace, trodden under foot Thy Blood, and Thy merits? Then denial and falsehood will no longer find a place, the truth will be made public and manifest. While the people were excusing themselves, the woman, abashed, remained concealed among the crowd, with her eyes cast down and keeping silence, anxious and uncertain what

she ought to do; but her doubt was soon enlightened.
3. An enquiry full of discernment. *When all denied, Peter, and they that were with Him, said, Master, the multitude throng Thee, and press Thee, and sayest Thou, Who touched Me? And Jesus said, somebody hath touched Me; for I perceive that virtue is gone out of Me;* a miraculous work hath taken place. Jesus distinguishes amongst those who followed Him, the crowd of people whose eagerness He approves, and whose failings He bore with, and then amongst the multitude, He distinguishes those fervent souls, who, though hidden in the crowd, did not share in their levity, inattention, and distraction. Let us be of that number, and let us know how to draw down upon ourselves, by secret impressions, by a deep recollectedness, and by an intimate communication, the favours of Jesus Christ.

2. The acknowledgement of the woman. 1. A prompt acknowledgement. Whilst Jesus was telling His disciples that a miracle had gone forth from Him, He was looking *round about to see her that had done this thing. The woman, knowing what was done in her,* saw then clearly that it was of herself that He spoke, and that, if she had been able to conceal her action from the knowledge of the people and of the disciples, she had not been able to hide herself from that of the Master. However great her fear and her confusion were, when she *saw that she was not hid,* she did not persist in her silence, but came trembling before Jesus, and presented herself before Him in order to confess all to Him. We shall see hereafter that the Divine Saviour will speak to the traitor Judas in a yet clearer and more precise manner, and that this unhappy man will not choose to understand His words. There is a great difference between a timid soul who fears to have done wrong, although without intending to do so, and a heart which is set upon the evil which it does, and which is given up to the excesses of its own evil passions. The one is attentive to every thing, and sensible to the least remorse: the other hears nothing, is hardened to every thing, and blinds itself

more and more. 2. A humble acknowledgement; *she came trembling, and fell down before Him, and told Him all the truth.* Her heart was yet more humbled before Him than her body. She accuses herself inwardly of rashness and temerity, and fears lest she is guilty of impiety and sacrilege. Ah! it is for me, O my God, to throw myself at Thy Feet, to be seized with fear at Thy judgments and with horror at myself, at the sight of the number and enormity of my sins. 3. A sincere acknowledgment. This woman, who had taken so much care to conceal herself, who feared nothing so much as to make herself known to all the people, who dared not even present herself before Jesus, now prostrate at His feet, surrounded by these very people, who have their eyes fixed upon her, *she declared unto Him, before all the people, for what cause she had touched Him;* that is to say, she declares publicly all that has taken place in her, the incurable malady with which she was afflicted, the secret artifice she had made use of, and lastly, *how she was healed immediately.* How good and loving is Jesus, and how profitable to us are the trials to which He puts us! If we did but know how to accuse ourselves before Him, with the trust, the humility, and sincerity of this woman, how pleasing to Him would such conduct be, and of what profit to ourselves!

3. The decision of Jesus. 1. A decision which the people were awaiting with eagerness. The people and the disciples had not understood any thing from the words of the Saviour; but what must have been their surprise at the account which this woman gave! After having heard her speak, they did not know what to think of her, they did not venture to judge whether she were innocent or guilty, they waited till the Master should decide, and they remained attentive to that which He was about to utter. 2. A decision which this woman accepts beforehand. After the acknowledgement which she has just made, what are her thoughts? what will her fate be? what will become of her? Will the health she has received be taken away from her again, because

she had, as it were, gained it by deceit? she does not believe it. Will she receive a public and severe reprimand? she believes herself to deserve it. Will her fault be forgiven her, and her error be excused? she hopes it. Whatever happens to her she places herself in the hands of her Judge, submissive to all, and ready to accept all which it may please Him to decide upon. 3. A decision in which the goodness and gentleness of Jesus are manifested. Happy woman! you will soon, by your own experience, learn to know your Saviour. You know already how powerful He is, how all-wise; learn now how good He is. The woman, healed and trembling, was not long left in uncertainty of her fate: the tender name of daughter which Jesus bestows upon her announces to her her happiness, and from that moment disperses all her fears. The answer which she received from Him was the praise of her faith, and the confirmation of her healing. *Daughter, be of good comfort: thy faith hath made thee whole: go in peace.*

Prayer. What peace, O great God! what peace! Happy fear, which leads to so delicious a peace! Inspire me, Lord, with the feelings of this woman, that I may draw down upon myself Thy mercy, so that I may obtain healing, and be made a partaker of that true peace which will be followed hereafter by eternal glory. Amen.

Meditation LXXIII.

DEATH OF THE DAUGHTER OF JAIRUS.

Death of the daughter of Jairus. S. Mark v. 35, 36. S. Luke viii. 49—56.

While He yet spake, there cometh one from the ruler of the synagogue's house, saying to him, Thy daughter is dead; trouble not the Master. But when Jesus heard it, He answered him, saying, Fear not; believe only, and she shall be made whole. If the faith of Jairus was to receive its perfect confirmation by the healing of this woman, it was subjected at the same time, and in the same place, to a severe trial. Jesus was still speaking to the woman who had been healed, when some one came to announce to the ruler of the synagogue that his daughter was dead, adding that it was not needful to weary the Master any more, nor to give Him the fatigue of a further journey. What a thunder-stroke for this father! He was walking with Jesus, Whom he had just beheld work a miracle; and just as he was feeling assured of the healing of his daughter, he is told of her death. Oh death! how many hopes dost thou not destroy, how many projects dost thou not overthrow! There is nothing but the hope which we have put in Jesus which thou canst not destroy. This death is a lesson for two sorts of persons in particular, and for every body in general.

FIRST POINT.

A lesson for young persons of her own sex.

Let them contemplate here the daughter of Jairus who is just dead, or some other of those whom they have seen die about the same age. She is dead, this only child, this rich heiress, this young girl; neither her noble birth, nor the position of her father, nor the riches of her family, nor her youth and charms have been able to preserve her from death. Hardly had she made her appearance in the world, and already she is separated from it for ever. Alas, if she has loved it, this world; if the desire to please it has made her forget God: if the care of her body has made her forget that of her soul; if she has cultivated her beauty out of love of admiration; if her adornments have been a stumbling block to pure and innocent souls; if the charms of her mind and of her person have only been employed as a snare to lead others astray; if, proud of her advantages, she has opened her heart to pride and has allowed it to spend itself in chimerical projects, and an aimless life, what misery for her, what folly! death has destroyed them all, her plans and wishes. Oh! how much more wise is a Christian maiden, whom the thought of death makes to despise alike all that the world can offer her that is pleasant, and all that she herself may have that is agreeable to others; who, sure that she must die, and that she may die soon, either leaves the world with joy in order to cling only to Jesus Christ, or enters into the world with fear, and in the sole desire to fulfil the will of God!

SECOND POINT.

A lesson for parents.

She is dead, this cherished daughter, the object of your tenderness, the happiness of your life, and the foundation of your hopes. If you have received her as a gift from the hands of God, as a loan which is entrusted to you, by One Who claims the right to take it back again when it pleases Him: if you have brought her up in the principles of religion; if you have formed her heart in the ways of holiness: if you have kept far from her every thing that might wound her innocence, then indeed you have lost nothing; her happiness is complete, and ought to form your consolation. But if, on the contrary, you have looked upon her as something which belonged only to yourselves; if you have brought her up only with ambitious views and for worldly glory; if, in order to enrich her, you have committed acts of injustice, or neglected the poor; if you have been the first to stifle in her the seeds of virtue which you thought contrary to your views, to disquiet her mind with regard to a devotion which was not according to your own tastes, to put an obstacle in the way of any call from God, which you had only the right to enquire into, but not to check; if you have given all your care to make her enjoy the world, and to take her to its assemblies, and its various amusements; if you have sanctioned books which were capable of corrupting both her heart and mind, if you have nourished luxury and vanity in her, or tolerated or even approved of dress, or light conversation, unbefitting a Christian maiden; if you have allowed her to remain in ignorance of the mysteries and the duties of religion, in an habitual distaste for prayers, and works of charity, and kept her back from Sacraments and means of grace; then indeed you are to be pitied. She is dead; your grief is without consolation; her death is a punishment from heaven both upon yourselves and her. Her misfortune is irreparable, and your's, that is to say, your sin, can only be repaired by a lifelong repentance.

THIRD POINT.

A lesson for every body.

Be we who we may, young or old, one day we shall die. One day it will be said of us, He is dead, she is dead. O inevitable necessity! Our Lord, who till then had said nothing to Jairus, hearing the tidings which were brought to him, and seeing what a deep impression they made on his heart, reanimated his trust and faith thus shaken, and says to him, *Fear not; believe only, and she shall be made whole.* Such are the needful feelings for us to have with regard to death, and with which we ought to inspire dying persons; feelings of faith and trust which the devil will omit nothing in order to deprive us of. Then our sins will come back to our memory in all their grievousness; our good works will present themselves before us only with all their imperfections; our confessions, our Communions, will become for us a new subject of fear: but have trust, especially if we have till then done what we could to guard our souls; let us believe then, let us believe only, and it will be saved.

Prayer. Yes, O my God, when at this last moment, I shall have done all that depended on myself, I will rest myself in Thy mercy, I will hold fast by Thy Holy Word. I will neither listen to my doubts as to the past, nor to my uncertainty and my fears as to the future; I will abandon myself in perfect trust in Thy merits, I will die in the faith which Thou hast given me, in the Church which Thou hast founded, believing firmly what she believes, and rejecting entirely what Thy Holy Catholic and Apostolic Church rejects; and then, I will wait in peace, for the fruit of those divine words, of those consoling words, which shall be to my soul the assured pledge of Thy glory, which Thou didst speak to Jairus: *Believe only, and she shall be made whole.* Amen.

Meditation LXXIV.

PREPARATION FOR THE BURIAL OF THE DAUGHTER OF JAIRUS.

Examine here, 1. what changes death brings into a house; 2. what idea religion gives us of death; 3. what judgement the world passes on those truths of religion. S. Matt. ix. 23, 24. S. Mark v. 37—40. S. Luke viii. 51—53.

FIRST POINT.

What changes death brings into a house.

And when Jesus came into the ruler's house, and saw the minstrels and the people making a noise, and seeth the tumult, and them that wept and wailed greatly, He suffered no man to go in, save Peter, and James, and John, and the father and mother of the maiden. And all wept and bewailed her. Jesus entered into the house of Jairus, but what did He find there? Much noise, a great tumult, loud cries, and great apparel; but noise, tumult, cries, and apparel far different in death from that which was to be found there in life. Instead of that smiling pomp which is to be met with in the houses of the rich, instead of those gay feasts which captivate and fascinate, nothing is to be seen there but the sad embellishments of funereal pomp; and preparations for a sumptuous burial; instead of those cries of merriment, which were formerly heard there, nothing is any longer to be heard but sighs and groans. O death! how afflicting and bitter are the changes which thou dost cause, but how instructive! How truly dost thou discover to us the vanity of earthly things! By what fascination does it come to pass that thou canst not undeceive us as to their value!

SECOND POINT.

What idea religion gives us of death.

Death is but a sleep. *And when He was come in, He saith unto them, Why make ye this ado, and weep? the damsel is not dead, but sleepeth.* The Israelites, in the use of their language, called the death of a person who had but newly expired, his rest, or his sleep. Moreover, the death of this young girl, who was about to be raised up again, was not in reality, like that of other persons; it was only to last as long as a light sleep lasts. By this expression, Jesus teaches us how we should sometimes conceal a good action, under a name which should hide its greatness. He recalls to us at the same time, that death, according to the language of Scripture, and the teachings of religion, is truly only a sleep, that is to say, that we do not die entirely and for ever; that we must one day rise again, and begin our life again by the re-union of our soul with our body, and that this re-union will be eternal; that then there will be a new order of things and another world; that we shall be great or abject there, happy or miserable, each according to his good and evil works; that happiness will there be perfect, and unhappiness extreme, and both eternal. Such is our faith and our hope; truths capable indeed of drying our tears at the death of our friends, and those near to us, capable indeed of assuaging the fears which the thought of our own death causes us, capable indeed of making us give up everything and employ every moment of our present life solely with a view of the future life which awaits us.

THIRD POINT.

What judgement the world passes on these truths of religion.

And they laughed Him to scorn, knowing that she was dead. The world mocks at that which is spoken to it of another life, as those to whom Jesus spoke, laughed Him to scorn, and mocked at Him; but they are unseemly and injurious railleries, unjust and ill-founded railleries, useless railleries, hurtful to those who utter them.

1. Unseemly and injurious railleries. They do not doubtless understand the meaning of the words of the Saviour, and they might appear to them strange: but the reputation of Jesus and the authority which He had gained for Himself by His miracles ought at least to have inspired them with respect, to have made them suspend their judgement, to persuade them even that there was some hidden truth under those words which they did not perceive? And it is thus that the disciples and the father and the mother of the girl reasoned. The profligate man mocks at the effects of death, he laughs at belief in another life, and all that he hears about it appears to him chimerical; but the authority of religion, of Holy Scripture, of the traditions of all nations and all centuries, have they then no weight? Has he studied that faith, that religion? Has he examined it, refuted it, and destroyed it? No: he does not give himself the trouble to do that, he turns it into ridicule, and makes a practice of turning everything into ridicule, and of making a joke of all belonging to it.

2. Unjust and ill-founded railleries. Those who laughed our Saviour to scorn, did so, because they knew well that the girl was dead; but they did not know that Jesus could, and willed, to bring her to life again. The father and the mother knew also well that their daughter was dead; but they did not cease to follow Him, and to wait to see what the effect of His words would be. The ungodly man has no other knowledge than that of his

senses; he sees only death, and believes that there is nothing beyond it; he sees only this world, and believes that there is no other: he only sees a small portion of things, and believes that he sees all. In vain does reason preach to him that God has not made men only to spend a short time on the earth, to be happy or unhappy there according to the caprice of a blind future, and thus to succeed one another eternally; that such a design could not be worthy of God, that it is contradictory to His greatness, His wisdom, and His equity: that this world is only the preparation for a new world, and this life, which is so short, is the germ of an immortal life. In vain does God Himself reveal to him these truths, and announce to him the magnificence of His works; he confines himself to what he sees; he would neither know nor believe anything besides.

3. Useless railleries, and hurtful to those who utter them. Jesus does not answer the railleries of these strangers, but He continues to act: He causes them to leave the house, and completes His work. Laugh, scoff, rail at and turn into ridicule as much as you will, ye unbelievers and profligates: in spite of you and independently of you, the work of God will advance, and will be accomplished. The Lord has raised up and has destroyed without your aid, in past centuries. By His order alone and independently of your own will, you have come into the world at the moment which He marked out: you live in it because He wills it; when He wills, you will groan under the weight of adversity, in the pains of sickness: lastly, at His will and independently of you, after having made you undergo all the infirmities of old age, He will mark out for you the hour of your departure from this world, and at the time prescribed by His will, you will go out of it; in spite of you, a new world will be formed; in spite of you, you will have the place in it which your works will have merited; in spite of you, sinners will be punished there, and the saints will be rewarded in a manner worthy of God, and you will see in all this the truth of His word fulfilled.

Prayer. As for me, Lord, who have been better instructed and more fully convinced of the truths of my religion, I will set myself to make a holy use of life in order to prepare myself for that death which is inevitable to all, and so desired by the true Christian. Help me to die, O my divine Saviour; to neglect nothing that may change those fearful sufferings which are laid upon the whole human race, into a sacrifice full of joy and love. Grant, O divine Jesus, that whether I live or whether I die, I may be always Thine: grant that the last sigh of my life may be a sigh of love which may conduct me into Thine eternal glory, there to dwell with Thee for ever. Amen.

Meditation LXXV.

RAISING OF THE DAUGHTER OF JAIRUS.

This resurrection may be looked upon as the image of the resurrection of a soul to the life of grace, or to a fervent life, and it will furnish us with five observations. S. Matt. ix. 25, 26, S. Mark v. 40—43. S. Luke viii. 54—56.

1. The preliminaries of the resurrection.

But when He had put them all out, He taketh the father and the mother of the damsel, and them that were with Him, and entereth in where the damsel was lying. Jesus caused the tumultuous crowd which filled the house of Jairus to leave it, and only kept with Him His three disciples, and the father and mother of the young girl: He entered with them into the room, and drew near to the couch on which the young girl was stretched motionless and lifeless. The first step towards the resurrection or conversion of our souls, is retirement and silence. Let us begin by banishing those cares, those occupations, those visits, those conversations, those useless books, that crowd of thoughts, of plans, designs, and desires which occupy us. Let us retain of all that, only what is absolutely necessary and requisite to our station in life, only that which is holy, and may lead us to good: then Jesus will come to us, He will enter into our inmost souls, where death reigns: He will drive it thence, and restore us to life.

2. The manner in which the resurrection is effected.

And He took the damsel by the hand, and said unto her, Talitha cumi: which is, being interpreted, Damsel, I say unto thee, arise. O powerful Hand! Thou dost join Thyself to a motionless hand, which death has rendered icy, Thou dost deign to touch a dead body, and Thou dost restore it to warmth, movement, and life! O life-giving voice! Thou dost pierce the deepest abysses: the empire of death is shaken by it, it recognizes its Conqueror, and Thou dost compel it to yield up again the prey which it had already seized. Touch my heart, O Jesus! speak to my heart, and life will be restored to it. There is none but Thou, O God, Who, by the application of Thy merits and the inward voice of Thy grace, canst bring me back to life.

3. In what resurrection consists.

And her spirit came again. At this voice of Jesus, the soul returned into the body which it had forsaken, and this young girl found herself full of health, strength, and life. Spiritual resurrection is the return of the Holy Spirit into our hearts, in order to shed abroad there the grace of justification and of holiness, in order to make us live a new life, fruitful in virtues and in good works. If we continue to conduct ourselves according to the spirit of the world, a spirit of pride, of dissipation, pleasure, impurity, avarice, revenge, then our resurrection has nothing real in it, it is a pure delusion.

4. The tokens of resurrection.

And straightway the damsel arose, and walked. And He commanded that something should be given her to eat. If we are truly raised from the death of sin, we ought to begin by leaving off our evil habits, that is to say, by renouncing our inordinate inclinations, by forsaking all occasions of sin, and overcoming our indolence and our lukewarmness in the service of God: we ought then to walk in the practice of virtue, and in the exact observance of God's commandments: lastly, after having proved and examined ourselves, we ought to eat the Bread of Life, to take delight in It, and partake of It as often as we have the opportunity.

5. The publication abroad of the resurrection.

And her parents were astonished: but He charged them that they should tell no man what was done. It would be impossible to describe better the surprise of those who were witnesses of so great a miracle. The disciples, although accustomed to the miracles which Jesus worked, had never seen any like this one. As for the father and mother, they were so besides themselves with joy, that they could hardly believe their eyes. Surprise, joy, gratitude, were mingled in their hearts, and deprived them of movement and of speech. Their transport would soon have burst forth publicly into praises and thanksgivings, if Jesus, anticipating their acclamations, had not imposed silence upon them, and forbidden them to make known to anyone what He had done for them. But the miracle shewed itself forth. Those who had seen the maiden dead, could not but recognize her when restored to life, *and the fame thereof went abroad into all that land.* The conversion of a sinner ought not to be published, either by him through whom it is effected, for that would be vanity; nor by him who is the subject of it, for that would be ostentation; nor by those to whom it has been confided, for that would be indiscretion: it ought to manifest itself of itself, in a simple unaffected manner. The soul which has been converted will reap a double advantage from his conversion. Some will scoff and mock, and that will serve as an expiation of the faults he has committed: others will be touched and edified by it, and that will serve as a reparation for the scandal which he has given.

Prayer. O divine Jesus, Who dost restore life to the sinner, and makest even the dead to hear Thee! speak to my heart as Thou didst to the daughter of

Jairus. Let Thy invisible and all-powerful Hand touch mine, so as to make it active in good works. Grant that I may rise, that I may walk, that I may receive with spiritual hunger the Food which Thou dost set before me, so that I may live of Thy Spirit by feeding on Thy flesh, and that by a holy life, I may attain to Thy glory. Amen.

Meditation LXXVI.

HEALING OF THE TWO BLIND MEN.

In the healing of these blind men, we may observe five circumstances which form their glory and our confusion. S. Matt. ix. 27—31.

1. Their zeal and our faintheartedness.

Jesus passes by them, and they follow Him. *And when Jesus departed thence, two blind men followed Him, crying, and saying, Thou Son of David, have mercy on us.* After the resurrection of the daughter of Jairus, Jesus left Capernaum in order to go to Jerusalem, and passed through the villages and towns which lay on His way. Two blind men, hearing the crowd which accompanied Jesus, understood and were informed that it was He who passed by. They did not lose the opportunity: they seized the moment, and set off to follow Him, crying after Him, and saying with a loud and moving voice, *Thou Son of David, have mercy on us.* Let us admire their wisdom and their earnestness; let us deplore our folly, our cowardice, and our misfortune; our folly, in letting all the moments of our salvation which God sends us, escape from us. Festivals, solemn times, holy seasons of Lent, inspirations, distaste of the world, longings after salvation, all these pass, and we remain always the same, always blind as to our truest interest, which is our sanctification. Our cowardice: we only lift at most towards Heaven some faint and imperfect sighs, instead of that strong and earnest cry which would rescue us from the sad state of blindness in which we are living. Our misfortune: we do not know our misery and the need we have of the mercy of God. We are blind as to our sins, our faults, our bad habits, our obligations, the dangers which surround us, the nothingness of the things of this world, and the importance of salvation. We are blind as to the ways of God and of perfection, the excellence of spiritual gifts, the value of the graces which God bestows on fervent souls, and the daily losses which we suffer of those graces: and far from perceiving our blindness, we pride ourselves on our pretended enlightenment. O Son of David! Messiah sent from God! Son of God, Saviour of men, have mercy on us!

2. Their perseverance and our levity.

Jesus Christ enters into a house, and they draw near to Him. *And when He was come into the house, the blind men came to Him.* Jesus, having entered with His disciples into the house where He was about to lodge, the blind men followed Him thither, and yielded to no discouragement until they reached Him. How happy they were when they knew themselves to be in His presence. With what joy, with what movements of hope were not their hearts animated. They could not see Him: but they knew Him to be present and they hoped soon to see Him. Let us admire their perseverance, and deplore our own levity. Jesus Christ is in His House, He is present in the Holy Eucharist; we have access to Him there, and the entrance is free; how do we profit by our opportunities? If we enter His House, is it in order to draw nigh to Him and ask Him for His grace? Present in body, are we not more often absent in heart and in mind? with what love, with what reverence, with what desire, with what joy, with what hope are we animated, when we find ourselves in His Presence? Alas! we hardly remember that we are there.

3. The warmth of their faith, and the feebleness of our's.

Jesus Christ asks them questions, and they answer Him. *Jesus saith unto them, Believe ye that I am able to do this? they said unto Him, Yea, Lord.* By this reply, they shew forth the power of Jesus Christ and the faith which they have in Him. It is as if they said, Yea, doubtless, Lord, Thou canst: yes, certainly we believe that Thou canst. Let us admire the warmth of their faith, and let us deplore the weakness of our's. Ah! when we pray, let us imagine to ourselves that Jesus Christ is putting the same question to us which He put to those blind men: *Believe ye that I am able to do this?* But let us remember that in asking us this question, this divine Saviour sees the depth of our hearts. If He asks for the acknowledgment of our lips, it is only in order that the expression of our words may increase yet more the feelings of our hearts. Let us then often utter with our lips the words of faith and confidence with which these blind men answered our Lord, in order to deepen more and more in ourselves the feeling we ought to have, that Jesus Christ can do everything, and that nothing is impossible to Him either in the order of grace, or in the order of nature. It is with this faith that we ought to draw near to Him, to address to Him our prayers, and to receive Him in the Holy Communion.

4. Their reward and our punishment.

Jesus Christ touches their eyes, and they recover their sight. After the confession of faith which these two blind men had just made, Jesus Christ *touched their eyes, saying, According to your faith be it unto you.* O happy blind men! O worthy reward of your faith! ye see Him at length, this divine Saviour; He was the first object upon which your eyes were fixed. What were then your transports! what was your love! Jesus Christ touches us, Jesus Christ comes to us and is within us, and we are not enlightened, but walk on always in darkness, and live on always in the same blindness. It is the punishment of our want of faith, do not be surprised at it, it is unto us *according to our faith.* Let us remember without ceasing this terrible truth: always and in every thing, it will be done unto us according to our faith; and that will be the measure of the grace which we shall receive. Do we desire then to merit and to obtain the mercy of God? let us encourage ourselves and stir up within us the feelings of the most lively faith. Now, we may distinguish four degrees of this faith to which we must strive to attain. The first degree is that by which we feel assured that we are in the presence of our God, and our Saviour, and then we shall act and feel both outwardly and inwardly in a manner which answers to this assurance. The second degree is that by which Jesus Christ makes us hear His voice in the depth of our hearts, and when we answer to Him. Sweet intercourse, full of charms and always too short! The third degree of faith is brought about by an inward touch, which stirs up in our heart motions which make themselves felt, and a devotion so tender, that we experience, so to say, in a tangible manner, that God makes Himself one with our souls, and our souls one with Him. The fourth consists in an abundance of insight into spiritual things, which seems to dissipate the darkness of our faith. We see Jesus Christ, or rather the veil which covers Him from us is, so to say, so transparent, that, without hiding this Divine Object from our sight, it only serves to conceal His splendour, so that the soul not being dazzled and intimidated by It, it may delight in its God with greater familiarity and delight.

5. Their gratitude and our ingratitude.

Jesus Christ forbids them to speak of this miracle, and they publish it everywhere, *And He straitly charged them, saying, See that no man know it. But they, when they were departed, spread abroad His fame in all that country.* How little we follow the example of Christ, we who like so much that people should speak of us, of the good which we do, or which is to be found in us; we who are perhaps the first to speak of it ourselves! How little we follow the example of these blind men, after they were healed, we who are little occupied with talking of Jesus Christ, of His Power, His Goodness, His benefits.

Prayer. Have pity on me, Son of David; open the eyes of my heart, disperse the darkness of my soul; I entreat Thee with earnestness, and I will persevere in prayer, until I shall obtain from Thee this miracle of Thy power. Increase in me the faith which is the source of this prayer, and the measure by which Thou dost proportion Thy gifts. Do not limit these Thy benefits, O Jesus, grant that after my prayers have been heard by Thee, I may imitate the gratitude of these blind men, that I may bless Thee without ceasing, that I may never forget Thy mercies, that Thy love may be always in my heart, Thy praises always in my lips; that I may leave nothing undone that lies in my power, in order that all may know Thee, love and glorify Thee in time and in eternity. Amen.

Meditation LXXVII.

HEALING OF A DUMB MAN POSSESSED WITH A DEVIL.

Observe 1. the sad condition of this dumb man; 2. the miracle which was wrought in his favour; 3. the remarks made upon this deliverance by the multitudes. S. Matt. ix. 32—34.

FIRST POINT.

The sad condition of the dumb man.

As the two blind men who had been healed *went out* from the presence of Jesus Christ, *behold, they brought to Him a dumb man possessed with a devil.* Whether this man was dumb from his birth, and possessed as well as dumb, or whether it was rather the devil who made him dumb, his condition was one the saddest that can be imagined.

1. Because, in this condition, he could not fulfil the greater part of the duties of life. Is it not through the power which the devil exercises over us, that we often fail in fulfilling the greater part of the duties of our Christian life ? 1. The duties of prayer. When it is a question of our prayers, are we not often dumb ? At Church or at home, in private prayer or in public prayer, are we not without words, without feelings ? If we repeat from habit or out of a sense of obligation some vocal prayers, is not our heart silent, does it take any part in them, and for the want of this language of the heart, although our mouth utters the words, is it not true that we remain dumb, and do not pray ? 2. The duties of our station in life. If we are obliged, from our position, to teach, to reprove, to correct, to set forth the truths of salvation, do we not dispense ourselves from doing so, and by so doing, do we not fall under the power of the dumb spirit ? 3. The duties of religion, justice, and charity. Do we not violate all these duties by maintaining a disgraceful and timid silence, when we ought to speak, when we ought to support the cause of God against those who attack the faith, or who speak words which are not convenient, and thereby wound innocent and pure minds : the cause of the innocent against those who oppress him : the cause of our neighbour against those who are slandering him ? Oh! how many duties does this dumb devil make us neglect daily! Oh! how many sins he makes us commit, with which perhaps we do not reproach ourselves, or are not conscious of!

2. Sad situation of the dumb man, because he could not remove his sufferings. In bemoaning our troubles to others, we seem to find relief: in making them known to others, we excite their compassion, and their sympathy seems to us a diminution of our trouble. In laying bare the nature of our sorrow, and the source of

our troubles, we may receive wholesome advice which may strengthen us, and point out to us the means either of receiving healing, or of alleviating our sufferings; but when we are possessed with a dumb devil, we are left to our own mercy, and all the severity of our fate. It is no longer by a real possession that the devil renders us dumb, for it is always in our power to break the fatal silence to which he desires to subject us: but it is for us to arm ourselves against his artifices, and not to fall into the snares which he lays for us. In matters of faith, in matters of morals, let us beware of any one who recommends silence to us. The first endeavour of an evil spirit, who seeks to lead us astray, is to close the mouth of him who listens to him, to recommend and require inviolable secrecy. Oh! how many souls this dumb spirit, this fatal secrecy has plunged into vice, error, and hell!

3. Sad situation of the dumb man, because he could not entreat to be healed, however much need he had to be healed. *They brought to Him a dumb man.* It is to the charity of those who presented him to Jesus that this man owed his cure. What these charitable persons did, we ought to do ourselves, and break at length the obstinate silence which has prevented us from having recourse to those who have received the power to heal us. Why should we suffer any longer, the poignant remorse of a conscience which we can only silence by speaking ourselves, and by sincerely confessing our sins? O dumb devil, how many souls dost thou torment, how many souls hast thou lost! Alas! even when we confess our sins thou dost tie the tongue, and hinder our speaking out: thou dost lead us to dissimulate, to disguise the truth, and to misrepresent our faults even whilst confessing them; and in place of the cure which we have come to seek, we make ourselves yet more criminal, and more possessed of the devil than ever. Are we not in one or other of these conditions? If we are, let us pray to Him who alone can deliver us from them; if we are not, let us pray for those who are: let

us imitate the charity of those who presented the dumb man to our Lord, and let us pray Him to heal them.

SECOND POINT.

Speech is restored to the dumb man.

And when the devil was cast out, the dumb spake.
There are four kinds of persons who speak.

1. Some speak, because the devil has been driven out of them. They are those who sincerely confess their sins, who pray with fervour, from whom are heard only words of gentleness, patience, resignation, humility, charity, and edification. Are we of this number?

2. Some speak, because the devil has not been driven out of them. They are those, whose conversation is, as formerly, filled with vanity and self conceit, with murmurs and impatience, with levity and dissipation; who speak without restraint, and who neither respect the holiness of religion, nor the rules of decorum, nor the inviolable acts of charity. Does not one or other of these vices enter into our conversation? Let us examine our words, and we shall know by our language with what spirit we are animated.

3. Some speak, in order to drive away the devil. Let us hearken to the word of God, and those who speak to us for our good and for the edification of our soul. Let us speak thus ourselves to others. Let us seek for pious conversations, let us love to read good books, and let us help others to share in them.

4. Others speak, in order to bring in or detain the devil. Let us avoid all seductive and scandalous conversation, let us give up reading all evil books, even useless books, which might make us lose our time, distract our minds, and dry up our hearts. Not only books, but also paintings, sculptures, engravings have their language, and a language so much the more pernicious and more fitting to bring in the devil, as it is more intelligible and perceptible to the senses.

THIRD POINT.

The remarks made by the multitudes on the deliverance of this dumb man.

1. *The remarks of men of upright hearts.* The multitudes marvelled, saying, It was never so seen in Israel. Such is the language of uprightness and good sense. Faith is always the same, and always preserves its character: and still now-a-days faith follows with simplicity the guidance of reason and good sense: it is founded on the evidence of facts, and it cannot deceive us. We say still to-day, when reading the Gospel; Never, in any other religion, has any thing been written like this: and in reading the history of the world; never, in any religion, has the like been believed. So just an admiration enraptures and exalts our faith, and renders it immovable.

2. *The remarks made by men of prejudiced minds.* But the Pharisees said, He casteth out devils through the prince of the devils. Could there be a more senseless prejudice? It is, nevertheless, all that men have found to oppose to the miracles of Christ during several centuries. If we appeal even to the unbelievers of our days, what do they think of such reasonings? What objections do they raise against miracles so evident? They deny them. Is it then now the time to deny them, when those who have seen them then did not dare to do so, and could not do so? Miracles which converted those who saw them, which converted the whole universe! it would be difficult to say whether of the two would be the most senseless, to deny them after seventeen centuries in which they have been believed, or to attribute them to the devil.

3. *The remarks made by men on the miracles of grace.* The same difference between the people and the Pharisees, in the judgement passed and the remarks made, is still to be found amongst people now-a-days, with regard to those whom God's grace delivers from the devil, and who are sincerely converted. Those who are

truly just and upright admire God's power, and bless Him for it: the ungodly mock at it, and attribute this change to human motives, or even to sinful motives, of which the devil alone could be the author. Let us abstain from similar language, or if such words are applied to ourselves, let us be none the less earnest in working out our own salvation, nor less occupied with our sanctification.

Prayer. Lord, Thou wilt open my lips, and my mouth shall shew forth Thy praise, and I will speak only of Thee, to Thee, and for Thee. O Jesus! drive away the dumb devil, that is to say, the evil spirit of pride, hatred, envy, and prejudice, and then I shall live and acknowledge with a glad heart all the good which Thou dost work in my brethren. Amen.

Meditation LXXVIII.

JESUS PASSES THROUGH THE CITIES AND VILLAGES.

Meditate here, 1. On the mission of Christ; 2. On the compassion which He showed to those who followed Him; 3. His words under these circumstances. S. Matt. ix. 35—38.

FIRST POINT.

The mission of Jesus Christ.

Observe His journeys, His labours, and His miracles.

1. *The journeys of Jesus Christ. And Jesus went about all the cities and villages, teaching in their synagogues, and preaching the gospel of the kingdom, and healing every sickness and every disease among the people.* Jesus passed on foot through the towns, cities, and villages. His zeal despises nothing, neglects nothing: it extends equally to great and small, towards the rich who dwell in the towns, and the poor who live in the country: thus He has willed that in His Church, large

places as well as the smallest, should be equally provided with ministers of the Gospel, who, in their apostolic labours should have Him for their example, their support and their helper in difficulties or in trials. Let us not, through our own fault, make the labours and the wearinesses of Jesus Christ and His ministers of no avail.

2. *The labours of Jesus Christ.* Why does He thus pass through *the cities and villages?* It is in order to *teach* there the knowledge of salvation, to *preach* there the *Gospel*, and to set forth there *the kingdom* of God. To this all His efforts are directed, and in this He seeks His only relaxation. Painful journeys, laborious missions signalised by the abundant outpouring of His mercies, such is the history of His life; He does nothing, He undertakes nothing but for the salvation of souls; He labours unceasingly at it. On the days of public assemblies, He teaches publicly in the synagogues: on other days, He teaches in all places and on all occasions, or rather always and at all times He devotes Himself to the painful exercise of His zeal and charity. Let us thank this divine Pastor, and let us imitate Him in His functions, each one according to our station.

3. *The miracles of Jesus Christ.* Everywhere where He went, He *healed every sickness and every disease among the people*, and shewed Himself in that, the true Saviour of Israel. The power which He exercised over the bodies of men was the sensible proof of the power which He had over their souls. Let us pray Him, this divine Saviour, to heal our souls, and let us present them to Him, such as He sees them, laden with *every sickness and every disease* which He alone can heal.

SECOND POINT.

Compassion of Jesus Christ.

But when He saw the multitudes, He was moved with compassion on them because they fainted, and were scattered abroad, as sheep having no shepherd.

1. Jesus had compassion on them, because they were

wearied, or rather yet more because they were tormented, afflicted, and vexed with sicknesses, infirmities, and miseries, from which they did not know how to draw forth any profit; because they were laden with the weight of their sins, which they did not seek to free themselves from; because they were led away, and taken captive by their passions, without having any means of fighting against them and overcoming them.

2. Jesus had compassion on them, because they were scattered abroad, or rather yet more because they were discouraged, downcast, bent down towards the ground, thinking only of things of this earth, only occupied with this present life, and their own interests, without any one to raise them up, and bring them back to thoughts of heaven, their soul, and eternity.

3. Jesus had compassion on them, because they were as sheep having no shepherd, abandoned to the fury of the wolves, that is to say, exposed to the corruption of evil example, to the seduction of vice and error, without having any one to forewarn them and to guard them against so many dangers. Alas! how many are there who find themselves in the same condition, in the same forsaken state! Am I not also myself in this condition, not from want of instruction, but from want of profiting by that I have received; not from want of pastors, but because I do not listen to those which have been given to me. And in truth, does not their zeal fatigue me? does not their care for my soul seem to me troublesome, and uncalled for? Do not I even go so far as to feel indifference, nay, even perhaps, hatred, or contempt for their ministry, and wish that I might be free from it?

THIRD POINT.

The words of Jesus Christ.

Then saith He unto His disciples, The harvest truly is plenteous, but the labourers are few; Pray ye therefore the Lord of the harvest, that He will send forth labourers into His harvest. Thus,

MEDITATION LXXVIII.

1. We ought to pray, in order that God may send forth labourers, that He may multiply them in His Church, that He may animate them with a spirit of zeal, that He may support them, and that they may gather in the abundant harvest which there is there. But do we enter into these words of our Saviour? do we feel the need which there is that labourers to preach the Gospel should be multiplied? do we pray God that He may send some? Are we not rather of the number of those politicians and philosophers, who only think of the present time, who look upon the ministers of God, as useless men, whose number cannot well be too limited? How far different will their thoughts be in eternity?

2. We must not seek to turn aside those whom God calls to His ministry, we must not put hindrances in the way of their vocation, nor prevent them from following it, but on the contrary, we should esteem them happy in that God calls them to so holy an employment, and if they belong to us in any way, we should look upon it as a blessing sent us by God. Those who feel themselves thus called by God ought to take great care not to resist His call; they must seek to overcome all obstacles, and prefer on this occasion the obedience which they owe to God to that which is due to men. But, on the other hand, they must feel convinced that it is God Who calls them, Who sends them. Woe be to those who of themselves, and from human motives, take upon themselves the sacred ministry! woe be to those who lead them to do so!

3. We ought not to trouble those whom God has sent, nor cross them in their undertakings, nor disquiet them so as to hinder their work, nor bring their work into disrepute, so as to hinder the success of their labours, but on the contrary, we should do all in our power to help, encourage, and cheer them. If it were not for the obstacles which the malice of men, and the fury of devils, have opposed to the zeal of the ministers of the Gospel, all the world would be Christian, all heathen countries would have embraced the Catholic religion, and piety

would flourish in all Christian lands. Woe then to those who shall have given their help to the devil, in order to furnish obstacles, and fight the battles of those who are opposed to religion? How overwhelming and terrible will be the judgment which will be pronounced upon them at the tribunal of Jesus Christ at the last day!

Prayer. I thank Thee, O my Saviour, for all the sufferings, and all the fatigues which Thou didst undergo for my salvation; suffer them not to be useless to me. O divine Shepherd of our souls! at the sight of Thy labours, of Thy painful journeyings, of Thy laborious missions, who would not blush to remain in idleness, to seek for repose, and to avoid every thing which brings work on them? Who would not desire to enter into the participation of Thy journeyings, Thy sufferings, and Thy toils? Happy they whom their station in life calls to such honourable duties! Grant, O God, that all those whom Thou dost call to the sacred ministry, may be multiplied in numbers, and strengthened in holiness, and may enter into a share of Thy labours on earth, and Thy glory in Heaven. Amen.

Meditation LXXIX.

CHOICE OF THE APOSTLES.

Consider, 1. the circumstances of this choice; 2. those who were chosen; 3. that which concerns the traitor Judas. S. Matt. x. 1—4. S. Mark iii. 13—19. S. Luke vi. 12—16.

FIRST POINT.

The circumstances under which this choice took place.

Examine what precedes it, what accompanies it, and what follows it.

1. What precedes this choice. *And it came to pass in those days, that He went out into a mountain to pray, and continued all night in prayer to God.* Jesus,

having sent away the people who were following Him, withdrew in the evening to a mountain, where He passed the night in prayer; thus He prepared Himself, by fasting, retirement, and prayer, for the important act which He was about to perform on the morrow. Who can imagine what this converse of Jesus Christ with God His Father must have been, with regard to the establishment and the growth of His Church, of which He was about to lay the foundations? It is thus we ought to pray ourselves, and seek counsel from the Lord in all our undertakings, especially if they are of any importance, and above all, if they regard the service of God, and the choice of the ministers of His Church. It is thus that the Church herself acts at the four seasons of ordinations. Let us then observe carefully the fasts which she appoints at these special times with this intention, and let us join our prayers to her's that God may give unto her worthy ministers. The glory of Jesus Christ, that of religion, the salvation of mankind, and our own in particular, depends upon this choice; can it then be indifferent to us?

2. How this choice was made. The people who knew whither Jesus had withdrawn, went there in crowds at break of day, and remained, waiting, at the foot of the mountain. *And when it was day, He called unto Him His disciples; and of them He chose twelve, whom also He named apostles, that they should be with Him, and that He might send them forth to preach.* First of all He called to Him His disciples, of whom some were to be chosen, and the others were to be witnesses of His choice: *He called them unto Him into a mountain*, in order to teach the ministers of the Church, that they were not to content themselves with the ordinary life of the people, but to seek to raise themselves up to Jesus, by a life, set apart, of holiness, and a high degree of perfection. Then He chose those *whom He would;* not those who wished it themselves, not those whom the assembly of disciples wished, not those whose relations or friends desired it, much less those who would only

have presented themselves with ambitious views, or with those of self-love, or self-interest. The will of God, such is the only rule which should be followed in the choice of the ministers of the Church. Lastly *of them He chose twelve.* The promises made to Abraham, and the figures which had announced them, are now beginning to be accomplished. Here is the Son, Who was promised to him, typified by Isaac, and in Whom all the nations of the world were to be blessed : here are the twelve heads of the twelve tribes, by whom a new and spiritual Israel is to be formed, and through whom the children of promise are about to multiply and to exceed the number of the stars of Heaven, and of the sand that is on the sea shore. We read the Old Testament, we see what takes place in the New : can we fail to be filled with admiration in contemplating here the works of God in the foundation of His Church ? To Thee alone does it belong of right, O my God, thus to order times and seasons, to announce by types, during several centuries, the effect of Thy promises, and to accomplish them in a glorious manner, at the time foretold. For nearly eighteen hundred centuries, do the Christian nations, spread throughout the world, where they are daily making fresh progress, acknowledge the authority given by Thy well-beloved Son, to the twelve apostles, to be its founders and teachers: what happiness for us to belong to this Holy, Catholic, and Apostolic Church !

3. What follows this choice. At first Jesus gave to the twelve disciples whom He had just chosen the name of apostles, that is to say, messengers, because they were to be His messengers to men, to announce to them the joyful covenant which God was making with them, and to teach them what they must do in order to have a part in it; the apostleship and mission which was to continue to the end of time, and without which no one has any lawful office in the House of God, and is only an intruder into the ministry, and his work is without authority. Such is the privilege of the Church, that the mission of those who teach in her can be carried back visibly,

by an uninterrupted succession up to the apostles, and through them, to Jesus Christ Himself. Then *He ordained these twelve apostles, that they should be with Him,* and so to say, under His direction, in order that He might send them to preach when and where He should see fit. Such is still the work of those who embrace the ministerial call: that they should be ready at all times to go and preach the kingdom of God, where He calls them. They must be constantly with Jesus by keeping themselves in a state of inner recollectedness, in order that they may hear His voice, and go, speak, act, at His command, and in order that pride may not bring them into distractions, nor success into vanity. Finally, Jesus, *when He had called unto Him His twelve disciples, gave them power against unclean spirits, to cast them out, and to heal all manner of sickness and all manner of disease.* Such are still the duties of Christ's ministers, to heal the sick and to drive away evil spirits, to heal the wounds of the soul, to nourish it, to strengthen it, to chase away its lukewarmness, to bring it into a state of health and strength, by instructions, exhortations, warnings, corrections, and by the administration of the Sacraments, to make a continual war against the devil, by driving away superstition, error, heresy, vices, and causes of offence. Happy he who sacrifices his life, his rest, his enjoyments, and his health to those divine offices!

SECOND POINT.

Of those who were chosen.

1. Of the twelve apostles in general. *Now the names of the twelve apostles are these; The first, Simon, who is called Peter, and Andrew his brother: James the son of Zebedee, and John, his brother; Philip, and Bartholomew: Thomas, and Matthew, the publican; James, the son of Alpheus, and Lebbeus, whose surname was Thaddeus; Simon the Canaanite, and Judas Iscariot, who also betrayed Him.* Who were these men

whom Jesus chose in order to found and establish His Church, to convert the universe, in order to unite all the people of the world in one common religion, in order to make them renounce their prejudices, their superstitions and their vices, in order to make them adore a God-man, poor, crucified, and dead for them? Men without name and without birth, without authority and credit, without worldly possessions and riches, without strength of arms, without letters or eloquence, without talents or gifts. If the enterprise had been wrecked from its commencement, we should not have been surprised; but when we see it, on the contrary, crowned with the most complete success, we cannot but exclaim; This is Thy work, O God: there is none but Thee, Who, with such feeble instruments, couldest have done such great things.

2. Of the eleven Apostles who were faithful to Jesus Christ, considered in particular. Piety and gratitude require of us that we should know who were our fathers in the faith, and that in the course of the year, we should celebrate the days which are set apart in honour of them, with deep feelings of love and reverence. The first mentioned of the twelve Apostles is S. Peter. S. Matthew and the other Evangelists place him first, although they do not follow the order in which the Apostles were called. The name of Peter was given him by our Lord, and we shall soon hear from His lips the meaning attached to this name. S. Andrew was the elder brother of S. Peter; he had known Jesus before him, and had himself brought his brother to Jesus. S. James and S. John were also brothers, both sons of Zebedee, and were surnamed Boanerges, that is to say, sons of thunder, in order to point out the strength and fire of their zeal. S. James is called the elder, in order to distinguish him from James, the son of Alphæus, either because he was the first to follow our Lord, or because he was the oldest. He is the first of the Apostles who shed his blood for Jesus' sake, and Spain recognizes him especially as her patron saint. S. John, surnamed the Evangelist, was the disciple so specially beloved of Jesus.

He was the youngest of the Apostles, and he died the last of them. These two brothers are, with S. Peter, the only three to whom our Lord gave a particular surname; they were the three who were the most intimate confidants of their Master, and they were with Him on several occasions to which the others were not admitted. There were besides two other brothers, with their cousin germain, namely, S. James, son of Alphæus, otherwise called Cleophas; S. Simon and S. Jude, surnamed Thaddeus. The three Evangelists put them always together, and call S. James, the son of Alphæus, which makes it seem as if he only were the son of Alphæus, or Cleophas, and of Mary, sister of S. Joseph, and that S. Simon and S. Jude were brothers, and sons of a person named James, who was married to another sister of S. Joseph, (*) from which these three Apostles are called the brethren of the Lord, because they were the nephews of S. Joseph, the supposed father of Jesus. This second S. James is called the less, in order to distinguish him from the first; it is he whom the Church at Jerusalem acknowledges as her first bishop; S. James wrote an Epistle; S. Jude wrote one also in which he calls himself the "brother of James," that is to say, his cousin germain. That which induces him to take upon himself this title, is, that S. James had already written a similar Epistle, and that besides, he was more known in Judea, in his office of bishop of Jerusalem. S. Matthew and S. Mark give to Simon the surname of Canaanite, which S. Luke interprets Zelotes. The three Evangelists place S. Philip in the fifth rank, and S. Bartholomew in the sixth. It was, in reality, the order in which they were admitted into the number of Jesus Christ's disciples, as we have already seen in S. John, which leaves no room for doubt that the Nathanael of S. John was the same as S. Bartholomew. We have also seen the call of S. Matthew, the

---

(*) Acts i. 13. There are several intepretations of this point which we do not profess to enter into, we keep here to the one which is most generally received.

son of another Alphæus; he alone, out of humility recalls here the remembrance of his former profession and calls himself, *Matthew the publican*, and puts himself after S. Thomas. The other Evangelists place S. Thomas after him. The latter, after having been, distinguished by his obstinate unbelief, signalised himself subsequently by the ardour of his faith.

3. Of the three Apostles who were not called at this time. S. Matthias was doubtless one of the disciples, who were witnesses of the choice which Jesus Christ made of His Apostles, and had no thought at that time that he should be one day raised to that high rank. It is to him that the place of the traitor Judas was given, which completed the number of the twelve. To these first twelve Apostles, who received on the day of Pentecost, the fulness of the Holy Spirit, two others were added afterwards: S. Paul, who is so often named in common with S. Peter, on account of the strangeness of his call and the greatness of his labours, and S. Barnabas, who was for a long time the companion of S. Paul in his journeys. Let us give due honour to these holy Apostles by whom the Gospel has come down to us, and, who at the end of time will judge the world with Jesus Christ. Let us commemorate them with fervour, and pray that at our death Jesus Christ may receive us with them into His eternal kingdom.

THIRD POINT.

Of the traitor Judas.

Judas, surnamed Iscariot, because he was from Cariot, a little town of Judea, and since, surnamed by just right, the traitor, because he betrayed Jesus, and gave Him up to the Jews; Judas furnishes us here with three subjects of the keenest surprise.

1. Is it not most surprising that, amongst a choice of twelve men, made by Jesus Christ, there should be one found who could have betrayed his ministry and his Master? That in so august a position, and in such

saintly fellowship, there should be found one soul so black, and one heart so perfidious? It is not always a sign that the choice has been ill-made, because he who has been chosen betrays his trust. However holy a state of life may be, it has its temptations and its dangers; however divine and inspired a calling may be, let us still always fear, and let us never think ourselves safe. The holiness of our state and of our calling may perhaps gain us honour in the sight of men, and dispose men's minds in our behalf; but it will not sanctify us in the sight of God, except so long as we pray and watch over ourselves, how we fulfil our duties. The fault of one ought not to recoil on the body of which he is a member; the body ought not to support and defend the fault of one of its members; but ought, on the contrary, to be the first to condemn it, and the most zealous to punish it.

2. Is it not surprising that a man who had begun so well, whose call came so evidently from heaven, who had responded to it with so much zeal, worked so many conversions and miracles, should have perished by the greatest of all crimes, and should have died a reprobate? It is not enough to begin well, we must persevere and finish well. The unworthiness of the minister does not affect his ministry. The virtue of Jesus Christ, of His word and Sacraments is the same in the most unworthy minister, and we should be equally guilty if we did not make use of them.

3. Lastly, can we hear without fear that he who had so long practised every virtue, overcome evil spirits, and all vices, should have let himself be overcome by the one from which of all others it would seem he had least to fear, namely, covetousness, that formidable monster, which disguises itself under the name of prudence and foresight for the future, but which makes itself completely master of the heart, and makes it look upon, as of no account, acts of cruelty, inhumanity, the most crying injustices, and the blackest perfidies?

Prayer. Alas! Am I in no way, in my position,

another Judas? All the hatred and the shame which this traitor has brought down upon himself, ought they not to fall upon me, who am a traitor, and perjured, faithless to my baptism, to my duties, to my engagements, to my promises? How often, O divine Jesus, have I not betrayed Thee? I return to Thee, Lord: I implore Thy mercy; suffer not that a fatal despair should fill up the measure of my treasons, rather, grant that imitating the holiness and following the examples of Thy holy Apostles, I may return once more to the duties of my station, and fulfil the obligations of my baptism, and make a faithful profession of Christianity which should be to me, as the ministry was to the Apostles, the path of labours, the profession of poverty, and the school of martyrdom. Amen.

END OF THE FIRST VOLUME.

TABLE OF THE MEDITATIONS CONTAINED IN THE FIRST VOLUME.

	Page
I. Of the disposition of mind with which the study and meditation of the Holy Gospel should be undertaken.	1
II. Appearance of the Angel Gabriel to Zacharias, in order to announce to him the birth of a son, who was to be the forerunner of the Messiah.	8
III. The Annunciation.	16
IV. Mary visits Elizabeth.	25
V. Hymn of Mary.	32
VI. Commencement of S. John Baptist's career.	39
VII. Hymn of Zacharias.	44
VIII. Genealogy of Jesus Christ on the side of S. Joseph.	51
IX. An angel announces to S. Joseph the Incarnation of Jesus Christ.	57
X. The birth of our Saviour.	63
XI. Adoration of the shepherds.	69
XII. The circumcision of our Saviour.	77
XIII. The adoration of the Magi.	83
XIV. The purifiation of the Blessed Virgin Mary.	90
XV. Continuation of the Purification of the Blessed Virgin Mary.	95
XVI. Conclusion of the Purification of the Blessed Virgin Mary.	101
XVII. Of the persecution of Herod.	106
XVIII. Of the childhood of Jesus Christ, up to the age of twelve years.	113
XIX. Jesus, at twelve years of age, asks questions of the doctors.	117

CONTENTS.

	Page
XX. The hidden Life of Jesus, from the age of twelve years, to that of thirty.	123
XXI. Commencement of the preaching of the gospel by S. John the Baptist.	128
XXII. Preaching of S. John Baptist.	135
XXIII. Jesus baptized by S. John Baptist.	145
XXIV. Genealogy of Jesus Christ on the side of the Virgin Mary.	151
XXV. On the Incarnation of the Word.	156
XXVI. The temptation of our Lord.	166
XXVII. Preaching of Jesus Christ in Galilee.	174
XXVIII. Jesus is present in the synagogue of the Nazarenes.	178
XXIX. Jesus comes from Nazareth to Capernaum, which He makes the centre of His missions.	186
XXX. The first witness which S. John Baptist bears of Jesus, to the deputies of the Jews.	193
XXXI. Second testimony given to the people by S. John Baptist, on seeing Jesus.	199
XXXII. Jesus begins to gather disciples around Him.	205
XXXIII. Two other disciples join themselves to the three first.	210
XXXIV. Of the miracle which Jesus worked at the marriage in Cana.	215
XXXV. Jesus prepares to go to Jerusalem.	221
XXXVI. First journey of Jesus to Jerusalem to the Feast of the Passover.	227
XXXVII. Conversation of Jesus with Nicodemus.	236
XXXVIII. Of the other mysteries which Jesus reveals to Nicodemus.	246
XXXIX. Third and last witness of Christ, given to His disciples.	253
XL. Conversation of Jesus with the woman of Samaria.	264
XLI. As regards that which preceded the conversion of the Samaritans of Sychar.	275

	Page
XLII. Conversion of the Samaritans of Sychar.	284
XLIII. Jesus, being at Cana, heals the son of a nobleman, who was sick at Capernaum.	288
XLIV. Healing of one that was possessed of a devil.	295
XLV. Jesus heals the mother-in-law of S. Peter.	301
XLVI. Several cures wrought by Christ on the evening of the same day.	307
XLVII. Jesus goes through Galilee.	314
XLVIII. Preaching of Jesus, and the miraculous draught of fishes in the ship of Simon Peter.	320
XLIX. Sermon on the Mount.	326
L. First continuation of the Sermon on the Mount.	333
LI. Second continuation of the Sermon on the Mount.	342
LII. Third continuation of the Sermon on the Mount.	351
LIII. Fourth continuation of the Sermon on the Mount.	358
LIV. Fifth continuation of the Sermon on the Mount.	369
LV. Sixth continuation of the Sermon on the Mount.	376
LVI. Seventh continuation of the Sermon on the Mount.	384
LVII. Eighth continuation of the Sermon on the Mount.	392
LVIII. Ninth continuation of the Sermon on the Mount.	401
LIX. Tenth continuation of the Sermon on the Mount.	411
LX. Conclusion of the Sermon on the Mount.	419
LXI. Jesus heals a leper.	424
LXII. Jesus heals the centurion's servant.	431
LXIII. Jesus departs in order to take ship, and pass over to the other side of the lake.	436

	Page
LXIV. Calming of the tempest.	442
LXV. The two men who were possessed of devils in the country of the Gergesenes.	448
LXVI. Of that which took place after the deliverance of the two who were possessed in the country of the Gadarenes.	454
LXVII. Jesus heals a paralytic man in the presence of the Pharisees.	459
LXVIII. The call of S. Matthew.	467
LXIX. Answer of Jesus to the complaints of the Pharisees and of the disciples of S. John Baptist.	474
LXX. Jesus confirms His preceding answer by three comparisons.	479
LXXI. The prayer of Jairus.	485
LXXII. Healing of the woman with the bloody issue.	490
LXXIII. Death of the daughter of Jairus.	497
LXXIV. Preparations for the burial of the daughter of Jairus.	501
LXXV. Raising of the daughter of Jairus.	505
LXXVI. Healing of the two blind men.	508
LXXVII. Healing of the dumb man possessed by a devil.	512
LXXVIII. Jesus passes through the cities and villages.	517
LXXIX. Choice of the twelve apostles.	521

www.ingramcontent.com/pod-product-compliance
Lightning Source LLC
Chambersburg PA
CBHW031947290426
44108CB00011B/702